INTERPRETATION
OF SCHIZOPHRENIA

Interpretation of
Schizophrenia

by Silvano Arieti, M.D.

Clinical Associate Professor of Psychiatry
State University College of Medicine
at New York City

New York, 1955
ROBERT BRUNNER
PUBLISHER OF PSYCHIATRIC BOOKS

to my Parents

Preface

In the last decade psychiatry has undergone very significant changes in its field material, scope and results, but schizophrenia has remained its main therapeutic and theoretical problem. In spite of the progress made, more hospital beds are occupied by schizophrenics than by patients affected by any other disease, and the number of people suffering from this condition is steadily increasing every year.

This book is the result of 10 years of study, observation, and thought on this subject. It is not intended to be a complete monograph on schizophrenia. Several notions, especially of a descriptive nature, which are found in the usual textbooks of psychiatry, are omitted or reduced to a minimum. This book was written in an attempt to increase the understanding of this disorder and to present some techniques of treatment. It is intended for the private psychiatrist who practices psychoanalytically oriented psychotherapy and treats ambulatory patients, as well as for physicians working in hospitals with the most advanced cases. People working in related fields, such as psychology, sociology, and anthropology, may also be interested in this work, which has borrowed so much from their sciences in the attempt to unravel this many-sided problem.

The different parts of this work will undoubtedly have different meanings to various readers, in accordance with their predominant interests. The psychiatrist will be concerned mainly with the parts which deal with psychodynamics and therapy, whereas the psychologist will find more interest in the part which expounds the formal psychological mechanisms. One of the main purposes of this book, however, is to present to the reader several avenues of research, even if his professional activities predispose him toward a unilateral approach.

I am well aware of the shortcomings and the controversial aspects of this book. Some parts of this vast subject, like child schizophrenia, have been omitted entirely, because I feel that I have not had enough experience with them. In these cases, the reader is always referred to the works of competent authorities on these specific subjects. At times, as in Chapters XXI and XXII, certain ideas have been advanced for which not enough empirical evidence is available. In those instances the reader is warned about the theoretical nature of what is expounded. In some cases repetition was unavoidable because the integration of the various approaches required some recapitulation of the material previously mentioned. The style may be resented by some since it may seem too plain and since it is shorn of almost all technical terminology, particularly in the part which deals with the psychodynamics of schizophrenia. To this possible criticism I must respond that in my life experience as a student and a teacher, as an analysand and an analyst, I have always felt that plain language conveys more meaning, especially in the field of human relations. Of course, when factual data are required, as, for instance, from the anatomo-physiological field, I do not hesitate to use the exact technical terminology, and in general, when new concepts are formulated, I do not refrain from the use of new expressions.

I know that this book does not solve the problems with which it deals, but I humbly present it as an honest attempt to move a little forward toward the goals of relieving human suffering and of increasing our understanding of the nature of man.

The work entailed in this writing could not have been carried out if I had not been helped in my training and experience by many teachers, colleagues, students, as well as by cooperative patients. First, I wish to thank the whole faculty of the William

Alanson White Institute of New York, where I received my psycho-analytic training, and especially Doctors Ralph Crowley, Janet Rioch, Rose Spiegel and Clara Thompson. My work in that school enabled me to acquire a deeper grasp of the psychodynamics of schizophrenia, as well as of the impact of social and cultural factors. Needless to say, any misinterpretation of the teachings of that school or any variations are my sole responsibility.

My thanks also go to Professor Howard W. Potter of the State University College of Medicine at New York City, who gave me the rewarding opportunity to teach this subject to residents, and offered me access to the patients of the psychiatric department of Kings County Hospital.

Many of the observations reported in this book were made during the years spent at Pilgrim State Hospital, under the inspiration of Dr. Newton Bigelow, who was then First Assistant of that hospital, and is now Commissioner of Mental Hygiene of New York State. Dr. Bigelow, by showing a deep personal interest in my clinical work and early research, gave me much-needed encouragement.

I am also grateful to my teacher of neurology, the late Professor Giuseppe Ayala, and to my teacher of neuropathology, Professor Armando Ferraro, of the New York State Psychiatric Institute, who provided the impetus for my clinical and experimental research during the years spent with them. Although the organic approach to which they exposed me was later to become a secondary one in my general orientation, it has remained an important part of what I consider a more complete integration.

I must mention once more Dr. Janet Rioch, as well as Dr. Eilhard Von Domarus and Dr. John Meth, who read the manuscript and offered valuable criticism.

I also would like to acknowledge the work of Miss Evelyn Kossoff and Mrs. Bernice Platt, who edited the manuscript, and Mrs. Lily Michael who prepared Figures 7, 8 and 9.

Jane, my wife, deserves special credit, not only because she helped me with several suggestions, but especially because she spent in solitude, somewhat reluctantly, the hours which I devoted to this work.

SILVANO ARIETI

New York City,
November 1, 1954

Acknowledgments

I wish to express my indebtedness to the authors and publishers of the works quoted in this book. All quoted works are listed in the bibliography. I am especially indebted to the publishers who have permitted the reproduction in this volume of long excerpts from the following articles of mine:

Special Logic of Schizophrenia and Other Types of Autistic Thought. Psychiatry, 11, 325–338, 1948.

The Placing into Mouth and Coprophagic Habits. Journal of Nervous and Mental Disease. Vol. 99, 959, June, 1944.

Primitive Habits in the Preterminal Stage of Schizophrenia. Journal of Nervous and Mental Disease. Vol. 102, 267, Oct. 1945.

The Processes of Expectation and Anticipation. Journal of Nervous and Mental Disease. Vol. 106, 471, Oct. 1947.

Autistic Thought. Its Formal Mechanisms and Its Relationship to Schizophrenia. Journal of Nervous and Mental Disease. Vol. 111, 288, 1950.

Primitive Habits and Perceptual Alterations in the Terminal Stage of Schizophrenia. Archives of Neurology and Psychiatry. Vol. 53, 378, May 1945.

Primitive Intellectual Mechanisms in Psychopathological Conditions. American Journal of Psychotherapy, Vol. 4, 4, 1950.

I wish to thank also Oxford University Press for permission to reproduce an excerpt from Hinsie and Shatzky "Psychiatric Dictionary."

Contents

PART THREE: THE PSYCHOLOGICAL STRUCTURE
             OF SCHIZOPHRENIA
             Study of the Formal Mechanisms

Illustrations

frontal lobe and, to a lesser degree, the right frontal lobe. B. The same brain after the hemispheres have been separated. Notice the extension of the destruction of the normal tissue in the right frontal lobe, pr The tumor extended from the rig

PART ONE

---

*The Psychological Approach
to Schizophrenia*

*Historical Review of the Interpre-
tation of the Psychosis and Introduction to the Present Study.*

CHAPTER I

The Psychological Approach to
Schizophrenia: Introduction

No other condition in human pathology has perplexed and challenged the human mind more than schizophrenia.

This book will pursue chiefly the psychological approach which, in the opinion of the author, so far has yielded results more significant than those of any other kind of research toward the solution of this problem.

Even in the limited field of psychology and psychopathology, there are various methods which may be followed, and all of them, to a varying degree, have been rewarding. The simplest psychological approach is, of course, the descriptive. With this method, the symptoms of the patients are collected, described, and labeled. Valuable as this approach was at a certain stage in the history of psychiatry, it is no longer satisfactory today.

The dynamic approach initiated a new era of greater and deeper understanding. The symptoms came to be interpreted as having a meaning; the symptomatology as a whole was seen as having a purpose and a genetic history as well, inasmuch as it could be related to the previous, generally early life, of the individual.

It is impossible to overestimate the value of the dynamic approach in schizophrenia, and, of course, in psychiatry in general. Nothing could be more important from a psychotherapeutic point of view. In schizophrenia, this dynamic study has not yet given results as gratifying as those obtained in psychoneuroses. However, the knowledge of this field is increasing every day, and the therapeutic results are improving, as the number of dynamically-oriented and trained psychiatrists who are becoming interested in studying and treating this psychosis increases. One of the major parts of this book will be devoted to this dynamic interpretation of schizophrenia.

And yet even this dynamic approach, in spite of its success, does not solve the mystery of this mental disorder. Even when the symptoms are explained in their symbolic language, even when their motivation is understood, even when their relation to early life situations has been established, there is still a great deal which needs explanation. Why is the schizophrenic pattern so different from any other? Why have the symptoms such peculiar aspects? Why does the patient experience hallucinations and delusions? Why does he present word-salad, catatonic postures, stereotyped activities, etc.? Even if we accept the fact, and we do accept it, that the psychological traumata in schizophrenia were more violent, more destructive, and occurred earlier than in patients who develop psychoneuroses, we are not able, with a dynamic approach, to understand the formal structure of the symptoms. When to the question, "Who was the first president of the United States?" a regressed schizophrenic replies, "White House," how is the disorder, implicit in the answer, to be interpreted? Bleuler would call the phenomenon a "loose association," but this is nothing more than a descriptive term.

Can a dynamic approach understand the process involved? Obviously not. An approach aimed at the understanding of the formal psychological structure is needed. The formal approach must then be related to the dynamic, of course, and the way in which dynamic factors use, exploit, and change the formal mechanisms must be determined.

The formal approach does not aim at a description, as the descriptive approach does, but at an understanding of the mechanisms of the psychological functions. This approach remains at a psychological level and is not necessarily concerned with, although it may lead to, studies of the organic basis of the psychic functions.

The dynamic and the formal (psychostructural) approaches differ also in certain other respects. The formal approach emphasizes what patients have in common, and the common psychological mechanisms which they adopt. The dynamic approach studies, not exclusively but predominantly, what is specific in each case; the more specific are the elements studied, the more accurate and therapeutically useful they are. Both approaches must be used since both are valuable. Every schizophrenic, like every man, is both similar to and different from other patients and men. Here again is that fundamental dichotomy, similarity and difference, on which all human understanding is based.

Whereas the dynamic approach remains predominantly a psychiatric study, the formal or psychostructural approach transcends the field of psychiatry. Prolonged excursions into other fields such as anthropology, sociology, logic, aesthetics, neurology, and general biology, are necessary. The results obtained concern not only psychiatry, but all the sciences which study the intrinsic nature of man. The third part of this book, which is devoted to the formal or psychostructural approach, will disclose the influences of people who have made significant contributions in various fields, such as

Giambattista Vico, Hughlings Jackson, George Mead, Ernst Cassirer, Kurt Goldstein and Susanne Langer.

Another psychological approach, one which is connected with dynamic psychiatry on the one hand, and with internal medicine and neurology on the other, is the psychosomatic. Extensive work has been done to demonstrate the psychogenic origin of functional and organic changes which occur in psychoneuroses, or in what are called psychosomatic conditions. The physiological and organic changes which occur in schizophrenia have been studied instead almost exclusively from the point of view of demonstrating the organic origin of this condition. They have not been viewed generally as psychosomatic, that is, as sequences of the primary psychological condition. Part V of this book will be devoted to the psychosomatic study of schizophrenia. It will also include the study of the functional alterations which may occur in the central and autonomic nervous system.

Another part of the book (Part IV) will be devoted to the longitudinal study of schizophrenia from the earliest to the most advanced stages. Many works have failed to offer a detailed description and interpretation of the gradual progression of the illness. In Part IV, interpretation of some individual symptoms, as well as of the whole phenomenon of regression, will be given.

In Part VI the psychotherapeutic approach to schizophrenia will be described. What has been learned predominantly from the dynamic, but also from the formal or psychostructural studies, will be applied to the psychotherapeutic procedure.

Before undertaking these studies, however, it is worthwhile to examine the evolution of our present concepts of schizophrenia resulting from the work done by the major contributors. This will be done in the next chapter.

CHAPTER II

Changing Concepts of Schizophrenia

I. Introductory Remarks

A critical review of the changing psychological concepts of schizophrenia will be attempted in this chapter. This review will not be a complete one; it will not include the pre-Kraepelinian conceptions, which now have only a historical interest, and it will omit entirely all those theories and contributions which have received transient and inconsequential consideration. The contributions examined here will be those of six men only, the six innovators who, in the opinion of the writer, are responsible for the evolution of our present concepts on schizophrenia. These men are Kraepelin, Bleuler, Meyer, Freud, Jung and Sullivan. A host of contributions, some of them very valuable, have been stimulated, directly or indirectly, by the works of these six men, and the reader who is interested may find an account of them elsewhere. (Lewis 173, Bellak 18, Bini and Bazzi 26).

Although our purpose here is to discuss the views of these

six authors on schizophrenia, it is obvious that their views in respect to this condition reflect their entire psychiatric conceptions and therefore we cannot help in several instances referring to their works in other psychiatric areas as well. These six authors have enlarged our understanding of schizophrenia through their work in the psychological field. Some of them have worked and theorized from an organic point of view also, but it is only their psychological work which is important. For instance, Kraepelin's hypothesis about metabolic-toxic disorders in schizophrenia did not produce the same repercussions that his clinical description of the psychological manifestations did.

In contrast with the relatively non-extensive but very constructive work of these six psychiatrists, is the immense amount of the work of countless researchers who have attacked the schizophrenic enigma from a predominantly organic point of view. These researchers have followed the assumption that in the study of schizophrenia, as in the study of other diseases in biology, one should follow Virchow's concept that any kind of pathology means organic or cellular pathology. Under the influence of this concept which, for a long time, has dominated the whole field of medicine, researchers have examined every possible spot of the body of the schizophrenic patient, from top to bottom, from the hair to the sexual glands, in a relentless attempt to find clues which would reveal the organic nature of this condition.

Even at present, the organic studies of schizophrenia outnumber by far the psychological ones, although in the United States the trend now is in favor of the psychological approach. In other countries like England, France and especially Germany and Italy, the organic studies receive almost exclusive attention. These organic approaches may be divided into six major groups: 1) genetic; 2) constitutional (including endocrine); 3) infective; 4) biochemical; 5) neurophysiological;

6) anatomical and neuropathological. It is not the purpose of this book to review these researches. The reader is referred to the highly informative books by Lewis and Bellak on this subject. Lewis' work covers 15 years of research, from 1920 to 1934, and includes 1,778 papers, monographs and books published in 12 languages (173). Bellak's book covers 3,200 papers written in many languages during the period 1935–1945 (18).

The quantity of these works and the variety of directions which they have taken, reveal that no headway has been made and that no constructive avenue of research has yet been found in the organic field. In spite of this fact, it would be unfair to ignore these works, some of which have been very revealing for various and unexpected reasons. Some of them will be examined in Part V of this book. At the present time, however, it is possible to state that the organic nature of schizophrenia has not been demonstrated. Genetic studies have failed to reveal, in a clear and uncontroversial manner, that schizophrenia follows certain genetic laws. Anatomical pathology, including neuropathology, has not ascertained any causal relation between organic factors and schizophrenia. However, today we are not in a position to deny an organic, predisposing constitutional factor. We are not in a position to deny it, not because it has actually been demonstrated, but only because medical knowledge has shown that such a factor exists in practically every disease, even in those which are caused by a specific agent. Not everybody who is exposed to the pneumococcus or to Koch's bacteria, develops pneumonia or tuberculosis. In addition to the specific cause, a state of receptivity or of non-immunity, based on a physical substratum, is necessary. It is possible, although by no means demonstrated, that the same is true of schizophrenia. At the present stage of our knowledge, the organic interpretation of schizophrenia cannot claim more than this.

II. Kraepelin

Emil Kraepelin (1855–1926) was the first psychiatrist to differentiate from the mass of intramural mental patients that pathological entity which he called Dementia Praecox. This name had already been used by the French psychiatrist Morel, but not with identical implications. For Morel, *praecox* meant that the demential state started early or precociously in life, in contrast to senile dementia, which occurred in old age. For Kraepelin the term praecox acquired an additional meaning: The state of dementia was supposed to follow precociously or soon after the onset of the illness. Thus even in the name of the disease, as used by Kraepelin, one recognizes his finalistic conception: The fundamental characteristic of the disease is its outcome, a prognostic characteristic.

The major contribution of Kraepelin consisted of the inclusion in the same syndrome, of catatonia, already described by Kahlbaum, hebephrenia and "vesania typica" also described by Kahlbaum, characterized by auditory hallucinations and persecutory trends. After examining and observing thousands of patients, and seeing them panoramically in space and time, Kraepelin was able to discern the common characteristics in these apparently dissimilar cases. The characteristic which impressed him most was the progressive tendency toward a state of dementia. The other patients who did not have this tendency, like the manic-depressives, would be separated from the praecox group, and subsequently recognized as having other differential symptoms also. Using this method of observation, Kraepelin could differentiate and define as dementia praecox a symptomatology consisting of hallucinations, delusions, incongruous emotivity, impairment of attention, negativism, stereotyped behavior, and progressive dilapidation, in the presence of relatively intact sensorium.

Once he defined this syndrome, Kraepelin tried his best to give an accurate description of it. Like a man working at a microscope, he described as many minute details as possible. His monograph, "Dementia Praecox and Paraphrenia," remains until today the most complete description of the symptoms of the schizophrenic from a phenomenological point of view (163). The symptom is described and accepted as it is, with no attempt being made to interpret it, either physiologically or psychologically.

Kraepelin divided the patients into three groups, the hebephrenic, the catatonic and the paranoid. Later, he accepted the differentiation of a fourth type, the simple, as suggested by Bleuler. He also separated from Dementia Praecox, a new nosological entity, "Paraphrenia." In this syndrome, too, the outcome is the fundamental consideration: In spite of the progression of the illness, there is no decay of the personality. As to the etiology, Kraepelin considered dementia praecox an endogenous illness, that is, one not due to external causes. At first he thought it was due to organic pathology of the brain; later he felt that it might be due to a metabolic disorder.

The great merit of Kraepelin consists in his having been able to synthesize successfully the works of Kahlbaum, Morel, Wundt, and others, and to organize them in his own system. We cannot fully appreciate his influence until we read a book of psychiatry of the pre-Kraepelinian era, and evaluate the confusing picture of psychiatry in those days. Today it is impossible, however, not to see the shortcomings of Kraepelin's conceptions of dementia praecox. The acceptance of the prognostic characteristic as the fundamental one cannot be considered a sound principle. First, as Kraepelin himself came to recognize, not all cases of dementia praecox end in dementia; as a matter of fact, some of them seem to make a complete recovery. Secondly, this finalistic or teleologic point of view is incompatible with the scientific method, which searches for the causes and not for the effects.

Although Kraepelin himself was probably unaware of this influence, this over-all prognostic concept reinforced the popular fatalistic attitude toward mental illnesses and discouraged therapeutic attempts. Reading his monograph on dementia praecox, one cannot help admiring the accurateness of his description; however, it is a description which is remarkable for its extension and completeness, not for its depth. The patient appears as a collection of symptoms, not as a person; or, if he appears as a person, he looks as if he belongs to a special species, to be differentiated from the rest of humanity, and put into the insane asylum. The psychiatric hospital is a zoological garden, with many differentiated species.

Kraepelin seems to see the patient as detached or to be detached from society. It never enters his mind that the schizophrenic may have been influenced by social forces, or may even be a product of society. Although his fundamental concept was the final outcome, that is, a temporal concept, he does not give a longitudinal picture of the patient. Except for the repeated mention of the fact that the patient decays progressively to reach a state of idiocy, we do not see in the Kraepelinian description different stages or any real movement, even toward regression. The patient is always seen in cross-section.

It is often said that Kraepelin was more concerned with the structure of the psychic phenomena than with the content, that he was more concerned with how the patient thinks, than with what he thinks. Undoubtedly, he was not concerned with the psychological importance of the content of thought, but it seems to me that he was also not concerned with the real structure of patients' thoughts. A mere description of the symptoms is not a structural understanding.

When we examine the negative qualities of Kraepelin's conceptions, we are bound to be too harsh with him. It is really too easy for us to see what he did not see. Nobody would criticize Galileo for not knowing the principles of electricity. If we concentrate on what Kraepelin did not give us, in comparison to others, like Freud or Bleuler, we are bound to minimize his accomplishments, which are immense.

Kraepelin may be viewed as the Linnaeus of psychiatry, in comparison to Freud, who may be viewed as the Darwin. But as Linnaeus and Darwin were necessary in the development of biology, so both Kraepelin and Freud were necessary in the development of psychiatry. A great deal of resentment toward Kraepelinian psychiatry, which may be noted in some psychiatric circles, is due actually not to an attempt to minimize Kraepelin's accomplishments, but to a displeasure with the tenacity with which his concepts have been retained, even long after more penetrating ones have been formulated. Zilboorg writes that "the system of Kraepelin appears to have become a thing of the past as soon as it announced its own birth in 1896." (280). In a certain way this is true, since it is in the same year, 1896, that Freud published his first outstanding book. On the other hand, one may say that even today, at the date of the publication of this book, Kraepelinian psychiatry is the best known in the world. Thousands and thousands of patients are still viewed and classified as Kraepelin taught and are still labeled with the name "Dementia Praecox."

III. Bleuler

Kraepelin's contributions were not accepted without objections. Among the well-known psychiatrists who opposed most of his views were Ernest Meyer, Korsakov, and Bianchi.

Eugene Bleuler (1857–1930), a Swiss psychiatrist whose

role in the history of psychiatry will remain an important one, accepted much of Kraepelin, but revitalized the Kraepelinian concepts and revised them, making a strong attempt, though not a thoroughly successful one, to go beyond a purely descriptive approach.

In 1911 Bleuler published a monograph on Dementia Praecox, which was the result of many years of study and research (30). He renamed the syndrome, "schizophrenia," implying that a splitting of the various psychic functions, rather than a progression toward a demential state, was one of the outstanding characteristics. He delivered a blow to the Kraepelinian concept of Dementia Praecox as a disease entity, inasmuch as he included in the schizophrenic group many syndromes which at that time no one was prepared to consider as being related to schizophrenia. Psychoses which arise in psychopathic personalities, alcoholic hallucinoses, prison psychoses, and cases of symptomatic manic-depressive psychoses he included in the schizophrenic group. Furthermore, he thought that the largest number of cases of schizophrenia are latent cases; these patients are never hospitalized because the symptoms are not severe enough, but show oddities of behavior which are attributable to an insidious schizophrenic process.

Bleuler classified the symptoms of schizophrenia in two sets of groups: the groups of fundamental and accessory symptoms, and the groups of primary and secondary symptoms. The fundamental symptoms are not necessarily the primary ones; they are the symptoms which are present to an extent in every case of schizophrenia, latent or manifest. The accessory symptoms are those which may or may not occur. Among the fundamental symptoms Bleuler included the disorder of the process of association, which he considered the most important characteristic of schizophrenia, and also a particular type of thinking and behavior which he called autism. Among the accessory symptoms he included the acute manifestations of the psychosis, like delusions, hallucinations, catatonic postures, etc. Primary symptoms are those which are directly related to the disease process; they are the necessary phenomena of the disease. The most important of them is again the association disorder. Secondary symptoms are caused by a combination of the action of the primary ones and the action of psychogenic factors.

The most important contributions of Bleuler were those related to his study of the process of association and disturbances of the affective life, the concepts of autism and ambivalence, and his interpretation of negativism.

The disorder of the process of association, according to Bleuler, involves every aspect of schizophrenia. In thought processes it may range from a maximum, which corresponds to complete incoherence, to a minimum, which is hardly perceptible. Bleuler described accurately the various degrees of this associative disorder, and related symptoms, such as blocking, elisions, logical errors, etc., but was not able to infer any underlying basic formal mechanism. He limited himself to the formulation that these symptoms were the result of a loosening of associations. As far as their motivation was concerned, Bleuler accepted Freudian mechanisms quite often. Blocking was seen by him as an exaggeration of repression. He felt that psychological complexes might explain the combinations of ideas in a condensed or bizarre pattern. He accepted Freudian symbolism especially in explaining hallucinations and delusions, but was evidently of the opinion that it was not enough to explain everything with dynamic processes.

Bleuler went further than Kraepelin; he wanted to explain symptoms in respect to their psychological content as well as their structure. As to the content, he accepted Freud's explanations. He realized, however, that these were not enough; and although he was not able to formulate clearly what was missing in the Freudian approach, it is obvious that he searched for a structural or formal explanation of the symptoms, that is, he would have liked to have known why the symptoms have specific manifestations in schizophrenia. He tried to solve the problem by assuming that the structural defect involved always the loosening of associations; but he could not go beyond this point, and therefore his formal studies remained as descriptive as Kraepelin's. Although he might have been influenced by Wernicke's "concept of sejunction," Bleuler did not attempt to give an anatomical interpretation of the symptoms. On the other hand since he could not explain everything with Freudian mechanisms, he could not dismiss the idea that schizophrenia might be due to an underlying organic disease. In his book he mentions the possibility that mental causes produce the symptoms, but not the disease. He states that the disease process may be due to some kind of toxin, like rheumatism. Thus, Bleuler himself is a good example of that ambivalent attitude which he was the first to describe; he expresses the feeling that schizophrenia is a psychogenic disorder, and yet he cannot dispel the idea that it may be organic in origin.

This concept of ambivalence, which Bleuler first described in psychotics, has since played an important role in psychiatric thinking, not only in reference to psychotics, but also in reference to neurotics and normal human beings. By ambivalence Bleuler meant the simultaneous occurrence of two opposite feelings for the same object, such as in the case of the husband who both loves and hates his wife. He found this symptom in every schizophrenic and thought that the most marked form of it was inherent in catatonic negativism.

Bleuler thought that the affective disorders which occurred in schizophrenia were not primary but secondary. He was one of the first to note that when patients' complexes were involved, the feelings of the patients were normal or even exaggerated. He also noticed that patients who appeared completely apathetic, were capable of complete or partial recoveries. He saw the apparent loss of affection as due to repression.

The concept of autism is another of the major contributions of this author. He used this term to refer to a certain tendency to turn away from reality, accompanied by a certain type of thinking. Autistic thinking, according to Bleuler, as opposed to logical thinking, does not represent occurrences in the outer world and their associations; as a matter of fact, it excludes many external and internal facts. The autistic patient tends to live in a world of fantasy, where symbolization is used constantly. Autistic thinking is not bound by the laws of logic and reality. "It is unlogical and permits the greatest contradictions with the outer world and in itself." The autistic person identifies wishes or fears with reality. "The fear of having enemies is for his autistic thinking identical with the fixed conviction that they exist." Autistic thinking flourishes particularly in schizophrenia, but it may occur even in normal situations, for instance, in children when they play; in subjects which are not sufficiently accessible to our knowledge and our logic, such as religion, love, etc.; or wherever the emotions "obtain too great a significance." (28).

Undoubtedly it is to Bleuler's credit that he defined and described this type of thinking which is so different from what is generally called logical thinking. However, it must be remembered that fundamentally Bleuler has given us only a description of it. Here again it should be stated that he accepted Freudian interpretations in regard to the content; from a formal point of view, he limited himself to saying that this type of thinking was not logical. He felt that his concept of autism nearly coincided with Freud's concept of autoerotism, and with Janet's "loss of the sense of reality."

As far as negativism is concerned, Bleuler thought that

it could not be explained solely as a motor phenomenon (27, 30). He was inclined to consider it as a psychological attitude. The patient considers all stimuli coming from the environment as hostile and disturbing, and therefore he tries to block them off. This psychological interpretation allows for the explanation of negativism as being expressed only at times toward certain persons. As was mentioned before, Bleuler saw the negativistic attitude as being related to the ambivalent attitude. He also felt that intellectual negativism might be based on a general tendency of ideas to associate with their opposites.

Thus, we may summarize the contribution of Bleuler as follows:

1. He saw the schizophrenic syndrome not as a progression toward dementia, but as a particular condition characterized mainly by a disorder of association, and by a splitting of the basic functions of the personality.
2. He enlarged the boundaries of what should be included under this syndrome.
3. He differentiated a new subtype, the simple type.
4. He emphasized that affectivity is not absent in schizophrenia, and that it plays a more important role than it was then thought.
5. He attempted not only to describe the symptoms, but to explain them. As to their psychological content, he accepted Freud's contributions. From a formal point of view, his efforts have remained unfulfilled.
6. He gave psychiatry the concepts of autistic thinking and of ambivalence.
7. He enlarged the psychiatric terminology by coining the well-accepted words, schizophrenia, depth-psychology, autism, ambivalence and dereism.

IV. Meyer

Adolph Meyer (1866–1950), a Swiss-born and -trained physician, who came to the United States in 1892, was to become and remain for several decades the leading American psychiatrist. Schizophrenia was one of his major interests, from the beginning of his career (176, 190–194). Meyer was dissatisfied with the role given to heredity and auto-intoxication in the etiology and pathogenesis of dementia praecox. He felt that perhaps the psychological factors, to which laymen and old schools of psychiatry had given so much importance in the past, should be reconsidered.

Kraepelin had given an accurate description of the disease, after the onset. Meyer advocated that the patient be studied "longitudinally"; from the beginning of his life, all the factors which might have contributed to the mental condition should be searched and examined. Meyer thus became convinced that dementia praecox was the result of an accumulation of habit-disorders or faulty habits of reaction. The individual who is not able to cope with the problems and difficulties of life, and who is confronted with failure after failure, may tend toward what Meyer called substitutive reactions. At first, these new habits appear as "trivial and harmless subterfuges," such as day-dreaming, rumination, decrease of interests, etc., but later they become harmful, uncontrollable and tend to assume definite mechanisms, like hallucinations, delusions, blocking, etc. These anomalous mechanisms, according to Meyer, are partially intelligible as substitutions for "efficient adjustment to concrete and actual difficulties." Meyer felt that it was possible to formulate the main facts appearing in the history of most cases as a "natural chain of cause and effect." He saw dementia praecox as "the usually inevitable outcome of 1) conflicts of instincts, or conflicts of complexes of experience, and 2) incapacity for a harmless constructive adjustment."

Meyer called his concept dynamic, inasmuch as it implied a longitudinal interaction of forces; he also called it psychobiological, inasmuch as it considered the psychological as well as all the pertinent biological factors. He renamed the disorder parergasia, which etymologically means incongruity of behavior. This term, however, has not met with success outside of his school.

An unbiased critic may find great merits and great pitfalls in Meyer's concepts. The greatest merit lies in his having reaffirmed the importance of "mental" or psychological factors in the etiology of schizophrenia. The longitudinal aspect of the process of maladjustment, before it reaches psychotic proportions, had not been adequately stressed before by any other school, except the psychoanalytic. In other respects, however, Meyer's formulations remain vague and inadequate in explaining any specific characteristics of schizophrenia. Accumulation of faulty habits and of repeated failures may already indicate some pre-existing abnormality, either organic or environmental. Meyer explains the progression of the habit-deterioration as caused by the gradual substitution of increasingly inferior and distorted material. Finally, the distortions are so great that they become full-fledged schizophrenic symptoms. The role that anxiety plays in this process is not clearly apparent from his writings. Furthermore, how and why these faulty habits lead necessarily to schizophrenia, and not to other psychopathological reactions remains unexplained. Meyer seems to believe that there is only a gradual or quantitative difference between faulty habits and clear-cut schizophrenic symptoms. He seems to consider the faulty habits only as the expression of maladjustment at a realistic level; he does not stress enough the point that what he calls substitutive habits often have a symbolic or non-apparent meaning. Moreover he does not emphasize that schizophrenic symptoms have an archaic or primordial aspect, which is lacking in prepsychotic faulty habits.

In addition, although some schizophrenic-like or symbolic manifestations may appear as faulty habits in everybody's life, a constellation of them, as is found in schizophrenia, seems typical or characteristic enough, even from a qualitative point of view. The faulty habits which we may find in human beings, are innumerable, but the schizophrenic symptoms, from a formal point of view, are strikingly similar in every patient. The patients do not appear only as caricatures or exaggerated expressions of their prepsychotic personality; the greatest number of their characteristics have undergone a drastic metamorphosis, and have been channeled into few and definite patterns. In other words, if a substitution of faulty habits occurs, it is because they are substituted by schizophrenic symptoms. Meyer's interpretation of schizophrenia as a substitution of faulty habits is therefore not an interpretation. In addition, these faulty habits found in the history of many schizophrenics, are found also in the history of many psychoneurotics.

Meyer is correct in considering schizophrenia a progressive pathological adjustment; however from his writings one does not learn when a patient with "faulty habits" is to be considered an overt schizophrenic. It may be asserted that the faulty habits of the schizophrenic disclose some kind of malignancy, which is not present in the faulty habits of the neurotic. This concept has led many psychiatrists to make an accurate search for those latent schizophrenic symptoms which seem to be psychoneurotic traits. A pseudoneurotic type of schizophrenia has even been described (Hoch and Polatin, 128). Since many of these patients do not move either toward a more or less psychotic condition, it remains for the individual observer to classify them in one way or the other.

No doubt this search for latent schizophrenia in apparent psychoneurotics has resulted in the early diagnosis of many schizophrenics. However, this tendency is perhaps exaggerated in some sectors and until recently may have had a deterrent effect as far as therapy is concerned. In fact, until recently in some circles a diagnosis of schizophrenia discouraged a psychotherapeutic approach, which Meyer himself usually found "negative and rarely clearly positive" in these cases. (194) Other types of therapy, like shock, etc., have been recognized by psychiatrists of every school as having no beneficial effect on these dubious or borderline cases.

Summarizing, we may state that Meyer's major contribution was his emphasis on a longitudinal study of the patient, and on the reaffirmation of the importance of the psychogenic factors. His approach must therefore be considered a dynamic one. Its dynamism, however, is somehow stunted by the fact that the early environmental factors, acting during the childhood of the patient, do not receive the proper stress, and by the fact that its symptoms are more or less considered from a realistic, that is, non-symbolic, point of view. The dynamic psychoanalytic point of view not only is more complete, but actually preceded the psychobiological one historically. However, in the first few decades of its existence, psychoanalysis devoted itself almost exclusively to the psychoneuroses, so that the psychobiological approach had an opportunity to gain a respectful place in the study of schizophrenia.

V. Freud

Whereas the German schools of psychiatry have been mainly interested in the psychoses, the French schools centered their interest on the study of the psychoneuroses. Sigmund Freud (1855–1939), himself an Austrian, after spending one year in Paris at the school of Charcot, felt the influence of the French school of psychiatry more than of any other. Thus we find that throughout his life, he paid only secondary attention to the study of the psychoses. Freud's influence on psychiatry as a whole, however, is of such magnitude and of such a revolutionary nature that even the field of psychoses had to be totally reviewed in the light of his contributions.

In one of his first psychoanalytic papers, written in 1894, nine years before the first dynamic interpretations of Adolph Meyer, Freud first described how unbearable ideas may give rise to hallucinatory psychoses (88). The unbearable idea is rejected by the ego, but the attempt to reject it is not successful. The idea comes back as an hallucinatory wish-fulfillment. The girl who could not accept the fact that she was not loved by a certain man, in her delusional system saw him and heard him near her.

In a paper published in 1896, Freud gives the dynamic interpretation of a case which seemed at first to be a case of chronic paranoia, but which later was recognized as a case of the paranoid type of dementia praecox (89). In this paper, for the first time in the history of psychiatry, the term "projection" is used and this mental mechanism is explained. Freud found that in this case, too, as in neurotics, the nucleus of the psychical mechanism was repression. However, in this case repression of self-reproach is "projected" on to others, who thus become the persecutors.

In another paper of paramount importance, published in 1911, which reported Schreber's case, Freud described other projection mechanisms (90). He showed that the rejection of a homosexual wish accounted for the persecutory complex. The proposition I (a man) love him (a man) is not accepted by the patient, who wants to deny it with the contradictory proposition "I do not *love* him, I hate him." "I hate him," by projection, becomes transformed into "He hates me." Thus from a homosexual wish a delusional idea is formed.

According to Freud in erotomania the mechanism is the following. The patient, who does not want to admit attachment to a man, forces himself to think, "I do not love him— I love her" (that is, I do not love a man, I love a woman). By projection, "I love her" becomes "She loves me." Delusions of jealousy in women have a similar mechanism. "It is not I who love women, but he (my husband) loves them." In every case, the delusion is a defense or an attempt to deny the homosexual wish.

In paranoia and in dementia praecox, Freud sees a withdrawal of the libido from the external world. Thus, catastrophic delusions of cosmic magnitude, like the experience of the "end of the world," often found in these patients, are interpreted by him as withdrawal of libido. Things become indifferent or irrelevant, and may appear ruined or dissipated. The delusion-formation is interpreted as an attempt at recovery, a process of reconstruction, inasmuch as it is a method used to recapture a relationship, though a distorted one, with the world.

In another paper on Narcissism, published in 1914, Freud explains in more detail the application of his libido theory to the interpretation of schizophrenia (91). The libido is withdrawn and is directed into the ego, giving rise to a state which is called narcissism. For instance, some patients suffer from megalomania and withdraw their interest from external objects. All the affective charge which was cathexed on external objects is now withdrawn and deposited on the patient himself, who becomes a megalomaniac. But megalomania is not a new phenomenon; it is found in primitive peoples and in children. The loss of the normal function of appreciating reality is brought about by the withdrawal of the libido. The libido may withdraw to one or more points of fixation, corresponding to various stages of regression.

By libido, Freud means sexual energy, although he actually speaks of the affective component of the mental processes. This withdrawal of libido to the narcissistic level can hardly explain the specific characteristics of schizophrenia. On the other hand, the concept of regression, as a return to earlier levels of integration, is acceptable to many authors, if it is separated from the concept of libido. The concept of regression has replaced that of deterioration in schizophrenia. The patient returns to infantile or archaic levels of integration because he is unable to function at a higher level. These levels, however, are not necessarily representative of earlier levels of sexual development, as Freud thought.

In the book "The Ego and the Id" which appeared in 1923, Freud wrote that neurosis is the result of a conflict between the ego and its id, whereas psychosis is the analogous outcome of a similar disturbance in the relation between the ego and its environment (outer world) (92). In a paper published in 1924, "Neurosis and Psychosis," he wrote that whereas in the neuroses, the ego, in virtue of its allegiance to reality, suppresses a part of the id, in the psychoses, the ego, in the service of the id, withdraws itself from a part of reality (92). In other words, the ego accepts part of the id. In a following paper (Loss of Reality, etc.) he wrote that in psychoses there is not only loss of reality, but also remodeling of reality (94). Psychosis substitutes something for what it denies.

Any attempt to give an adequate account of the importance of Freud's contributions to the field of schizophrenia remains somewhat unfulfilled because the whole psychoanalytic theory would have to be repeated, each part of it having a direct or indirect relevance. Perhaps of all the contributions of the founder of psychoanalysis, the most important in relation to schizophrenia is the concept of symbolization, although it was not originally formulated in connection with this disorder. According to this concept, the symptoms are no longer accepted at a phenomenological level, but as substitutes for something else which they symbolize. The repressive forces of the ego transform the symptoms in such a way that they are no longer recognizable to the patient as attempts to fulfill objectionable wishes. The study of symbols, which Freud made in his masterful book on dreams, was later extended, especially by Jung, to the field of schizophrenia.

Freud's important concepts such as those of the unconscious, repression, and transference have a great value when they are also applied to schizophrenia. Rather than to attempt in this book a too sketchy account of their significance, the reader is referred to the usual textbooks of psychoanalysis and especially to those by Fenichel (75), Thompson (258), and Freud himself (95). It is important, however, to mention here that the significance of these concepts in schizophrenia is somewhat different from that derived from their application to neuroses. For instance, the unconscious decreases in extension in schizophrenia, as a consequence of a partial return to consciousness of what is generally repressed in psychoneuroses and normal conditions. The concept of transference is applied by Freud to schizophrenia in a negative way. According to him, all the libido in the schizophrenic is withdrawn from external objects, and therefore no transference, no attachment for the analyst, is possible. The result is that the patient is scarcely accessible to analytic treatment. This idea of Freud's discouraged many therapists from attempts to treat schizophrenics, although, as Fromm-Reichmann writes (105), Freud hoped that future modifications of the analytic technique would make schizophrenics too amenable to treatment.

Freud was the first author who really succeeded in explaining the content of this psychosis in psychological terms. He was also the first to disclose in a convincing manner the importance of psychological factors in the etiology of this condition. He did not limit himself, as Meyer did, to the interpretation of the symptoms as faulty patterns, but also uncovered their symbolic meaning.

Freud was also successful in explaining, at least partially, the formal aspects of several symptoms, such as projections. His concept of regression remains a fundamental one in the field of schizophrenia. However, the excessive importance given by him to sexual frustrations as the cause of the regressions, did not permit him to give enough consideration to the patient's total interpersonal relations, the sexual manifestations being only one aspect of them.

VI. Jung

Of the psychoanalysts who deviated from Freud, Carl G. Jung (1875–   ) was the first one who made outstanding contributions to the field of schizophrenia. His book, *Psychology of Dementia Praecox,* was written in 1903, nine years before his break with Freud (143). In this book Jung described the importance of the autonomous complex. The French authors, and in particular Charcot and Janet, had already postulated that a series of ideas, removed from consciousness, maintain a more or less independent existence. Janet attributed the phenomenon to the so-called "abaissement du niveau mental." Jung added that the dissociation of this autochthonous group of ideas, was dynamically determined. Word association tests convinced him that the dissociated ideas were emotionally charged, and that the defense mechanisms which isolated them were the same as those described by Freud in hysterical patients.

Jung felt that delusions, hallucinations and other schizophrenic symptoms were due to the activity of the complex, which could not be under the control or correction of consciousness. He criticized those theories which interpreted the apparent incongruity between the ideational and affective functions of the schizophrenic as due to psychic ataxia (Stransky, 247). The "belle indifference" of hysterics is a reaction to oversensitiveness; why not accept the same mechanism in dementia praecox? He thought, however, that the hysterogenic complex causes manifestations which are reparable, whereas the effects of dementia praecox are not. He thought also that possibly the emotional disturbance in dementia praecox engenders an anomalous metabolism or toxin which injures the brain in a more or less irreparable manner, so that the highest psychic functions become paralyzed.

Jung is thus the first author to conceive of the possibility of a psychosomatic mechanism in schizophrenia. According to him, it is not an organic disorder which produces the psychic disorder; on the contrary, the emotional disorder produces an abnormal metabolism which causes physical damage to the brain. This fact is particularly interesting in that, for the first time, the nervous system itself is considered the victim of a psychosomatic disorder. Jung, however, considers this possibility as a mere hypothesis, and does not exclude the idea that a change of metabolism may be primary, as Kraepelin suggested. On account of this metabolic disorder, the last accidental complex may become "clotted" or "curdled" and thus determine the content of the symptoms.

Jung stated that the "essential basis of our personality is affectivity." Thought and action are only "symptoms" of affectivity. Affectivity is the dynamic force of the complex, which may occupy the whole mental field and disturb many of the ideational processes. Jung referred to the disturbances as he noticed them in his experiments on associations, but did not give a complete explanation of the formal mechanisms of schizophrenia. According to him, the autonomous complex disturbs the concentration of the patient and paralyzes all other psychic activities. Recognizing that the psychological mechanisms of dreams are closely related to those of dementia praecox, he wrote, "Let the dreamer walk about and act as though he were awake and we have at once the clinical picture of dementia praecox."

In 1908 he stated that some unknown factor of predisposition may produce a non-adaptable psychological function which can develop into manifest mental disorder (140). In its turn the mental disorder may determine organic degeneration with its own progression of symptoms. In the same paper he wrote that there is overwhelming proof that a primary psychological fault in function exists from the time of childhood. He also added that borderline cases of dementia praecox had been restored to normal life with analytic treatment.

In 1913 Jung differentiated his psychological types, formulating a concept which was to have great importance in psychiatric thinking (141). His first thoughts about a psychological classification actually originated from his effort to compare hysteria and dementia praecox in every possible way. He felt that whereas in hysteria one always finds an "extravert personality," as he called it, with an exaggerated emotivity, and psychic energy directed centrifugally, that is, toward the environment, the opposite is true in dementia praecox. In dementia praecox the psychic energy is centripetal, that is, directed away from the environment and toward the self, the emotivity is decreased, the personality as a whole is what he called "introvert." These early studies of Jung stimulated a subsequent series of studies of the personality of the schizophrenic. Others, like Kretschmer, added a physical counterpart to Jung's psychological description. According to

Kretschmer the introvert has an asthenic and the extravert a pyknic constitution (164).

Another of Jung's concepts which was important in his interpretation of schizophrenia, was his hypothesis of the collective unconscious (142). Jung was very much impressed by the similarity of myths all over the world, in spite of geographical, historical or racial differences. He explained this similarity as the manifestation of a general or collective unconscious which stores the primordial images or *archetypes* that have been deposited there as a result of numerous recurrences of identical situations. Thus our personal psyche rests on a deep impersonal psyche. Jung thought that it was not enough to interpret the symptoms of the patient as Freud did, from the information derived from the detailed personal history of the patient, but that it was necessary to go beyond. For instance, a person's image of parents cannot be attributed only to his memories of his parents from childhood. The images of father and mother acquire a stronger value and intensity on account of the archetype parental image which is stored in our collective unconscious.

The error Jung made was that of minimizing the effect of culture and society on the individual psyche. Some of the patterns that he attributes to the collective unconscious are the effect of the impact of culture on the individual. The individual's image of his mother is not only the result of what he thinks and feels about his own mother on account of his memories of her, but also the result of what culture teaches him that mother is.* Certainly in pathological conditions and especially in schizophrenia, archaic modes of thinking and feeling resurge. However, only the formal mechan-

---

* Jung has taken into consideration the effect of cultural factors, but only in the engendering of the *analogues*. The analogue is an equivalent of the archetype, after culture has modified its appearance. Jung's archetype, however, is not just a formal structure; it has also a content which is determined by the collective unconscious.

isms, or rather the propensity for those formal mechanisms, may be attributed to non-acquired factors. We may call these factors functions of our nervous system or of our collective unconscious, as we wish. The content of those emotions and thoughts, and the motivation of those emotions and thoughts, however, originate in the environment of the individual, that is, in the family and in his culture. The explanations of symptoms go beyond the study of the personal history of the patient and the environment to which he was exposed. Jung is right in this respect; however, what is not explained by personal and environmental factors is only the *formal* aspect of the symptom.

Jung's theoretical formulations force one to attribute more importance to congenital or hereditary factors than to environmental ones. In my opinion, these formulations are incorrect, but have not led to major therapeutic errors. In certain cases, therapy may solve psychological problems, no matter whether we think they are due to the collective unconscious or to social forces. Thus, the Jungian approach has helped many psychotics, and especially borderline cases (Baynes, 16).

In a paper read in 1939 at the Psychiatric Section of the Royal Society of Medicine, Jung reiterated some of his previously expressed ideas and added a few others (149). He criticized the concept of latent psychosis. A latent psychosis is nothing else than the possibility that an individual may become temporarily mentally ill at some period in his life. The existence of unconscious material in his mind proves nothing. Such material is found in neurotics, artists, poets and normal people. According to Jung, "The possibility of a future psychosis has nothing to do with the peculiar contents of the unconscious mind. But it has everything to do with the question whether the individual can stand a certain panic, or the constant strain of a psyche at war with itself." Jung states that the psychosis is generally interpreted from two points of view, either as a primary weakness of consciousness or as an "inordinate strength of the unconscious." He believes that the second theory "cannot be easily dismissed, since it is not unthinkable that the abundant archaic material could be the expression of a still existing infantile, as well as primitive, mentality. It could be a question of atavism." He adds, "I seriously consider the possibility of a so-called *development arrêté,* where a more than normal amount of primitive psychology remains intact and does not become adapted to modern conditions."

We may summarize Jung's major contributions to the study of schizophrenia as follows:

1. He was the first to apply psychoanalytic concepts fully to schizophrenia. He described the existence of the autochthonus complex in this condition, and felt that affectivity was the dynamic force of the complex.

2. He was the first to see the possibility of psychosomatic involvement of the central nervous system in schizophrenia, although he did not formulate his concept in these words.

3. He attempted a description of the basic personality of the schizophrenic, which he identified with the introvert type, contrary to the personality of the hysteric, which he identified with the extravert type.

4. He advanced the theory of the collective unconscious. According to him, many symptoms of schizophrenia were the reproductions of the archetypes deposited in our collective unconscious.

5. He thought that schizophrenia was due to unusual strength of the unconscious and that an abnormal number of atavic tendencies did not adjust to modern life. With this last point, Jung seemed to reaffirm the importance of congenital factors and to minimize greatly the role played by environmental or interpersonal forces.

VII. Sullivan

Harry Stack Sullivan (1892–1949) is the American psychoanalyst who has made the most valuable contribution to our understanding and treatment of schizophrenia.

The full evaluation and assessment of this man in the history of psychiatry have not yet been accomplished. Too recent are his contributions; too many are his writings which have not yet been published posthumously and therefore are unknown to those who had no direct contact with him;* and last, but not least, too difficult is the interpretation of some of them, as Sullivan was not endowed with a clear style or with facility of expression. In the last few years, however, his contributions have gained much wider acceptance, and his influence has been rapidly expanding, even in non-psychiatric fields. His theories are now an integral part of social psychology.

The great contribution of Sullivan is his interpretation of psychiatry as the study of interpersonal relations. According to Sullivan, the psychiatrist must be more concerned with what goes on between people than with the intrapsychic. As a matter of fact, according to him nothing is intrapersonal or intrapsychic; everything evolves from the individual's relations with other people, especially people with whom he has lived in his childhood, his parents or parent-substitutes, whom Sullivan calls "the significant adults" in the individual's life. Everything is interpersonal; all our thoughts and phantasies deal with people, either real or imaginary.

One might say that every type of dynamic psychiatry is interpersonal. Isn't Freud, for instance, studying what goes on between parents and children, when he describes and interprets the oedipal situation? This is true only to a limited degree. Freud focused his attention not on the interpersonal

---

* All the works by Sullivan are now in the process of being published by W. W. Norton & Co., Inc.

relations but on the fight of the individual against his instincts.
The parents are seen by Freud, mostly as a source of sexual
strivings which the child has to inhibit. In his early writings,
Sullivan, too, under the influence of Freud, gives considerable
attention to these sexual strivings and stresses sexual maladjustment as the precipitating factor of neuroses and psychoses. Later, however, he comes to recognize the importance
of the parent-child relationship in its totality. Sexual difficulties may enter, under exceptional circumstances, as the cause
of the abnormal interpersonal relations. Generally they are
the effect, not the cause, of a poor parent-child relationship.

According to Sullivan, the attitudes of the parents determine the responses of the children. The personality, or the
"self," of the child is built from "reflected appraisals," that is,
appraisals coming from the parents. The anxiety of the
mother, or her anger or disapproval, brings about discomfort
and anxiety in the child, too. He may be badly hurt in the
course of the development of his self-esteem; he may dissociate from consciousness what is unpleasant, and throughout
his life may resort to "parataxic distortions." By parataxic distortion Sullivan means distorted interpretation of an interpersonal situation. The distortion is due to the fact that the
patient identifies the other person involved in the relation
with somebody else, or with a person who exists only in his
fantasy. If the parataxic thinking is not corrected, the patient
will obtain less and less "consensual validation," that is, less
and less recognition from others of the validity of his statements. This lack of recognition will increase the difficulty of
the interpersonal relations.

A complete examination of Sullivan's contributions and
theories will not be attempted here. Some of his concepts will
be illustrated in Part II of this book. For a more thorough
understanding of his impact on modern psychiatry, the reader
is referred to other works. (Mullahy, 200–202), (Thompson,

258–259), (Sullivan, 254–255). In this section some of his contributions in the field of schizophrenia will be examined briefly.

In his first paper on schizophrenia, published in 1924, Sullivan states that the foundations of his work and his concepts of this disorder are pluralistic, but that he has accepted three conceptions particularly in the interpretation of his data (248). The first is the postulate of the unconscious, as formulated by Freud. The second is the teleological vitalist hypothesis (Nunn's concept of hormic energy). The third is "the genetic hypothesis of mental structure and functions, which implies a vital sequence of experience."

In this paper Sullivan writes that "the disorder is one in which the total experience of the individual is recognized." He acknowledges the eruptions of primitive functions of thinking, and, even in this first paper, he mentions the fact that there is a profound alteration of the sentiment of self-regard. He criticizes Bleuler's formulation of the disorder as based on impairment of the association of ideas, and reaches the important conclusion that the primary disorder in this illness is one of *mental structure*. He writes that the mental structure is dissociated in such a way that "the disintegrated portions regress in function to earlier levels of mental ontology."

Although in this important paper he seems to have great regard for the works of Lévy-Bruhl, Jung and Storch, and refers more than once to the appearance of primordial or archaic concepts, Sullivan tries to explain the schizophrenic symptomatology as a return to infantile and fetal mental functions exclusively. In other words, according to him there is no necessity for accepting the notion of phyletic regression of mind structure. The phenomenology is subsumed in the "ontogenetic psychology." Although, to my knowledge, Sullivan is the first psychiatrist to speak of *mental structure* in a formal non-organic sense, his predominant interest in the dynamics of schizophrenia prevents him from conceiving that some of the phenomena, even from a formal point of view, are determined by factors which transcend the history of the patient. Thus, already in this first paper, his conceptions seem diametrically opposite to those of Jung.

Sullivan is not clear, however, in understanding the schizophrenic mental *structure* to which he refers. From a dynamic point of view, his first paper is a good forerunner of the great contributions that he was to make later. We have already mentioned his realization of the alteration of the sentiment of self-regard in the schizophrenic. He also outlines in this paper simple therapeutic procedures: there should be no free associations; the patient should be asked simple questions; the psychotherapist should have recourse to primitive forms of thought exchange.

In a paper, published in 1925, Sullivan states that according to his experience, the complex etiology of the disorder has invariably culminated in a situation in which the sexual adequacy of the individual, according to his own ideals, was acutely unsatisfactory (249). In the same paper he writes that there is no good reason for believing that all or most of that which is not fairly accessible to awareness is sexual. He feels, however, that many things, particularly undeveloped impulses which finally escape inhibition, may acquire a sexual coloring.

In a very important paper, published in 1929, Sullivan writes that after thirteen years of study of schizophrenics, his conclusion is that the existing interpretations of this disorder are misleading (250). He feels that the current researches, such as genetic, organic and psychoanalytic, have been inadequate. The schizophrenic has to be seen as a total person. Prenatal and childhood environmental factors are very important. He reminds the reader of the peculiarity of the parents of the schizophrenics, and states that psychiatrists have usually noted that they cannot secure a good history of a schizophrenic from his mother. He regards schizophrenia as a condition characterized by a) "regressive preponderance" in implicit fantasy life; b) a "regressive preponderance" of overt irrational activity, like ritualistic and magical behavior; c) an extraordinary preponderance of motivations which normally receive only occasional expression. He states that this concept of schizophrenia implies a genetic-evolutionary view and eliminates all considerations of duration of the process and of the outcome. He feels that the problem of motivation is the fundamental one. He writes that in the history of every case which he studied, he found a point at which there occurred "a disaster to self-esteem." This event often was experienced by the patient as a state of *panic*.

Sullivan expands the study of psychological, social and therapeutic factors in other papers (251–253), but it is in his *Conceptions of Modern Psychiatry* that most of his contributions are reformulated and integrated (254). The theory of interpersonal relations is expanded more adequately here. The sequence of events which leads the schizophrenic from the state of panic to a full-fledged symptomatology, is dynamically illustrated. He describes the resurgence of what was dissociated, more from the point of view of the subjective experience of the patient than from the point of view of the observer. In all the writings of Sullivan, even in those that deal with abstract conceptions, the patient is seen not as a clinical specimen, but as a person who cannot relate to his fellow human beings without a hard struggle. When the patient is examined or treated by Sullivan, he is no longer alone in his subjective world; Sullivan shares his suffering and sees his frightening vision of "reality." In the therapeutic situation Sullivan is not predominantly an *observer*, but, as he emphasized, a *participant*.

In many of his papers, Sullivan gives instruction about

his psychotherapeutic treatment of schizophrenics, but his methods have not yet been described or collected in an organized manner. Thompson (259), White (273), and all others who had the opportunity to work with him or to observe his work, have witnessed the high level of his results. Frieda Fromm-Reichmann is now continuing the therapeutic work of Sullivan, to which she has added many remarkable contributions of her own (101–105).

Summarizing, one may state that Sullivan's contributions to the field of schizophrenia are the following:

1) He demonstrated that schizophrenia, as well as any other psychiatric condition, is engendered by poor interpersonal relations, especially parent-child relations. In doing so, he opened up new vistas and included psychiatry in the realm of social sciences. His achievement in this field has not been contrasted by two limitations which, for sake of objectivity, must be taken into consideration. First, even he, the creator of the theory of psychiatry as the field of interpersonal relations, felt that the chronic insidious cases of schizophrenia must be organic in nature. This idea, however, to my knowledge, was never elaborated and, fortunately, got lost in the midst of Sullivan's great contributions. Secondly, as Murphy and Cattell (203) wrote and Mabel Cohen (55) reemphasized, although Sullivan made a social science of psychiatry, he did not study the over-all sociological forces which derive from the structure of our society and which, by acting upon the individual, may predispose him to mental illness. Undoubtedly, Sullivan had been exposed to the anthropological and sociological influences necessary for such a study (Sapir, George Mead, Benedict, etc.); as a matter of fact in the last few years of his life he devoted himself to the psychiatric study of international relations. It is to be assumed that if untimely death had not interrupted his work, he would have

expanded his interpersonal approach to include the impact of society as a whole on the engendering of psychiatric conditions and of schizophrenia in particular.

2) More than any of his contemporaries, Sullivan felt that schizophrenia could be treated psychotherapeutically. He made the psychotherapeutic treatment of the schizophrenic the primary work of his life.

PART TWO

The Psychodynamics
of Schizophrenia

CHAPTER III

Frequent Psychodynamic Patterns
Leading to Schizophrenia

I. Early Exposure to Anxiety-Producing Interpersonal Relations. General Primary Defenses.

In this chapter some of the most frequent psychodynamic developments which lead to schizophrenia will be taken into consideration from a general viewpoint. The reader who prefers the study of individual cases is advised to read the subsequent chapters of this part, and to return to this chapter afterwards.

❖ The fundamental concept of the dynamic interpretation of schizophrenia may be summarized in the following sentence: *Schizophrenia is a specific reaction to an extremely severe state of anxiety, originated in childhood, reactivated later in life.* It must be added that this specific reaction occurs when no other solution, no other possibility of adjustment, is any longer available to the patient.

This is not a definition of schizophrenia. A definition must include an understanding of the specificity of the reaction, and will be attempted later on in this book (page 384). The above statement is only a preliminary concept, the results only of the dynamic studies which are presently to be reported.

A characteristic unique to the human race, *prolonged childhood,* is at the basis of this mental condition, which is also specific for the human race. The newborn of many species are helpless and dependent on parental care for survival. They have certain needs, like food, sleep, rest, warmth, and contact with the body of the mother, which must be satisfied. When these needs are met, a state of "satisfaction" follows (Sullivan, 254). The young human being, however, on account of his more complicated organization, has an additional, equally important need: the *need for security,* or for the *feeling of being secure.* This particular need for security is first felt at the end of the first year of life when, contrary to what happens in other species, the human baby is *still* dependent on others. Both the feelings of satisfaction and of security depend on others, that is, on the relations that the child has with the few adults who take care of him. The lack of satisfaction of the physical needs, which were mentioned above, may bring about a state of anxiety, one which is also experienced by animals under similar conditions; but lack of security determines a type of anxiety which is characteristic of the human species (see page 239).

What does it mean to be secure or to feel secure in childhood? This feeling, or state of being, cannot be expressed adequately by the child, and is difficult for the adult to recapture. It is connected with the development of the self-image; it is a state of being which involves the present and the future.

The child needs love, care and approval in order to feel secure. The child who is loved realizes that he is wanted, that the parents enjoy him, that they take care of him not because they must, but because they wish to do so. With the feeling that he is wanted, he gets the feeling that he is worthy of being wanted and loved, that he belongs, he is a part of the family, and at the same time he is recognized and accepted as an individual in his own right.

As Sullivan emphasizes, the child needs approval in order to feel secure. Somehow the child is almost immediately involved in our evaluation of things as good and bad. Having no system of his own, he depends on the parents to establish what is good and bad. Good is what receives approval, bad what receives disapproval. The child wants to be approved; his self-esteem is built up by the approval he receives. If the parents have a warm, loving, respectful and sympathetic attitude toward the child, he will develop the same attitude toward himself and later on toward others.

The child learns also to conceive his own role in life from the standpoint of all the participants in his interpersonal world. He learns to look upon his own behavior and upon himself as an individual from the points of view of all these people, because it is through them that he organizes his behavior and develops his sense of self. Appraisal from others will build his own self-esteem; understanding of the roles assigned to him and acceptance of them as well as identification with the surrounding adults will enable him to organize a sense of self-identity. The image that the child builds of himself consists of self-esteem and self-identity, in addition, of course, to the body image, which is not considered here.

At times, however, the child is not surrounded by this atmosphere of love, acceptance and approval. His strivings toward self-esteem and self-realization are thwarted by the destructive influences that the surrounding adults have upon him. His security is attacked and anxiety originates. Inasmuch as he needs these adults in order to survive, he has to accept their destructive influences, which he may take for granted and consider necessary. The parents may be as confused as the child and may use their destructive influences, believing that they are constructive, and necessary for the growth of the child. If the parents are hostile and disparaging, the child will acquire the same attitude toward himself and toward society. Disapproval brings about discomfort, fear of punishment, anxiety. Anticipation of disapproval engenders further anxiety.

Each child has to be disapproved at times; but if he meets an atmosphere of constant scolding, criticism, nagging, he will grow up with the conviction that there is something bad in him, that he is worthless. This inner feeling of worthlessness may accompany him throughout life and may be reinforced, even by minor failures. Preference for other children, unfulfilled promises, ridiculing of first creative activities, lack of encouragement, disappointments, instability of parents so that the values of what is right and wrong are continuously changing, are some of the factors which produce anxiety. Violent scenes of alcoholic and psychopathic parents are causes of anxiety in children; however, from my experience, I have found that they are not as dangerous as a subtle, often unconscious, hostile attitude which is disguised by a mask of love, and finally succeeds in breaking the child's will and in undermining his belief in himself. The mother of one of my patients used to tell him, "You are a horrible child. Only mother can love you!"

Parental affection may also become a cause of anxiety if there are "strings attached" to it, if the child feels he will have to pay too high a price for it or, in other words, if he feels that the parents will increase their expectations beyond his ability to live up to them.

These anxiety-producing parents are generally severely maladjusted. They are people who are not able to give. At times, they appear to be willing to give a great deal of themselves, but in reality what they want in return is to live their children's lives by infiltrating into all their activities and by replacing their children's wills with their own. Consequently, the children cannot develop a sense of initiative. When they have to do something on their own, they feel anxious and irreparably lost.

Parental affection may also become a cause of anxiety because it may stimulate incestuous sexual feelings which are disapproved of in the environment. This point will be discussed later in this chapter.

The child who is confronted with this atmosphere of discomfort and anxiety will make strong attempts to protect himself by finding a *modus vivendi*, a compromise. The defenses he resorts to are multiform. Some of them will be found as responses to abnormal early interpersonal relationships, regardless of whether the individual will later follow a psychoneurotic or a psychotic pattern of behavior.

A type of defense consists of the removal from consciousness of many unpleasant experiences occurred in early childhood. These experiences, however, will remain as parts of the unconscious and will continue to influence the behavior of the individual with unconscious mechanisms. What is retained in the unconscious does not consist only of repressed episodes, but also of unconsciously assumed beliefs, attitudes, and, especially, *generalizations*. For instance, the attitude that the person throughout his life has toward women may be determined to a large extent by the repressed experiences he had with his own mother during his early childhood, and by the beliefs and generalizations which he unconsciously assumed on account of these experiences.

Another important development consists of the organization of the self-image of the "bad-me" (Sullivan, 255), or of being the bad child. It may be surprising to find included among the so-called defenses the development of the self-image of the bad child, which obviously has unfortunate aspects in relation to the self-esteem of the individual; but, as we are going to see, this image also has defensive elements which favor its occurrence.

The child who suffers on account of his contacts with the rejecting parent, generally the mother, tries desperately to preserve a good image of the parent, often the image which he built during the first year of life, when only the needs for satisfaction (see page 44) were taken care of by the parent.* After the end of the first year the child wants to retain this image. He wants to feel that the parent is good. If the parent is punitive and anxiety-arousing, it is not because she is malevolent but because he, the child, is bad: Mother is right in being harsh and strict with him and showing how bad he is. The child who is raised in this environment and wants to maintain the image of the mother as a benevolent person, tends therefore to accept her negative appraisal of him. By accepting this negative appraisal, he develops the self-image of the bad child, that is, he considers himself inadequate, bad and has little self-esteem.

The preservation of the good image of the parent is made possible by the removal from consciousness of the most unpleasant traits of the parent. This removal from consciousness is often made easier by the acceptance at face value of the apparently loving and warm manner of the parent. The child is deceived by these superficial manifestations and by a process of selective inattention remains unaware of subtle or even not so subtle hostility.

Thus, the child will have two images of the parent: the good image, which is conscious, and the bad image, which will remain unconscious. The good parental image appears in

---

* The tendency to preserve the "lovableness" of mother and the consequences of such tendency have been considered by Suttie in a different frame of reference (256).

myths, legends and dreams as God, the fairy, the magic helper, the protector. The parental bad image appears as the witch, the stepmother, the bad man, etc.

Why does the child need to preserve the image of the good parent? We must realize that in early childhood the parent, generally the mother, is the person who connects the child with the world; in a certain way, is the only representative of the world. The child must accept her in order to fulfill his inborn potentialities toward full maturation and socialization. If she is not good, his need and desire to accept the world will be thwarted and certain tendencies toward autism and arrested socialization will manifest themselves (see page 294). In the cases in which the mother is not the almost exclusively important adult, this need to preserve her good image is not so strong.

There are other reasons for wanting to preserve the image of the good parent. It is more tolerable for the child to think that he is punished by the good parent because he deserves to be punished than to think that he is unfairly punished. If he is punished, although he is not bad, he will have a feeling of despair; the situation will seem to him beyond remedy, hopeless. Maybe he is so horrible and worthless that he must be punished even without being bad. Some children actually force themselves to do "bad things" in order to be bad, because they want to be punished for something that they have done rather than for nothing. By being "bad" they preserve the self-image of the bad child. In addition, if mother is good, the child thinks that she will love him even if he is bad.

Except in cases which will be described in the next section, the child raised in this atmosphere does not feel hopelessly bad and makes repeated attempts to regain some self-esteem.

Most of the developments just described occur at a non-

verbal or preverbal level. The child is not able to verbalize
his feelings which remain very confused, inconsistent and
often self-contradictory.

Other developments may occur in connection with the
parental images and the self-image of the bad child; but we
shall limit ourselves to a brief discussion of them in order not
to be distracted for too long from our main topic. When we
use the word "parent" we generally mean the mother who in
our culture almost always has the predominant parental role.*
The need to preserve the good image thus applies much more
thoroughly or exclusively to the maternal image. At times, in
fact, the child, who has repressed the bad image of the
mother, does not repress at all the bad father image, of which,
on the contrary, he remains fully conscious. This generally
occurs when the child feels that the more powerful parent,
the mother, wants to see him as an ally in her war against
the father. For the same reasons the child may repress the
good image of the good parent (mother or father), if the
good parent is a weakling dominated by the spouse and the
child feels he must ally himself with the strong parent.

Another development found frequently in psychopathology is the repression of the self-image of the bad child. The
patient professes great confidence in himself, but if he undergoes therapy, he discovers the underlying derogatory self-
image.

Images of siblings are also formed, but generally they do
not require many dissociations from consciousness, unless
these siblings assume parental roles, as in the cases of parental
death or desertion.

In addition to the organization of these conscious and unconscious images and to the dissociation from consciousness
of many unpleasant experiences, the child who is raised in

* For a clear exception to the usual parental roles of the mother and
the father, see the cases of Peter and Gabriel (pages 88–108).

this anxiety-producing environment develops relatively fixed patterns of behavior in his interpersonal relations. Although he considers himself bad, he wants to obtain parental love. A frequent method by which he tries to obtain this love is by complying with his parents' requests and denying his own wishes. He may see that there is no other way out, that the parents, although "good," never yield; he may obtain love or approval, and therefore maintain some self-esteem, only at the price of compliance. The child then becomes a compliant person.

Other children find out, instead, that their parents, although "good," yield only if they continue to cry or to have temper tantrums, if they insist and argue for what they want. They learn from experience that the fight will be rewarded. They develop an aggressive, hostile personality.

Other children learn that the best way to avoid anxiety is not by complying or by fighting (parents will not give in to these methods), but by keeping away from their parents as much as possible, by maintaining an emotional or physical distance. They develop an aloof, detached personality.

An important defense thus consists in developing one of these types of personality (compliant, aggressive or detached) or a mixture of them, (if by personality we mean the prevailing pattern of relating to others). Horney was the first to describe these three types of personality and to understand fully their consequences in the whole life of the individual (129, 130). As far as I know, however, she did not write that the *specific type of personality is determined by the specific type of relationship that the child has with his parents*. It is the specific type of this most important early interpersonal relationship (parent-child) which determines which one of the three types of relatedness the child will develop. Since there are two parents, and they are not consistent in their attitudes, a mixture of different types generally results with one type, however, predominating. At times these types of relatedness alternate in such an abrupt or "stormy" way as to become an important aspect of another type of personality to be described later (page 58, and page 74).

The developments which have been mentioned are not sufficient protection if the child is exposed to an atmosphere of severe anxiety. Additional defenses are needed. Neurotic symptoms will develop, such as hysterical symptoms, phobias, obsessions, etc. To enumerate all these possibilities would mean repeating the whole field of dynamic psychiatry. Instead, we shall limit ourselves in the next section to the consideration of those circumstances and factors in childhood which are most apt to lead to a schizophrenic disorder.

II. Factors Likely to be Found in the Childhood of Schizophrenics

In many cases, it would be impossible to predict from the early history of the patient whether he would develop a psychoneurosis, a psychopathic condition or a psychosis. In fact, the fundamental feature, presence of anxiety in childhood, is common to these three types of psychiatric disorders. However, from the history of the childhood of schizophrenic patients we learn that in that period of life the anxiety of the patients was of such tremendous intensity that no sufficient self-esteem and sense of self-identity could be built and that certain trends of psychological development prevailed over others.

Although it is the mother who contributes mostly in producing the conditions which we are going to describe, we usually find in the history of schizophrenics that both parents have failed the child, often for different reasons. Frequently the combination is as follows. A domineering, nagging and hostile mother, who gives the child no chance to assert himself, is married to a dependent, weak man, too weak to help the child. A father who does not dare protect the child because of the fear of losing his wife's sexual favors, or simply because he is not able to oppose her strong personality, is just as crippling to the child as the mother is.

Occurring less frequently in the United States, but still frequently enough, is the opposite combination: A tyrannical father is married to a weak mother, who has solved her problems by unconditionally accepting her husband's rules. These rules do not allow her to give enough love to the child.

At times, one parent dies or is away because of divorce, separation, war, etc., and the child is completely at the mercy of the destructive parent, generally the mother.

In these very unhealthy home atmospheres a state of intense relatedness exists between the preschizophrenic child and his parents, especially the mother. The child is actually overwhelmed with feelings, but this relatedness, these feelings, are extremely anxiety-provoking and destructive.

The disturbance created by this situation is often considered a one way stream flowing from the parent to the child. Actually this is a simplified view of the situation. Although it is true that the disturbance originates on account of the parent's personality, it soon becomes more complicated or a two-way stream. The child, who at this period is intensely emotional and often overactive, with his behavior causes out-of-proportion anxiety to the already over-anxious parent. The parent expresses her anxiety in the form of hostility toward the child, who will then be more adversely affected. He will respond with behavior which will be even more objectionable to the parent. Furthermore, the mother often feels guilty for her hostility and this guilt-feeling increases her anxiety. A circular process of ominously vast proportions thus originates.

It is during this period, generally from the end of the first to the end of the fifth year of life, that the unpleasant experiences described in this section, the "uncanny" experiences, as Sullivan calls them (255), take place.

On account of the intensity of these experiences, the preschizophrenic child finds difficulty in organizing the defenses which were described in the previous section. It is his awkwardness in developing these defenses which is often a prelude to a later schizophrenic disorder. We have seen, for instance, that the child who grows in an atmosphere of exposure to anxiety tries nevertheless to preserve the good image of the parent. The preschizophrenic child may find difficulty in preserving an image which is so remote from reality. At times, in order to maintain this good parental image, which is the one he built when he was a baby, he tends to act like a baby or will manifest strong regressive tendencies toward babyhood. He feels that his only fault was to grow as an independent person; if he is a baby, if he is completely taken care of and has no will of his own, mother will be good to him. Mother then will appear again not only as good, but as omnipotent, doing everything for the child, out of her generosity, and the child will tend to maintain a parasitic attitude. Any real or symbolic separation from mother is capable of producing great anxiety even much later in life. I have found these tendencies to a more or less pronounced degree in several preschizophrenics and schizophrenics, but in my experience they are not the most common or the usually predominant trends in the psychodynamics of schizophrenia.

In the majority of cases one finds that the good image of the parent cannot be preserved. In these cases the patients do not tend to regress to a stage of being completely taken care of like babies, possibly because even when they were babies they could not build a good parental image. The preschizophrenic remains to a certain extent conscious of the bad qualities of his parents. Even he, however, represses in large measure their worst characteristics. Only in a minority of cases is the child's rejection of his parents complete or almost complete. Possibly these are the cases of early infantile autism (see page 266, and page 296) and of child schizophrenia. In the overwhelming majority of cases the child represses the fact that he was hated, falsely accused or the innocent target of hostility. He remains, nevertheless, with the feeling that the parents are bad, and he harbors hostile thoughts of them. At the same time he thinks he should love them and therefore he feels guilty. Often he alternates in believing in his own values and in those of his parents. When he prefers his own he feels guilty; if, on the other hand, he follows the orders and values of his parents he feels crushed, victimized, compelled to surrender.

Often the child is afraid that people can read his thoughts, see his hostility for his parents and will punish him. Even normal young children have the feeling that adults know their thoughts or steal their thoughts (Erikson (67), Kasanin (153), Piaget (212)). In preschizophrenic children this impression is enhanced by their fear that the parents may know the feelings of hostility the children harbor for them.

One would think that the inability to repress totally the bad image of the parent would have a beneficial effect, inasmuch as the child would not need to build the self-image of the bad child (page 47). Actually this is not the case in preschizophrenic children, and for several reasons. In some cases the image of the bad child is built early, when the bad image of the parent is repressed, that is before the bad parental image becomes conscious again. More often, however, the preschizophrenic child believes that although the parent is bad, he, the child, is worse. No matter how bad the parent is, she or he is willing to take care of the child. The child is willing, to a certain extent, to accept the bad parent but, as we shall see shortly in more detail, he tries to detach himself emotionally from the "badness" of the parent.

In some patients the situation is even more complicated. The attitude of the parent is so inconsistent and the conscious parental image is so frequently vacillating between being the bad or the good one, that the child cannot even develop the self-image of the bad child, as at least something solid and sure in his life, even if negative. He suspects that he is bad, but he is not absolutely sure. He will be in a state of anxious uncertainty and will develop an image of himself which, for lack of a better expression, may be called the image of the presumably-bad-child. This image will predispose him to a particular type of prepsychotic personality, namely, the stormy personality, as we shall see shortly.

The atmosphere described in this section is gloomy indeed. A redeeming feature is the hope often harbored by the child that when he grows up things will be different. Although he has given up the hope of obtaining parental approval, he still makes attempts to learn how to avoid disapproval. But even learning to avoid parental disapproval is an impossibility for him, on account of the parents' hostile and inconsistent attitude.

Since the child is in constant expectancy of disapproval, and tries desperately to anticipate possibilities of disapproval in the futile attempt to avoid them, he becomes very sensitive to the slightest sign of the oncoming reproach. Thus the preschizophrenic develops the sensitive personality which has been described by many authors. This sensitivity to disapproval persists until it is covered by other defenses. The preschizophrenic is never able to tolerate even minor frustrations, because frustrations mean disapproval from other human beings.

Like other children, the preschizophrenic, too, will attempt to find ways of relating to others which will decrease his anxiety. Often he learns that complying, as the person with a compliant, dependent character does, or that being aggressive and hostile, like the hostile person, does not pay. His parents may not accept either compliance or hostility. Only by detaching himself emotionally will he avoid further attacks on his self-esteem. Furthermore, by detaching himself emotionally, it will be easier for him to tolerate his own image of the bad child and to accept the partially conscious bad images of the parents. Moreover, the hostility for them will produce less guilt feeling. Thus, very often, but by no means in all cases, he develops the character changes which are found in a person with a schizoid personality.* He becomes aloof, cold, inactive. It is to be remembered, however, that the fundamental fact is that *in every preschizophrenic who develops a prepsychotic schizoid personality such development is chronologically secondary to the mentioned intense relatedness.*

We do not want to convey the idea that all persons who develop a schizoid type of relatedness are candidates for schizophrenia. On the contrary, we have seen in the previous section of this chapter how frequently even people who never become psychotic find in this form of relatedness a convenient pattern of dealing with others. It is true, however, that people who later develop schizophrenia are particularly drawn toward this type of relatedness. It is also correct that not all individuals who become schizophrenic develop a detached personality or a schizoid character armor. Many of them find this condition unsatisfactory. In their attempt to escape anxiety, they alternate between extreme submissiveness, hostility and detachment, to find that none of these states removes their difficulties. They will develop what I have called the

---

* Forerunner of the characteristics of the schizoid personality may be what Sullivan has described in infants as "the dynamisms of apathy and somnolent detachment" (255). The uncomfortable tension produced in the infant by lack of satisfaction of certain needs may be reduced or warded off by either apathy or falling asleep. There is no proof, however, that the infants who resort predominantly to these mechanisms are the same who later develop a schizoid personality.

stormy personality (see page 74). But before going on with
the description of the schizoid or the stormy personality, it is
important to give particular attention to certain traits which,
although they may be present even in normal children, assume
particular significance in children who, later in life, develop
schizophrenia.

Lack of warm social contacts induces in these children
a rich fantasy life, and excessive brooding about certain subjects, one of them being their own sex identity. As many
authors have described, the preschizophrenic child has some
indecision as to what his sex is going to be. The impossibility
of any frank conversation about sex because of cultural mores,
and because of the apprehension about having any discussion
with the parents, encourages these ruminations about sex.
Children who know that they are boys or girls, are not sure
that they will maintain their sex throughout their lives. Boys
may lose a penis; girls may grow one. Although many children have these thoughts, in the preschizophrenics they
assume the form of serious uncertainty, for several reasons.
In many cases the uncertainty is due to the fact that children
somehow connect the hostility which surrounds them with
their belonging to a given sex. If they were girls instead of
boys, or boys instead of girls, they think their parents would
be more pleased with them. If the most disturbing parent is
of the opposite sex, the child would like to be of the same
sex as this parent, so that he could resist him or her better.

In my opinion, the most common cause of this uncertainty
is the fact that the child who is rejected by both parents tends
also to reject both parents and therefore has difficulties in
identifying himself with either one of them. I have not found
the fixation of the Oedipus complex to be an important or
frequent cause of the anxiety which leads to schizophrenia.
Even the most orthodox Freudian analysts have found that
the psychic early traumata in cases of schizophrenia have

occurred before the onset of the Oedipus complex. As we have seen in this section, hopelessness about obtaining parental love and approval and not fear of castration is, in my experience, the frequent cause of the anxiety which starts the dynamic developments leading to schizophrenia. However, in families or cultural environments where sex is strongly expressed and repressed, the Oedipal situation may in certain cases increase the already existing anxiety and make the occurrence of schizophrenia much more probable. The child attributes his sexual desires to his being bad.

A combination which I have found in several preschizophrenic girls is the following: The girl has been rejected since birth by the mother who, in rejecting her, rejects herself. The same mother has a different attitude toward "her boys." Later, the girl is afraid of closeness to the father because of her incestuous strivings. She will reject the father or will manage to be rejected by the father, in order to escape her sexual desires. In this situation, too, we see that the pre-existing rejection by the mother is the most important factor, and has sensitized the girl to such a degree that she will not be able to cope with her incestuous feelings.

A mechanism which English and Pearson also find frequently, and which we shall describe here in the case of a girl, is as follows: The girl is rejected by the mother who imposes ill treatment on the child (66). The child turns from the mother to the father, thus heightening the heterosexual strivings which, however, are hampered by the fact that an identification with the mother has been impossible, on account of the mother's unpleasant characteristics. Rejection by the father complicates the situation; it inhibits heterosexual strivings, increases the homosexual ones (love for mother), prevents further identification with the mother and predisposes to an identification with the father which, however, will be unsuccessful because of his rejection. Thus, not homosexuality but a state of sexual confusion and indecision is engendered. If accidentally, seductions by people of the same sex occur, this uncertain orientation of the child may become homosexual. Homosexuality, however, will never be entirely accepted because of the child's rejection of the parent of the same sex; thus it will be repressed or projected. Often the described confusion or the homosexual tendencies are repressed, and the child's identification with his own sex is achieved later in childhood. These repressed tendencies will come back to the surface after the onset of the illness.

In addition to this confusion and uncertainty about his own sex, the preschizophrenic child has, to an exaggerated degree, that feeling of omnipotence described by many authors even in normal children. (Ferenczi [76], Kasanin [153], Silverberg [237, 238]). The normal child has feelings of omnipotence and lives in a world which he thinks exists for him only; but whereas a child who has normal relations with his parents is gradually corrected by them with their approach to reality, because he wants to accept their reality, the preschizophrenic child cannot depend on his parents for this correction. The reality which they show him, the reality of the world, is their unpleasant reality. The child is reluctant to lose these feelings of omnipotence; when he succeeds in losing them, to a more or less conscious degree he still has the desire to go back to them. Together with this tendency toward the feeling of omnipotence, there is the tendency toward a unique, or very subjective outlook. The child has tendencies to use his own language, with expressions he has coined. (See page 294.) All these tendencies, which are called autistic, are more or less suppressed and repressed but will become conscious again during the psychosis. They will be discussed later again in more detail (page 266, and page 296).

Some of the tendencies and traits described in this section could be corrected at least partially if the child were exposed to some healthy influences, like close relations with friends and distant relatives. Unfortunately, in many cases the personalities of the parents of schizophrenic patients are such as not to encourage extrafamily social intercourse, so that what has been described as the "ingrown family" is constituted. Compensatory interpersonal contacts are lacking, and the children are dependent for psychological development on their unfit parents, even more than children usually are dependent on parents.

III. The Schizoid Personality and its Outcome

We have already mentioned that the two types of prepsychotic personalities which are of particular interest to the student of schizophrenia are the schizoid and the stormy personalities.* These two types of personality are established in childhood, as a result of the relations that the individual has with his parents, but they become progressively more marked and acquire a definite pattern after puberty.

In this section we shall describe first the schizoid personality in general, that is, not exclusively the *prepsychotic* schizoid personality. Then we shall illustrate the cases in which, on account of the particular developments described in the second section of this chapter and on account of other factors, the schizoid personality leads to a schizophrenic condition.

The person who has a schizoid personality appears aloof, detached, less emotional than the average person, less concerned and less involved. Actually, at an unconscious level the schizoid is very sensitive, but he has learned to avoid anxiety in two ways: first, by physical distance from situations which are apt to arouse anxiety and, second, by repress-

---

* The possibility is not excluded that other preschizophrenic personalities will be differentiated in the future.

ing emotions. This physical distance is maintained by avoiding interpersonal relations or avoiding doing things which will evoke an unpleasant reaction from other people\Often, when the schizoid person is in the latter part of his childhood, he would like to do things, but he still remembers from early childhood that action does not pay because it provokes a storm of intense and threatening emotional responses in the surrounding adults. Anticipation of actions means anticipation of a repetition of these emotional storms. The patient therefore becomes underactive. In some cases the parents have actually encouraged him not to do things; doing nothing meant being a good child, "because" what the child did was "always bad." The patient may grow with a deeply-rooted pessimism about the outcome of his actions.

In several instances these schizoid people seem to be relatively active. On close observation they reveal, however, that they do things because they cannot resist the pressure of somebody who pushes them, generally the parent. This occurs not only in childhood and adolescence, but even later on, when the patient has to select a profession, clothes, marital partners, apartment, furniture, etc. More often than not, this parental pressure is exerted not directly, but in a subtle way. Under the pretense of helping the child, a parental invasion of the child's personal prerogatives takes place. Ironically, many of these parents boast about their liberality and non-interference in their children's lives. The children protect themselves from this parental invasion with further detachment.

Contrary to what the compliant person does under parental pressure, the child who has developed a schizoid personality prefers not to comply. And yet, to the observer, he quite often gives the impression of being extremely compliant. Actually he complies in a perfunctory way. He goes through the motions of the imposed act, but without being emotionally involved. He prefers to do this because he has learned that this is the best way to avoid anxiety. If he succeeds in being emotionally uninvolved, his resentment and hostility will be deeply repressed. Should he later become schizophrenic, the resentment and the hostility may be displaced toward non-parental figures who may become the persecutors.

\The person who develops a compliant personality has much less difficulty than the schizoid, because he learns to accept emotionally the values of his parents. Of course, at a deep level of unconsciousness he may also retain the bad image of them and not accept them. Only later on in life, or if he is analyzed, he may dethrone his parents.\The compliant person complies in order to please; the schizoid complies in order not to displease. The schizoid is often partially aware of the conflict between himself and his parents. The character armor of indifference will remove to a great extent the unpleasantness of the conflict, but will not succeed entirely in repressing the awareness of the conflict itself. The schizoid character armor will remove the consciousness of anxiety to a large extent, but will never confer on the patient the feeling that he is really wanted, approved, accepted.

Often the schizoid acquires a certain insight into his personality. He recognizes that his detachment is a very unsatisfactory solution and indeed he is justified in feeling that way. The compliant and the aggressive persons find some kind of solution, although at a high price. The compliant person gets approval, while the aggressive person generally manages to get at least some kind of substitute for what he really wants. The schizoid reaches a pseudo-solution by denying a great part of his life, but by doing so he may make that part of his life which he continues to live more awkward and unstable. His unconscious hostility and resentment increase; his emotional and social isolation are never complete enough to protect him entirely from anxiety; on the other hand, he harbors

secret desires to reconnect himself with that emotional and
social life from which he has tried to detach himself.

His lack of emotion is not due to simple repression of
feelings; it is also a reaction-formation to too much sensitivity,
not only to the sensitivity of the preceding intense relatedness
to the parents, but also to the sensitivity which still exists at
an unconscious or preconscious level. The dreams or phantasies of the schizoid often reveal great emotional potentialities; they are very dramatic, have great intensity of feelings
and vivacity of actions. They transport the patient into an
adventurous life, and often in storms of affect. With his actions, on the other hand, the schizoid person tries to be as
static as possible. Often, if he acts, he will be very impersonal
and will try to avoid communication by direct contact.

A nine-year-old schizoid girl used to write letters to her
parents, in which she would explain what she did not dare to
tell them directly. These schizoid persons prefer to write letters, rather than make telephone calls, and even when they
write, they do so in a cold, formal, business-like manner. In
his school work, the schizoid learns much more from a book
than from the direct presentation of the teacher. Written
material conveys meaning to him much better than spoken
material, because a direct interpersonal experience is eliminated.

In spite of this apathy and aloofness, there are little signs
which indicate how the sensitivity of these schizoid persons is
ready to come back to awareness. One of them is that they do
not have a sense of humor. They cannot stand a joke or anything humorous said about themselves. Sensitized as they are
to environmental hostility, they see in the joke a pungent
remark made against them. In this interpretation they are
right, because many jokes and humorous remarks have an
element of hostility (98, 12). However, this element of hos-

tility is so mild that it is not only tolerated but often perceived as a pleasant experience by the normal person. For the schizoid, a joke is a serious rebuff. For the same reasons, schizoids are poor losers at play. Defeat is another proof of their inadequacy and increases their already strong reluctance to do things with other people.

Schizoid persons succeed without difficulty in decreasing their needs to an almost unbelievable extent. Many of them live alone in furnished rooms, away from their families, away from social contacts of any kind, except those which are absolutely necessary. As we have already mentioned, phantasies, sexual or otherwise, replace their need for action. The phantasies often involve objectives which cannot be attained; therefore, any possibility of action is removed. When they are confronted with a situation which does require some action, they convince themselves that it is not necessary or worth while to act. They are able to work, but they do not let any emotion enter into their activities. Often they select a type of work, like mathematics, which is impersonal and which may be performed without any emotional involvement.

On the other hand, the schizoid, some time during his life, may even become concerned over his lack of feelings. In spite of his detachment he knows that his life is dull and gray. He would like to become emotionally involved but he cannot. At times, he feels that he must pretend to have feelings and is afraid that people may "see through" him, and recognize that he has no emotions. Actually, once he is successfully analyzed, he will discover not that he has pretended to have feelings, but the opposite, that he has pretended to have no feelings. The analysis itself is very difficult, first because of this lack of conscious feeling, and secondly because when the patient becomes aware of his feelings he is afraid to bring them up. He fears lest they be used against him to demonstrate how bad he is, just as he originally feared his parents would do. He is still afraid that feelings will bring about rebuff, anxiety and attacks on his self-esteem.

What happens to the person who has developed a schizoid personality? The most frequent occurrence is that he will remain schizoid during his entire life, unless, of course, timely therapy or unforeseen circumstances diverge him toward a different adjustment.

In this category are included even many people who had those "uncanny" experiences described in the second section of this chapter. Some of these people respond to the difficulties of life with further detachment; their character armor becomes so pronounced that many psychiatrists consider these patients preschizophrenic or cases of latent schizophrenia. In reality, the greatest majority of them never develop schizophrenia. They live socially permissible, though inadequate lives.

On the other hand, for many individuals who underwent the experiences described in the second section of this chapter, the schizoid personality is not a sufficient protection from further anxiety and maladjustment. The difficulties become more apparent after puberty, for several reasons. The defenses that the patient was able to mobilize were somehow adequate in his childhood, when he had to contend exclusively or predominantly with his family. Later, not only his family but the world at large makes demands on him and would like him to relinquish his detachment and withdrawal. The school situation, the emerging sexual desires and the search for a position in a competitive world, put his character armor to serious strain. The average person is able to overcome these difficulties, but not the preschizophrenic patient. First of all, his schizoid character armor not only does not protect him, but actually handicaps him when the forces of the environment compel him to do things in spite of his withdrawal. He feels "pushed around." He does things haphazardly and half-heartedly and cannot exploit his full potentialities. The reduction of spontaneous activity confers on him a certain awkwardness and inappropriateness. His lack of experience in dealing with people increases his fears. When he succeeds in evading his schizoid attitudes and in doing things, the old sensitivity tends to come back, and tremendous anxiety is experienced. The early uncanny experiences which the patient has forgotten continue to alter or to give a particular coloring to his present experiences. The persons he has to deal with are, symbolically speaking, other parents, and he has never learned to deal adequately with parents. The world appears to him to be populated by millions of authorities, ready to criticize him. Symbolically, every interpersonal situation is a reproduction of the old parent-child relationship; a compulsive attitude quite often compels the patient to make this reproduction more similar to the original situation than is actually required. Furthermore, in spite of his detachment, he maintains the image of himself as the bad child; but to be bad now means to be incapable, inadequate, worthless. His awkwardness seems to prove to him that he is really inadequate. The competitive spirit of our society, where everybody is supposed to assert himself or to show how good he is, makes his predicament worse. Handicapped as he is, it is no wonder that he fails. Any additional failure increases his feeling of inadequacy and predisposes him to subsequent failures. The series of failures and disappointments which Adolph Meyer was the first to describe takes place. The patient undergoes a progressive maladaptation, and needs to withdraw into a stronger armor, with more defensive mechanisms.

This progressive maladaptation has many different aspects and courses. At times, although it is very pronounced, it is not noticed by the superficial observer. On the contrary, the lack of emotional involvement and the slow tempo confer a certain poise on the individual which may even be appealing to some who do not recognize the underlying unrest. In other cases an insidious maladaptation leading to schizophrenia may become apparent even to the superficial observer, but only in some areas. For instance, the scholastic record may reveal a steady decline. The patient was a good student in grammar school, less than average in high school and could not function in college.

At other times the maladaptation is not continuous but is arrested or enhanced by favorable or adverse circumstances, to resume the original course later. The maladaptation generally undergoes a rapid development if it has become apparent abruptly, shortly after puberty. At this age the preschizophrenic starts to harbor ideas and feelings which further discourage him and remove the last remnants of hope. When he was a child, he maintained some optimism as far as the world and the future were concerned; he thought that the world at large would be good to him, once he grew up (see page 56). After the onset of puberty he gradually develops the opposite feeling. He projects to the world, or to society at large, the feelings that he had for his family, but he is not aware of this projection. He finds out that the family situation could have been much better for him; he also feels that the world is going to be bad, and bad for *him only*. What is "bad" involves not only the present, but the past, the present, and the future. The sexual urges which for the first time are experienced very strongly, and the hopelessness about satisfying them in an acceptable manner, increase his utter discomfort.

These more or less conscious realizations which occur after puberty are important; they cause a state of desperation which has an ominous prognostic meaning. The realization that the world is bad only for the patient cannot occur in certain cultures, like those described by Ruth Benedict, where all children are exposed to the same hostility (22). In these cultures, children very seldom develop schizophrenia; however, they develop character traits which are not acceptable in our society. Also, in certain situations like defeats, famines, and national catastrophes, as have often occurred in Europe, there is no increase in the incidence of schizophrenia, because in those circumstances people feel that the world is *bad for everybody,* and this consideration does not cause a lowering of individual self-esteem.

When, on the other hand, the patient realizes that the world is bad for him only, he also feels that the world is bad for him because *he* is bad or worthless. He feels that if he has always done wrong, it is because there is something wrong *with him.* He feels that if he has not been loved, it is not because love does not exist in this world, but because *he* is not lovable. The malevolent authorities which populate the world are malevolent only toward him and with good reason. He must hate himself more than anybody else hates him. His self-esteem undergoes the most injurious attacks.

The defense mechanisms become more and more incapable of coping with these situations. Anxiety is not covered any longer; on the contrary it is felt more and more and finally it is experienced with the same violence with which it was experienced in early childhood. Through generalization it spreads like fire to all situations which are similar to the original unpleasant situations. The behavior becomes more and more symbolic; it continues to be distorted by the power of the repressed experiences. Finally the anxiety is experienced as actual panic, unless other defenses—this time psychotic—are mobilized.

We have rapidly surveyed the patient from the establishment of the schizoid personality to the psychotic outbreak. There are, however, other points which have to be taken into consideration: First, certain specific factors which may delay or even avert the psychosis; then, some factors which enhance its occurrence.

Among the factors which may delay or avert the psychosis is the ability of the patient to resort to additional neurotic defenses. Even from the study of his early childhood one could have detected that, although prepsychotic traits were present, the patient also had many neurotic trends and that there was the possibility of a development toward the neurotic pattern of maladjustment. These conditions will not be discussed here in detail because the relation between schizophrenic and neurotic symptoms will be the subject of Chapter VIII. Here, however, it suffices to say that often the schizoid person tries to defend himself from the growing anxiety with psychosomatic and obsessive-compulsive mechanisms. In some cases, these additional defenses will protect the patient from the psychosis, but in others they will not. The obsessive-compulsive symptoms which are found in those who eventually develop a psychosis, are usually general in character, and not limited to a single situation. They actually tend to exhaust the reserves of the patient. For instance, the patient has to repeat every single act twice, or is concerned with every movement of his body, etc. The psychosomatic symptoms of the preschizophrenic are also general in character, including a generalized hypochondriasis, implying some distorted conceptions of the body image.

Often in our culture the schizoid patient who does not find sufficient protection in his defenses, resorts to unusual, drastic action at a reality level, rather than to *obvious* neurotic symptoms. He may enter a monastery, where he will be away from the dangers of life; he may join the Army where he will be forced to respect authority; he may select some kind of work where he has to display no initiative whatsoever. In a considerable number of cases, he may devote himself more and more to religion. In the belief and practice of religion he will try to get the comfort which he could not find elsewhere. Religion and God are the good parents, whom he substitutes for the bad parents. They are the parents who accept even the inadequate and worthless children. The patient is unwilling to submit to the authority of his parents, but may respect the authority of God. He is not able to relate to people, but is able to develop some kind of relatedness to God. People don't give love, but God does. In some cases this escape into the church is a protection which may delay the psychosis. On the other hand, if in the association with the church the patient does not come into contact with some human beings and receive warmth and comfort from them, he may receive no help at all. Abstract concepts often do not provide what he needs. Some religious conceptions are too near to the delusional material of some patients and therefore dangerous to entertain; they may slip into real delusions. On the other hand, since they are so near to delusional material, they may make delusional material unnecessary. From a practical point of view, the religious fervor may push the patient in two directions. The patient may retain the religion of his parents but become much more involved in it than they were, or the patient may change his religion. By converting to a new religion, he fulfills several goals: 1) he rebels against his parents; 2) he tries to find in the new religion a solution to his problems, which he thinks cannot be solved if things remain unchanged; and 3) he tries desperately to make some satisfactory interpersonal relationships, though they have to be in a very unusual form (convent, missionary work, etc.). Generally, the change in religion occurs from the more rational and abstract religion to the more mystical.

In many instances the patient who escapes the psychosis does not need to resort to these drastic measures in order to protect himself from anxiety. He succeeds in channeling his unfortunate experiences and his tendencies into ways which are acceptable to society and which will raise his self-esteem. His tendencies toward desocialization and autistic expressions may direct him successfully toward an artistic career (see page 310). The feeling of having been unfairly accused by his parents may stimulate in him interest in defending people, and he may become a successful lawyer.

On the other hand, the situations which enhance or hasten the occurrences of the psychosis are episodes which all of a sudden cause violent injury to the self-esteem and tremendous increase in anxiety. In spite of his detachment, the patient is not capable of avoiding these episodes. At times he does not do anything to avoid them. As we have mentioned before, he harbors secret desires to experience feelings again and does not dislike the idea of making excursions into life. Occasionally, in a sudden fit, he takes active steps which are completely incongruous with his previous attitude. Oftener, however, he lets himself be pushed by the events.

A schizoid young woman may be induced by her mother to get married, although she is psychologically unprepared for that step. The husband, actually selected by the mother or by the incorporated image of the mother, may be experienced as another parent who will evoke the old infantile anxiety.

A schizoid man, who has lived in a single room of a boarding house for many years, practically in isolation, may come in contact with another tenant, an aggressive, domineering woman. By her aggressive methods, she may succeed in overcoming his shyness, and then later in convincing him to marry her. Sexual urges or other considerations may induce the patient to accept the marriage proposal. After the marriage, the patient's anxiety is apt to increase because he finds in the wife a new parent. He will make serious attempts to adjust to the spouse's new way of living but will find that task insurmountable. Because of what he considers blatant proof of his failure in living, he can no longer hide from himself the feeling of worthlessness which he has been able to check, up to that point in his life.

The intimacy of marriage is often very threatening for the patient because it tends to reproduce situations similar to those which have caused him so much anxiety in his childhood.

Another frequent occurrence which will make the defenses of the schizoid personality insufficient protection from anxiety is the unexpected development of a friendship or of some social contact with a person of the same sex. Strangely enough, the patient succeeds, for the first time in his life, in establishing a more meaningful interpersonal relationship, but homosexuality, which had been repressed for so long on account of the social attitude toward this form of sexuality, and on account of the patient's rejection of the parent of the same sex, threatens to come to the fore again and causes deep anxiety.

In many cases, the anxiety of a woman increases very much after the birth of a child and produces the so-called post-partum psychosis, generally as a result of a double identification with her child and with her own mother. A few days after the birth, but at times even several months later, the patient feels, even consciously, that she wants to leave husband and child and escape from the situation. She alternates between thinking that she does not love the child and thinking that she loves the baby very much but is not able to take care of him. If she is not treated properly and in time, she may develop a full psychotic attack, often catatonic. If she is treated adequately, she will realize that in her relation to the child she relives the anxiety of her former relationship with her own mother. The patient is afraid that she too will be as bad a mother as her mother was. In addition to this feeling, there is the other feeling that she is worthless, not even good enough to be a mother. In these cases, the husband generally is not able to supply or to compensate for the increased emotional needs of the patient. In reality it is difficult for the husband to cope with her increased needs because the patient, on account of her personality difficulties and increased anxiety, is not apt to stimulate in him an attitude of warm understanding.

Zilboorg thinks that childbirth represents castration to these women, and that the psychotic reaction is due to a recrudescence of the penis-envy. He thinks that for these women the child has "more the value of a lost male organ than anything else." Zilboorg's patients experienced an inadequate motherly relation to the child, and for that reason, he thinks, they turned to masculinity (278, 279). Deutsch has found that it is more difficult for emotionally deranged, schizoid women to preserve their psychic balance when the maternal relationship must be spread to several children than when it is concentrated on one child (64). In my experience with post-partum schizophrenic psychoses, I found the first birth to be the precipitating factor, at least as frequently as subsequent births.

IV. The Stormy Personality

We have mentioned that in addition to the schizoid there is another type of personality which is frequently found in persons who are apt to become schizophrenic. This type I have designated as the "stormy personality."

We have seen how often preschizophrenic children, in their attempts to avoid the unpleasantness of their relationships with their parents, become detached, and distant, and develop a schizoid personality. They find in detachment a better protection than in either compliance or rebellion. The persons who develop a stormy personality, however, do not find a solution in this state of detachment. In their attempts to gain parental approval and love, and to avoid disapproval, they try all types of attitudes, and all of them to an extreme degree. They have to try all possible means of defense and reactions, because none of them seems actually able to remove the existing anxiety. This uncertainty about the way of reacting is enhanced by the inconsistency of the parents. Thus, the early environmental situation promotes in them a capacity to change their attitudes toward life repeatedly. The changes may be slow or abrupt; oftener, they are sudden, violent and drastic.

Another characteristic which is found much oftener in stormy than in schizoid personalities is a certain inability to build a relatively stable self-image. These are the persons who, as we saw in the second section of this chapter, cannot even build the self-image of the bad child, but only the image of the presumably-bad-child. They also cannot establish a relatively stable sense of self-identity. As we have already mentioned, with this term we do not mean only identity as far as belonging to a certain sex is concerned (see page 45), although this sex-identification is an important part of the meaning of the term (see page 58). We mean also that the patient is not able to answer certain fundamental questions which he asks himself. Who is he and what do his family, his acquaintances, society at large, expect from him? What does he expect from himself? These questions are not asked in a philosophical sense. Philosophical questions of this kind are normal occurrences in bright adolescents and in adults. The preschizophrenic, and especially the stormy person, is concerned with these problems in a more concrete way and in reference only to his own specific social situations. When we say that he asks himself these questions, we do not necessarily mean that he literally asks them of himself, although that may also happen. Often these questions and the inability to answer them remain at a non-verbal level, as a feeling of drifting aimlessly, a feeling of not being able to find oneself.

In the child who will develop a stormy personality, this sense of self-identity could not receive the proper organization for several reasons. First, the child could not properly identify with either of his parents, for the reasons mentioned on page 58. The conception of his sex identity and of his role as a male or female was thus seriously undermined. Secondly, he was uncertain about the role that the parents and siblings assigned to him in the family. He could not make out what *he* meant to each of the surrounding persons, especially adults, but also siblings. He felt *inconsistently unwanted,* the meaning of his identity or presence in the home remaining not well established, unless connected with overt rejection. As we have seen, even his general attitude toward others (one of either compliance, aggressiveness, or detachment) could not become well established. This uncertainty about the role attributed to him is due not only to the fact that the parents were inconsistent and torn by opposite feelings, like hostility, and a sense of duty. It is due also, and perhaps predominantly, to the fact that the child tried not to become cognizant of the role the parents attributed to him because he was too frightened to do so. He also sensed that the parents consider him "bad," but he did not want to see himself consistently in that light; it would be too devastating to his self-esteem. Somehow he knew that he was not accepted, but he was not sure that he would be rejected entirely. He vacillated between all possible points of view. He saved some self-esteem, but at the expense of a stable sense of self-identity.

The organization of the senses of self-esteem and self-identity generally go together in the individual, and it is only through a process of abstraction that we may separate them. In both schizoid and stormy personalities self-esteem and self-identity are impaired, but self-identity seems more impaired in the stormy personality.\The schizoid person is to a certain degree more certain of his own identity because he has accepted, at least, the self-image of the bad child. He resorts to detachment to defend himself; he becomes an inconspicuous follower, a wallflower, an isolated person. But the stormy person cannot compromise that way. He is forever busy searching for his role, although he does not meet with success. He still tries to "reach" people, although he is hurt every time he tries. He still harbors ambitions, although he becomes increasingly more discouraged.

In adolescence his difficulties increase, as his inability to find his place extends beyond the family circle and involves his peers, his acquaintances, and the community in which he lives. What role does he play with them? What do they think of him? When later he enters the working world, the same uncertainty creeps in as inability to find himself as a member of a certain profession or trade. These feelings are further increased by the competition which he senses all around him. Although feelings of this kind are experienced by neurotics too, they are much more pronounced in the prepsychotic individuals who have a stormy personality.

\ As we have already mentioned, patients with stormy personalities often are compliant to a degree of extreme submissiveness; at other times, they are aggressive and hostile; more seldom, they withdraw into an ivory tower of complete detachment. When they are not detached, they are very anxious; anxiety governs their lives. They are like schizoid persons who have been deprived of the protection of the schizoid defenses. They are, therefore, very vulnerable; every little event has the power of unchaining a crisis. The life of these persons in general is a series of crises.

In some instances these patients do not show sudden changes in character but appear almost constantly either submissive or aggressive. Their submissiveness, however, consists of that pseudo-compliance which we have also found in schizoids (see page 62). Their aggressiveness consists mostly of loud manners void of results. These attitudes of pseudo-submissiveness and pseudo-aggressiveness seem to increase the anxiety and precipitate more and more crises. These patients often live in an atmosphere of catastrophe and doom. On the other hand, they show an extreme resiliency, as mentioned before, and seem able to recover strength, spirits and good humor easily. Generally, however, they do a poor job in covering up the underlying unrest with this gay, shallow and effervescent attitude. When they are in a relatively good mood, they harbor grandiose phantasies and even paranoid tendencies. They are going to be great and successful, if they are just given a chance. They are going to get married to wonderful persons, etc. They like extremes only. For them, everything is black or white. Acceptance means devotion and love; non-acceptance means utter rejection and hate. There are no nuances in their lives. If the analyst accepts them, he must give all of himself to them. If they feel that the analyst rejects them, they go into a state of despair or detachment.

The changes in mood and attitudes do not relieve these patients. They often resort to excessive use of drugs and alcohol. The crises they go through often weaken them progressively. These crises are frequently precipitated by little happenings, magnified by the patients, who unconsciously see in them symbolic reproductions of the original situations which produced anxiety. At other times, the crises are really due to critical situations which the anxiety of the patients precipitates by forcing them to inappropriate actions (marriage, love affairs, absurd jobs, etc.). Things do not just happen to them, as they seem to happen to schizoid persons. They seem to search actively for a meaningful way of living. They actually live a stormy life, in a certain way comparable to the life which appears in the dreams of schizoid persons (page 64).

The schizoid personality has many points in common with the stormy personality, but enjoys the protection of the emotional detachment. Some schizoid persons whose character defenses become insufficient or who finally make excursions into life resemble stormy personalities. All gradations or mixtures of schizoid and stormy personalities are found.

Some types of stormy personalities are the quiet kind, who seem sociable and friendly, but whose anxiety is of terrific proportions. Also, in my opinion, the category of stormy personalities should include some of the patients who are considered by other authors as belonging to the pseudo-neurotic type of schizophrenia. Some of these "pseudo-neurotic" patients at times, by means of hypochondriacal rationalizations, maintain intense conscious anxiety which cripples their lives. They differ from schizoid persons inasmuch as they are openly anxious and in a state of unrest. Because in many of them no conversion of symptoms into actual psychotic manifestations occurs, I prefer to consider them stormy personalities, who may or may not become psychotic.

Even after the onset of the psychosis, the stormy personality maintains that resiliency which has been mentioned. Attacks are generally shorter than those in patients who have had a schizoid personality. On the other hand, stormy personalities with predominantly hostile and defiant traits, may be very resistant to any treatment and difficult to manage in hospitals.

V. The Psychotic Solution

All the defenses have now collapsed or have been recognized as futile, and the patient is unable to cope with his state of anxiety. If the development of events follows an acute course the patient falls into the state of panic which has been so well described by Sullivan (254). The patient has done everything possible to defend himself, and everything has failed. The schizoid personality no longer protects him; the stormy personality produces another crisis from which he cannot resurge. He cannot compromise with reality any more; now he has to change "reality." He will do so by entering the psychosis.

In many cases, however, a conversion of schizoid or stormy traits into active psychotic symptoms occurs gradually and very slowly. In some instances, one sees that this gradual conversion started at the time of puberty or even before.

The psychosis may be viewed as the ultimate attempt on the part of the patient to solve his difficulties. From a psychodynamic point of view it offers many apparent advantages, which vary in each case as to quality, quantity and interrelationship. The most common are the following: the difficulties appear to the patient no longer general in character, but restricted to specific situations. He is not the self-pitied victim of his own general inadequacy and worthlessness, but the victim of the malevolent doing of other people. Whereas before the onset of the psychosis the patient felt that millions of malevolent authorities were justified in having a low opinion of him, now he feels that a few malevolent, powerful people are unfair toward him and cause his troubles. There is thus a return to a situation similar to the one which existed in his childhood, when a few powerful people were responsible for the difficulties of the patient, but there is a displacement in attributing the responsibility. In the majority of cases, not the parents but other people are considered the wrong-doers. This displacement permits, even during the psychosis, a partial repression of the bad image of the parent. In a subsequent period the displacement does not involve a few people only, but may be generalized again to a vast category of persons who are identified with the original wrong-doers.

Another advantage which the psychosis offers is the elimination of the self-image of the bad child, which later events had strongly reinforced. Now the patient does not consider himself "bad" but unfairly accused of being bad.

The schizoid character armor, which proved insufficient in protecting the patient from anxiety-arousing feelings, including hostility for others, will be replaced by a much more pronounced process of desocialization, which will imply a gigantic removal from the psyche of symbols obtained from others.

The individuality which the patient felt was crushed by others will finally emerge. Guilt and disapproval will be apparently eliminated in numerous ways.

In the third part of this book, we shall study the formal processes which make possible these psychotic developments. In the fourth part we shall find out that, unless successful therapy or other fortunate circumstances occur, the difficulties of the patient are not eliminated by the psychosis but replaced by others. No real solution is found at any stage of the illness, but only pseudo-solution.

In the remaining chapters of this part we shall illustrate the dynamic developments of individual cases, pointing out the factors which predispose to each of the four types of schizophrenia (catatonic, paranoid, hebephrenic, or simple).

VI. Criticism of the Above-Mentioned Concepts

We shall now offer some criticism of the concepts expressed in this chapter.

The above outline of the chain of causes and effects which lead to schizophrenia, like every outline, has both good points and bad. Although it may clarify the development of many cases, it does not fit every case; even in cases which it does fit, it leaves out much which is important.

Many cases are a mixture of the examples given here. A few cases do not conform to the pattern at all. No dynamic development can be exactly duplicated, since each case is in some respects unique. The cases are all similar only in that a severe state of anxiety, originated in childhood and symbolically spread later in life, has not been resisted by other defenses.

Some people may debate even this point. In fact, one often hears that cases of schizophrenia have occurred in the best environment, in children who have received a great deal of love and security from their parents. In these cases, the impression of love and security may be received from brief interviews which the psychiatrist has with the parents of the patient. Actually, one should be aware that the more the parents of the schizophrenic give the impression of genuinely caring for him, the more subtle was the behavior which undermined his security. As we have mentioned, in certain cases the parental love was available, but it was a love which, for some reason, produced great anxiety.

One often encounters anxiety-ridden parents who give the impression of being genuinely interested in the patient. In many cases, the anxiety is actually due to a strong unconscious guilt feeling. The parents try to exert pressure on the psysician, to get reassurance from him that everything possible is being done to restore the patient's health. I have witnessed several instances where the doctor, although non-analytically oriented, has detected this guilt feeling in the parents and has tried to reassure them. "Parents should not feel responsible; schizophrenia is a mysterious disease; it can happen to everybody." But the parents are generally not reassured. As a matter of fact, they know better than the physician. They know the truth in a vague way, as a feeling which cannot be verbalized well and therefore gives the impression of being irrational. These guilt feelings often lead parents to more irrational actions. In a vain attempt to undo what they have done or what they feel they have done, they take the patient home from the hospital, in spite of an advanced state of regression. Consequently the activities of the family are thwarted or actually paralyzed, and care of minors at times is curtailed because of the enormous amount and unusual kind of care that the psychotic at home requires.

Another criticism which may be made of the opinion expressed in this chapter is that many persons, in spite of unhealthy environmental conditions, similar to the ones described in this chapter, have not become schizophrenic, but only psychoneurotic. This criticism will be discussed fully in Chapter VIII.

Another controversial point in the outline offered in this chapter is the fact that much more importance is given to the anxiety caused by lack of security, which starts at the end of the first year of life, than to the anxiety due to unsatisfied early needs, which may occur during the first year of life. In a minority of cases of schizophrenia the parents managed to retain a fairly adequate parental role, when the child, being less than a year old and not yet a center of independent will, had not yet caused them excessive anxiety and hostility. Those are the patients who tend to return to the dependency of babyhood and who tend to retain the image of the omnipotent mother, as mentioned on page 54.

For the majority of cases, however, this point of the importance of the first year of life in engendering schizophrenia is more of theoretical than practical interest. Undoubtedly many parents who expose the child to severe anxiety at the end of the first year have already exposed him to it during the first year of life. In this outline more importance was given to the anxiety which may be experienced toward the end of the first year of life and afterwards, because, as we shall see again later, only a type of anxiety which requires high symbolic processes may engender schizophrenia. This long-circuited anxiety cannot occur during the first few months of life.

A point which has not been taken into consideration in the outline presented here is the impact of sociological and cultural factors in the engendering of schizophrenia. There is no doubt that such circumstances as the presence of an industrial culture rather than a pre-industrial, an urban location rather than a rural, the emigration to a foreign country rather than living in a native land, etc., are all factors which predispose to schizophrenia as well as to other mental disorders. Many of these important studies have already been made at a sociological level (Faris and Dunham 68, Malzberg 183), as well as at an epidemiological level (Felix and Kramer 74), but many more are needed.

This admission of the importance of these sociological factors may seem a contradiction on the part of the author, who has given so much prominence to dynamic factors, and especially to the early family relations, but it is only an apparent contradiction. The culture may act in at least two ways: 1) by its impact on the internal organization of the family, on the assignment of specific roles and emotional values to its members and, more specifically, on the determination of most of the methods by which children are to be brought up; 2) with certain specific mores by which it may inflict adverse psychological pressures on the individual, causing him to be under greater strain and causing his psychic reserves, which might have compensated for the forces leading to schizophrenia, to be no longer sufficient. These sociological studies seem to indicate that even in the presence of those unfavorable psychodynamic developments which have been mentioned in this chapter, the individual has immense resources, which should not be underestimated and which will try to protect him from schizophrenia. When society at large cooperates in some way with certain destructive trends of the early family environment, the defenses will break down more easily. At the present time, psychiatrists are more prepared and more willing to study personal psychodynamic factors, but it is to be foreseen that in the near future sociological and cultural forces will receive appropriate consideration.

Another criticism, which is connected with the previous one, is that the outline presented in this chapter is contingent on conditions in the United States, or in Western countries, in the middle of the 20th century. At different times and in different places, an extreme state of anxiety, leading to schizophrenia, may be engendered by another set of factors. The author considers this criticism justified, as he believes that every generation of psychiatrists in a given culture has to revise the psychodynamic conceptions of the previous generations or of different cultures. The formal mechanisms of the psychiatric conditions, however, do not seem to vary with geography or history.

CHAPTER IV

Patients Studied With the Help of Members
of Their Families

In this chapter, we shall begin to study individual cases of schizophrenia. We shall start not with the direct study of schizophrenic patients, but with an evaluation of the dynamic factors operating in their lives, as they appear from the treatment of a close relative. I find this to be a very good technique at the beginning of the treatment of several schizophrenics, when the advanced stage of disintegration makes direct contact with the patient difficult.

A simple anamnestic history obtained from a relative quite often gives a distorted or oversimplified account of the facts. If, on the other hand, the therapist has a sibling or a parent of the schizophrenic under treatment, a great deal of information will be obtained which will be of great importance in the treatment of the schizophrenic himself. Of course, the disadvantages of treating two members of the family at the same time are known to everybody. However, in cases of advanced schizophrenia the advantages outweigh the disadvantages by far. This recommendation of simultaneous treatment of a relative of a schizophrenic by the same therapist refers to the treatment of a sibling or of a parent. Treatment of the husband or wife of the patient by the same therapist is not recommended.

When it is impossible to have two members of the family treated by the same therapist, it is advisable to suggest treatment by two different therapists who will be in close contact with one another and able to exchange information. Often it is even necessary to exert pressure on siblings or parents of a schizophrenic in order to convince them to undergo treatment. At times they are induced to accept treatment because they recognize that by doing so they will help the patient. Eventually, however, they will discover that the results of the treatment are rewarding for them, too.

Rose Spiegel has developed a special technique for young schizophrenics who refuse to be treated directly (240). She sees the parents in weekly sessions and through them, examines and evaluates what goes on in the parent-child relationship.

By the study of two or more members of the family of the schizophrenic patient, the psychological factors which were discussed in the previous chapter may be easily determined, and other problems may be clarified. For instance, two opposite and apparently self-contradictory facts, both of which paradoxically have been used in support of the hereditary nature of schizophrenia, can be re-evaluated. The fact that, at times, two or more cases of mental illness occur in the same family has often been mentioned as proof that the family is tainted by a hereditary gene. This circumstance, of course, can easily be explained if we study the family psychodynamically, and see that the parents had very destructive effects on several children. If the parents themselves were schizophrenic and lived with their children, their influence may have been even more destructive. It is important that in many instances of multiple cases of mental illness in the family, not every case is affected by schizophrenia, but by other psychiatric conditions.

The opposite fact, that often only one of the siblings is affected by schizophrenia, has also been taken as proof of the hereditary nature of the illness. In fact, siblings do not necessarily inherit the same genes but are exposed to the same environment. The weakness in this point of view can easily be demonstrated. The parents and the family environment are the same for all the siblings, only in a physical, not in a psychological sense. The parents, in their feelings, and in their conscious and unconscious attitudes, are different for each child. They may be very destructive toward one child, less destructive or not destructive at all toward another one. Siblings, in their attitudes and feelings, are also different toward one another, so that actually for each member of the same family the play of interpersonal forces is different.

This will be clearly illustrated in the cases presented in this chapter, which concern two brothers, Peter, who became a severe neurotic with some schizoid traits, and Gabriel, who became a full-fledged schizophrenic. The information concerning both patients was obtained from Peter, since Gabriel was never seen by a psychotherapist. I feel, however, that the information obtained through the analysis of Peter is highly accurate. The presentation of Gabriel's case in this form also has the advantage of eliminating the technical difficulties which are inherent in direct work with schizophrenics, and is therefore didactically suitable as the first report of a case of schizophrenia. After the two cases have been presented, some comments will be made concerning both.

PETER*

Peter is a 23-year-old man of Jewish extraction, born in Central Europe. After the German invasion of his native land,

---

* All names of patients in this book are fictitious and identifying data have been altered.

his family moved to a South American country, where they have resided since then. Peter started to complain of nervous symptoms about a year prior to the beginning of psychiatric treatment. After trying every kind of physical treatment in South America, the parents felt that a trip to the United States would do him some good. In the United States Peter continued to be distressed by his symptoms and consulted a physician, who advised him to see a psychiatrist.

During the first interview, the patient appeared morose and preoccupied. He could hardly talk English and expressed himself mostly in Spanish. He said that he perspired all over, that he had repeated attacks of diarrhea, and could not sleep, and that he always felt tired and tense. These symptoms abated somewhat when he was not in the company of others. He added that when he was very tense, his nose would first become clogged, then red and swollen. He was worried lest people would see this disfiguration of his face. He also said that he felt guilty over the death of his brother Gabriel who had been affected by schizophrenia and had recently committed suicide. Peter felt that maybe he too was affected by an organic disease of the brain, and that maybe "a bad heredity ran in the family." He was very disturbed.

Psychoanalytic treatment was recommended, to which Peter agreed. For many sessions the main topic was the patient's parents. The mother, 43-years-old, was described by Peter as a fearful person, who had no confidence in herself. Although she was very well educated and spoke many languages, she always claimed that she did not know anything, and did not want to participate in any discussion. When the family moved to South America, she was so afraid to make social contacts that up to the present time she had not succeeded in making one friend in the new country. When she was introduced to people, she blushed, and was so nervous that she could not even pronounce her own name. Peter felt that he could never confide in her. To use his own words, he never heard one thing from her that he liked to hear. Talks between mother and son would usually end in fights. She criticized everything he did: his work, his girl friends, his attitude toward his father, etc. On the other hand, she never praised him. When he was a child, she hit him repeatedly; during the beatings he would smile at her in defiance. She put him to bed at 6:30 every night until he was six years old.

Peter never experienced any feeling of closeness for his mother; on the contrary, he always had contempt for her. In the beginning of the treatment, he thought that maybe he loved her, but then he understood that he really did not. It was difficult for him to make such an admission; he felt guilty for not loving her. He had forced himself to love her, because a child should love his mother, but no real warmth or love had existed between them. Peter did not remember, except in very rare instances, having been kissed or hugged by his mother. She had been equally cold and distant, or even more so, toward Gabriel.

Peter's mother had always been unhappy, more so after the death of her second child. Peter knew that his grandmother had treated his mother badly, and that she had married his father to escape from her parents. At first she did not care for her husband, but finally she "adjusted" to him. Now she was the father's most powerful ally in any controversy between him and the patient.

Peter's father, now 51 years old, has played the most important role in his life. According to the patient he is a mechanical genius. In Europe he was a farmer, and mechanical engineering was his hobby, but in South America he had gone into the business of building machines for farmers. With little means, he had built marvelous machines and has had a few new agricultural implements patented.

Peter's father has peculiar habits. He gets up at six in the morning, works the whole day without any relaxation and goes to bed at six in the evening. He eats in bed, speaks to his wife about business for a few minutes and then goes to sleep. He is also as fearful as the mother is, but in a different way. Ever since Peter was a baby, he has heard his father say that they have to be careful, because "People are bad. They are ready to cheat you and steal from you, if you are not careful enough." Peter's father has cultivated no friends. His only interest has been to save money. "Save, save, save everything," was his motto. For instance, when he brushed his teeth, he used the minimum amount of tooth powder. Peter consequently was proud of his father because he knew that to save was a good thing. Another of his father's mottos which he liked to hear when he was a child was, "Foolish people make shit of gold; wise people make gold of shit." Peter's father would also praise wise people who were able to overcome the innumerable adversities of life. Peter listened to him with great admiration and was always convinced that his father was right. His father never told him "You have to do so and so," but he merely said, "I did so and so" and that was enough for Peter. The paternal examples were an unbreakable code of behavior for him.

Peter's father had been very considerate of Peter since the day he was born; he seemed to concentrate his attention on him and to neglect Gabriel. He used to tell Peter many stories, whose purpose, Peter thought, was only entertainment. But, as Peter discovered during treatment, his father, with his stories, had been constantly seeking admiration from the child. His father would say that many of the stories were episodes from his own life. Peter remembers that when he was four, his father had already told him of his adventures during the war against Russia. He had many scars on his arms and would exhibit them and say that they were the results of wounds sustained in fighting against a large number of Russians. Peter would listen in ecstatic reverence, but, at the age of six, he heard from an uncle that his father had never been in the war. Later he even found out that his father had been a deserter, and for several years, during the war, he had hidden himself in a cellar. Peter was ready to excuse his father, feeling that he had to lie to "undo the truth," and preserve the honor of the family. The other stories which his father used to tell him concerned children who had been massacred in wars; some were about gypsies who had stolen children, and had cut their throats with a sharp knife, after which the children had died a slow death, having been in agony for hours and hours. Peter's father used to tell Peter these stories while he was sitting on his lap, and would often simulate a cutting knife with his hands, laughingly saying, "we have to *schecht**" this child."

The stories which Peter's father told emphasized the evilness of life; the world was terrible; Peter had better be careful and stay near his father for protection. Father, or a paternal figure, was the hero and the protector, who would solve all the problems. For instance, Peter's father would often mention how he had eliminated the economic difficulties of his own parents by working hard since he had been a child. What a good child he had been and what a wonderful man he had become! In Peter there was a strong desire to emulate him, but at the same time he experienced anxiety because he felt that he would not be able to be a good child, according to his father's standards. His father never seemed to be satisfied; he often complained of how much the family was making him suffer; too much money spent, too little work was accomplished, and so on. He never seemed to be pleased, and never praised Peter or any other members of the family. Moreover, he often made impossible demands. Peter remembers that once when he was four and a half he went for a walk with his father in the country. They came to a narrow brook.

---

* Jewish word for cutting or slaughtering.

His father wanted to go to the other side of this brook, but since there was no bridge, he decided to pick Peter up and throw him over to the other side on the grass. However, he did not succeed in doing so, and Peter fell into the middle of the brook and got all wet. For a second, the child was scared, and looked at his father. There he was, laughing. Why did his father laugh? Peter thought he did so to reassure him; but was it really so? During the treatment, Peter realized that there had always been a double meaning in what his father did. That was what had confused him more than anything else.

Peter's father also had had the habit of simulating William Tell. He used to ask Peter to hold a piece of wood in his hand, while he would shoot at the wood with a real gun from a distance of a few yards. While this was happening, Peter's mother would be infuriated and scream from the window of the house, horrified at the possibility of an accident. The patient felt that his mother was a despicable coward who did not want to give him a chance to prove his courage and heroism to his father.

Much later, when Peter was working for his father on a farm, and was using a big agricultural machine, the little finger of his right hand got caught in the teeth of a large cogwheel. The wheel was moving only in one direction, so that it was not possible for the finger to be freed unless the whole machine was dismantled. Peter decided immediately to keep the machine moving, even if it meant losing a finger. He tolerated the pain very well, as the machine was amputating the last phalanx. After receiving first aid, he left the farm and ran to his parents' home, proud of himself, hoping that he would receive admiration for his heroic gesture. But even then he was disappointed. His parents did not seem to be pleased.

At other times, the patient would expose himself to dangers in the jungle, hunting snakes and other wild beasts, in an attempt to obtain recognition from his father. The few times that he got recognition, his anxiety was not relieved, because he felt that now he had a bigger task, that is, he had to retain that level of attainment. He felt that the demands on him would increase. He was therefore always in a state of self-perpetuating anxiety, caused by a feeling of non-fulfill-ment. In his own words, he was "running after an escaping goal, like a child runs after the moon." This anxiety, which originated in relation to his father, increased with his con-tacts with other persons, whom he experienced as father sub-stitutes.

The father never paid enough attention to Gabriel, who never admired him as Peter did. Somehow, the father did not seek as much admiration from the second child.

Apparently Peter was not fully aware of his own anxiety and state of unhappiness. He lived with a modicum of stability, conferred on him by the security he obtained in trying to ful-fill his father's demands. But, to use his own words, "to sustain myself on father was like sustaining myself on quick-sand . . . but even quicksand is better than nothing. Without that quicksand there would have been only emptiness."

The situation remained about the same until an important event occurred in the family. At the end of the second World War, a cousin, Miriam, and her husband, Leo, arrived from Europe. Through the good offices of Peter's father, they had been able to obtain a visa to immigrate to South America. After their arrival, it was decided that Peter and Leo would go to a farm, owned by the father, to work together. Father was enthusiastic about the farm, and told them that they could become millionaires. It was agreed that Leo would get one-half of the profit, Peter one-quarter, and his father one-quarter. Peter started to work with great enthusiasm and hope.

They had to chop away the wild vegetation of the jungle, cut the trees, seed new plants, remove stones, build cabins, etc. Leo, Peter, and a group of natives worked an average of sixteen hours a day. But the father was never satisfied. Now and then, he would come from the city to inspect and would always have a great many criticisms to make. Since it was new land, not yet cultivated, he had to invest money. He resented that, and was incapable of waiting for the results. Father started to talk against Leo, telling Peter how lazy Leo was, what a bum he was, how incapable he was of fulfilling his obligations.

But now, for the first time in his life, Peter had been exposed to close contact with another adult, and could no longer accept the derogatory attitude of his father. Leo seemed to be a very nice man. Peter often compared him with his father and could see how much better Leo was. Leo knew how to enjoy life; he knew how to work, but also how to play. He would talk not about money exclusively, but also about sports and women. A friendship grew between the two. For the first time, Peter discovered the world; he knew that a different life existed and realized that his home had been a "living grave." At the same time he was torn by conflicts. Maybe his father was right. Leo was too self-indulgent; maybe he could think about trivial things because he was a mediocre man, not a genius like Peter's father. Three months after they had started to work, Leo told Peter that his father wanted to change his verbal agreement and give Leo only one-third of the profit. Peter became very indignant and went to the city to argue with his father. It was the first time in his life that he opposed his father. Violent verbal fights resulted. Father told mother, "Peter is not our son; he is Leo's son." Peter tried to persuade his parents to change their opinion of Leo, but it was not possible to convince them. He went on working for a while with Leo but the altercations continued. This situation deteriorated rapidly so that the work on the farm had to be stopped, and the farm was sold.

From that time on, Peter's symptoms became manifest. He became aware of a state of anxiety whenever he had to perform a task. When in company, he was afraid that his nose would become swollen. Often he was tormented by acute pain in his chest and stomach. He would perspire conspicuously.

During the course of treatment, Peter had gradually improved. Many months were devoted to the analysis of his relations with his parents. Whereas in the very beginning he had claimed that he loved his father and mother, later his real feelings for them became obvious. He had phantasies in which he was imagining that he was quarreling with his parents. At first these phantasies would occupy all of his free time. All his thoughts had only one purpose, to show his parents that they were wrong. He also realized that his actions always had one of two purposes, either to fulfill his father's expectations, or to prove that he was wrong. In order to act, he would have to give himself an order: "Do this, do that; you don't do well enough." He recognized that these were the words of the incorporated father. Every action was loaded with anxiety. He had many dreams, which repeated almost the same scene. He was doing something wrong; his father was dissatisfied, but ostensibly seemed to approve. In the dream Peter had the feeling that his father did not mean to approve and felt worse than if he had openly disapproved.

He had recurrent dreams in which sharks appeared. One of these typical dreams is the following: Peter is in the ocean, riding on the back of a shark. There are many other sharks in the water, so that it is safe to be on the back of one of them. The shark he is on goes up and down, in and out of the water, producing in Peter a fear of drowning.

Another one of the dreams is as follows: Peter is pushed

into the water by an invisible force. In the water he sees many sharks devouring human beings. A shark comes toward him. At first he is afraid, but then he sees that the shark is smiling and is going to kiss him. Peter laughs, and also kisses the shark, but has the feeling of degrading himself.

Peter remembers that he has had dreams about sharks since the age of four, at which time he liked the company of Irving, a much older cousin, who would tell him stories. His father did not want him to stay with Irving; he would say, "Don't stay near him; I don't like him. We don't know him well enough. He may be a bad man. He may even have syphilis." Peter remembers that his father would say the same thing about any person with whom he would associate. He was apparently jealous, and wanted Peter's admiration only for himself.

One day Irving explained about sharks to Peter. "Sharks are animals who seem very tame and nice; but finally in a treacherous way they come near you and eat you up." After that, Peter's feelings for Irving changed. He felt distant from him; he felt that his father had been right, and that maybe Irving had syphilis. He could not understand why his feelings changed, but in the course of treatment, he realized that he had unconsciously identified the shark with his father, and that he had wanted to reject this identification which Irving, with his talks, had made possible. In the dreams, Peter realized, father is an evil shark, but a protecting one, who defends him from the other sharks who populate this horrible world. At the same time, this protecting shark causes anxiety too (jumping up and down, in and out of the water, indicating uncertain approval). In order to survive, he has to debase himself, to kiss the shark, to submit himself to the horrible father.

During treatment, Peter has acquired gradual understanding and the intensity of anxiety has decreased. The psychosomatic symptoms have all disappeared. In situations which represent an unusual task for him, however, the anxiety recurs. He has integrated better socially, but is still uncertain about the future. He goes out with girls, and has had some successful sexual relations. He still has the tendency to lean on strong people, whom he accepts as authorities. He has intellectual insight about his dependent attitude, and succeeds in controlling it to a certain extent. He has been able to immigrate to the United States with a permanent visa and is still under treatment. His parents continue to reside in South America.

GABRIEL

This is the story of Gabriel, as it was reconstructed from the information obtained during the treatment of his brother, Peter.

Gabriel was born two and one-half years later than Peter. The mother's attitude toward Gabriel was the same as toward Peter; she was a cold and hostile person whose main role was a punitive one. On the other hand, the father's attitude toward Gabriel was very much different from the one he had toward Peter. Gabriel and his father did not seem to care for each other. In the beginning of treatment, Peter felt that Gabriel never had had much interest in their father; but later on he discovered that their father had had no interest in Gabriel. He seemed to have had his needs satisfied by the admiration and love that he received from Peter, and did not seem to have needed Gabriel. He was much cooler toward the second child. Gabriel would seldom come to listen to his father's stories, and did not show any admiration or enthusiasm for him. In return, his father gave him practically no affection. A different pattern was thus established, one of detachment. The very few times that the parents showed consideration for Gabriel, they did not evoke a satisfactory response. On the other hand, the attitude of Gabriel toward Peter was different. Gabriel was rather shy, and had difficulty in making friends. He wanted to lean on Peter for companionship, but Peter resented that, and was not willing to please him. Peter was jealous of his friends; he had the feeling that Gabriel wanted to steal them from him, and used to tell him to find his own friends. Gabriel sometimes wanted to play "cops and robbers" with Peter and his friends, but was not good enough. Peter used to make fun of him, and would often refer to his funny ears, which would greatly embarrass Gabriel.

Peter felt that Gabriel did not belong in his company and used every possible means to show that Gabriel was inferior to him. He remembers that up to the age of twelve Gabriel used to cry loudly for long periods of time. He would cry in fury, and Peter would make fun of him. Whenever Gabriel went to his father to complain about his brother, the father would scold Peter, but not in a forceful way. Peter knew that his father did not mean to punish him and therefore was not fearful. Gabriel soon used to forget the fights with Peter, and after a short time would go to his brother again for companionship; he wanted to follow Peter, as Peter's own shadow did, but was almost always rejected.

Gabriel showed no enthusiasm for anything; he was quiet, spoke very little and often nobody knew that he was there. He would never ask for toys and never got anything. The father used to say that Gabriel was not even interested in toys; when Peter got the toys and Gabriel tried to touch them, however, he was rebuffed by Peter. There were moments, however, when Peter and Gabriel understood each other, and enjoyed their mutual companionship. The very few times that Peter fought with his parents, he sought out Gabriel, and felt love for him. Gabriel was glad to be on Peter's side and give him support.

In school, Gabriel was a very good student. The teachers would say that he learned much better than Peter. He was particularly good in writing and drawing. At home, he was a very obedient child; he would never rebel. Both Peter and Gabriel complied, but in a different way. Peter's was an active compliance, Gabriel's a passive one. Peter participated actively, was emotionally involved with what the parents expected of him, he, himself, expecting a reward or praise from them. Gabriel obeyed blindly, without openly objecting, but without enthusiasm. Often he would not even say a word. He seemed to be interested only in playing chess, and showed remarkable aptitude for that game from early childhood.

When the parents decided to emigrate to South America, their disinterest in the children increased. They were concerned about their own future, were extremely anxious, and had long discussions about their plans for South America. Peter tried to add some words to the discussions, to show approval for his father's plans, but Gabriel took no part. If he did, no attention was paid to him, anyhow. He was like a shadow, always present and, in a certain way, always absent, unable to separate himself totally and unable to participate. On the ship to South America, Peter made some friends. Gabriel did not, but he followed his brother, to be repulsed again with, "Go away, don't follow me, find your own friends."

At the age of thirteen, Gabriel started to do less well in school than he had before. One of the teachers remarked that he used to be such a good student, and that now he was much less attentive and diligent. The mother began to be a little concerned and wanted to find the cause for this; the father did not care. At times, in Gabriel's presence, the parents used to discuss what to do with him, because he was not good in school. In these discussions, he would listen without giving any opinion. He was changed to a business school, but after a year it was decided to have him transferred to an agricultural boarding school, with the hope that he would do better there. He remained there until he was fifteen and a half. He visited the family only twice during the time he attended that school. The second time he came home, he had grown tall and looked like an athlete. After supper, the two brothers went for a walk. Peter asked, "Tell me something about your girls." Gabriel did not answer; then, suddenly, as Peter repeated the question, he said, sighing, "You don't know what is happening there." Peter asked, "What's happening? Tell me, I am your brother." Gabriel replied, "I cannot tell you." Later he mumbled something about experiences with prostitutes. A few months later, Gabriel came back unexpectedly. He had a peculiar expression on his face, and smoked one cigarette after another. Suddenly he said, "I don't want to be in the school anymore. I am tired of being without money. I want to work."

After that, he worked in a few places but without success. The parents became more alarmed, and more critical of him. The father bought a small farm near the city and told him, "Gabriel, this farm is for you." From that day on, however, Gabriel was showered with much advice from his father and mother. They would always tell him what to do or not to do on the farm. He had no right to change anything or to give any orders. He was very tense and insecure, but he would never complain. He talked less and less. He wanted to plant according to the instructions he had received from the school, but his mother would interfere and even tell him in which order he had to plant the vegetables. Gabriel had difficulty in expressing himself, could not argue, and yielded to his mother's relentless pressure.

One day Gabriel suddenly said, "I don't want to go to the farm anymore. It is too far." The parents exploded. "What? Who do you think we are? Millionaires? We are still working for you. We worked hard to buy you this farm." Peter joined in this criticism. Gabriel was considered a parasite, the black sheep of the family. He walked around the house, smoking incessantly, writing his name on sheets of paper, and reading pornographic books.

The father bought another farm where Gabriel could stay without the necessity of commuting, but his work did not improve. Gabriel gave wrong orders to the workers, who made fun of him. He would barter his food for their cigarettes. Once a month he would go to the city to see his parents. He was sloppy, did not shave, would laugh occasionally without cause. He used to beg for cigarettes. Occasionally he would pick up cigarette butts from the street. He would go for long walks alone. He used to play chess with Peter at night, and he seemed to enjoy that. Peter had the impression that Gabriel liked to stay with him, in spite of the fact that Peter had sided with their parents in criticizing him for not working. Gabriel was told, "The Nazis used to kill people who did not work. Now you are here, free, and you don't want to work." After these long sessions, Gabriel would smile and mumble some words. Once, during lunch, he suddenly stood up, with tears running down his cheeks, and with a convulsive voice told his father, "I know what you want to do to me. You can't. You will see what I'll do." Then he went out of the room, crying loudly. A few days later he started to say that the radio was broadcasting news about him—that his father had given the radio station orders to talk about him.

One day, Gabriel sold a gold watch and his coat at a ridiculously small price. When he was asked by his parents why he had done so, he replied, "I thought that at least these things belonged to me and that I could do what I wanted with them." Even at this point, the parents did not consider the possibility of having him treated; on the contrary, they would mention the possibility of sending him to a psychiatric hospital as a threat. "You do a foolish thing once more and we shall send you to the insane asylum."

After Gabriel had been away from home for a period of twenty-four hours, a psychiatrist was finally consulted. During the examination, done in the presence of the whole family, Gabriel spoke incoherently about trains and "locomotives." He divided the word "locomotive" into "loco" and "motive." "Loco" in Spanish means crazy. "He wonders about the motive which drives him crazy," said the psychiatrist. He made the diagnosis of schizophrenia, and recommended hospitalization. Gabriel was hospitalized in a private mental hospital, where he received a series of shock treatments. After two months he was discharged, though no improvement was made. When he came home, his hostility toward the parents increased. He would call his mother "poisonous snake"; to his father he would often say, "One day, I'll show you what I shall do." He did not show any hate for Peter; he continued to follow him and to play chess with him. Peter continued to lecture him, asking him, "Why do you laugh in that silly way?" Once Gabriel replied, "Don't be a fool; don't you see, it is my nerves, it is not my fault."

After a few months, Gabriel was hospitalized again in a public psychiatric hospital. He was there only three months. He was very unhappy and begged the parents to take him out. His father used to tell him, "How can I take you out? You will do the same foolish things again." When Peter visited him, Gabriel begged him to stay a little longer. He used to talk about his delusions. He would often say that in the hospital there was a pilot who had come down with his plane. He wanted to die, but he cannot die. They beat him in the hospital; he has no peace. The father finally yielded and took him home. At home, Gabriel walked aimlessly, and talked to himself. In the evening he used to play chess with Peter. By this time, he played very badly. Occasionally, in some moves, he would show a spark of brilliance, reminiscent of the way he used to play, but then with wrong moves he would spoil the game.

Gabriel was sent to a doctor for vitamin injections. One morning there was an argument with his father. He wanted to go to another doctor he knew, not the one his father had selected. He did not want vitamins any more. His father and mother again coerced him to go, saying, "It is good for you; you need the injections." Gabriel went. When he came back, he said he wanted to go to the farm, and left for the country. When he arrived there, a girl who was working on the farm said, "Here comes the 'loco.'" Gabriel went into a room where a rifle was kept, took it, and aiming it at his frontal region shot himself. He died instantly.

This account of Gabriel's illness is a very incomplete one. It gives us only what Peter observed at a behavior level. No access to Gabriel's inner experiences has been possible. However, if we add to this account what we have learned from Peter about the parents, we are in a position to reach some understanding.

COMMENTS

The cases of these two brothers are enlightening because they reveal how different attitudes of the parents determined different illnesses in the two children: a severe psychoneurosis in Peter, a fatal schizophrenia in Gabriel.

The attitude of the mother did not show great variation in relation to one child or the other. This woman who had married to escape from the tyranny of her own mother, found herself tied to a man she detested. Seeing herself trapped, and too weak to fight a husband with a strong-willed personality, she gradually succeeded in deceiving herself. She became able to believe that her husband was a good man, and she learned to submit to all of his wishes. Unconsciously, of course, she was full of hostility toward this man, hostility which was discharged on the defenseless children. She went to the extent of allying herself with her husband whenever a disagreement arose between the father and children. Overcritical, petulant, and, at the same time detached, she gave the children neither love nor support.

It is the father, however, who played the predominant parental role in these cases, and who, with his different attitude determined the different illnesses in the two children. We have enough proof that he had very pronounced narcissistic and sadistic traits. Although maladjusted to a marked degree, he managed to survive by succeeding in manipulating the lives of the people around him, and creating his little neurotic world in which he could satisfy his own mental aberrations. He succeeded in overwhelming the personality of his wife to such a point that, though she detested him, she became his faithful servant and ally; he made Peter a tool with which to fulfill his tremendous desire for admiration, and completely ignored Gabriel, who was thus exposed only to hostility or to indifference.

The father showed great interest in Peter, but what kind, and for what purpose? Was that a genuine love, based only on the interest of the child? By depicting the whole world as a horrible and dangerous place, populated only by criminals (the sharks), the father enormously increased Peter's dependency on him. The father became the hero, the savior, the only one who would rescue him from the dangers. His desire for admiration and for being worshipped like a God were thus fulfilled. The price Peter had to pay for such protection was his complete submission to the paternal authority. That was an impossible task, since his father's demands were insatiable and unattainable. Peter was constantly afraid that he could not fulfill the requests of his father, and that his father would punish him. The father, too, symbolically became a shark; he might punish him by withdrawing what little love he had offered him, a love that was very little and not genuine, but the only love available to Peter in his whole life, and therefore extremely valuable. The father's interest was not demonstrated by manifestation of affection, but by continuous stimulation toward fulfillment of goals, which quite often could not be attained. Peter could have detected, through these manifestations of pseudo-love, the underlying hostility and narcissism, if this need for love had not blinded him.

Peter's anxiety, which originated from his relationship with his father, spread to all persons who had authority, and finally to everybody. Every human being became an irrational authority, a shark, who would reject him or actually injure him, unless he showed either superhuman ability, or extreme compliance, or obliging self-destruction (as in the case of the mutilation of his finger).

The security which he obtained by living as he did was only partial, and in a certain way renewed his anxiety, repeating a vicious circle. As he himself put it, he felt that **he was living** on quicksand, but that without that quicksand there would be nothing else, only emptiness.

Gabriel did not get even that quicksand. By concentrating on Peter, the father's narcissistic requirements were satisfied in a certain way. He obtained enough admiration from the elder, very compliant son. It was not necessary for him to spend energy and renew the same effort with Gabriel when he was born. Thus, he showed no interest, not even pseudo-interest in Gabriel, although at the same time, he asked for strict compliance from him, too. Gabriel did comply, but as we have already mentioned, in a different way from Peter. Peter believed in his father, wanted to comply, because he would get something in return, though very little, and tried to accept his father's wishes and his conception of the world. Gabriel complied passively, went through the motions of the requested acts and in order to do so had to learn to detach himself. This detachment was a necessity for him, the only possible defense, since it would have been too painful not to be detached. The adults were insufferable people; it was better not to be involved with them. This detachment, at the time was very realistic; but, for him it somehow became a boomerang, because it made his father even more detached from him. The father would say that Gabriel was not interested in anything, not even in toys; why, then, should he bother with him, why should he tell him stories, buy him things, spend time with him, and so on? A self-perpetuating, vicious circle was thus established. Furthermore this detachment did not abate the parental bad images (see page 54). As we have seen, Peter also retained a conscious bad image of the mother, but had repressed entirely the bad image of the father. Gabriel, on the contrary, retained in consciousness the bad images of both parents.

Unfortunately we do not have as much detailed information about Gabriel as we have about Peter, but we know enough to be able to picture him in his years of development, in a very unhealthy atmosphere. He had no chance to assert himself; his will was always crushed by his parents, who gave him nothing except material care. Since early childhood he made strong attempts to cope with the situation by detaching himself, but that defense finally proved inadequate. His adolescence was a crescendo of frustration, anxiety, and injury to self-esteem. The only person who theoretically could have saved Gabriel from the psychosis was Peter. In fact, we have seen how many times Gabriel had tried to get close to him. He needed him desperately, but was almost always rebuffed by Peter, too. Peter was too sick himself, too deprived, too worried about complying with his parents' de-

mands, too much in need to assert his superiority, in respect
to a weaker person like his brother, to be able to help him.

When the first symptoms of the psychosis occurred,
these symptoms were interpreted as manifestations of laziness
and rebelliousness. Even when the illness was already at an
advanced stage, the parents did nothing about it. This attitude,
of course, cannot be attributed to ignorance. Both parents
were well-educated people; they could not see, as usual, because they could not accept the facts. They remained as blind
as they had always been to any psychological manifestations.
When the illness was advanced, Gabriel asserted himself in
a psychotic way. He sold things which belonged to him. He
undersold them, but they were his; by underselling them, he
proved that he could do what he wanted. In his delusional
system, his father was the persecutor; he had given orders
to the radio station to talk about him. There was no displacement of the original wrongdoer, as occurs in the majority
of cases, and not even partial repression of the bad image
of the father. He identified himself with the pilot of the plane
which had fallen down, unable to live and fly and yet unable
to die. He felt that people were torturing him.

After his discharge from the hospital, Gabriel gave several indications that he wanted to kill himself. No steps were
taken to remove the weapons from his surroundings, however, and he finally killed himself. His last act was a libera-
tion for himself and a revenge against his parents.

CHAPTER V

Study of Catatonic Patients

Catatonia, from a psychodynamic point of view, is perhaps the most typical form of schizophrenia. The overt symptomatology, however, has features so specific as to make some psychiatrists consider this condition a separate illness, unrelated to the other types of schizophrenia. These specific features are the motor phenomena, which have made several authors consider the possibility of a neurological disorder, based on an organic pathology, or on some kind of intoxication, such as the one produced by bulbocapnine in experimental animals (59–61).

In this chapter, catatonia will be studied from a psychodynamic point of view. The formal aspect of the symptomatology will be discussed in Part III (pages 222-238).

The cases of Sally and Richard will be reported here. At a clinical level they are not the most typical cases of catatonia, because, in addition to catatonic symptoms, they had many recognizable obsessive-compulsive features. In the opinion of the writer, however, this atypical aspect makes them particularly suitable for a psychodynamic presentation.

SALLY

Sally is a 23-year-old Jewish, married woman, who lives in a small town in the vicinity of New York City. She was referred to me by a psychiatrist who had attempted electric shock therapy. After shock treatment, the patient seemed to make some improvement, but the symptoms returned very shortly. Psychotherapy was tried for a few months, with no appreciable results. The psychiatrist felt that the patient should try another therapist and referred her to me.

The first time she came, she was accompanied by her parents, who gave the following history: The apparent beginning of the illness occurred when the patient was twenty-two, a few days after her marriage. During the honeymoon the patient had been anxious, disturbed, and had wanted to go back to her parents' home. When she returned and went to her new apartment, she became increasingly distressed by obsessions. She gradually became slower in her motions, and finally lapsed into a catatonic stupor. She had to be dressed, undressed, and spoon-fed, and she defecated and urinated in bed. She was unable to move and hardly answered questions; often she answered in monosyllables. The striking feature in this case, however, was that this catatonic state was not constant. The patient occasionally was able to move freely, especially outside of her own home. However, when she was not in a catatonic posture, she was distressed by obsessional symptoms, which will be described later.

When I saw the patient for the first time, she gave me the impression of a typical catatonic. She was asthenic, very much undernourished and pale, and maintained the same posture throughout the interview; the mimic musculature of the face was practically paralyzed, except for an incongruous smile which appeared now and then. She gave the impression of being totally flat emotionally. Contrasting with this picture, however, was her ability to talk in my presence. She spoke rather fluently, and she expressed herself very well, but her speech was cold and rigid, without any emotional inflections.

Sally gave me an accurate description of her symptoms. When she was not in a catatonic state, she had the impression that small pieces or corpuscles were falling down on her body or from her body. She preferred not to move, because she was afraid that her movements would cause small pieces to fall. She had to reassure herself constantly that pieces were not falling down, and she had to look around constantly in an obsessive way. If she moved, even if she made the smallest movement, she had to think about the movement, dividing it into small parts to reassure herself that each part of the movement had not been accompanied by the falling of small bodies. This task was terrific; it kept her in mortal fear of any movement and compelled obsessive thinking from which she could not escape. She used to ask her relatives to help her do the searching for her, to reassure her that no bodies were falling down.

In the beginning, her relatives refused to give in to her symptoms. When she felt unable to satisfy the obsessions and became overwhelmed by them, she lapsed into a catatonic stupor. Later on, at the suggestion of the first psychiatrist who treated her, the relatives were much more tolerant. They did a great deal of looking for her, and consequently she was not in a stupor so often; but if she was not in a stupor, she was extremely compulsive, always looking around or asking other people to look for her. Even when she could move, she tried to reduce her movements to a minimum, because each motion would entail a tremendous amount of compulsive looking and thinking. Therefore, everything had to be done for her; she had to be dressed, undressed, fed, and even wiped when she went to the toilet. If other people did these things for her, the movements which were necessary for these activities were not "so much" her "responsibility." She spent most of her time in bed and was fed only once in twenty-four hours.

The following is a brief description of the family background and personal history as obtained later on from Sally herself. Her mother was a seemingly warm person, very much interested in the welfare of the patient. She was, however, overprotective, overbearing and domineering. With the pretext of helping the patient, and giving good advice when it was needed, she did not allow Sally to develop the capacity to make a choice. Sally's mother was always choosing for her; until Sally was in her teens she was not allowed to cross the street alone, for fear of the traffic; when the other children were going to a picnic or ice-skating, and Sally wanted to join them, her mother would never let her go: "It is better to listen to Mommy; those activities are dangerous and must be avoided." Sally was even told what friends to have. When she was older and wanted to go to art school or take dancing lessons, her mother was very discouraging, she believed that those things were not practical. If Sally needed to buy clothes, even at the present time, her mother wanted to be consulted in their selection. A few times Sally had bought a dress by herself and had been strongly criticized. The mother had rigid norms for everything. For instance, when the gas had to be turned on, the flame had to be of a certain size. If Sally made it a little higher or lower, she would incur her mother's disapproval. The mother also had always put tremendous emphasis on cleanliness. She was not very religious, but kept a strictly "kosher" home.

Sally constantly felt under pressure from her mother, always believing that her mother must be obeyed, that her advice must be good, even if unpleasant, and must be followed.

Sally's father was different from her mother in that he was not domineering, but weak. Sally felt that although he had the same point of view as the children quite often, he always supported her mother in her requests, maintaining a united front with her. The father was too weak to oppose the strong-willed mother, and always yielded to her wishes. Sally, therefore, had even more contempt for him than for her mother; he was the one who could help her, and instead he was her mother's ally in crushing her desires. Sally experienced a sense of suffocation and pressure when her parents were around. Her only happy time had been at night when everybody was in bed. Then she could feel free to do what she wanted. But even then her freedom did not last long. Soon she would hear the voice of her mother saying, "Sally, it is late. Go to bed." To prolong this time of solitude, she would take long baths and showers. She remembers, however, that quite a few times, when she purposely prolonged her baths, she had the impression that her mother came into the bathroom and stabbed her in the back with a dagger. If the water was running from the faucet, making noise, she was particularly afraid her mother could come in, and she would not even hear her. But she knew that this was just a phantasy, and she tried to dispel it, although some fear remained.

The patient had two siblings, a sister and a brother, who were older. She had never been close to them. Living with the parents was an aunt, her mother's sister, who had been married a few years before, but had gotten a divorce a few weeks after her marriage. At the time of the divorce the aunt had not sold her new furniture, but had put it in storage to be used again if the opportunity arose. This detail is relevant, as we shall see later.

At the age of eighteen, Sally had started to go out with a young man, named Robert, with whom she very soon became infatuated. Robert was different from her parents; he was intellectual, spoke about science, the arts, and especially about modern art. They would go to museums together. For

Sally, he represented the artistic and intellectual life of New York City, in contrast to the life of the small town where she lived. Sally and Robert had satisfactory sexual relations.

As soon as they had started to talk about marriage, Sally's parents had began a campaign against Robert. He was not the man for her. He was not practical enough; he was a dreamer. At first, Sally tried to resist her parents, but it was too great a strain and created too much suffering for her. Soon she became convinced that Robert was not the man for her, and she severed the relationship. A year later she met another young man, Ben, who became interested in her. Ben lived in the same town as she, and had the same views about life that her parents had. Her parents liked him very much and encouraged her to marry him. She became convinced that that was a good thing to do and she agreed to marry him. The wedding was soon arranged. Since the couple did not have much savings, Sally's parents felt that they could use the aunt's furniture, which was still new, although it had been kept in storage for several years. Sally did not like the idea, but she and Ben soon realized that this was the most practical thing to do, since the aunt was generous enough to give them the furniture. Sally agreed to accept her aunt's furniture, with one exception. The aunt had a painting that Sally did not like at all. That painting was not to enter her new home.

The parents told her that they would fix up her new apartment while she and her husband were honeymooning, and that they would find everything would be ready when they returned. During the honeymoon, Sally did not feel well, and the newlyweds returned sooner than they had anticipated. When they walked into their apartment, Sally's parents were arranging the furniture, and what were they doing at that moment? They were hanging the painting which Sally detested over the headboard of the bed. When Sally saw that, she became very distressed. When I asked her to explain why she disliked the painting so much, she said, "It was an old paint-ing, representing French aristocrats in wigs; it was a tradi-tional painting, so different from modern art." In other words, the painting symbolized for her the life of her parents and of Ben, in contrast to the life with Robert.

Soon Sally became afraid that she would not be able to fulfill her duties as a wife, that she would not satisfy Ben's expectations. She became slower and slower in her actions, and unable to do the work in the house. The parents became worried and asked her and Ben to come to live with them, so that Sally would not have to take care of the apartment. In her parents' home, Sally became worse and gradually fell into a state of catatonia.

Later on, when Sally could explain her symptoms, she said that she could not move because if she moved, she felt guilty, inasmuch as she was always afraid of doing the wrong thing. Later, when she resorted to compulsions, this feeling of doing the wrong thing was at least partially removed, if she could assure herself that she was accurately following her compulsive ritual. The compulsive ritual consisted of reassur-ing herself that bodies had not fallen. In going back over her movements in her thoughts, she followed this formula, "Do, feel, done, on, off, see, hear, think, and what else." This formula meant that she should think or revisualize in her mind what she had done, how she had felt, what she should have done, whether or not anything was on her, whether or not anything had fallen off, what things she had seen, what sounds she had heard, what thoughts she had had. "What else" stood for a final mental check-up.

All these symptoms, including the tendency not to move at all, were much more marked in the presence of her parents and Ben. Even in the first few months of treatment, the patient became aware, after discussion of many small epi-sodes, that her symptoms had something to do with her feelings, especially the feelings of guilt and resentment toward her parents and Ben. She was able to understand this relationship when she was reassured that she did not have to feel guilty with the analyst, and was willing to accept his support. She realized that she was afraid to act, because no matter how she acted, she would incur the disapproval of her real mother, or the disapproval of the mother that she had incorporated. When she would snap out of immobility, she could do so only with the protection of her ritual. Her ritual was not only a protection against guilt, but also a retaliation against her relatives. She realized that when she was particularly angry at her parents or Ben, her ritual increased and produced a disturbance for the whole family. They had to take care of her, and do the looking for her, no matter how reluctant they were to do so. This was the only way she was capable of expressing anger.

Although Sally acquired this degree of insight early in treatment, she could not refrain from indulging in her symptoms. Thus, it became obvious to me that no improvement could be expected from the treatment alone; her living conditions reactivated her anxiety and made it necessary for the symptoms to occur. Therefore, I decided that it would be better for her, at this stage of the treatment, to be in a situation where she did not need to be as guilty and resentful. Five months after the beginning of treatment, arrangements were made for Sally to live with a social worker, who would devote herself entirely to the patient.

When Sally went to live with this social worker, whom we shall call Barbara, a dramatic change occurred in the condition of the patient. For the first time since the beginning of the illness, she started to do things by herself. Barbara gave her progressively difficult tasks, which the patient was able to undertake, with some effort. Thus she started to dress and undress, and to do a little work in the house. It was necessary to give her a great deal of praise. In the beginning, she felt that Barbara was a great friend; they were two girls living together in mutual friendship. Her entire outlook toward life changed. The necessity to resort to her ritual decreased, and there was a progressive reawakening of her emotions. Her face was no longer mask-like, but responded emotionally to the surroundings. She also started to eat by herself and gained a lot of weight. This state of affairs, however, did not last very long. After a few weeks, Sally began to think that Barbara was making too many demands on her, that she was not patient enough with her slowness, that she was pushing her even more than her own mother had. Possibly there was some truth in these allegations. Although Barbara is an excellent social worker who has undergone intensive psychoanalytic treatment, and who has a great deal of understanding for mental patients, perhaps she was not the best person to work with someone like Sally. Being a very active person, Barbara experienced some kind of frustration at Sally's slowness.

Sally herself decided to return to her parents, called up her husband, and insisted that she be taken back immediately. When she returned to her parents' home, there was some relapse, but the symptoms did not reacquire the severity which they had had. It was obvious, however, that Sally was retrogressing, especially in the presence of her parents. It was then arranged that a young woman psychologist, Rhoda, would visit her in her parents' home every weekday, from early in the morning until 5:30, when Ben came home from work. In the company of this psychologist, Sally continued to improve and was able to accept and fulfill bigger and bigger goals. Whereas she had not been able to assert herself with Barbara, whom she had felt obligated to obey, no matter how reluctantly, she was able to reveal her anger to Rhoda, whenever she felt that the latter had slighted her. She felt equal to Rhoda, and a feeling of warm friendship developed. Rhoda was able to avoid becoming a mother substitute; by praising Sally a great deal, as one would do with a little child, Rhoda gradually built Sally's confidence in herself, confidence that she had never had. The patient became willing to do things, and dared to accept bigger and bigger goals. Occasionally, tendencies to misinterpret and the desire to put Rhoda into a mother's role again occurred. During treatment these tendencies were worked out.

Both a prolonged relationship with a healthy human being and psychotherapy with the psychiatrist were necessary. One of the purposes of the treatment was to examine this new, healthy, interpersonal relationship and to see to it that the old patterns of the patient did not force her to misinterpret it and spoil it. Sally became progressively more assertive, and dared to ask questions and to disagree. After a year of treatment, she was able to leave her parents' home and to have her own apartment with her husband. She started to take piano lessons and showed considerable interest and talent in playing that instrument. Her relations toward her husband improved to a great extent as she progressively became aware of the fact that she identified him with her mother and acted toward him almost exactly as she had acted toward her mother. Many of the bad qualities, which she had projected on him, were the result of this identification. She also learned to consider herself not as a shadow of her mother, but as a person living in her own right.

After two years of treatment the patient was able to secure a position as a saleswoman.

Sally continues to come for treatment, and the tendency is toward progressive improvement. She herself feels that she has never been so well. The illness, in spite of the symptoms ranging from catatonic immobility to distressing obsessions and compulsions, has made her a different person. She finally has been able to free herself from those conditions which she never accepted. Her interests in various aspects of life have expanded and she is able to sustain these interests, not only without shame or guilt, which she had formerly, but with confidence and inner feeling of great satisfaction.

RICHARD

Richard is a 23-year-old white Protestant, single, unemployed man who sought psychiatric treatment a few months after his discharge from a state hospital. His immediate problem was that he had a tremendous desire to commit himself to the state hospital again. He remembered the time he spent there with great pleasure. He felt that in the hospital he had spent the best time of his life; he had had nothing to worry about, everything had been taken care of for him, he had been able to work, and had had no difficulty in getting along with people. When he expressed to his family his desire to return to the hospital, they became worried and encouraged him to seek private treatment. Richard himself had had this intention, but the family had previously discouraged him from doing so.

The following is a brief family and personal history, as obtained from the patient himself in the course of treatment. The father was born in Europe. After a few years spent in the United States, he returned to his native country where he married and had two children. He returned to America with his family a few years later, against the wishes of his wife. In Europe he was a farmer, but in this country he worked as a cook and kitchen helper, and waiter. He is described by the patient as a very quiet man, submissive, and entirely dominated by his wife. He had little contact with his children, since he worked at night and slept during the day. The mother is described as a very unhappy person, hypochondriacal, and a constant nagger. She is always complaining of pains and

aches, and has undergone several operations. She has always
been dissatisfied with Richard. He remembers violent scenes
which occurred in his childhood. His mother was utterly dis-
gusted with him when he did not want to obey her. She would
even spit at him, kick him and throw dishes and other objects
at him. She never praised him, but nagged him constantly.
If he turned on the radio, it was to the wrong program; if he
looked for a job, it was always for the wrong job, etc. His
mother used to tell him that he had been a pest since his
birth, and that when he was an infant he had always cried,
causing her terrific headaches.

During the course of treatment, Richard realized that the
marriage of his parents was a very unhappy one. His mother
was taking out on the children, and especially on Richard,
who was the elder, the resentment that she had toward her
marriage. When there were open arguments between the
children and the mother, his father usually was not there
because he was working, or the few times when he was present, he would offer only a very weak defense for the children.
Richard remembers that when he was a small child, once at
the age of five, and another time when he was eight, his
mother went to the hospital for operations and he was taken
to a children's shelter. He retains a very happy memory of the
two times spent in the shelter, which he considers the best
experiences in his life. He was very unhappy when he had to
go back home. Later in his childhood and in early adolescence, he became very religious and had the intention of
becoming a minister. He used to pray quite often; he prayed
to God to let him win a ball game, have a girl friend, be
successful on a job, etc.

In high school, Richard was an average student. After
graduation from high school, he was drafted into the army,
where he felt unhappy because the other enlisted men bragged
about their sexual exploits and he was not able to offer any-

thing in that field. After his discharge, he wanted to enter some kind of musical career, but gave up the idea because it did not offer financial security. He had several jobs as a delivery boy, elevator man, hospital helper, etc. He could not keep a job for any length of time because he was very sensitive to criticism and always afraid that he would not satisfy his bosses.

Richard remembers this period, after the discharge from the army, as one of the worst in his life, even worse than his childhood. Throughout his life he had been very sensitive, he had always taken things too much to heart, but after his discharge, when he was supposed to do things on his own and show what he was able to do, his sensitivity increased. He was "eating his heart out" for unimportant reasons; any, even remote, anticipation of disappointment, was able to provoke attacks of anxiety in him. He could never be indifferent or detached, but was very much involved in everything. After his discharge from the army his life had become a series of crises.

Approximately two years after his return to civilian life, Richard left his present job because he became overwhelmed by these feelings of lack of confidence in himself, and he refused to go look for another one. He stayed home most of the day. His mother would nag him that he was too lazy and unwilling to do anything. He became slower and slower in dressing and undressing and taking care of himself. When he went out of the house, he had a compulsion "to give interpretations" to everything he looked at. He did not know what to do outside of the house, where to go, where to turn. If he saw a red light at a crossing, he would interpret it as a message that he should not go in that direction. If he saw an arrow, he would follow the arrow interpreting it as a sign sent by God that he should go in that direction. Feeling lost and horrified, he would go home and stay there, afraid to go out because going out meant making decisions or choices that he felt unable to make. He reached the point where he stayed home most of the time. But even at home, he was tortured by his symptoms. He could not act; any motion that he felt like making seemed to him an insurmountable obstacle, because he did not know whether he should make it or not. He was increasingly afraid of doing the wrong thing. Such fears prevented him from dressing, undressing, eating, etc. He felt paralyzed and lay motionless in bed. He gradually became worse, completely motionless, and had to be hospitalized.

In the state hospital, Richard was diagnosed as a case of schizophrenia, catatonic type, and electric shock treatment was recommended. He remembers that prior to the shock treatment, even in the hospital, he had to interpret everything that occurred. If a doctor asked him a question, he had a sudden impulse to answer, but then feared that by answering he would do the wrong thing. He tried desperately to find signs which would indicate to him whether he should answer or not. An accidental noise, the arrival of another person, or the number of words the questions consisted of, were indications of whether he should reply or not.

Being undecided, he felt blocked, and often would remain mute and motionless, like a statue, even for days. He had always been more or less afraid of being with people because he did not feel strong enough to take their suggestions or to refuse them; in the hospital such fear increased.

After shock treatment, which consisted of a series of twenty-one grand mal seizures, the patient felt much better. He found in the hospital an environment which he liked very much, and where he was not afraid. He became very friendly with other patients, helped them, liked his doctors, followed their guidance, and participated in occupational therapy classes; when he was in the process of doing things, he was not tortured by the previous horrible anxiety. In the hospital he was told what to do by authorities whom he was willing to accept. He improved so rapidly that the doctors wanted to discharge him. He begged them not to do so, because he was very happy there, much happier than outside, but after many delays they discharged him, nevertheless. Outside the hospital, his difficulties tended to return, and therefore he sought treatment.

For many reasons, this patient presented several difficult problems in the therapeutic situation. First of all, he was exposed again to the influence of the family. His mother was nagging him to find a job. The same acrimonious scenes were going on between the constantly disapproving mother and the patient. The economic conditions of the family were such that it was impossible for Richard to live by himself, or to have an additional person, as Sally did, who would work with him.

Although Richard was afraid to do things, his "stormy personality" pushed him again to act a great deal and try new things, in spite of his fear. He would go out quite often; he was eager to start friendships with girls, but later he would feel extremely frustrated and rejected by them, at the least provocation. Although he was afraid to have sexual relations, he would proposition girls who he knew were virgins and modest, and would feel painfully rejected when they did not accede to his request. He worked as an attendant in a general hospital, and there he was afraid that the nurse in charge of the ward did not like his work. He was very active and ambitious, in spite of his fears and anxiety. Thus, he decided to register in a school of music, where his tuition would be paid by the government under the G.I. Bill of Rights. At school his difficulties greatly increased. At first he did not know which instrument to choose; later he felt that the teachers were dissatisfied with his work, and were not friendly enough. At the same time, his mother was criticizing him for his interest in music and his lack of practicality. His anxiety increased in the same proportion as the wish to be back in the state hospital.

One afternoon, when he was supposed to be in my office for a session, I received a telephone call from an admitting physician of the state hospital, who told me that the patient had entered the hospital again on voluntary admission. He stayed in the hospital a few months. This time he was not as satisfied as he had been the previous time; when he was discharged again, he did not return for psychotherapy. He decreased his ambitions and was able to make a subliminal adjustment. The therapy of this patient was not entirely successful, although it prevented the occurrence of another catatonic attack.

COMMENTS

These two cases confirm what was described in Chapter III and add particular factors which are frequently encountered in states of catatonia.

Both Sally and Richard had very unhappy childhoods and were raised in very unhealthy atmospheres. In both cases, both parents were not able to fulfill adequate parental roles. Coincidentally, in both cases the mother was the actively destructive parent, whereas the father was a weakling, who was unable to compensate for the mother, even to a minimum degree.

In both cases, the patients complied with their mother's wishes, not really because they wanted to. Contrary to what happens in the person who develops a compliant neurotic personality, these two patients never accepted their mothers' way of living. They did what the mother wanted at all times, but they secretly rebelled. Richard was so unhappy when he was with his mother that he remembers the time spent in the children's shelter as the best in his childhood. Later on, when he wanted to go back to the state hospital, he tried to repeat the same situation, to go away from his mother, from the place where he had to be active and therefore disapproved. In other words, going to the state hospital was not only an escape from his mother, but also an escape from action; we may say that it was a partial catatonia. At the same time, going to the hospital meant going to an omnipotent overgenerous mother, who would take care of him completely; a mother who corresponded to the image of the good mother which he had possibly conceived when he was a baby.

One finds that in cases of catatonia, more than in the other types of schizophrenia, the parents not only have imposed their will on the reluctant pseudo-compliant children, but also have prevented the children from developing the capacity to will, and therefore, to a certain extent, the capacity to act according to their own wishes. These children are unable to accept their environmental conditions, and at the same time they are unable to fight them. The situation which produces the least anxiety in them is one of *ostensible acceptance*, that is, compliance in spite of themselves. If, on the other hand, they act according to their own wishes, they are either afraid or they feel guilty. Their ability to will, to make a choice, will always remain impaired. They will always experience indecision and ambivalent attitudes. If these patients make their own decisions, they feel that the mother will be angry, or that the action will turn out to be wrong, and they will feel responsible for the failure. The ambivalent attitude is due to the conflict between their own wish, which they do not *dare* to accept, and the parental wish, which they do not *want* to accept. Later on in life, when the parents are not physically present, the incorporated image of the parents (the Freudian superego) continues to argue against the patient's own wishes. One of the frequent methods by which they try to solve their difficulties is by giving up their will and putting themselves completely at the dependency of another person, a symbolic omnipotent mother, who will do everything for them. At times the omnipotent good mother is represented by an organization or institution (Army, religious order, etc.).

If these solutions cannot be found and the difficulties of living pile up, the inability to make decisions, to will, to act, will also increase. The patients will try to protect themselves from anxiety in any possible way; one frequent method, such as was used by both Sally and Richard, is to resort to compulsive rituals. The ritual sanctions the actions. If the ritual is not enough to eliminate anxiety, catatonia will occur and will abolish action. The anxiety that the patients experience at first in performing certain specific actions, which would be disapproved by the real parent, or by the incorporated image (superego), is generalized later to every action. All actions which are willed by the patients may arouse in them either guilt or fear, and are therefore eliminated. This process of generalization is responsible for the state of catatonic stupor. The patients may allow themselves to undergo movements imposed by another person, or may obey even absurd requests, because they do not will them and therefore are not responsible for them. However, the patients may remain in a state of waxy flexibility because they cannot will any change in the position of their bodies.

This generalization of the anxiety to every possible action would not take place, however, and would not precipitate the catatonic stupor, if there were not a general return to a primitive mechanism of willing and acting, which attributes to the person who wills a feeling of responsibility and guilt. This mechanism, which will be discussed in Part III (page 222), is generally repressed, but is reactivated by the anxiety of the patient.

As I said before, the state of catatonia, by eliminating

actions, removes any guilt or fear which is connected with them. One of the fears which has not as yet been considered, but which is present in almost every catatonic, is the fear of his own hostility. The action he contemplates may be a violent action against the parent or parent substitute. Another fear, which I have found several times in European patients but very seldom in Americans, and which has been frequently described by other authors, is the fear that each and every movement has a sexual meaning. This fear increases the guilt of the patient, because he feels that at least one of his incorporated parents will disapprove of his allegedly sexual actions, which are still connected with his original incestuous strivings. Ferenczi mentions a patient who spontaneously explained to him that with all his catatonic postures and movements he was seeking to defend himself from erotic sensations in the various parts of his body (77). In the same article Ferenczi reports another patient, whom he strangely considered a case of paranoid paraphrenia. The patient, a talented young artist, had become interested, to a fanatic extent, in Ostwald's natural philosophy, which preaches that one should accomplish as much as possible with as little expenditure of energy as possible. This patient went to extremes in following this philosophy. At first he made exact plans for the day, allotting a definite time for every kind of bodily and mental activity. Later he felt that he ought not to perform any work at all, except thinking. He requested that his relatives respect his absolute rest during his mental work. In his efforts to work "with the most favorable coefficients possible," he neglected the common tasks he was supposed to attend to. With the excuse of acting in the most economic way, he gave up acting altogether. Finally, he lay inactive for hours in peculiar positions, which Ferenczi regarded as catatonic postures. We have in this case a progressive withdrawal from action, in the beginning rationalized with ideas taken from a philosophical system, then followed by compulsions and finally catatonic symptoms.

It is important to understand the symbolism of the obsessive-compulsive rituals and of the catatonic symptoms. In the case of Sally, the ritual about making sure that small pieces had not fallen down may be interpreted in various ways. At a very superficial level it represents the compulsive necessity to obey her mother again. Sally's mother was concerned about cleanliness to a punctilious degree. What a calamity if she were to discover some dust in a remote corner of the house! Only by making sure that she was complying with her mother's wishes, could Sally move. On the other hand, those little bodies may represent parts of the bodies of the relatives for whom she had so much hostility. She wanted to reassure herself that the parts of bodies did not fall down. At an even deeper level, the corpuscles may mean the world which was falling down. She had come to the realization that she had given up everything; the world she expected to live in was going to pieces. She saw herself only as a shadow of her mother, as a desire of her mother. There is also an additional possibility: Toward the end of the second year of treatment, she began to use the phrase, "feeling like falling to pieces," when she was confronted by a difficulty. At this time, however, she was able to overcome her difficulties. It could be that earlier in her illness her symptoms were only a concrete representation of her subjective feeling of falling apart, of disintegrating as a willing person. Only by lapsing into a catatonic stupor could she avoid this catastrophe.

Why did Sally and Richard become sick at the time they did? In the case of Sally, the interpretation is easier. By marrying Ben, she saw herself as being compelled to give up her own individuality and to live as her mother wanted her to for the rest of her life. Ben was a symbolic mother, who was able to reactivate the old anxiety, at a time when the patient, after a series of disappointments, was least able to cope with it.

In the case of Richard we see a progression of events leading to the psychosis. He did not have a schizoid personality, but rather a stormy one, although not typical. He was very sensitive, tried to protect himself by escaping from action, withdrawing, avoiding the guilt, the feeling of responsibility and the anticipation of rebuff. On the other hand, he did not accept the withdrawal and made excursions into life which progressively increased his anxiety and his feeling of hopelessness. In the case of Sally, the marriage was the important culminating factor which precipitated the psychosis. In the case of Richard, no final precipitating factor could be found, but there was a long chain of causes and effects which progressively reactivated the childhood anxiety.

CHAPTER VI

Study of Paranoid Patients

According to the majority of writers, paranoid states are not always schizophrenic in nature. At times these syndromes are classified as paranoid conditions or reactions, paranoid type of involutional psychosis, paraphrenia, paranoia, etc. Some psychiatrists feel that all of them should be included in the paranoid type of schizophrenia.

The author is not going to embark here on a diagnostic or nosologic dispute. From a psychodynamic point of view there seems to be no fundamental difference between these cases. Of course, the defense mechanisms that these patients present are multiform. It is this multiplicity of the defense mechanisms which, together with the differences in age, makes it possible to distinguish several clinical entities.

Many of these paranoid states are subtle and never recognized; others are recognized only by the expert. A description of the wide range of all these possible paranoid conditions with their specific individualities and possibilities will not be given in this book. Paranoid symptoms will be examined and discussed in Parts III and IV. In this chapter a relatively simple case will be presented; then some comments will be made on this case and on paranoid patients in general.

LAURA

Laura is a 40-year-old married woman. A few weeks prior to her first examination, her husband had noted restlessness and agitation, which he had interpreted as being due to some physical disorder. A physician who was consulted prescribed a tonic. Later, Laura started to complain about the neighbors. A woman who lived on the floor beneath them was knocking on the wall to irritate her. According to the husband, this woman had really knocked on the wall a few times; he had heard the noises. However, Laura became more and more concerned about it. She would wake up in the middle of the night under the impression that she was hearing noises from the apartment downstairs. She would become upset and angry at the neighbors. Once she was awake, she could not sleep for the rest of the night. The husband would vainly try to calm her. Later she became more disturbed. She started to feel that the neighbors were now recording everything she said; maybe they had hidden wires in the apartment which would record every word she was saying. She started to feel "funny" sensations. There were many strange things happening, which she did not know how to explain; people were looking at her in a funny way in the street; in the butcher shop, the butcher had purposely served her last, although she was in the middle of the line. During the next few days she felt that people were planning to harm either her or her husband. In the neighborhood she saw a German woman, whom she had not seen for several years. Now the woman had suddenly reappeared, probably to testify that the patient and her husband were involved in some sort of crime.

Laura was distressed and agitated. She felt unjustly accused, since she had committed no crime. Maybe these people were really not after her, but after her husband. In the evening when she looked at television, it became obvious to her that the programs referred to her life. Often the people on the programs were just repeating what she had thought. They were stealing her ideas. She wanted to go to the police and report them. At this point, the husband felt that the patient could not be left alone, and after a brief telephone conversation with the family doctor, a consultation with me was arranged.

When I saw Laura, she repeated all her allegations to me. She was confused, agitated and afraid. Everything seemed to have a hidden meaning, but she did not know how to put all these meanings together. She was very distressed and unwilling to explain. If the husband or someone else doubted the validity of her beliefs, she would become infuriated.

Laura was hospitalized the same day. In the hospital several attempts were made by the members of the staff to treat her psychotherapeutically, but to no avail. As a matter of fact, it seemed that every such attempt made her worse. The patient was in a state in which every interpersonal approach would increase her anxiety to an enormous degree, and would promote the development of defensive paranoid symptomatology. For instance, she manifested paranoid attitudes toward every nurse who took care of her. Inasmuch as a non-anxiety-producing interpersonal relationship could not be established, the staff agreed to treat her with shock therapy. She received four electric shock treatments, during the last of which she sustained a minor fracture of a lumbar vertebra. It was felt, then, that insulin therapy should be instituted. After 15 comas, the patient seemed to be free of overt symptoms, was discharged from the hospital, and came to my office for treatment, as previously agreed. At this point she was no longer afraid of contacts. On the contrary, she was eager to come for treatment, although she was a little resentful about telling her past. She realized that she had had a nervous breakdown and attributed it to her present difficulties with her husband. In the course of the treatment she was able to give an adequate account of her past history.

Laura was born in Vienna, Austria, of Jewish parents. Her father, a painter, died while fighting in the first World War. She does not remember him, but from a picture her grandmother had once shown her, she knows that he was a handsome man. Her mother soon remarried, it seems, even before the end of the War, and went to live with her second husband in a small town in Germany. The early period in the life of the patient is somewhat confused. She sees her youth, from as early in her childhood as she can remember to her late teens, as a sequence of changes of residence back and forth, from Germany where her mother lived, to Austria, where her maternal grandparents were. It was not absolutely clear to the patient, in the beginning of treatment, why she had had to move so many times, perhaps once every six months. She remembered later, however, that she was not happy living with her mother. Her mother was interested in her own personal affairs, but not in the child. Laura remembers her stressing the fact that she was sending her daughter to the best nursery schools and other schools since she was very little. Later the patient came to realize that this was a device her mother used not to have her around. Laura's mother was not very affectionate, and yet always blamed the patient for not being affectionate towards her. She used to say, "I buy you clothes, toys, and still you give me no affection." On the other hand, when Laura would try to kiss her mother and sit on her lap, her mother would say, "Don't be silly." Her mother's attitude was so inconsistent that Laura did not know what to do. Most of the time, however, she preferred not to show any signs of affection, because she was afraid that her mother would think she was not sincere. Thus, she gave the impression of being cold and distant.

Her mother would also accuse her of lying. The patient does not remember what specific lies her mother accused her of, but she does remember that she was accused several times. Laura remembers her disagreeable voice saying, "This child is lying." She felt unjustly accused, and was very unhappy. She was very obedient, but she obeyed only in order not to be accused, not because she felt that her mother's instructions were right. She often expected to be accused. Whenever she was accused, she felt guilty, even if she had not done anything. At the same time, she had a feeling of repulsion for her mother.

Laura liked to have pets. Once she had a dog, and another time guinea pigs. On one of her returns from Vienna, she found out that the dog had died. She became very depressed about it, asked her mother about the death of her dog, and was given many contradictory explanations. Her mother told her once that the dog had had a heart condition and had died of a heart attack; another time, that he had run away; still another time, that the animal had contracted a terrible disease and had to be destroyed. According to Laura, her mother forgot each time what she had told her before about the dog. The result was that she knew that her mother had ordered the dog destroyed, against Laura's wishes.

The guinea pigs also disappeared one day, and the mother said that they had just died of a "sun stroke." Laura felt that her mother had ordered them killed because it was too much trouble to have them in the house.

Her stepfather, according to Laura, was a nice man, but disinterested in her. Her mother, also, was much more interested in him than in the child. Every time she was in Germany, Laura felt unhappy; she wanted to go to live in Austria with her grandparents. Sometimes she even threatened suicide, if she were not sent to Vienna. When she was in Vienna, she would feel better, but she was not happy there either. Her grandmother was relatively tolerant, but her grandfather would often say, "This is not your home. Children must stay with their mothers." When she was sent back to Germany, the same cycle would begin again. Moreover, the German children considered her a foreigner, a stranger, and she felt alone.

Laura's desire was to become independent and leave home as soon as possible. Throughout her childhood she attended dancing schools and she became a professional dancer at the age of twenty. In the meantime, her mother and stepfather moved to South America, and soon they stopped corresponding with her. Laura does not know whether they are alive. Her grandparents died and she continued her theatrical career. She was very successful and was booked for vaudeville theaters in many European countries, but she performed mostly in Germany. Her occasional encounters with men were not too important.

It was during one of her tours in Germany that Laura met her husband. He was a French tourist, a business man, who became interested in her acting. He would often go to Germany from France just to see her. He overwhelmed her with his consideration and interest, and Laura felt that she liked his attention. She had some qualms about leaving her theatrical career and marrying him, but finally she decided to do so. They were married and went to live in a small French provincial town, where the husband's business was. Laura felt like a stranger immediately, being in an environment so different from her own, and not being accepted by his family. There were realistic grounds for her feelings. They considered her a foreigner, and could not forgive her for having been a dancer, and not a "regular girl." She spent a year in that town, and was very unhappy. She felt that when there were arguments or controversies, her husband always took the side of his family, and never took her part.

Finally, because of the uncertain political situation in Europe, Laura and her husband decided to emigrate to the United States, along with her husband's sister. Laura did not get along well with her sister-in-law and again felt that her husband showed favoritism toward his sister.

The years spent in America have not been easy ones. Laura and her husband have not been happy together. They had different points of view about many things, and the gap, due to their different backgrounds, was never closed. Laura's husband became more and more intolerant of her attitude and started to neglect her. Nothing would irritate her more than his lavish attentions to his sister. They had no children and Laura again showed interest in pets. She had a dog to whom she was very devoted. The dog became sick and partially paralyzed, and veterinarians felt that there was no hope of recovery. The dog required difficult care, and her husband, who knew how she felt about the animal, tolerated the situation for several weeks. But finally he broached the problem to his wife, asking her, "Should the dog be destroyed or not?" From that time on, Laura became restless, agitated and depressed. As we know, her symptoms became progressively worse until the time of her hospitalization.

COMMENT

This case is not too difficult to understand. The childhood of this patient was bad enough to produce excessive anxiety, and to give her the feeling that she was not wanted and not loved. It is interesting that although Laura's mother did not love her, and was unwilling to give her care and affection, she blamed the child for not loving her. The patient felt guilty, probably on account of the hostility she had toward her mother. She felt that when her mother accused her of lying, she referred to her hostile thoughts, rather than to her actions. Actually, the mother was the one who lied. The example of the dog indicates that Laura had realistic reasons for becoming suspicious and anticipating hostility from the surrounding adults. At the same time, the mother was suspicious of her. Laura was not criticized for her actions, as people who become catatonics generally are, but for her intentions. She had to defend herself by anticipating these false accusations. At times, she would deny them; at other times she would accept them because her guilt about her own feelings of hostility did not allow her to reject them.

Laura's suspicious personality was determined by the actions of her mother, whose inconsistencies provoked uncertainty and anxiety in her. She was very badly disappointed by her mother; she trusted her, and her trust proved to be unfounded. There is enough here to establish the basis for a paranoid personality.

However, the patient probably could have compensated for all this anxiety, if fortunate circumstances in her life had helped her. In fact, not everything was negative or destructive. She received a more than tolerant attitude and possibly some love from her grandmother. Her stepfather did not seem to resent her. In addition, Laura was able to find a field, classical dancing, in which she could express herself, and from which she received acclaim and gain in self-esteem. Her marriage, however, was an unfortunate event. At the same time that it deprived her of her theatrical career and artistic expression, it placed her in a situation where she again felt anxious and unwanted. Going to France, a foreign country, to live in a small town, was like going once more to Germany, after one of her visits in Vienna. Her mother-in-law and sister-in-law were other women in authority, ready to find fault with her actions, but mostly with her intentions. A woman coming from the theatrical world was not to be trusted. Her husband also vacillated in his attitude, and favored his family. too much.

The situation did not improve in America. The patient felt more frustrated and disappointed. She had no interest in motherhood, possibly because the example of motherhood she had seen in her own mother was not an inspiring one. Her discontent and anxiety increased. These problems were accompanied by the realistic difficulties that the patient and her husband had to face in settling in the United States. Furthermore, living with her husband was a constant threat to her already unstable security. He was more and more critical of her, as her mother had been. She oscillated between believing him and increasing her self-image of the bad, worthless person, and repudiating him and defending herself from the accusations.

When the dog became sick and the patient's husband proposed having it destroyed, she identified the present situation with the one which had occurred with her dog in her childhood, which had caused her so much distress. She experienced horror. Now she could believe that she was not worthless, but that somebody was against her and against what was dear to her. Her anxiety greatly increased. At the same time, however, she shifted the anxiety-producing role from her husband to other persons, generally women, who could better be identified with her mother. The neighbor was reading her thoughts, as she once felt that her mother had done. The neighbor was doing even more; she was making a recording of her words and thoughts. Finally, there was a wide generalization when she thought that people were accusing her, that even the televised programs were referring to her.

This case is fairly typical, and it reveals the basis for a selection of the paranoid pattern, rather than the catatonic or hebephrenic. The factors which predispose to the paranoid type are the following: The parents of the paranoids do not criticize the patients for their *actions*; they generally *accuse* the patients for their *intentions* or for *lying*. The child learns to defend himself, either by anticipating these accusations, and therefore becoming anxious and suspicious, or by developing a facility for rationalizations. He has to find almost a legal or technical way to protect himself from insinuations and accusations.

There are various trends which may develop. The patient may become a submissive person who, although suspicious and living with the anxiety of being attacked, hurt or accused, feels some guilt at the same time. As a matter of fact, he often oscillates between feeling misunderstood, guilty, inadequate, and "not-good," and feeling unjustly accused, the victim of lies. He is generally compliant and fairly cooperative. These cases generally are benign and respond well to therapy.

In other cases, what predominates is the desire of the patient to defend himself; there is a certain pride and complacency in the way the patient defends himself from the accusers. Rationalizations and pseudo-logical defenses are built up. Some of these persons may never become psychotic in a manifest way; on the contrary, their tendencies to find legal reasons for protecting themselves or accusing others, may be channeled successfully into certain professions. At times, their hostile allegations, based on half-truths and on distortions, may meet with popular favor, and may help their careers. When they become psychotic, these patients are generally defiant and resistant to treatment. One of these types of paranoids is the "querulous paranoid." He feels that injustices have been perpetrated on him, and he resorts to the law to defend himself. When he is defeated, he does not surrender, but appeals as many times as the judicial system permits. With his pride in his knowledge of the law, and his fanatic belief in his rights, he acquires at times almost a grandiose and maniac flavor. Sometimes the diagnosis of manic-depressive psychosis with paranoid trends is made. French writers (Serieux and Capgras, 234) consider the querulous paranoids "maniaques raisonnants." According to Mayer-Gross, this type is not as common in England as it is in Germany (186). He states that the difference in incidence may be due to the fact that the Common Law does not elicit this type of reaction the way the codified system does; or that it may be due to the fact that the pathological nature of these reactions is not as easily recognized in Britain as in Germany. In my own experience, I have found that this type of paranoid is not rare in the United States. I have come in contact with several cases.

Other cases, instead of focusing their attention on their pseudo-rational defenses, seem to sense or magnify any kind of hostility in the environment. At times, this hostility is real and is caused by the attitude of the patient; at other times it is just a mild hostility which accompanies many actions of normal people. The paranoid is sensitized to this hostility; he magnifies it and generalizes it. He feels *pushed around,* pressured. The pressure which, as a child, he experienced as coming from the malevolent, hostile and inconsistent parent, is now generalized to a great part of humanity. In some of these cases any interpersonal relationship increases the anxiety, and enhances paranoid developments. This tendency may make psychotherapy very difficult or impossible.

There have been reported in the classic psychoanalytical literature many cases of paranoid states in which a latent homosexuality was found. Latent homosexuality is a frequent cause of paranoid conditions, but it is not a necessary factor; it leads to paranoid conditions, not because it is an inherent part of the paranoid process, but because homosexuality engenders a great deal of anxiety in many people. The latent homosexual tries to deny his own homosexuality because this form of sexuality is not accepted by society. In certain situations, however, as when he encounters a person to whom he is particularly attracted, he cannot deny this feeling to himself. He feels that he is succumbing to his impulses, and in order to avoid doing so he may resort to psychotic denial. The loved person becomes the persecutor, as Freud illustrated in Schreber's case. The patient no longer accuses himself of any homosexual desires, but other people do accuse him of awful things as, for instance, of being a spy. The parents or their symbols enter the picture again; they accuse him of being a "bad child." He is bad, he is homosexual, he is a murderer, a spy. All these accusations are emotionally equivalent. No homosexuality, even at a latent stage, would have originated if the patients had had healthy interpersonal relationships with their parents or parent-substitutes. Not all persons who deny homosexuality become paranoids; not all paranoids are latent homosexuals. Furthermore, in a society where this form of sexuality were more acceptable, there would be fewer persons who, on account of these latent leanings, would develop the intense anxiety which leads to psychosis.

In my experience, many paranoid cases, especially those which are diagnosed as the paranoid type of schizophrenia rather than other paranoid conditions, have been found to show an uncertainty about their own sexuality and a general sexual maladjustment, rather than a clear-cut homosexual pattern (see page 60).

Under the paranoid classification are to be included the cases of *folie à deux* or *folie à trois*. In these instances we have the simultaneous occurrence of two or three cases of paranoid conditions in the same family or household. The situation is generally the following: The first one to become sick is usually a person with a strong, overbearing, arrogant personality. He is able to make the spouse, or the child, or a friend living on the same premises, accept his own delusional system. The recipients are generally weak, submissive persons who find it easier to accept the ideas of the donor, even if they are psychotic, than to fight them. The unshakable conviction of the donor, as well as the anxiety that a rejection of his authority would provoke in the recipients, make the latter accept his delusions. Of course, the recipients must be predisposed by their own psychological difficulties (such as an extreme state of dependency, etc.) to accept the psychotic burden of someone else. Gralnick (119) has made an accurate dynamic study of these cases. The prognosis is good for the induced cases, if they are separated from the donor and receive adequate therapy.

I am also inclined to classify with paranoid conditions certain cases which, from a legal point of view, cannot be considered psychotic. These are persons who, because of unusual circumstances, or because of their ability to organize, succeed in changing and manipulating their environment according to their bizarre wishes, and therefore have no need to develop overt paranoid symptoms. These are cases of *acted-out* or *externalized psychoses*. For instances, people like Nero or Hitler were able to alter the environment in accordance with their own wishes, no matter how bizarre these wishes were. As long as they were able to do so at a realistic level, they had no need to become psychotic in a clinical or legal sense. In history we find many examples of externalized psychosis. We do not need to believe, however, that this condition may occur only among prominent people, such as kings and leaders who, on account of their positions, are able to effect changes in their surrounding world. In my opinion, this condition is often found even among ordinary people, especially in families of schizophrenics. For instance, the father of Peter and Gabriel, who was discussed in Chapter IV, seems to me to be a case of externalized psychosis. Through his manipulations, he was able to organize a little world where everybody else had to respect his eccentric wishes. These persons often create situations which will precipitate or engender psychoses in other people, whereas they themselves remain immune from overt symptoms.

CHAPTER VII

Study of Hebephrenic Patients

The hebephrenic type of schizophrenia in some ways is the most difficult to define and to diagnose. It is supposed to be characterized by generalized shallowness of affect, poorly organized delusions, often concerning the body, silly behavior and mannerisms, incongruous giggling, and a tendency toward rapid regression. Actually, the differential diagnosis is often controversial. In cases where there are many delusions, it is difficult to differentiate the hebephrenic from the paranoid type. In other cases, the absence of delusions and hallucinations makes it appear to be the simple type. However, in the simple type, there is more impoverishment than distortion of mental functions; clang associations and thought disorders are more prominent in the hebephrenic. When the patient is overactive a differential diagnosis with the catatonic excitement is also difficult.

Summarizing, patients who do not fit into the other three types, for one reason or another, are generally classified as hebephrenics. Actually it is doubtful whether an important difference exists betwen the psychodynamics of the paranoid and the hebephrenic types. The only difference may be the fact that hebephrenic patients regress more rapidly.

In this chapter the case of a patient suffering from an acute hebephrenic disorder will be reported. This report will be concerned mainly with the more recent precipitating events, rather than with the early environmental factors, as was done in the previous presentations.

ANN*

Ann was a 26-year-old, white, Catholic, married woman, who was brought to the hospital for observation.

The present illness had begun a week and a half prior to admission. The patient had been going dancing frequently with her sister. About this time, she had met a young man at the dance hall and they had danced together. One evening she came home from dancing and told her mother that she was going to give up her husband, marry Charles, the man with whom she had danced, go to Brazil with him and have twenty babies. She was talking very fast, and saying many things, several of which were incomprehensible. At the same time, she also told her mother that she was seeing the Virgin Mary. She then went to her mother-in-law and told her to take back her son, Henry, since he was too immature. The following day, Ann went to work and tried to get the entire office down on their knees with her to recite the Rosary. A few days later, her mother took her to a priest, whom she "told off" in no uncertain terms. She finally spit at him. A psychiatrist was consulted, and he recommended hospitalization.

Part of the following information was obtained from various members of the family, since the patient was too disturbed

* By courtesy of Dr. Murray Lieberman, who treated this patient.

on admission. Ann was born in the United States to parents of
French lineage. She was the second of four siblings, having
a brother six years older and two younger sisters. Her birth
was not planned. The relationship between Ann and her father
is not too well known. The family can recall that the father
was very fond of Ann, and apparently had never punished
her, leaving any discipline to the mother. When the patient
was 4½, her father died as a result of pneumonia. He is described as having been an easy-going, quiet, friendly person.
He was about thirty years older than the mother and was sixty
when he died.

The mother was fifty-four years of age at the time the
patient became ill. She tried to be friendly and pleasant, but
rambled in her talk. She seemed somewhat confused and dis-
played a rather shallow affect, particularly when discussing
serious matters. The physician who interviewed her in reference to the patient had the impression that she herself was
psychotic, and maybe affected by a mild form of schizophrenia. When she attempted to put into writing what she considered important aspects of her daughter's history, she disclosed some scattering of thought processes. She felt that at
the time of her pregnancy with the patient she had gone to
see a horrifying film about a man trapped in a burning building. She suggested that this prenatal influence might have
played a part in the patient's present illness.

The mother was the disciplinarian in the family, although
she never resorted to actual physical punishment. What she
would mete out was a stern look and a hand upraised as if to
strike, but she never did strike. She was very strict in the
patient's training. She was always very prudish about sexual
matters and never discussed them with Ann. Shortly after the
father's death, an uncle (a brother of the father) came to live
in their house, but would not have much to do with the patient. Ann's older brother seems to have been the most serious-

minded member of the family. He would frequently take care of the patient in her early years, but saw less and less of her as she grew older. The younger sisters played a minor role in Ann's life.

Ann was graduated from high school and from a school for commercial art. She was a very persistent student, very punctual in her study habits, and even in her early childhood showed a talent for drawing and painting. Following her studies in commercial art she obtained several jobs which were not commensurate with her ability. She even did factory work.

The patient apparently had been kept fairly ignorant of sexual matters until the age of about seventeen, when her older brother explained to her in a didactic manner "the facts of life." She began to menstruate when she was about thirteen and apparently became very anxious at this time. She went to her mother for an explanation of what had occurred and was reassured. The patient had had several acquaintances throughout her life, but no deep friendships. In the whole household a deep religious atmosphere prevailed. At the age of eighteen she met a man, ten years her senior, with whom she became infatuated. They went out on frequent dates, but this man was inducted into the Army. The patient then began going out with Henry, the younger brother of the inducted man, who was a year younger than Ann.

They became engaged shortly thereafter and went out together frequently until their marriage, which took place three years prior to Ann's hospitalization. There had been no premarital relationships. During married life they indulged more in mutual masturbation than in regular intercourse. They seemed to enjoy this form of sexuality. Regular intercourse was practiced once every two or three weeks. The husband often became irritated at the patient for her apparent joviality during sexual relations. On a few occasions, while he was on the point of having an orgasm, Ann would crack

jokes, upset him and prevent him from continuing. This
would result in arguments afterwards. Married life was considered a boring routine by both Ann and Henry. There was
very little conversation between them.

Family life became more and more monotonous, and Ann
had to resort to outside activities to have some fun. A year
prior to the onset of the illness she had had the desire to go
out West where her father had lived, and to find out from
his relatives facts about his life which she had never known.
She went there and visited his grave, but did not learn much
about his life.

Ann's disappointment in Henry increased. They had nothing in common; she was artistically inclined, whereas he had
only an ordinary, conventional outlook toward life. It was at
this time that she started to go dancing, and that she met
Charles. Her interest in him increased, but she knew that she
was married and that a divorce was not compatible with the
precepts of the Catholic Church. Her conflict grew, and put
her in a state of great agitation. A few days before she became
openly disturbed, she wrote a long letter to a priest. Here are
some excerpts from this letter:

> Dear Father L.,
>
> I have to start out with the most daring words that
> I could ever tell a priest or anyone.
>
> I have no right to wear a wedding ring.
>
> It's most peculiar that when you become an *adult* in
> the eyes of *God* you can begin to see *NOT* with your
> own but *HIS* vision—and be able to tackle life's prob-
> lems (sufferings) in only *one* way which is his order.
>
> For all my years, I went into this marriage as a
> skeptic and knowing and not knowing, mind you, that
> I didn't love my about to be husband.
>
> When a person is at peace with himself and knows
> he's done his best he can sleep.

I can't feel this way and remain married to Henry. It is no marriage, but self-inflicted torment on my part. I know that God didn't mean it to be this way. If Henry and I cannot *grow* together in marriage the way it should be, we have nothing but emptiness.

I look at Henry with my newly found values of life and see a great big cold handsome person. One that represents my old values. He is only cold to me because he has always sensed that I don't love him. (I could never put this into words before.) I know that if I could learn to love him, I would never have another complaint. He is that good! I can't bear the thought of him being hurt. *It* hurts. What looks right in the eyes of this world is not what is right at all.

People get so used to living their own narrow, inhibited life ("nobody's going to tell me what to do" attitude), they never get along with the right time—and they can't see it. It's wrong for themselves because it can *only* be done with God's help.

Speaking of interpretation I have only been able to come to my drastic conclusions through the Blessed Virgin Mary's reaching God for my betterment. How I would like to be able to say *our* betterment—Henry's and mine. I can't.

I know all my answers now—as I repeat through Mary's intervention. For three years I couldn't live without a struggle. I didn't have much religion then but because of my struggle and not being able to reach Henry I turned to it—my now greatest value in life.

I have found the greater your struggle for truth—no matter how low or miserable—the greater your reward.

Rather than cross the sex boundary from which you cannot return—I have crossed into a spiritual intellect world that knows no turning back unless all my beliefs and *present* values are wrong. In that case I belong in an insane asylum. (And many would say, "Ha, I always thought so.")

How can I ever have children or *ever* begin to live in marriage if *I* with these thoughts do not possess love. I have no foundation. All my great building which I have in my power is to no avail without love as the basis.

In a nutshell, I violated God's law of marriage! It has taken three years for me to be beaten into submission. This is my case, it is for you, as a priest, to tell me whether or not I am married!

Nobody can go against God's law, otherwise they suffer unnaturally so. (This is what happens to non-believers—the poor souls.) Just the way he can make your cross lighter (for it shall always be there) with your *full* cooperation so is suffering made *worse* than sin (if such a thing can be) without his help.

These three years served only as a means of helping me to grow up. It furthered everything about *ME* (which sounds so selfish). The good Lord knows how many times I could not express myself but only feel that gap between Henry and I. Why did I feel so selfish all the time *knowing* what a good guy Henry is with his being so unselfish? Why couldn't I take intercourse? Why was I so lopsided in my mind as to make jokes at a *serious* time like that and hear Henry's exclamation of "No cooperation"—"I've done my part," "What's the matter now?" "What's wrong with you?" For three years *we* lived like this. Just like two kids on a perpetual date always parallel with each other—never coming together.

For the first time in my life I *feel* that I have become an adult. Marriage was instituted for adult people that *know* what they are doing—not kids. Why doesn't the church put out a questionnaire that states DO *NOT* marry if not for love? Know what you are doing—scare people. I'd say the church is so lax on this issue, it *takes for granted* that its pets will do the right thing. The church is strict on divorce. Fine but it should BE *MUCH* stricter BEFORE entering marriage.

Why can't people know that religion with all its

binding laws is what makes a man free—no longer a
slave to himself but a sincere natural person?

Faith is the answer.

How does a person acquire it?

Dependence on God through Mary.

I'm the luckiest person in the world. I used to possess blind faith. It is not so blind any longer. It makes a
lot of sense. I humbly thank God and Mary for it.

You, a priest, is next in line—for who else would
understand and not consider me off the beaten path but
on it.

Ann, however, did not have the courage to mail this letter.
Instead she went to her mother, hoping to find in her compre-
hension and advice. She told her that Henry was a wonderful
guy, but that she could not live with him, and was going to
leave him. Her mother told her that she absolutely could not
leave him, that the Church would not permit it. When, for
the first time, the mother heard the name of Charles and of
Ann's love for him, she became very upset and said, "You
can't do this. What God joins together no man separates. God
doesn't want you to separate. That's the devil." Then the
mother kissed Ann, and Ann returned the kiss. Later Ann
went to see her mother-in-law, became increasingly disturbed,
and the events which led to her hospitalization took place, as
has already been noted.

When the patient was first seen in the ward by the examiner, she was dashing around the room, singing and laughing.
She was markedly agitated; frequently she would cry one
minute, and then laugh in a silly, impulsive manner, or suddenly slump over and become mute. Her speech would be
incoherent at one time, because she mumbled, and at another
time she would shriek very loudly. She would be irrelevant,
or circumstantial, and she frequently rambled, her thoughts
being completely unrelated to one another. Her affect would
vary from extreme liability to complete flatness. She was

hallucinating in auditory and visual spheres quite vividly. She was saying, "I was judged insane and others felt that this was the place for me. I am too weak. You look to me like Uncle Joe, and he is so far away. He knew how much I loved him. We could always get along. I never meant to be disobedient to you. The darn SOB, you couldn't smile at me. You are the Pope and I must be obedient to the Pope. He is the only one I must be obedient to. You didn't flinch when I said SOB. You are trying to help me. All the others are different. That I can't fake in your presence, my lord. You will understand me as my friends didn't. Russia is the only Catholic country. Russia is to the rest of the world what God is to the Pope."

Later, the patient became more agitated and required strong sedation. Her illness seemed to proceed toward more advanced disintegration. She laughed in an inappropriate manner, and her whole behavior appeared silly. She was restless, confused, and talked to imaginary persons. Her productions consisted of word-salads and clang associations. During the therapy session, however, she acted calmer and maintained a fairly relevant conversation. During painting sessions on the ward, she would frequently smear herself deliberately with fecal-colored paints. Frequently she would make loving gestures at other patients, particularly Negroes, and would hug and kiss them.

During the therapy sessions, she appeared friendly and seemed to like the therapist. However, her productions were still disconnected. One day she said to the therapist, "We have come to a draw. This is the end of the line. You are a man and I am a woman. You are a Jew and I am a Catholic. We both like music." The patient seemed to have some anxiety about her friendship for the therapist and therapy was therefore conducted on the ward. When her mother was mentioned, she would refer to her as the "Blue Mother." About a month and a half after admission, the patient became more negativistic, refused to enter therapy sessions, and was extremely hostile towards the therapist and other authority figures about her. She was, however, extremely friendly towards the patients. Frequently, she would smear food over her body as well as paints. She made statements to the nurse on the ward that she might be pregnant since she had had intercourse with a fellow. Around this time, the patient began to urinate and defecate in bed. When questioned about this, she stated that the nurse did not bring her a pan and she could not control herself. Shortly thereafter the patient became very disturbed on the ward; she would take her feces and smear them on the walls, attempting to draw murals. She would run around the ward laughing, screaming, and acting in an incongruous manner. Two months after admission, it was felt that the patient should receive shock therapy in addition to psychotherapy. She was given a series of fourteen electric shocks, which was completed three weeks later. At this point, the patient seemed much quieter, friendlier, developed amnesia of her earlier behavior on the ward, and would speak in a fairly relevant and coherent manner. She was no longer inappropriate or silly. She apparently did not hallucinate but occasionally seemed to have some ideas of reference and vague ideas of persecution.

Therapy was continued for a few weeks. During this time Ann became more and more lucid and was able to verbalize her conflicts about her marriage. She was soon discharged from the hospital, and therapy with another physician was instituted. It is more than a year now since the patient left the hospital and she seems to have made a good adjustment.

COMMENT

In this case we shall limit the analysis to the acute episode. Why did it have to occur? Of course the early environmental factors are important in this case, too. We know that Ann's father died when she was only 4½ and that thereafter she was exposed exclusively to the influence of her mother. We do not know much about the mother, but what we know does not seem constructive, from the patient's point of view. At the time of Ann's illness, her mother also seemed psychotic, and possibly had been for a long time. The fact that she married a man thirty years older than herself seems to reveal an unusual oddity. Her ideas about prenatal influence seem to be due more to a certain paranoid frame of mind than to ignorance. When Ann was in the most critical situation of her life, at the time when she wanted to leave her husband, and went to her mother for support, the latter was not able to help her at all. On the contrary, she reinforced Ann's religious conflicts.

The patient had an ambivalent attitude toward her mother. Not only was her mother the person whom she sought during her marital crisis, but possibly the Negro patients whom she hugged and kissed during her psychotic attack were concrete symbols of her "blue mother." She liked them, but at the same time they were Negroes and, according to social prejudice, inferior, like her mother. Mother was blue in her mood; they were dark in their skin color. Her feelings for her mother were found to be frustrated, since her mother disappointed her again and again, even in the most crucial moment in her life. After disappointments in her artistic career, she had rushed into this marriage with Henry and had found herself disillusioned again. The letter that she wanted to send to the priest is an excellent document of her state of mind at that time. She seemed to have remarkable insight about her situation. However, paranoid developments were already functioning. She tried to solve her conflicts with the help of the Church, but she could not go against the Church. She felt that the priest to whom she wrote would be able to help her. The Church, God, and the Virgin Mary (all symbols of good parents) would be able to help her. Rather than divorce

Henry and marry Charles (that would be tantamount to adultery in her religious conceptions), she tried to immerge herself in religious feelings and to obtain the approval of the Church.

"Rather than cross the sex boundary from which you cannot return, I have crossed into a spiritual intellect world that knows no turning back unless all my beliefs and *present* values are wrong. In that case I belong in an insane asylum." The spiritual intellectual world of the Church could not help her. The Church could not make her love Henry, and could not declare that she was not married. She understood this, and therefore did not send the letter to the priest. Instead, she made an attempt again to seek help from her real parent, her mother, and again she was disappointed. She had to turn back and, as she had mentioned in her letter, she turned toward insanity. Although at the beginning of the attack she manifested paranoid conceptions as concretizations of religious concepts, an arrest at a paranoid level was not sufficient to allay her anxiety. Harboring paranoid delusions still would mean being part of a "spiritual intellect world" from which she had to turn back also. Her escape had to be more pronounced, and therefore it reached hebephrenic proportions. Her words became incomprehensible most of the time; her behavior was that of acute regression, but not antagonistic. Therapy with a male physician did not decrease the anxiety, and the staff decided to submit her to shock treatment. With this type of treatment, the anxiety about the recent developments in her life was eliminated; she became accessible to psychotherapy and was able to reintegrate. Many cases of hebephrenia do not have an acute onset, such as this patient did. On the contrary, there is a slow, insidious beginning of the illness, at times even before puberty.

The hebephrenic type occurs mostly under two sets of circumstances: either when an arrest at a paranoid level does not remove anxiety (as in the case of Ann) or when the environmental factors do not predispose to the development of those paranoid defenses which were mentioned on page 139.

In this second eventuality, it may be difficult to distinguish hebephrenic from simple schizophrenics. As a matter of fact, a mixture of these two types may be found in some patients. Frequently, in the development of the simple type of schizophrenia, in addition to poor child-parent relationships, I have found another dynamic factor. The patient has had to compete with a younger sibling who, on account of superior intelligence or of favoritism from the parents, has had a better chance to develop. The patient abandons the fight; he not only accepts the younger sibling's supremacy, but wants to remain in an inconspicuous role, and refuses to grow psychologically. He may remain a shadow of the sibling and obtain some security as long as he does not try to compete with him.

CHAPTER VIII

Averted Schizophrenia. Relation Between
Psychosis and Psychoneurosis

As has been mentioned before (page 83), one is often impressed by the fact that schizophrenia has not occurred in certain individuals, in spite of what seems to the psychiatrist to be the most unfavorable environmental circumstances. The apparent contradiction with what has been explained in this book may be understood, if the psychodynamic investigation is carried on beyond a superficial level. If, for instance, a statistical report shows the incidence of schizophrenia to be lower in broken homes than in non-broken homes, this report cannot be interpreted as demonstrating the non-psychogenic origin of schizophrenia. A home broken by death, divorce, or desertion may be less destructive than a home where both parents are alive and always directing hostility toward the child. Adversities at a predominantly realistic level do not produce as much anxiety and lowering of self-esteem as does the hostile attitude of the parent or the parent-substitute.

In other cases, we discover that in apparently very destructive set-ups, fortunate compensatory events have altered the situation. A grandmother, a teacher, a maid, an older sibling, an aunt, may have given enough affection and created enough self-esteem to compensate for the deficiencies of the parents. At times, only a fantasy to which the patient has clung tenaciously may have replaced a good parent. For example, a very neurotic patient was a child of divorced parents. Until he became an adult, he lived with his mother, who hated him. In childhood he had a fantasy that his father, who had gone to live in a distant part of the country, still loved him. One day the father would come back and rescue him from the distressing situation. Although this fantasy was irrational, at the same time it had a strong reassuring quality which possibly saved the patient from a worse mental disorder.

This point is debatable. One may ask why the patient was capable of creating such a fantasy. Here again circumstances helped. The paternal grandmother, although not a loving person herself, would often mention the father, and his alleged great deeds, with the implication that one day he would come back. Thus, the grandmother was not able to give much love, but at least gave hope to which the child could cling.

The more accurately we study the early family situation, the more we understand the fortuitous circumstances or the unforseeable developments which in many cases directed the patient toward a psychoneurosis and diverted him from a schizophrenic outcome. It is only in this respect (in that a neurosis may prevent a psychosis) that the often-expressed idea of an antithesis between neurosis and schizophrenia may be upheld. If the character neurosis or the psychoneurosis do not protect the patient sufficiently, a full-fledged psychosis may follow. There are no intrinsic qualities in neuroses and psychoses which would make one of these conditions eliminate the other. They are both abnormal compromises, created to deal with certain distressing factors. If the neurotic compromise is not sufficient, the shizophrenic one may follow. In

many cases, however, the neurotic compromise is sufficient.
In other cases, which today are increasing in number, pre-
ventive psychiatric treatment averts the psychosis.

Three case histories will be presented in this chapter. In
the first two, the character neurosis and the psychoneurotic
symptoms protected the patients from the psychosis, in spite
of very adverse early environments. In the first case, one can
see that from early life the patient followed a definite psychoneurotic pattern and that the question of schizophrenia never
arose. In the other two cases, instead, quasi-schizophrenic
manifestations were already in evidence and the psychosis was
averted by a narrow margin. In the third case the psychosis
seems to have been averted by treatment only.

LOUIS

Louis came for treatment with the following complaints:
"I think I am falling out of love with my wife. I love my wife
very much and yet I feel I am going to desert her or that
something will happen which will make me separate from
her." He was over-anxious, weepy, trembling, and his voice
was unsteady in spite of an effort to control it. He added that
these ideas came to him all of a sudden while, in the company
of his wife, he was seeing a picture with Ingrid Bergman. He
mentioned also that two years previously he had had a fear
that he was going to kill everybody, especially his wife. He
was also afraid that his father would die.

The patient was a 37-year-old printer, Jewish, of asthenic constitution, who looked a little older than his age. His
father was 65 years old, born in Europe, and owned a sta-
tionery store. The father always had put emphasis on work
and education, had been a good provider, but had not spent
much time with the children. He was never satisfied. If a
child's grade was 95 at school he would say, "Even marks

like 100 are made for people." The only time he spent with the children was at the dinner table from five to six, at which time he would always emphasize school and intellectual accomplishments. He never played with them or showed them any affection.

Louis was extremely afraid of his father. The latter would often beat him on account of his poor scholastic achievements and say, "You will grow up to be a taxi driver, you will never be a professional man." These words appeared almost prophetic for the patient, who is the only one in the family who did not become a professional man. At the same time that he was afraid of his father, Louis admired him, thought that he was very intelligent, always right, and that his predictions would come true. The father was always worried and anxious, and somehow was able to impart his anxiety to Louis. Whereas the father was a tyrant in respect to the children, he was completely submissive toward the mother.

The mother was a rather energetic business woman, who had always been disinterested in the family. She spent most of her time in the store. At four o'clock she would go home to prepare supper for the family, and at five o'clock would go back to the store to return home late at night with her husband. The children were left alone; occasionally one or another of the neighbors was asked to keep an eye on them.

The family consisted of six children, Louis being the second oldest. A sister, six years older than Louis, was the favored child. She worked hard in the store, and the parents seemed to appreciate her. Louis was envious of her, and used to incite the other children against her. The third child, Roy, was two years younger than the patient and Louis had the impression that Roy was ashamed of him. Roy, a good student, was sociable, had nice friends, and made a better impression. Though Louis was older, he always felt inferior to Roy; he felt that Roy did not want to introduce him (such a shy, scared-looking and shameful brother) to his friends.

The other three siblings did not play a very important role in the life of the patient. All of them, however, appeared to him to be better than he, to be preferred by the parents, and somehow to have a disparaging attitude toward him.

The atmosphere at home was very tense and insecure. Louis felt that he could almost never obtain the approval of his parents. At the age of fourteen, he had to leave school, because he was falsely accused of stealing a knife. He did not have the courage to defend himself in front of the teacher, and he was considered guilty. He could not face the class again and refused to go back to school. His parents did not insist that he go because they were discouraged by his poor academic achievements. Louis grew up with the idea that he was the black sheep of the family, that he was not only the most stupid member of the family, but very stupid—"not even intelligent enough to go to school," his father said. Louis tried to compensate for his scholastic failures by doing a lot of work in his parents' store, carrying heavy packages, doing everything he was asked to do, etc. He never rebelled, but felt that no amount of work which he did was enough to redeem him in the estimation of his parents. He felt inferior, hardly tolerated, and tried to make himself as inconspicuous as possible in the family. He would never talk, for fear of being ridiculed. Later he was afraid to associate with young men and especially with girls. He never had premarital sexual relations.

When Louis left his native city and came to live in New York, through friends he met a girl who became interested in him. He was pleased by her attention, and they were married. This woman actually offered love to Louis, who accepted it enthusiastically and reciprocated. However, she always tried to mother and dominate him in a more or less subtle way. As has already been mentioned, when Louis came for treatment, about ten years after his marriage, he had developed the idea that he was falling out of love with his wife. After a few sessions he admitted that he was afraid he was going to kill her. He was also afraid that his father was going to die.

During the first year of treatment, the family situation was explored. The parents, who in Louis' eyes were still "very good and nice parents," were dethroned and he eventually understood the origin of his anxiety. He would still insist, however, that his marriage was perfect and that his wife was a superior woman. During the second year of analysis, he came to the realization that he resented being dominated by his wife, whom he saw as a new parent. Domination was the price he had to pay for her love. When this situation was understood, and he was able to express his resentment, he became more anxious for a while. Gradually however he became more assertive, less resentful and lost the fear of killing her.

Toward the end of the second year, I felt that the treatment was successfully progressing toward a solution. And yet at the beginning of therapy, when I was not aware of many factors, I was rather pessimistic, wondering why this patient, although very sick, was not even sicker. With an early atmosphere as threatening as his, with parents apparently so oblivious of their children's needs, with additional difficulties coming from the siblings, with such a desire to make himself inferior and inconspicuous, with this lack of self-esteem and despair of pleasing his parents, I felt that the patient could very easily have gone into a schizophrenic reaction. The more I understood the dynamics of this case, however, the more I realized that this case could not develop into schizophrenia.

Several months after the beginning of treatment, the patient said that he was still suffering from a disturbing symptom which he had not mentioned to me as yet because he was too ashamed of it. He had peculiar food habits. There were many foods which he could not eat. These foods, which he excluded from his diet, did not follow any apparent pattern. Some of the foods which he refused to eat he had never eaten, not because he did not like them, but just because he did not want to eat them. He was not even aware of any anxiety or fear associated with the act of eating them. He assumed that they were very good, but he could not make himself eat them because he had never eaten them before. He could not explain the origin of this habit, which was very distressing and led to embarrassing situations when he was invited to dinner at his friends' homes, and refused almost everything. His wife had to comply with his absurd likes and dislikes and could never prepare some of the foods which she liked. He later remembered that this peculiarity had existed since his childhood. No matter how severely he was punished for refusing to eat, he would not eat the "forbidden" foods. *On this point he did not comply with his parents' wishes.* His mother had to go to the trouble of preparing special foods for him every day, so that he would not starve. During the course of treatment, Louis gradually realized that his motivation was the following: He was forcing his mother, who was reluctant to do anything for him, to do this, at least to prepare special food for him. He forced her to do this extra work, which she was very reluctant to do. This may be interpreted as a manifestation of hostility and retaliation on his part. Certainly there was a big component of hostility in this attitude, but at the same time Louis got the feeling that he was not completely neglected, forgotten, or allowed to die of starvation; his mother was doing something for him, too; she loved him then, gave him care and love as she did the others. This compulsive habit thus prevented him from developing that feeling of utter despair, of complete emotional isolation which is harbored by the person who feels completely unloved and unlovable. That is why he had to cling to this habit so tenaciously; it was proof that he too got something, some love, from others. But he was not aware of the motivation of this habit, which therefore became a symptom. When he got married, he maintained the symptom which served the same purpose. After the symptom had been interpreted to him and he had already accepted the fact that he was really loved by his wife, and when he had learned to assert himself even with her, the symptom disappeared.

One may conjecture that until the patient was psychologically prepared for an interpretation, this neurotic symptom had a useful purpose; without it the patient would have been much sicker. This is probably so; however, it would be erroneous to go so far as to think that without this protective neurotic symptom the patient would have developed schizophrenia, when, after his marriage, his difficulties with his wife reactivated the old anxiety. In fact, there are other indications in this case that schizophrenia was not likely to occur. But first, let us reconsider this symptom of not eating certain foods. The mother actually allowed this symptom to exist. It is more than doubtful that the patient would have died of starvation if he had not been given the special foods. Sooner or later he would have eaten the food that the others ate. Somehow Louis felt that his mother would respond to such a threat. On certain occasions, his mother would respond, would do things only for him. In other words, he could "reach" his mother, although with neurotic mechanisms.

In addition, the general attitude of this patient is not the one found in the person who becomes schizophrenic. It is true that as a child he was withdrawn and tried to make himself as inconspicuous as possible; however, even when he separated himself from the others in a physical sense, he was very much involved emotionally in the interpersonal relationships of the family. He did not become apathetic or unemotional; the opposite is true. He was always emotionally involved. Furthermore, although he felt rejected, he tried, in spite of his skepticism, to gain the approval of his parents. He complied excessively, as when he helped them in the store. He did not comply in a passive way, in order not to displease them, but in an active way, in order to regain the affection which he had allegedly lost on account of his poor scholastic achievements. Thus he developed a fundamentally compliant personality, not a schizoid or stormy one. Finally, he never doubted the values of his parents; at a conscious level he always felt that his parents were right and good, especially his father. A certain degree of identification with his father was possible. It was only when he was under treatment that he could see his parents in a different light. If we remember what was expounded in Chapter III, we can deduce once more that the dynamic pattern followed by this patient, and especially the reaction to his parents, is not the one usually conducive to schizophrenia. This patient instead followed a pattern which led to a psychoneurosis of severe intensity.

ANTHONY

Anthony was a 32-year-old mathematician, single, Catholic, of asthenic constitution. He complained that while he had been preparing for some examinations for his Ph.D. degree in mathematics, rather suddenly he had felt unable to do his work. He felt that he could not cope with the situation any longer. The problems appeared insurmountable to him. He had not as yet finished his thesis, in spite of his recognized ability in mathematics. At his age, when he should have been married, his relationships with women had been very few. He had never had sexual relations. He had always found excuses for not going out with girls; he was too busy, he had no money, etc. In social situations he felt very tense and awkward. He was afraid that people would see the gold filling in one of his teeth and therefore consider him maimed. He was also very much afraid to eat in front of people. He felt that while he was drinking a cup of coffee or a glass of water his hand would shake and people would notice and make fun of him. At times after eating, he had attacks of nausea. A few times he had vomited after eating in the company of other people.

While working for over two years on his thesis, Anthony would always find difficulties, which would delay the completion of the work. Finally, he decided to change to another college and write another thesis. He also had other symptoms. When he went to a high building, he was afraid of falling; if he was in the lobby of such a building, he was afraid that the building would fall on him. He felt very dissatisfied and lonely.

Anthony was the second of four children of poor European immigrants. The first child died when the patient was very young. The other two children were also boys. The father of the patient was an illiterate laborer. At home he spoke his native language, not having been able to learn English in spite of having lived in the United States for about forty years. He has never been very close to the patient or to the other children. He seems to have shown some interest only in their scholastic achievements. He was not cruel, but apparently disinterested. He was never home, and in later years he had taken to drink, and quite often came home intoxicated.

The mother was described as a very ignorant and very domineering woman. She was ignorant to such a point that she believed in the flatness of the earth. She had never praised the patient; she never seemed satisfied either with her husband or with Anthony. She seemed less antagonistic toward the other two children, and Anthony always had felt as though he were the most disliked person in the family. His mother always told him what to do. To be with her at mealtimes was particularly unpleasant, since she would take that opportunity to impose one criticism after another on him. His table manners were not good, he had not helped her enough with the housework, he had done so many things wrong, etc. His mother was also very strict about the children's observance of all the rites of the Catholic church; she made sure that no one transgressed, and she sent the children to a Catholic school, directed by nuns. Guilt and sin were concepts always present in the teachings of that school. The atmosphere at home and in school was intensely colored by this religious feeling; life was just a preparation for death; the only purpose of living was the salvation of the soul. The patient remembers his very intense feelings and ideas about religion since childhood. He recalls an extraordinary experience which he had at the age of twelve, when he looked up at the sky and felt that a voice was reaching him, saying, "You must become a priest." He interpreted this voice as a message from God. He never had a similar experience either before or after that one. He staggered; he was perplexed, and astonished, but decided not to tell his mother or anybody else what had happened. He wanted to enter a Catholic Seminary, but his parents discouraged him. After that experience he worried for months. He was afraid to look up at the sky for fear of receiving messages again. At the time this happened, he felt that the future was dissolving because he did not want to become a priest, but that he had to obey God. He felt sure that God wanted him to become a priest; however, he felt that as long as he did not get married, he could always postpone becoming a priest, and would eventually become one. When he was an adolescent, he felt that one of the reasons for not going out with girls was the knowledge that he had a mission from God to become a priest, in spite of his desire not to do so. Even at the beginning of treatment, when the patient was thirty-two, doubts about this religious experience remained. Even then

Anthony felt that it was a genuine religious experience. "If such things exist, if people receive messages from God, then this was one of those instances," he would say.

Anthony also had obsessions, religious in content. Before Communion one is not supposed to eat. He was afraid that some nasal drip or swallowing of his saliva would constitute eating and therefore make him unsuitable for Communion. He was also afraid of committing sins, in the interval between confession and Communion, when one is supposed to remain pure. These sins were sinful thoughts about his mother, which consisted of believing that his mother wanted to get rid of him and put poison in his food. Often he did not want to eat his meals, fearing that his mother had poisoned them. He felt ashamed of these ideas; a good son should not have such thoughts about a loving mother. Twice he revealed these thoughts to the priest during confession. The priest agreed that those were sinful thoughts.

The patient remembers some fantasies which recurred during his late childhood and adolescence. He was the slave of a cruel queen. This queen would make him do degrading things, such as washing her feet, kneeling in front of her, and doing many humble forms of work. He would always obey, gladly, to please the queen at any cost.

The patient remembers some sex talk among the boys in grammar school, but during adolescence he never spoke about sexual matters. Attainment of sexual gratification was considered by him absolutely beyond the realm of possibility and very sinful. He started to masturbate at the age of twenty-eight, as far as he remembers.

At school the patient had always been a very good student. During the war, he had been deferred from service, because of the position he had as a mathematician. After the war, he resumed his studies toward a Ph.D.

The personality of this patient has to be described in more

detail. He had always cultivated very few friends, and had spent most of his time by himself, avoiding social contacts as much as possible. At the same time he felt lonely and ashamed of being alone. He had always found pride and comfort in intellectual achievement. At the beginning of treatment, he felt quite lost, when during the session he was requested to say just what came to his mind. He wanted to follow an outline, or at least be given a topic. Often he would ask for a book where he could learn what to talk about during the session. The inability to prepare in advance for the analytic hour was very disturbing to him. When he was asked to describe a certain feeling that he was experiencing, he would beg the analyst to give him a list of possible feelings so that he could recognize the one which he was experiencing. He had to anticipate the direction in which the analyst or the treatment was aiming, and as a result he had difficulty in making contact with the present feeling. In other words, he felt completely at a loss when he had to do something spontaneously. He had acquired a certain degree of security by doing everything as it should be done, according to a certain routine. Everything had to be planned or known in advance. He would often point out the superiority of the mathematical method as compared with the psychoanalytic. This psychological attitude also had some repercussion on his mathematical views. For instance, he did not accept quantum theories because they leave room for unpredictability and uncertainty. In the beginning he was disappointed that the analyst, after knowing his symptoms, had not been able to classify him properly, and thereafter follow the most economic and efficient methods to elicit the other symptoms and the causes. He felt that the analyst should be able to classify him in a certain category and by doing so, know everything which was to be found in him.

Although many other interesting facts concerning this

patient have to be omitted, we are now in a position to understand several processes which have occurred in his life. Again we have an unhappy childhood. The father, with his detachment, the mother, with her hostility, were both destructive. One wonders whether or not the events described by the patient, such as hearing the voice of God and being afraid of being poisoned by his mother, were full-fledged schizophrenic symptoms. Feeling so rejected and hopeless about obtaining his mother's approval, the patient needed to believe that God had accepted him and wanted him to be a priest. Maybe God in heaven was a symbol of his emotionally distant father, from whom he wanted, but could not get, a message of love and encouragement. God would accept him if he became a priest, and stayed away from women, that is, from his mother. In an environment permeated by religion, such as the one in which Anthony was raised, the idea of having a mission from God is not necessarily a delusion. It must be admitted, however, that the anxiety and distress of the patient must have been very intense, if they caused him to develop this non-realistic belief. Whether the experience was a real hallucinatory one or not cannot be fully ascertained. An uncertain belief in the reality of this experience remained until the patient was at a fairly advanced stage of treatment.

As for the fear of being poisoned, we have to remember that it occurred only at mealtimes. During these times, Anthony's mother used to shower her nasty criticisms on him. To be near her during lunch or supper was an ordeal. In a metaphorical sense she poisoned his food. In the symptoms, this metaphor was changed into a concrete act; mother might actually have poisoned his food. Even in this case, however, the patient was doubtful; most of the time he felt that it was not true, and felt guilty for having such a belief. Later in his life, when the symptomatology changed and followed a more psychoneurotic picture, he felt extremely anxious during meals, especially if he ate in company. He attributed the anxiety to his bad table manners, and fear of criticism. Again, symbolically, the people who watched him were mother-substitutes, who saw how worthless he was. From the time of adolescence, many of these ideas disappeared; the patient improved, and in certain areas, like the scholastic, he made a good adjustment. One wonders why this situation, which in early life seemed oriented toward a schizophrenic breakdown, took a turn for the better and changed into a psychoneurotic one.

If we re-examine the childhood, we see that already there were elements more typical of the psychoneurotic than of the schizophrenic pattern. The patient never lost the desire to please his parents. The recurrent fantasy about the cruel queen indicates his desire to placate his cruel mother at any cost. In other words he had not become hopeless about obtaining her approval. He was concerned about obtaining this approval, no matter what it entailed, and therefore there was no complete emotional detachment. The fantasy about receiving the order from God to become a priest is also something of the same nature. In the fantasy of the queen he is the slave who has to do horrible things to please her; in the fantasy of God he has to become a priest and keep away from women. It is true that he has to submit reluctantly, but at the same time he has been chosen by the queen as the servant, and by God as his minister. In a certain way, he has been accepted and approved. We see indications that he will develop not a completely detached personality, but elements of a dependent, compliant character which will play an important role in his make-up.

The desire to gain the approval that his siblings had already obtained gave him the stimulus to go further in life than they did, and to become the most educated, and the most advanced, professionally, in his family. He chose the field

of mathematics, which requires very little emotional involvement, and in which every step necessarily follows the previous
one, and can be predicted. He also developed schizoid traits,
characterized chiefly by removal of spontaneity. Any spontaneous act might incur the disapproval of his incorporated
mother. If he did what he was "supposed to do," he would
remove anxiety. He had removed sex entirely from his life; he
had no respect for his emotions, which he tried to repress all
the time. At the age of thirty-two, he wanted to look for a
wife, because at that age a man "should" marry. This combination of a compliant and schizoid personality has protected
the patient from the anxiety which could have engendered
a schizophrenic reaction. By removing spontaneity, he became
withdrawn and apathetic; but by doing what he should do all
the time, he manifested his willingness to comply with the
authority in his family and in his society.

ARTHUR

Arthur is a 25-year-old white man, who sought psychiatric
help because of an apparent lack of emotions, obsessive ideas,
compulsions, occasional stuttering, and "peculiar thought disorders." The "peculiar thought disorders" were the symptoms
which distressed him mostly. He did not know how to explain
them, and attributed them to a serious mental disease. He
noticed that often normal thinking was impossible for him,
because it was replaced by a strange form of thinking which
he recognized as abnormal. This disorder occurred not only
while he was thinking, but in talking and reading. Here are
some examples taken verbatim:

"I see in the paper 'Camera Fotoshop' and I read 'Campo
Formio,' which is the name of a peace treaty. I see 'Triumph'
and I read 'Truman.' While walking on the street I saw a
girl with a button on her blouse on which a word was written

beginning with a large F. I immediately read it as 'Frustration' but on coming closer I saw it was 'Fieldston,' the name of a school. When I meet people who have a certain appearance and manner, a name will often flash into my mind and I will think of this name each time that I see the person subsequently. The name 'Higinio' flashes into my mind whenever I see a certain fellow whom I recently met. He is short, and the black hair on his head sticks up like a porcupine's. All this seems to me to be so much more appropriately expressed by the name 'Higinio' than by his actual name . . . ."

"I once saw a letter on my uncle's desk in which were the words 'Lyon's velvet.' I immediately thought that the letter must have come from England. The fact that the letterhead and the stamp showed it to have been sent by an American firm did not cause the feeling to vanish; the facts, on the contrary, seemed inappropriate because they contradicted what I somehow felt should be the truth. Now the word 'Lyon's' rather suggests England to me; it seems an English rather than an American name. There is a chain of restaurants in London called 'Lyon's restaurants.' Moreover I have always associated the manufacture of textiles, such as cotton and velvet goods, with England. So I had a definite feeling that the letter must have come from England and been written by an English firm . . . .

"When I lie in bed at night or early in the morning, long strings of words, many of which are meaningless, will pour into my mind. These appear to have a meaning sometimes. Other times completely meaningless sentences come up; for instance, 'Spain for a half-inch sword.' "

At the beginning of treatment, the patient described other experiences which had a disturbing effect on him. He generally took a bus to come to my office. At times when he got off at the stop nearest my office, he had the impression that the other people who got off at the same time were also coming to see me. He recognized the unreality of such an idea and did not *believe* that the other people came to my office, but he had a *momentary feeling* that they were doing that. Occasionally, when he was riding in buses or subways, if he saw people talking, he had the feeling that they were talking about him. He realized almost immediately that it could not be so, and actually he did not think that they were talking about him, but for a fraction of a second he had that feeling.

The patient also complained of emotional indifference and apathy. He used to say repeatedly that he had lost all his emotions. He could not become involved in anything. When he had to do something, he was going through the motions of what he had to do without any emotional participation. Life appeared colorless to him. He could not force himself to do anything; he just wanted to be left alone. On account of this thought disorder and apathy, he could not concentrate on his studies. He had intended to get his M.A. in mathematics, but had to give up the idea. He would not go out with girls, since it was too much of an effort to ask for a date. Never in his life had he had sexual relations. He would go into parks, hide behind bushes, and masturbate at the sight of girls lying on the grass.

Arthur was born in England. There was no history of mental or nervous disorders in his family. The father had died about ten years ago of cancer. The patient did not love him; as a matter of fact, he had experienced relief when he died. Arthur remembered attempts he had made during his childhood to get close to his father. His father used to take him to restaurants or to movies occasionally, and would tell him stories. However, whenever the patient started to feel a little warmer toward him, his feelings were generally changed by his father's subsequent nagging attitude. Arthur felt that it was better not to allow himself to get close to him and never confided in him.

During adolescence, Arthur's father appeared to him as a tyrant who was always after him, like a policeman, to investigate whether he had masturbated or not. If the patient had a pimple on his face, or was pale, the father would say that these were signs of masturbation, and that terrible things would happen to him. Since the patient had actually masturbated, he felt guilty; he felt that his father could read "through him" and was afraid that he would develop serious diseases. He was also afraid of actual punishment from his father.

The patient hardly remembers how his mother appeared to him during his early childhood; he rarely saw her, since he was almost always cared for by a governess. He does not remember having been caressed or kissed by his mother, or having done anything with her in his early years. For several years he was taken care of by a governess, who later developed the paranoid type of schizophrenia. Later on, when the parents came to the United States, they could not afford maids, and Arthur had more contact with his mother. At the same time, however, he had the impression that his mother was much more concerned with his sister, who is his only sibling and four years younger than he. Arthur considered his mother a very weak person. She was not tyrannical, like his father; however, when the latter bitterly criticized and punished Arthur, she never came to his defense, but was always on his father's side. After the father's death, when Arthur was fifteen, his mother tried to get close to him, but it was too late. Somehow the patient did not trust her.

Arthur remembered both parents, from his early childhood on, with a sense of annoyance or disgust. Being near them was unpleasant. He felt that they were ugly; he even had the impression that an awful odor emanated from their bodies. He had to obey all the time, to avoid his father's punishment; he never put up a fight. He tried rather to detach himself from them. To use his own words, he felt that "Those adults were intolerable naggers who never understood you. Why bother to defend yourself?" He did not play much with children of his own age, and stayed by himself most of the time. He had vivid fantasies which persisted throughout adolescence, and kept him busy when he was alone. In his mind he had constructed an imaginary world made up of countries of different periods in the recent or remote past, that he had learned about in history.

Ever since childhood he had also been disturbed by obsessive thoughts. The following is a verbatim description of some of them:

"I was very impressed by religion from an early age and my obsessions consisted of horrible ideas about Jesus Christ, that he was unclean, or that I should urinate or excrete upon him or upon his mother. I also had similar thoughts about God, and often I would fantasy that God or Jesus or his mother would perform similar defiling actions upon one another. I also remember compulsions to fill all my pockets and to perform all kinds of actions an even number of times. For instance, if I spilled some soup by accident and was reprimanded by my parents, I would nevertheless feel obliged to repeat the act in order to make an even number."

From the time when he was sixteen, Arthur fell in love periodically with girls. These loves were never manifested. For one reason or another these girls were unattainable, or he imagined that they were unattainable (they lived in different cities, were of a different religion, etc.). These unmanifested loves were so intense that they caused relatively important changes in his life. For instance, while he was attending college, he took courses which were unnecessary in his curriculum, wasting time and energy, only because the girl he loved was taking them. He had always been an excellent student, but in the last few years there had been a decline in his scholastic achievements and finally he had had to interrupt his studies.

Many other things could be said about this interesting patient, especially in relation to treatment. However, we have to limit ourselves to the consideration of what is relevant to the subject of this chapter. Here again is an example of an unhappy childhood. The early uncanny experiences have been very well repressed by the patient who has very little recollection of the role played by his parents during his early childhood. He did not succeed, however, in repressing entirely the bad images of his parents, for whom he always had hostile feelings. He remembers his past life from the age of five or six. Reality was so unpleasant that the child had to isolate himself emotionally. He did not dare to put up a fight; it was useless to fight the adults; the best thing to do was to disregard them. While he was detaching himself, he was also preserving his own individuality. At the same time these difficulties with the significant adults in his early life did not help him to become an integral part of the social world in which he had to live.

He was living in his own world, made up of fantasies. As was mentioned in Chapter III, and as will be further discussed in Part III, this detachment gave momentum to autistic tendencies, which were retained by the patient up to the time he came for treatment. Even during the second year of treatment, autistic tendencies, represented mostly by thought disorders, tended to come back when he was faced with a situation which provoked strong anxiety.

By detaching himself from his parents, Arthur succeeded in finding a more or less stable equilibrium. He became aloof, reserved and pseudo-compliant. After puberty, however, the situation changed. His father, with his own obsessive thoughts about sex, did not allow him to be aloof and detached. This attitude increased the patient's hostility toward the father and stimulated further detachment. After the death of his father, Arthur was confronted with new problems: guilt about having wished his death; inability to gratify his sexual urges, and feelings of inadequacy when he attempted to establish social relationships. His mother could not help him. Although she was finally willing to get closer to him, he was somehow afraid of her "smothering" attitude and he had to reject her.

The situation deteriorated to such a point that the picture presented by the patient when he came for treatment consisted not of just a strong or very rigid schizoid personality. Especially in anxiety-arousing situations many autistic phenomena were occurring. Some of them did not seem of too serious significance. He read "frustration" instead of "Fieldston" on the button pinned on the girl's blouse. Girls represented frustrations to him, or his frustrated attempts to love. Everything which was associated with England, where he spent his childhood, was charged with great emotional tone for him. Thus, when he read Lyon on a letter found on his uncle's desk, he thought that the letter came from England. Some other symptoms gave almost a schizophrenic appearance to his condition. For instance, he had pseudo-ideas of reference, tendencies toward neologisms, and pseudo-word-salad phenomena. I use the prefix pseudo here, because these experiences were not accepted by the patient as reality, but were immediately recognized as abnormal manifestations. It was only the preservation of the ability to test and disprove their reality, however, which distinguished them from full-fledged schizophrenic symptoms. The formal structure of the symptoms was the same as in cases of schizophrenia. The patient also presented symptoms of depersonalization. He did not experience emotions; at the same time, he was aware of his emotional bluntness and was afraid of developing schizophrenia, the symptoms of which he had read in psychiatric books, which he had studied avidly.

Indeed, Arthur was very close to schizophrenia, and it is a fair guess that if he had not come for treatment at this point, the psychosis would have developed. Many psychiatrists,

I am sure, would have diagnosed this case as a schizophrenic one. The typical background for a schizophrenic psychosis was present: rejection by both parents; development of a strong schizoid personality with great propensity for autistic phenomena; inability of the patient to defend himself from the increasing difficulties after puberty, in spite of the rigidity of the schizoid personality. There were also, however, some favorable signs, which may explain why the patient did not develop a psychosis. First, his father's rejection of him was not complete. The father did make some effort to reach him. The patient, however, did not trust these efforts and preferred detachment. Later he felt that if only he could abstain from masturbation or from sexual desires, he could obtain acceptance from his father. The sexual urges were very strong, however, and he had a feeling of hopelessness about being able to suppress them. A second relatively favorable sign was the fact that from early childhood this patient protected himself not with detachment exclusively, but also with compulsive symptoms. Although some of them could have had the purpose of retaliating against the parents (spilling the soup twice) they also protected him from anxiety.

The treatment of this patient has been long and laborious. He is still under therapy after six years, but has made steady progress. There has been an affective reintegration, and he is aware now of his anxiety, especially in social contacts with the opposite sex. The autistic phenomena have entirely disappeared. He has been able to resume his studies and is preparing for a Ph.D. in mathematics, at the same time that he holds an important position as a mathematician.

PART THREE

The Psychological Structure of Schizophrenia

Study of the Formal Mechanisms

CHAPTER IX

The Escape from Reality

In the second part of this book we have studied the psychogenic factors which usually lead to a schizophrenic disorder. We have seen how an extreme state of anxiety, originated in early childhood, produces a vulnerability which lasts for the whole life of the individual. We have seen how desperately, even heroically, the patient attempts to maintain contact with reality, and how, under certain conditions of stress, his defenses become increasingly inadequate. Confronted with overpowering anxiety, he finally succumbs, and the break with reality occurs. In other words, when he cannot change himself any longer, not even in a neurotic way, he has to change reality. But reality cannot change, and he has to change himself again in order to see "reality" in a different way.

In this part of the book we have to examine with what mechanisms the patient now attempts to envision reality in a less frightening manner. The mechanisms that he has at his disposal are, from *a formal point of view,* fundamentally the same in every patient; they are inherent in his human nature.

These mechanisms, in addition to those which he shares with the neurotic and the normal person, are mechanisms which were used by the human race in the process of becoming the species that it is today. In other words, they are obsolete, archaic mechanisms, buried long ago in unconscious processes.

The capacity of resorting to primitive mechanisms is a quite common occurrence in pathology. For instance, in diseases of the heart, when the auriculo-ventricular bundle is injured, the more ancient sino-auricular node takes over its functions. Much more will be said in Part V about this biological aspect; at the present time we shall remain at a purely psychological level. Of course, as in other fields of pathology, in psychiatric conditions also, the use of less evolved mechanisms for functions which require higher processes may bring about peculiar situations, most of which have never occurred normally in previous stages of phylogenesis. This fact may reinforce the point of view, even expressed by some competent psychiatrists, that these interpretations are nothing else than phylogenetic phantasies. Psychiatrists who make that statement have not yet understood the difference between the dynamic and the formal mechanisms. I myself believe that it would be nothing more than a phantasy to explain phylogenetically the dynamics of the single case of schizophrenia. This is the mistake Jung made. Jung thought that the collective unconscious could explain the motivations of the individual. As we have seen, this is not the case. It is only when we want to understand the formal or psychostructural aspect of psychiatric conditions that we must transcend the ontogenetic level.

One of the most important groups of archaic mechanisms, which occur in schizophrenia consists of characteristic intellectual processes. Psychodynamic studies are predominantly concerned with the emotional life of the patients. There are no emotions however, in human beings, which are not accompanied by intellectual processes. The intellectual process may be unconscious, or automatic, or distorted, but it is always present. As it is true that no human activity is completely deprived of emotions, because emotions accompany us everywhere and to a great extent determine our lives, it is also equally true that there are no naked emotions, but that emotions are always accompanied by some kind of intellectual process. By intellectual process is meant some kind of organized mental activity, by virtue of which an understanding of the situation involved is attempted. Emotions, however, have the power to distort the intellectual processes, and this type of distortion has its most typical example in schizophrenia.

In neuroses the distortion occurs to a much lesser degree. But more important than the degree of the distortion is the recognition that such distortion occurs. In the neuroses such recognition on the part of the patient exists, or if it does not exist, it may relatively easily gain consciousness with psychoanalytic treatment. It is not so in schizophrenia. Let us take, for example, the case of an obsessive patient, who has the obsession that if he does not wash his hands three times at each meal, his children are going to become sick and will die. This patient fully recognizes the absurdity of such an idea. It is true that a power stronger than himself will continue to compel him to wash his hands three times, but he has retained sufficient logical power to recognize the unreal nature of such an obsession. Usual psychoanalytic therapy will help in explaining what unconscious emotional factors have determined this symptom. Instead, in the case of a deluded schizophrenic patient, who thinks that he is the king of Egypt, let us say, usual analytic procedure may also uncover the unconscious emotional factors which have determined this delusional idea. It will not explain, however, why such an idea is accepted as reality by the patient, in spite of the most complete contradictory evidence. In other words, it does not explain what change has occurred in the logical powers of the patient so that he is no longer able to test reality. To limit ourselves by saying that the ego of the schizophrenic is disintegrating under the stress of the emotions is to cover the unknown with a semantic screen. We must make an effort to understand why the disintegration has that particular aspect, why it deprives the patient of the power to test reality.

We have already mentioned that the schizophrenic adopts different intellectual mechanisms. By that it was meant that he does not think with ordinary logic. His thought is not illogical or senseless, but follows a different system of logic which leads to deductions different from those usually reached by the healthy person. The schizophrenic is seen in a position similar to that of a man who would solve mathematical problems not with our decimal system, but with another hypothetical system, and would consequently reach different solutions. In other words, the schizophrenic seems to have a faculty of conception which is constituted differently from that of the normal man.

As we shall see in the following chapter, this different faculty of conception or different logic is the same as that which is followed in dreams, in other forms of autistic thinking, and in many manifestations of men living in prehistorical and certain other cultures. It was consequently called *paleologic* to distinguish it from our usual logic, which is generally called Aristotelian, since Aristotle was the first to enunciate its laws.* The laws of paleologic, especially as they are de-

---

* Lévy-Bruhl used the term "prelogical" for the method of thinking which preceded the Aristotelian. Von Domarus used the term "paralogical," which is a term usually adopted by professional logicians. I prefer not to use the term "prelogical," because, as I shall explain shortly (page 193), I consider paleologic thought organized or logical too. I also do not like the term paralogical, because this kind of logic is not pathologic in itself, but is an archaic form of logic. I have thus designated this form of logic as paleologic (from the Greek *palaios,* ancient and old), meaning ancient logic.

Significant works on schizophrenic thought are also those by Vigotsky (264), Kasanin (152), and Bychowsky (38).

duced from the study of schizophrenic thought and dreams, will be examined in detail in the following chapter. Here it is sufficient to emphasize again why the patient abandons the Aristotelian way of thinking and adopts a primitive type. He does so in order to escape anxiety; as long as he interprets reality with Aristotelian logic, he is aware of the unbearable truth, and a state of panic may ensue. Once he sees things in a different way, with a new logic, his anxiety will decrease. This new logic will permit him to see reality as he wants to, and will offer him a pseudo-fulfillment of his wishes. Once the patient sees things in a different way, with a new logic, no Aristotelian persuasion will convince him that he is wrong. He is right, according to his own logic.

The adoption of this paleologic way of thinking is predominant in that type of schizophrenia which has been termed hebephrenic. However, not all thinking in hebephrenics follows paleologic modes. Islands of logical thoughts remain, but they are more and more overwhelmed by the paleological way of thinking. In the paranoid type of schizophrenia a peculiar situation occurs: Aristotelian thought is preserved to a considerable extent, but, as we shall see later in detail, it is often strangely used to support the conclusions reached by paleologic thought. This situation is, to a certain degree, reminiscent of those defenses of the ego which in many neuroses protect or reinforce unconscious complexes.

Another mechanism by which the schizophrenic breaks with reality is the withdrawal from action. This mechanism is particularly pronounced in the catatonic type, following complicated processes which are connected, as we shall see later, with "psychological causality."

In the simple type of schizophrenia the mechanisms mentioned above are not present, or present only to a minimal degree. Rather than change reality, the simple schizophrenic limits reality. He narrows his horizon to a large extent, so that he will be able to make some kind of compromise with what is left of reality, without having to resort very much to paleologic or to withdrawal mechanisms. What he leaves out of his life is generally what pertains to the abstract. Since life in our present cultural environment, however, cannot be deprived of this increasingly important aspect of thought, the simple schizophrenic cannot successfully compromise. He will appear bizarre, odd and inappropriate.

Each of the mechanisms which have been mentioned, though predominantly found in one particular type of schizophrenia, may occur to a greater or lesser degree in every type of this illness. Transitional stages and different combinations of the various mechanisms are commonly found. In addition, there are two other mechanisms which are common to all types, the impairment of affect and desocialization. All of these mechanisms are, of course, interconnected, and possibly only different expressions of one process. In this part of the book, they will be considered separately for didactical reasons, but their interrelation will always be considered. This approach should not be interpreted as a return to psychological atomism. We are fully aware that the human psyche functions as a whole, but the problem under consideration is so involved that no other study of it is feasible except the examination of its parts separately. A synthesis will be attempted in Chapter XIII.

CHAPTER X

The Retreat of Reason

I. The Principle of Teleologic Regression

In this chapter the various intellectual alterations which occur in schizophrenia will be examined.

In this first section, however, it will be shown that intellectual distortions do not occur exclusively in schizophrenics, but occur in a much larger group of individuals than is generally assumed. These distortions never reach the intensity of the schizophrenic distortion, except in dreams. If we take mathematical thinking at one extreme, as the most typical example of pure logical Aristotelian thought, and schizophrenic thinking at the other extreme, we can also find all possible gradations between the two. Generally, the greater the intensity of the emotion involved, the greater may become the necessity for resorting to some kind of intellectual distortion. The amount of the distortion, however, is not proportional to the emotional need.

The most common of these distortions is what is generally

called *rationalization*. Rationalizations are found in normal people and neurotics as well as in psychotics, and consist of attempts to justify logically actions or ideas which in reality are directed, not by reason, but by an emotional need. These rationalizations are often not unrealistic at all from an intellectual point of view; as a matter of fact, they are supported by pure Aristotelian logic. For example, a patient was suffering from feelings of rivalry for his brother, who was a singer. The patient used to warn his brother in a paternal and affectionate tone of voice, "Don't sing so often at clubs and private parties. You will ruin your voice!" This was a correct recommendation. The singer had also been told by many experts that he should not strain his voice with too much work. Actually the motivation of the patient in repeating this recommendation was a different one: He was jealous of the consideration and honor that the brother was receiving when he sang, and wanted to prevent them.

Often the rational foundation which sustains the idea or action is less plausible. Some element of plausibility, however, must remain. As we have seen in one of the previous chapters, the patient, Peter, justified his father's saying that he had been a hero during the first World War, although actually he had been a deserter. According to Peter, his father had to say this in order to remove all doubts about his participation in the war, and by so doing, he was saving the honor of the family. Peter's need to consider his father a venerable authority compelled him to resort to such a fantastic rationalization. His brother, Gabriel, when he was already psychotic, sold a gold watch and some other valuable objects for a few cents. When he was questioned about it, he justified himself with the following rationalization: "These things were mine. Can't I do what I want with my things?" He switched the problem from the advisability of the act to the permissibility of the act, in an attempt to justify it. Actually, the motivation was different. In a latent way he was saying to his parents: "I had to become crazy in order to assert myself. You never let me do what I wanted. Now I can."

From these examples, and from many others which could be cited, it is evident that an attempt is always made to maintain an element of plausibility or logic, even when the wish to have one's way is very strong. As was mentioned before, human beings cannot accept anything which to them seems irrational. The need for rationality is as powerful as the need to gratify the irrational emotions. If rationality is never completely abandoned, a certain *level* of rationality, however, is often lost, especially in situations of emergency, and a regression to a lower level is often resorted to, even by normal human beings. Similar regressions have occurred innumerable times in human history. For instance, if diplomatic discussions do not bring about certain results, much more primitive methods, such as wars or persecution of minorities, may be resorted to.

This regression occurs so often that this process can be defined in the form of a principle. *If, in a situation of severe anxiety, behavior at a certain level of intellectual integration cannot take place or does not bring about the desired results, a strong tendency exists toward behavior of lower levels of integration in order to effect those results.*

The reader should note that the word "tendency" is used. In other words, this principle is not like a physical law, which must operate without exceptions. There is just a propensity toward its occurrence, but it may not occur, as for instance, in cases where something unexpected intervenes. It should also be noted that a situation of severe anxiety *must* be present.

By resorting to lower levels of integration, the human mind turns again to methods which were used in the past, but which were discarded when new methods had been adopted. It is a repetition of history in reversed chronology. This happens not only to human beings, but to animals as well. Mowrer has demonstrated this principle in rats with a very ingenious experiment (199). The animals learned to protect themselves from an electric current by sitting on their hind legs. Later, the rats learned a much better way; they discovered how to turn off the current by pressing a pedal. When this habit was well ingrained, it replaced the previous one. Later, the pedal too was charged with electricity, and the rats had to face another shock, if they continued to press it. At this point they went back to the method of sitting on their hind legs. Thus, they reverted to the earlier and inferior method.

When experimental animals have learned to solve a problem with the mechanism of insight and, for some reason, can no longer solve the problem with this method, they revert to the method of trial and error. In other words, there is a tendency toward a reversed hierarchy of responses,* from the highest to the lowest. I propose to call this principle *the principle of teleologic regression: regression* because less advanced levels of mental integration are used; *teleologic* because this regression seems to have a purpose, namely, to avoid anxiety by bringing about the wanted results. As a matter of fact, studies in abnormal psychology have revealed innumerable instances in which the mind in distress does not necessarily follow scientific thinking (events are the effects of previous causes), but rather teleologic thinking (events have a purpose). Thus, dreams, hallucinations, symptoms, delusions, etc., seem to have a purpose, even though they themselves are the results of previous causes.

More often than not, of course, thinking which follows the principle of teleologic regression does not effect the desired results, but will decrease the anxiety, at least temporarily.

---

* The emphasis here, however, is given not to the response in a behavioristic way, but to the central process which is responsible for the response.

Legends and myths frequently reveal the adoption of this principle. For instance, the Jews, as described in the Bible, had reached that high cultural level which permitted them to worship an abstract God. When, however, they were under the stress of anxiety caused by the sudden disappearance of their leader, Moses, they reverted to the worship of the Golden Calf. When Moses reappeared and the anxiety was relieved, they went back to the cult of the abstract God.

At this point, a question of terminology must be clarified. The reader may be confused by the use of the words "logical," "rational," "intellectual," to indicate thoughts or actions which appear irrational and illogical. These terms are used because these thoughts or actions are intellectually organized, as explained on page 186; in other words, on careful examination they reveal an intellectual process or effort, even if this process does not correspond to the one used in our common logic. In a rationalization, for instance, there is an intellectual or logical effort to justify something, even though this actual intellectual process may be at fault from our common point of view.

The difficulty that some people may experience in calling these processes intellectual or logical is in a certain way similar to the difficulty that some philosophically-minded people experienced in calling the unconscious mechanisms discovered by Freud "psychological." They thought that a necessary characteristic for a psychological phenomenon was that it be conscious; without consciousness a phenomenon could not be psychological. In a similar way, we call a process intellectual if it has some kind of intellectual organization, although it may not necessarily follow the Aristotelian logic (the only one known to us, usually) and may therefore appear to us very illogical. *What may seem to us as forms of irrationality are instead archaic forms of rationality.* As a matter of fact, we shall find more and more that intellectual organization is always present. As I have mentioned above, it is as difficult to escape from some type of intellectual organization as it is to escape from emotions. Even the most nonsensical, bizarre, and irrational thoughts have some kind of intellectual organization. When we understand the type of intellectual organization and its content, we understand the meaning of the process. In other words, it is possible to translate the archaic thought into an Aristotelian thought. Even the so-called "word-salad" of the schizophrenic is not just a bizarre, whimsical *sequence* of words. When we understand it, we discover that it is a *consequence*. (See page 260).

II. Von Domarus' Principle

Paleologic to a great extent is based on a principle enunciated by Von Domarus (265, 266). This author, as a result of his studies on schizophrenia, formulated a principle which, in slightly modified form, is as follows: *Whereas the normal person accepts identity only upon the basis of identical subjects, the paleologician accepts identity based upon identical predicates.* For instance, the normal person is able to conclude, "John Doe is an American citizen," if he is given the following information: "Those who are born in the United States are American citizens; John Doe was born in the United States." This normal person is able to reach this conclusion because the subject of the minor premise, "John Doe," is contained in the subject of the major premise, "those who are born in the United States."

On the other hand, suppose that the following information is given to a schizophrenic: "The President of the United States is a person who was born in the United States. John Doe is a person who was born in the United States." In certain circumstances, the schizophrenic may conclude: "John Doe is the President of the United States." This conclusion, which to a normal person appears delusional, is reached because the identity of the predicate of the two premises, "a person who was born in the United States" makes the schizophrenic accept the identity of the two subjects, "the President of the United States" and "John Doe." Of course, this schizophrenic has an emotional need to believe that John Doe is the president of the United States, a need which will arouse anxiety if it is not satisfied. He cannot think that John Doe is the president of the United States if he follows Aristotelian logic; thus, following the principle of teleologic regression, he abandons Aristotelian logic and follows Von Domarus' principle.

A patient thought that she was the Virgin Mary. Her thought process was the following: "The Virgin Mary was a virgin; I am a virgin; therefore, I am the Virgin Mary." The delusional conclusion was reached because the identity of the predicate of the two premises (the state of being virgin) made the patient accept the identity of the two subjects (the Virgin Mary and the patient). She needed to identify herself with the Virgin Mary because of the extreme closeness and spiritual kinship she felt for the Virgin Mary.

A patient, quoted by Bleuler, thought that he was Switzerland (28). How can one explain such a bizarre thought? Even at the time of Bleuler, Switzerland was one of the few free countries in the world, and the patient had selected the name of this country for the concept of freedom with which he had the impelling need to identify himself. "Switzerland loves freedom, I love freedom. I am Switzerland."

The mechanisms or successive steps of this type of thinking are not necessarily known to the schizophrenic, who automatically thinks in this way, just as the normal person automatically applies the Aristotelian laws of logic without even knowing them. For instance, a schizophrenic patient thinks, without knowing why, that the doctor in charge of the ward is her father, and that the other patients are her sisters. A common predicate, a man in authority, leads to the identity between the father and the physician. Another common predicate, females in the same position of dependency, leads the patient to consider herself and the other inmates as sisters. At times, the interpretation of this type of thinking requires more elaboration. For instance, a patient of Von Domarus thought that Jesus, cigar boxes, and sex were identical. Study of this delusion disclosed that the common predicate, which led to the identification, was the state of being encircled. According to the patient, the head of Jesus, as of a saint, is encircled by a halo, the package of cigars by the tax band, and the woman by the sex glance of the man.

At times paleologic thought is even more difficult to interpret because the principle of Von Domarus is applied only partially; that is, some partial identity among the subjects is based upon partial or total identity of the predicate. For instance, a person who is conceived of by a schizophrenic as having a quality or characteristic of a horse may be thought of with a visual image consisting of part man and part horse. In this case, one subject, the person, is partially identified with the other subject, the horse, because of a common characteristic—for instance, strength.

It is well known how frequently similar distortions and condensations appear in hallucinations and drawings of schizophrenics. Similar conceptions appear in mythologies of ancient peoples and of primitives of today. As a matter of fact, anthropologic studies may disclose to the careful reader how often the principle of Von Domarus is applied in primitive thinking. Numerous studies, outstanding among which is the one by Storch (246), have emphasized the similarities between primitive and schizophrenic thought, but the common underlying principles of logic which rule this thought have received no mention. Werner writes. "It is one of the most important tasks of the developmental psychology to show that the advanced form of thinking characteristic of Western civilization is only one form among many, and that more primitive forms are not so much lacking in logic as based on logic of a different kind. The premise of Aristotelian logic that, when a thing is A it cannot at the same time be B, will not hold true for the primitive." (270). "A Congo native says to a European: 'During the day you drank palm wine with a man, unaware that in him there was an evil spirit. In the evening you heard a crocodile devouring some poor fellow. A wildcat, during the night, ate up all your chickens. Now, the man with whom you drank, the crocodile who ate a man and the wildcat are all one and the same person.' " (from Werner, quoting Lévy-Bruhl). Obviously a common characteristic or predicate (having an evil spirit) led to the identification. Werner rightly states that "this kind of interpretation is rooted in an altogether different mental pattern, a differently constituted faculty of conception, from that exhibited by the scientifically thinking man." He adds that this primitive mode of thinking is neither illogical nor prelogical. It is logical in a different sense. Werner, however, does not attempt to enunciate the principles of a different logic. He does not add that for the primitive A may be B if A and B have only a quality (predicate) in common, although in his outstanding book, *Comparative Psychology of Mental Development,* he gives numerous examples proving this fundamental fact. It is not necessary to give other examples here. The reader may be convinced of the universality of Von Domarus' principle, just by reading a book of anthropology. The student of myths, legends, folklore, traditions, fairy tales, etc. will also be impressed with the same finding.

Young children, too, have the inclination, although not the necessity, to think in accordance with Von Domarus' principle. Max Levin, who compares schizophrenic thought to that of young children, concludes that the patient, as well as the young child, "cannot distinguish adequately between a symbol and the object it symbolizes" (169). For example, a middle-aged schizophrenic, speaking of an actor whom she admired, said, "He was smiling at me." The patient had seen, on the cover of a magazine, a picture of the actor in the act of smiling. Thus she had confused a picture of the actor with the actor himself. Levin reports that a 27-month-old child, drinking milk while looking at the picture of a horse, said, "Give milk to the horse." At 25 months, the same child, looking at the picture of a car, tried to lift the car from the pictures and said to his father, "Daddy, get car out!" For the child the pictured objects were real. Levin is correct in his observations. However, he has not seen them in the light of Von Domarus' principle. What appears to us as a symbol of the object for the schizophrenic or for the child is not necessarily a symbol, but may be a duplication of the object.

Levin makes other exceptionally interesting observations which do not receive complete interpretation, however, and he is led to the conclusion that infantile and schizophrenic concepts "are the result of amusing mixtures of relevant and irrelevant." For instance, he reports that a child, twenty-five months old, was calling "wheel" anything which was made of white rubber, as for example, the white rubber guard which is supplied with little boys' toilet seats to deflect urine. The child knew the meaning of the word wheel as applied, for example, to the wheel of a toy car. This child had many toy cars whose wheels, when made of rubber, were always of white rubber. Thus, he came to think that the word wheel included not only wheels but also anything made of white rubber. Levin concludes that this example "shows how associations of the most ephemeral nature are permitted to enter into a concept when the child is too young to appreciate the non-essentiality." In view of what has been said before, it is obvious that an identification had occurred because of the same characteristic, "white rubber."

In my experience, children have a propensity to indulge in paleologic thinking especially from the age of one and a half to the age of three and a half or even four. Thus, children around two years of age, if shown a picture of a man, will quite often say "Daddy," and if shown a picture of a woman will say "Mommy," no matter whom the pictures represent. A girl, three years and nine months old, saw two nuns walking together, and told her mother, "Mommy, look at the twins!" She thought that the nuns were twins because they were dressed alike. The characteristic of being dressed alike, which twins often have, led to the identification with the nuns.

The foregoing does not imply that young children or that the so-called primitives of today *must* think paleologically. They just have a greater propensity to do so than adult Western men. This greater propensity should not be interpreted as proof of inferiority; it is based on reasons which will be discussed in one of the following sections. We shall discuss here instead another point of more direct importance to the psychiatrist, the application of Von Domarus' principle to the understanding of the structure of dreams.

Freud has shown that a person or object *A* having a certain characteristic of *B* may appear in the dream as being *B* or a composite of *A* and *B*. In the first case there is identification, in the second, composition. The whole field of Freudian symbolism, from *a formal point of view,* is based on Von Domarus' principle. *A symbol of X is something which stands for X, but also something which retains some similarity with X—a common predicate or characteristic.* Thus, snake or fountain pen may symbolize penis because of the similar shape; king may symbolize father on account of the position they both enjoy; box may symbolize vagina because both box and vagina are apt to contain something in their cavities, etc. The wife of a dreamer appeared in a dream as having the physical appearance of the dreamer's boss. The two persons were identified in the dream because the dreamer was concerned with a predicate common to both of them (their domineering attitude). The boss was selected as a symbol because it was more tolerable for the dreamer to be dominated by his boss than by his own wife. A male patient, obsessive-compulsive, had the obsession that he was homosexual, or that he was going to become homosexual. Once he would be known as homosexual, all women would reject him. He had the following dream: He was resting, lying on a couch, when a beautiful woman appeared and told him, "I like vinegar too!" He was pleasantly surprised and woke up. The dream made no sense to him. I asked him what came to his mind when he thought of vinegar. He replied, "Something bitter and disgusting." Then I asked him what came to his mind when he thought of something bitter and disgusting. He replied, "Homosexuality." Thus it is obvious that in the dream vinegar and homosexuality were identified because they had the common characteristics of being bitter and disgusting. The beautiful lady who appeared in the dream was telling him in paleologic language, "I like you even if you are homosexual." Thus the dream was a reassuring one; it removed the anxiety about being rejected by women. Another patient, 18 years old, also an obsessive-compulsive with schizoid traits, was a devout Catholic who wanted to become a theological student and be ordained a priest. At the same time he struggled very hard against his sexual instincts. He had the following dream: He is undressing a young woman with sexual intentions, when suddenly he realizes that her vagina looks like an umbilicus. He wakes up. In his associations, the patient remembers that when he was a child, he believed that children were born from the umbilicus. Thus, in the dream, vagina and umbilicus are identified because they are thought of by the patient as organs having the common characteristic of giving birth to children. The dream serves a purpose; the vagina is seen not as a sexual organ, but solely as an organ which gives birth to children. The patient, after having been stimulated sexually, tries to make a reconcilation with the precepts of the Catholic church, which prefers to consider the sexual organs as organs of reproduction rather than organs which give carnal pleasure.

One may conclude that Von Domarus' principle, or the first principle of paleologic, gives an important clue not only to the understanding of the schizophrenic way of thinking, but also to the understanding of the mechanisms of dreams and of some infantile and primitive thinking. However, Von Domarus' principle and the other paleological laws which will be mentioned shortly, do not explain these phenomena dynamically, but only formally. In other words, the study of paleologic may explain the essential structure of this type of thinking, independently of the content of thought. The content of thought varies with the various emotional factors which can be studied fully only by psychoanalytic procedures. The study of formal mechanisms reveals *how* we think and feel. The study of dynamic or psychoanalytic mechanisms reveals *what* we think and feel and the motivation of our thinking and feeling. Both the formal and the dynamic approaches are necessary if we want to understand psychological phenomena fully.

Although the purpose of this book is to expound only what pertains to schizophrenia, it is not possible to avoid references to other conditions, normal or pathologic, when archaic mental processes are studied. Thus, in this section we could not help calling to the attention of the reader the tremendous role played by Von Domarus' principle in all non-Aristotelian thinking, a role that transcends by far the schizophrenic process.

Von Domarus formulated his principle in connection with schizophrenia in 1925. In 1910 Lévy-Bruhl, as a result of his studies on what he termed "the prelogical functions of inferior societies," had formulated the so-called law of participation, which may be considered a harbinger of Von Domarus' principle (170, 171). According to this law, for the primitive mentality "the objects, the beings, the phenomena, in a way incomprehensible to us, may be at the same time themselves and something else." This law, which Lévy-Bruhl applied *only to collective or social manifestations** is correct but very indefinite, because it does not state the essential condition for the identification of different objects, namely, the necessity of a common characteristic. The formulation of Von Domarus' law was a great step forward, inasmuch as it permitted the linking of this archaic logic to the phenomenon of Freudian symbolism. Von Domarus himself, however, did not see this connection; it was several years after his discovery, in 1947–48, that my research indicated this relationship.

III. Further Discussion of Von Domarus' Principle

The study of Von Domarus' principle in schizophrenia, as well as in other instances which have been mentioned, requires more consideration of the predicate which determines the identification. In fact, it is obvious that the predicate is the most important part in this type of thinking.† In Aristotelian thinking only identical subjects are identified. The subjects are immutable; therefore, only a few and the same de-

---

* The fact that Lévy-Bruhl applied the law of participation only to *social* manifestations is very important. Many authors have neglected to take this point into consideration and have thus misinterpreted and unduly criticized Lévy-Bruhl. This social aspect will be discussed again in section 10 of this chapter.

† That the predicate is the most important part in primitive language is confirmed by other facts. For instance, in aphasia nominorum and other aphasias, the patient does not remember the names of objects but remembers their functions (predicates). For example, if shown a key and asked to name it, he will say "to open." If shown a cigarette, he will say "smoke," etc. History of languages also reveals that things were first named according to their function.

ductions are possible. In paleologic thinking, on the other hand, the predicates lead to the identification. Since the predicates of the same subject may be extremely numerous and one does not know which one will be chosen by the patient in the process of identification, this type of thought becomes bizarre, unpredictable, individualistic and often incomprehensible. For instance, in the example quoted from Von Domarus, the characteristic of being encircled was the identifying quality. Each of the three subjects which were identified—Jesus, cigar boxes and sex—had a potentially large number of predicates, but the patient selected one which was completely unpredictable and bizarre. The Congo native, quoted by Lévy-Bruhl, chose the characteristic, "having an evil spirit," in order to identify the man, the crocodile and the wildcat, thus giving the European the impression that his reasoning was bizarre, unpredictable and illogical.

The predicate which is selected in the process of identification is called the "identifying link." Why a certain predicate, out of numerous possible ones, should be selected as the identifying link can be found out only by the study of the emotional factors involved. In other words, emotional currents may determine which one of the predicates will be taken as the identifying link. It is obvious that if John Doe thinks that he is the president of the United States because he was born in the United States, he must wish to think so. His emotional needs direct him toward the selection of that predicate, being born in the United States, out of many other possibilities. If a patient thinks that she is the Virgin Mary, just because she is a virgin, she must have a strong urge to identify herself with the Virgin Mary.

The emotional factors operating in paleologic thinking are, of course, the same as those described by Freud in "Psychopathology of Everyday Life," (97), and by Jung in "Psychology of Dementia Praecox" and in his works on word associations (138, 139, 143). However, a study limited to the consideration of emotional factors will not explain the formal manifestations of this type of thinking. Conscious or unconscious emotions are only the directing motivation or the driving forces of thoughts which, in accordance \ ith the principle of teleologic regression, acquire a paleologic mould. It is thus obvious that the principle of teleologic regression operates only inasmuch as Von Domarus' principle permits a psychodynamic selection of the predicate.

Since predicates will be discussed again when we examine the disturbances of thought-associations in schizophrenics, it is important that an accurate definition of them be given. A predicate is, by definition, something which concerns the subject. One is accustomed to recognizing as predicates abstract or concrete qualities of the subject or something which in a certain way is contained in the subject, for instance, the characteristics of being white, red, honest, attractive, suspicious, big, small, of having a tail, and infinite other possibilities. These are called *predicates of quality*. There are, however, other characteristics which paleologically are conceived of as pertaining to the subjects and, therefore, are considered predicates, although they are not contained in the subject, for instance, the characteristics of occurring at a certain time or a given place. These are the *predicates of contiguity*. For instance, if a patient accidentally ate a certain exotic food on a day in which he had a pleasant experience, he may dream of eating that special food again, because he wishes to revive the pleasant experience. Special food and pleasant experience are identified in the dream because they happen to have been perceived at the same time. The identifying link in this case is a *predicate of temporal contiguity*. The predicate of contiguity may be not only temporal, but also spatial. For instance, a patient may dream of being in his summer home in the country. A woman he loves lives near his summer home.

Summer home and loved woman are identified because they both have the characteristic of residing in the same place. In this case the identifying link is *a predicate of spatial contiguity*. In many other cases the identifying link is a mixture of predicates of the two different types, quality and contiguity.*

If the identifying link is a predicate of quality, it will be relatively easy to understand the meaning of what the patient expresses. What are referred to in psychoanalytic literature as universal symbols are generally objects whose identifying links are predicates of quality. If the identifying link is an accidental predicate of contiguity, obviously the symbol may be specific for the individual, and many details concerning his life history may be necessary in order to understand its meaning. For instance, only the patient mentioned could identify the girl he loved with his summer home in the country.

Now, if we go back to Aristotle's traditional logic and to its four laws of thought—law of identity, law of contradiction, law of excluded middle, law of sufficient reason—we may easily conclude, as we shall soon see, that the first three are annulled by Von Domarus' principle. Before discussing the paleological logic in comparison with the Aristotelian, however, the author wishes to point out that he does not necessarily imply that the Aristotelian logic is the model of correct thinking in *an absolute sense*. This implication would require long philosophical discussions which are inappropriate here. The author is aware of the criticisms which have been made of the Aristotelian logic at different times. He has used Aristotelian logic as a system of reference, because it is most commonly accepted as representative of normal thinking. It is only in this relative sense that the effect of Von Domarus' principle on the first three laws of Aristotelian logic is exam-

---

* In a previous article (10), I distinguished a third type of predicate: predicate of finality. I feel now that this additional group is not necessary, as the predicates of finality may be included in the group of predicates of quality.

ined. The physician or psychologist who is unfamiliar with the subject of logic need not worry. This discussion will be extremely brief and simple.

The law of identity says that A is always A, never B. Now, according to Von Domarus' principle, B may be A, provided B has a quality of A. The law of contradiction states that A cannot be A and not be A at the same time and place. Now, if the patient follows Von Domarus' principle, he may see A as A and at the same time as B (that is, non-A), if he concentrates on a quality which A and B have in common. The law of excluded middle says that A must be A or not be A; there cannot be an intermediate state. In its tendency to condense several subjects, paleologic thinking seems to neglect this law of excluded middle. Things are often seen as a composite of A and B. For instance, in schizophrenic drawings one often sees a human figure, who is half man and half woman. The person represented in the drawing may be conceived by the schizophrenic as having a characteristic of the opposite sex. Also the emotional difficulty the schizophrenic has in identifying himself with one sex may be revealed formally by his non-adherence to the third law of thought. Similar composition (that is, abolition of the third law of thought) occurs quite commonly in dreams. The neologisms of the schizophrenic are due to composition of different verbal symbols.

The philosopher Vico, who published his major works at the beginning of the eighteenth century, advanced similar ideas about the origin of the mythological figures, such as satyrs and centaurs (263). He wrote that the Ancients, being unable to abstract the same property from two different bodies, united the bodies in their minds. Vico explained mythological metamorphoses in a similar way. If a subject acquires a new property which is more characteristic of a second subject, the first subject is conceived as transformed into the second. For instance, if a woman who used to travel or to change in many ways, finally stopped at a certain place, and no further change occurred in her life, in the myth she might appear as transformed into a plant. Even today, angels are usually represented with wings because they are supposed to be in the sky (heaven) like birds. Vico's interpretation of myths may be applied also to dreams, and to schizophrenic thinking.

The study of Von Domarus' principle may also explain other peculiarities of thought in schizophrenia and in dreams. For instance, it is not too difficult to understand how in these types of thinking, the part may symbolize the whole and the whole may symbolize the part. In fact, according to Von Domarus' principle $a = a + b + c$ etc., because the two terms of the equation have a part a in common. Therefore, in dreams and schizophrenic delusions we find that a person, either the patient or another person, may be identified with a part of himself, so that he may at the same time be symbolized by (identified with) several people, each of them having a quality that he has.

Von Domarus' principle often leads to delusions of identification of the patient with another person. The formal mechanism is the following "If A may be identified with B because they have a common quality, it will be sufficient for me to acquire a quality of the person I want to be identified with, in order to become that person." The deluded patient discovers in himself a quality possessed also by a hero, a saint, a general, and identifies himself with the person who has that given quality. Other deluded patients try to acquire identifying qualities, or to confer them on others. A paranoid schizophrenic wanted her child to become an angel. Since angels are nourished only by "spiritual food," she did not feed her child for a few days—that is, until her relatives became aware of her acutely developed psychosis.

The converse of Von Domarus' principle is also applied

in paleologic thinking, as well as in primitive and infantile thinking. If A has not a given quality of A', A cannot be A'. I'll mention again one of the interesting examples given by Levin (168). The content of this example is similar to the one reported (page 199), inasmuch as it also refers to twins. A bright six-year-old boy asked Levin whether twins are always boys. He replied that they may be either boys or girls, or a girl and a boy. When the child heard that twins may be a girl and a boy, he asked with surprise, "Then how could they wear the same clothes?" Levin concludes that the child had seen identical twins dressed alike, and that his concepts of twins included an irrelevant detail, identity of raiment. If we apply Von Domarus' principle in reverse, the mental mechanism seems to be the following: "Twins have a common quality, identical raiment. If two persons have not or cannot have identical raiment, they cannot be twins!"

Not all delusions can be explained by Von Domarus' principle because many are based only on the Freudian mechanisms of projection, or because they imply other paleologic rules which we have not yet examined. Some of the more complicated mechanisms of delusions will be examined on pages 299–304.

I shall mention one here which implies both projection and Von Domarus' principle. Why may the homosexually loved person become, in the delusional system of the patient, the persecutor? The mechanism may be as follows: *This man produces something very disturbing in me and causes me a lot of misery. He must be a persecutor.* The persecutor and the loved person are identified because they both have the quality of producing in the patient a very disturbing reaction, or homosexual love and hate themselves are identified, because they produce the same disturbing effect in the patient. The patient, of course, prefers to think that the person involved is a persecutor, and harbors hate, not love, for him, because in this case he will not feel guilty of the socially unacceptable homosexuality. Freud's formulation, "I do not love him—I hate him, because he persecutes me," may be simplified in the following formulation, "He disturbs me, therefore he persecutes me." The part "He disturbs me," replaces or summarizes "I love him—I don't love him, but I hate him." (Identification of love and hate because they are both disturbing.)

Another important occurrence of Von Domarus' principle, which will be mentioned again when therapy is discussed, is found in the transference situation, not only in psychotics but in neurotics as well. The analytic situation appears to the patient as a repetition of the relationship with his own parent, not only because he has the emotional need to repeat the relationship, but also because the two situations have several characteristics in common. Later the patient will realize that the relations are not the same (he was deceived by Von Domarus' principle), and the transference will evolve toward a more fruitful development.

IV. Connotation, Denotation, Verbalization

Before proceeding with the examination of paleologic thinking, I wish to remind the reader of what is traditionally meant in logic by different aspects of terms, that is, by connotation and denotation. Let us take, for instance, the term, *table*. The connotation of this term is the meaning of the term, that is, the concept *article of furniture with flat horizontal top, set on legs*. The denotation of the term is the object meant, that is, the table as a physical entity. In other words, the term *table* may mean table in general or it may mean any or all particular tables. Every term has both these aspects. It means certain definite qualities or attributes and also refers to certain objects or, in the case of a singular term, to one object which has those qualities. The connotation is, in a certain way, the definition of the object and includes the whole class of the object, without any reference to a concrete embodiment of the object.

I feel that, in addition to the two aspects of the terms which are traditionally considered in logic, one has to consider a third aspect, if one wants to understand the problem better from a psychological point of view. This is the verbal aspect of the term, the term as a word or verbal expression. I propose to call this aspect of the term *verbalization*. For instance, the term *table* may be considered from three aspects: its connotation, when one refers to its meaning; its denotation, when one refers to the object meant; its verbalization, when one considers the word as a word, that is, as a verbal representation independent of its symbolic value.

Now it is possible to formulate a second important principle of paleologic. *Whereas the healthy person in a wakened state is mainly concerned with the connotation and the denotation of a symbol but is capable of shifting his attention from one to another of the three aspects of a symbol, the person who thinks paleologically is mainly concerned with the denotation and the verbalization, and experiences a total or partial impairment of his ability to connote.* In view of this principle, two phenomena have to be studied in schizophrenia and other types of paleologic thinking: first, the reduction of the connotation power; second, the emphasis on the denotation and verbalization.

However, before proceeding with this study, it must be reemphasized that these paleological principles do not have to be interpreted or applied as rigidly as physical laws. These principles probably are nothing else but special formulations which help to interpret certain processes. The important thing, I think, is to have a methodology which shows not only how the paleologic mind differs from the normal, but also how its way of thinking may be interpreted and predicted.

REDUCTION OF CONNOTATION POWER

For the person who thinks paleologically, the verbal symbols cease to be representative of a group or of a class, but are representative only of the specific objects under discussion. For instance, the word "cat" cannot be used as relating to any member of the feline genus, but only in reference to a specific cat, like "the cat sitting on that chair." Oftener there is a gradual shifting from the connotation to the denotation level.* This gradual regression is apparent if we ask a not too deteriorated schizophrenic to define words. For instance, the following are some words which a schizophrenic was asked to define, and her replies:

Q. Book.

A. It depends what book you are referring to.

Q. Table.

A. What kind of table? A wooden table, a porcelain table, a surgical table, or a table you want to have a meal on?

Q. House.

A. There are all kinds of houses, nice houses, nice private houses.

Q. Life.

A. I have to know what life you happen to be referring to— *Life* magazine or to the sweetheart who can make another individual happy and gay.

---

* The statement made by many logicians that there is an inverse ratio between connotation and denotation does not hold true if the problem is considered from a psychological point of view. In other words, a decrease in the connotation power is not accompanied by an increase in the denotation power and vice versa. Many logicians, too, have criticized this concept of inverse ratio, because objects (denotation) can be enumerated, but qualities and meanings cannot be measured mathematically. I might add that the study of primitive thought discloses that what would be called terms with great connotation (with meaning of specific objects) preceded terms with greater denotation, which originated at a higher level of development.

From the examples, it is obvious that the patient, a high school graduate, is unable to define common words. She cannot cope with the task of defining the word as a symbol of a class or a symbol including all the members of the class, like all books, all tables, and so on. She tries first to decrease her task by attempting to break it into little pieces, that is, by limiting her definition to special subgroups or to particular members of the class. For instance, she is unable to define the word "table" and attempts to simplify her problem by asking whether she has to define various subgroups of tables— wooden tables, surgical tables, and so on. In the last example, she wants to know whether I am referring to one of two particular instances, *Life* magazine or the life of the sweetheart. This reply, which reveals impairment of connotation power, is also complicated by the emphasis on the verbalization, as will be demonstrated in the following section.

A similar inability to formulate or use words or concepts which include whole classes has been noted numerous times among primitive people, by anthropologists. For instance, Steinen reports that primitive people of Brazil have a group of expressions for different species of parrots, but the generic name "parrot" is lacking in their language (244). Smith reports that the Australian aborigines have no class names such as bird, tree, or fish, but on the other hand they have special terms for particular species of birds, trees and fishes (239).

The philosopher Cassirer, in his book, *Language and Myth*, has described very well the difficulty or inability of the primitive mind in connoting (51). Cassirer does not seem to have become aware of other important paleologic laws, like Von Domarus' principle, but rather has concerned himself with this reduction of the connotation power. He has emphasized that when the concept is separated from the class, the single experience remains isolated, loses expansion, but acquires emotional concentration or "intensive compression." The immediate sensible experience increases in power. In a certain way the universe of the schizophrenic, of the primitive, and of the child is closer to the immediate perception, to the phenomenological world, and at the same time it is farther from the truth than ours because of its extreme subjectivity.

According to Susanne K. Langer many of the psychological phenomena that caught Cassirer's interest arose from the psychiatric work of Kurt Goldstein on cases of cerebral damage caused by physical accidents (166). More recently, Goldstein has dealt with this decrease of the connotation power in schizophrenics too (113). In the color-sorting test, one of Goldstein's patients picked out various shades of green, but in doing so he named them—peacock green, emerald green, taupe green, bright green, bell green, baby green. He could not say that all of them might be called green. Another patient of Goldstein said in the same situation: "This is the color of the grass in Virginia, this is the color of the grass in Kentucky, this is the color of the bark of the tree, this is the color of the leaves." The words used by the patients in naming colors belonged to a definite situation. "The words," Goldstein writes, "have become individual words, i.e., words which fit only a specific object or situation." In other words, the meaning or the connotation of the word includes not a class but only a specific instance. There is, therefore, a definite restriction of the connotation power.* Goldstein calls this phenomena expressions of "concrete attitude." This tightness to the denotation prevents the schizophrenic from using figurative or metaphorical language, contrary to what it may seem as at first impression.

It has already been stated by Benjamin that the schizo-

---

* Many logicians, on the other hand, would say that the connotation is increased. This point of view is psychologically wrong.

phrenic is unable to interpret proverbs correctly (23). He will always give a more or less literal interpretation of them. Figurative language increases the use of the term which acquires an unusual denotation and connotation. If one says, "When the cat's away, the mice will play," a normal listener will understand that by cat is meant a person in authority. A schizophrenic patient gave the following literal interpretation of that proverb: "There are all kinds of cats and all kinds of mice, but when the cat is away, the mice take advantage of the cat." In other words, for the schizophrenic the word "cat" could not acquire a special connotation.

The inability of the schizophrenic to use metaphorical language is also revealed by the following replies of a patient who was asked to explain what was meant when a person was referred to by the names of various animals, for instance:

Q. Wolf.

A. Wolf is a greedy animal.

Q. Fox.

A. A fox and a wolf are two different animals. One is more vicious than the other, more and more greedy than the other.

Q. Parrot.

A. It all depends what the parrot says.

Q. Peacock.

A. A woman with beautiful feathers. By the way, *Woman* is a magazine.

Many beginners in the field of psychiatry get the impression that schizophrenic language and thought are highly metaphorical and poetic. In reality it is not so. This impression is due to misinterpretation of the phenomena which were explained above in terms of Von Domarus' principle. For instance, a schizophrenic will be able to *identify* a man with a wolf on account of a common characteristic, greediness, but will not be able to accept the concept *wolf* as a symbol of greedy men. Two different mechanisms are employed. In the first instance, a very primitive paleologic mechanism is necessary; in the second instance a high process of abstraction is at play. The primitive and the schizophrenic use metaphors out of necessity, not for esthetic reasons. The artist may exploit archaic processes to intensify the emotional tone of his expression, but at the same time will retain that power of abstraction which has been lost by the schizophrenic and which has not been sufficiently used by the primitive.

Now a question may occur to the reader. If these reversions to primitive mechanisms have a teleologic function in psychopathology, what is the purpose of this loss of connotation power in the schizophrenic? This is an important point. The answer, however, requires knowledge of other aspects involved, which are taken into consideration in Chapter XI.

EMPHASIS ON DENOTATION AND VERBALIZATION

When the word has lost its connotation power, its denotation and verbalization acquire greater significance. The word, disrobed of its connotation, in a certain way remains isolated from a logical context but increases its emotional tone, acquires more subjective value, a uniqueness which is connected with the subjective sensorial image of the individual. In other words, it becomes much nearer to the perceptual level. Ideas are, therefore, quite often expressed with words which describe sensory images. Storch has described this phenomenon in schizophrenia at length (246). One of his patients spoke of "a heap of truth," another of an "idea" as being "smaller than a flea," etc.

In many cases, when the connotation value is lost, the

attention of the schizophrenic is focused on the verbalization, or on the word merely as a word. When this happens, several different situations may ensue:

1) Often mental processes occur which are stimulated only by verbalization.
2) The verbalization becomes the identifying link in identifications.
3) The verbalization becomes confused with the whole or part of the denotation; that is the word and its characteristics may be taken as identical with the thing and its characteristics.

As an example of the first possibility, I'll mention a patient whom I examined during the second World War. During the examination, she told me that the next time the Japanese would attack the Americans it would be at Diamond Harbor or Gold Harbor. When she was asked why, she replied: "The first time, they attacked at Pearl Harbor, now they will attack at Diamond Harbor or at Sapphire Harbor." "Do you think that the Japanese attacked Pearl Harbor because of its name?" I asked. "No, no," she replied. "It was a *happy* coincidence." Note the inappropriateness of the adjective *happy*. It was a happy coincidence for her, because she could prove thereby the alleged validity of her present paleologic thinking. Her train of thought was stimulated by the words "Pearl Harbor." A literal connotation was given to the word "Pearl," which aroused in the patient associations with precious stones.

As we shall study in more detail in a following section, even simple associations of ideas occur in the schizophrenic, on account of this emphasis on the verbalization. A schizophrenic who was writing words as they would occur to him, wrote the following sequences, "C, see, sea" "Y, why, Y." These are so-called sound associations.

The second possibility which we have mentioned merely

states the application of Van Domarus' principle with the verbalization as the identifying link. Different things are identified because they have names which have a common characteristic. The identification is particularly prone to occur if the names are homonymous. Two otherwise different things are identified, or considered together, because they have the same verbalization, that is, the same phonetic or written symbol. In one example mentioned above, the patient put together *Life* magazine and the life of the sweetheart. Another schizophrenic was noticed as having the habit of wetting her body with oil. When asked why, she replied, "The human body is a machine and has to be lubricated." The word *machine*, applied in a figurative sense to the human body, had led to the identification with man-made machines. It is obvious that for the schizophrenic the term may be not a symbol but a characteristic, a quality or a predicate, or a whole duplication of the object which is symbolized. The identification due to similar or common verbal expression is based not only on Von Domarus' principle, but also on the second principle of paleologic, that is, on the emphasis on the verbalization and the decreased importance of the connotation.

These two mechanisms, application of Von Domarus' principle and emphasis on the verbalization, are quite often used by normal adults in jokes and witticisms. Some of the examples mentioned above, such as the schizophrenic who was wetting her body with oil, have definite comical characteristics. The important point, however, is that what is comical for the healthy person is taken seriously by the schizophrenic. In a separate publication I have described the use of paleologic in wit in detail (12). Freud, in his important monograph on wit, described many mechanisms involved in the technique of witticisms, and compared them to the mechanisms in dreams (98). He did not see them, however, as an expression of a special logic.

The emphasis on verbalization also appears in many dreams, as revealed first by Freud in his monograph on dream interpretation (96). The following is one of the numerous examples he gives. C. dreams that on the road to X he sees a girl bathed in a white light and wearing a white blouse. The dreamer had begun an affair with a Miss White on that road. The following example is also instructive. The wife of a patient dreamed that she had intercourse with Mr. X., a friend of the family. Motivated either by guilt or hostility, she revealed this dream to her husband, my patient. The patient was hurt but did not say anything because, after all, "it was only a dream." The following night the patient dreamed that his wife was unfaithful to him, but to his great surprise he found out that the man she had relations with was her own brother. The patient, in the dream, was thinking: "After all, it is not so bad. It is true that she has intercourse, but only with her brother. Sex with a brother does not count." The patient did not know how to explain the dream, but suddenly it occurred to him that Mr. X.'s first name was Carl, the same name as that of his brother-in-law, who had had relations with his wife in the dream. Thus it seems that in the dream Mr. X. and the brother-in-law were identified because they had the same name, Carl. The dream reported by the wife apparently hurt the patient very much. By the identification which occurred in his own dream, his anxiety was diminished, because "Sex with a brother does not count, cannot be too pleasant."

The third point mentioned concerns the tendency of the verbalization to become part of the denotation, when the connotation has been lost; that is, the schizophrenic sees the verbal symbol as part of the thing which is symbolized. Cassirer, too, has noted that in primitive thinking there is an essential identity between the word and what the word denotes. The word is not a mere conventional symbol, but is merged with its object in an indissoluble unity. Thus word magic originates. The word of an object acquires the same property of the object, and may be substituted for the object when the latter is not available. The name of a god is as powerful as the god himself. Werner and many other authors have reported identical observations.

Piaget has observed that children, too, experience names as fused in the objects they denote (210). Piaget asked children not older than six, "Where is the name of the sun?" and he elicited the following responses: "Inside! Inside the sun!" or "High up in the sky!"

V. Psychological Causality and the Formal Mechanisms of Catatonia

It was mentioned in one of the previous sections that the first three laws of thought of traditional logic were eliminated by Von Domarus' principle. On the other hand, there is something retained in paleologic thinking similar to the fourth law, the law of sufficient reason: We must assume a reason for every event. Something "similar" to the fourth law, we say, because actually the methods by which a reason for, or a cause of, an event is searched for by the paleologician are different from those used by the normal person. The paleologician confuses the physical world with the psychological. Instead of finding a physical explanation of an event, he looks for a personal motivation or an intention as the cause of an event. Every act, every event, occurs because it is willed or wanted, either by the person himself who seeks an explanation, or by another person, or by something which becomes personified. In other words, causality by logical deduction, often implying concepts involving the physical world, is replaced with causality by psychological explanation. Moreover, causality by psychological explanation may be divided into two types: 1) projected psychological causality and 2) introjected psychological causality.

Some of the conclusions expressed in this paragraph have been suggested by the works of Piaget on the mentality of the child (210-212), and by several anthropological works, especially "Society and Nature" by Kelsen (157). Correlating the observations of these authors with my observations on schizophrenics, additional conclusions can be set forth. It is the feeling of the writer that these conclusions are particularly useful in understanding the formal mechanisms of schizophrenia, and especially those of the catatonic type, which so far have eluded the efforts of many interpreters.

Explanation by projected psychological causality is encountered particularly in the paranoid type of schizophrenia. It simply means that everything which occurs is interpreted as due to the will of a person. If a person is killed, if a storm occurs, if the wind blows, it is so *solely* because somebody wants it so. This method of interpreting events is much more primitive than the one by logical deduction. Piaget has described this method very well in young children (210-212). Children, examined by him in Switzerland, thought that God made the thunder in the sky, that Negroes were made the way they were because they were naughty when they were little and God punished them, that there were a great and a little Salève Lakes, because some people wanted to go into the little one and some into the great one. Werner reports other examples (270). A boy five years of age thought that in the evening it got dark because people were tired and wanted to sleep. The same child thought that the rain was due to the fact that the angels swept the heavens with their brooms and lots of water. The intentions are ascribed first to other people, then to things. The moon follows the child, the sun goes up in the sky, the rivers run. An animistic and anthropomorphic conception of the world originates. Things become animated; they either have a will of their own, or are moved by the will of somebody. The same conception of psychological causality is found by many anthropologists in primitive cultures.

Man living in a primitive society has the need for explanation just as civilized man has. The need for explanation is one of the basic needs of the human race, and is to be found in every member of Homo Sapiens. However, man living in a primitive culture is entirely satisfied when he can think that some person, or a personified entity, is responsible for an event. The moral point is not more important than the casual link; it is the *only* aspect taken into consideration: *to be responsible for an event means to be the cause of the event.* The concept of impersonal force is a scientific abstraction which requires a much higher level of thinking. Many magic practices of primitive societies consist of attempts to change or modify the will or intentions of the people who are responsible for (causers of) the event. Study of myths reveals the same thing. If Ulysses is wrecked, it is because Poseidon, the God of the Sea, is angry at him. If the Greeks are afflicted by epidemics, it is because Phoebus wants to punish Agamemnon. Anthropological and mythological examples of projected psychological explanation could be multiplied indefinitely. The reader who is particularly interested is referred to the quoted works. (Vico 263, Lévy-Bruhl 170, 171, Werner 270, Kelsen 157).

In dreams, too, events are engendered by wishes, intentions, or psychological motivations. Paranoiacs and paranoids interpret almost everything as manifesting a psychological intention or meaning related to their delusional complexes. If the nurse looks at the patient in a special way, if a certain food is given at a certain meal, if a certain noise is heard, etc., each of these things has a special meaning. They are willed by other persons in that specific way for reasons which involve the patient. In many cases, practically everything which occurs is interpreted as willed by the persecutors of the patient. In many other cases, especially when the delusions are not well organized, the patient does not even ask himself why the alleged persecutors commit these acts against him. He simply accepts the fact that they do so, that those acts are willed by somebody. If those acts were not willed they could not occur. Of course, in these ideas of reference, two mechanisms are at play: not only is there the belief that each event is willed, but also the belief that each event has a special reference to the patient himself.

More difficult to understand, perhaps, are the concepts of introjected psychological causality. Although this type is psychological causality related to the person himself who thinks, and therefore not essentially dissimilar from projected psychological causality, it implies much more and requires the study of other aspects of the problem. Again I refer the reader to the study of primitive races. One of the first things man became aware of was that he was able to will. Whereas infra-human animals *react* to events, men *act*, that is, they have a choice, or at least they believe they have a choice as to what to do. Men understood this fact before they grasped the concept of physical causality, that is, the concept that a given physical event is the cause of another event. As a matter of fact, as has been mentioned in this section, every event was considered to be caused by the will of men or anthropomorphized beings (gods, animals, rivers, etc.). We have also seen how the person who caused the event was also considered responsible for the event; that is how responsibility and causality were confused. If the event was harmful, and most events in those days were harmful, since man could hardly protect himself from nature, the person who was responsible was guilty. The concepts of *guilt* and *cause* are confused in many primitive languages. Even in early Greek, the word *aitia* (from which is derived the English word "etiology") has both the meanings of guilt and cause. The individual primitive man as an actor, as a doer, must have felt guilty quite often. To do was to be potentially guilty, because after all, you could not know the event which will follow what you were doing. The event might even have an effect on the whole tribe; its repercussions might be enormous, like an epidemic or drought. Kelsen has well illustrated the relation between *to do* and *to be guilty* (157).

How do primitive men act in order to diminish their feeling of guilt? They refrain from acting freely; they perform only those acts which are accepted by the tribe. For any desired effect, the tribe teaches the individual what act to perform. Ritualism and magic thus originate. The life of primitive man is not as free as many philosophers and romantic writers believe. It is completely regulated by a tremendous number of norms and restrictions. The individual has to follow the ritual for practically everything he does. By performing the act according to ritual, the primitive believes that he will avoid guilt for that act. The anxiety, which is due to the uncertainty connected with the expectation of something that has not as yet occurred, is removed. The ritual reassures the individual that the effect will be good. In summary, primitive men feel extremely guilty for their individual actions, performed of their own free will. In order to avoid the anxiety of the unknown effect and the feeling of guilt, they devise rituals, ways of acting accepted by the group, which are supposed to ensure that the events will turn out favorably.

Now, if we translate the foregoing into psychiatric terminology, we may state that an extreme state of anxiety is alleviated by the adoption of an enormous system of compulsions. What would happen if the primitive would not follow the ritual? He would be overwhelmed by tremendous anxiety, not only because he is afraid of being punished by the tribe but also because he feels guilty or responsible for his free acts. He may seek punishment, or remain anxious. If the anxiety is intolerable and as intense as panic, he may eliminate action entirely. Actually that happens very seldom; the man living in a primitive culture faithfully follows the ritual.

Going back to our patients, let us consider again the case of Richard, already cited in Part II of this volume (see pages 119–129). When he was in a state of extreme anxiety and in the process of developing a catatonic attack, he presented the following strange phenomena. More and more he realized that it was difficult for him to act. He did not know what to do. He did not know where to look, where to turn. Any motion that he was inclined to make appeared to him as an insurmountable problem, because he did not know whether he should make it or not. This problem presented itself when any act was to be performed; it was an exasperating, horrible experience. The overwhelming fear of doing the wrong thing, which would either hurt or disappoint him, seemed to possess him to an increasing degree. Therefore, he preferred not to eat, not to dress, not to wash himself. He preferred to be motionless, almost paralyzed, to lie in bed or on a chair for a long time. However, before he developed the symptoms of immobility, when he realized that it was becoming increasingly difficult for him to do things and had the feeling that he was lost, or losing himself, he tried desperately to hold on to something. That something was, to use his own word, "magic." For instance, when he was walking and would see a red light, that was interpreted by him as a sign that he should not go ahead; God was guiding him and was telling him to stop. If he saw an arrow, he would go in the direction of the arrow. He felt that he *must* go in that direction. If he discovered no signs, a terrific hesitation tortured him. When he was motionless, he had to "interpret" everything. Every occurrence seemed to have a special reference to him and was an indication of whether he should do the thing he wished to do or not. When he was asked questions, he tried to answer, but an accidental noise or other occurrence was interpreted by him as a possible sign or order for him not to respond. The number of words the question consisted of was interpreted as a possible sign not to answer. Even before he had become so sick, he had tried to find signs for guidance. One day he saw a girl working in a hospital, an indication to him that he should work in that hospital. As the anxiety increased, his reliance on these signs did not help much, and he gradually sank into a complete catatonic stupor.

In this case I have related these experiences almost verbatim, as given by the patient. Very few patients are able to recollect the experiences of precatatonic panic as well as this patient did. I was very fortunate indeed to be able to recapture them from him. They are dramatic and frightful experiences of tremendous emotional intensity, and are often completely forgotten by the patient. At times, the patient who senses that he is sinking into stupor because he is afraid to act, tries to prevent this by becoming overactive and submerging himself in a manic-like sequence of aimless acts. This is the so-called catatonic excitement which precedes or follows the catatonic stupor. During this period of excitement the patient acts in the opposite way, that is, as if he were not concerned at all with responsibility or as if he would defy previous concepts of responsibility. He may become homicidal, suicidal, and destructive. Indeed, the catatonic excitement is one of the most dangerous psychiatric occurrences, more dangerous by far than the manic excitement.

Now, let us re-examine the case of Richard in view of our knowledge of the primitive mechanism of introjected psychological causality. We have seen that because of the traumatic environment of his early life, whenever Richard was in the act of doing something, he would be possessed by anxiety. Mother was always there, either in her physical reality or as an incorporated image, to tell him that he was doing the wrong thing. When the difficulties in living, which were described on page 121 further increased his anxiety, the problem of acting became even more difficult. Action automatically produced either guilt or at least further anxiety. In other words, the patient was in the same predicament as the primitive man, when confronted with this new and portentous weapon, the choice of action. Like the primitive, he tried to protect himself by resorting to neurotic compromises, compulsions and obsessions, which correspond to ritual and magic.

. If the prepsychotic patient knows what to do, if a sign is given to him, he will not feel guilty or anxious. The future will be controlled, he feels, the effect may be foreseen, the result will be good. Often, however, this compromise or defense is not sufficient, either because the anxiety is too overpowering or the patient is not able to find enough signs, that is, is not able to fabricate compulsions quickly enough. He is actually in a much worse situation than the primitive. The tribe protects the primitive by giving him all the signs he needs (magic and ritual), but the patient has to fabricate all of them by himself at an increasing speed, and the more acute the spell of anxiety is, the more difficult it is for him to do so. He has only one other resort, the last, with which to escape anxiety, not to act. He will not act and will fall into catatonic stupor.

This sequence of events also explains why many catatonic attacks occur acutely or semi-acutely. If the anxiety does not increase in an acute manner, there is the possibility of building a compulsive defense, which may prevent the psychotic breakdown. But, before interpreting other psychotic symptoms and the relations between catatonia and obsessive-compulsive psychoneurosis, it may be useful to reexamine briefly the case of Sally, which was discussed on pages 110–129.

As in the case of Richard, Sally grew up in an atmosphere

of recrimination and suffocating parental interference. Her fear of doing the wrong thing was always present. She either did what mother wanted, or had to face anxiety. However, after her marriage, when the anxiety increased to a tremendous degree for the reasons noted on page 115, the fear became uncontrollable. We have seen how, at other times in her life, she resorted to compulsive defenses. After her marriage, with the precipitation of events, she sank into a catatonic stupor. Like Richard, she was able to describe what happened. She was afraid to make any movement. Any movement she made might be wrong. For that reason, she could not dress herself, get up from bed, eat, etc. If she were dressed by others, and if she were spoon-fed, the responsibility would rest on others. Even talking was an action, and she wanted to avoid it as much as possible. This catatonic condition lasted for a while, but later, when she was less insecure, she was able to transform the catatonic symptoms into compulsive ones. If she acted in a special way, that is, by examining every movement and seeing that pieces were not falling, she might be allowed to act. She might do a few things, but at the expense of tremendous ritual. Each small trivial act had to be made licit by the application of the ritual. This was so cumbersome, however, that she often preferred absolute immobility to the action. That is why, during the first few months of treatment, the patient alternated between compulsive activities and catatonic postures.

From both these cases, one sees that there is a major difference between the primitive and the patient. Whereas the primitive has the support of the authority (the tribe) and therefore may indulge in the ritual with a certain facility, the patient does not have such support. On the contrary, the authority (parents) is generally the one which predisposes the patient to revert to the stage of introjected psychological causality. This explains why obsessional neuroses are absent in primitive societies (Carothers 49, 50). The culture itself is obsessive-compulsive. "It is only when the individual stands alone and must develop his own ethical code that this neurosis can develop." In the ten years spent in Kenya as a psychiatrist, Carothers has never seen a single case of obsessional neurosis. He did see, however, 32 cases of catatonia. We do not know the dynamics of those cases. One may venture to guess that the culture did not protect them any longer with the ritual, and that they protected themselves with a catatonic armor, just as people in our culture may do.

What has been mentioned explains other characteristics encountered in cases of catatonic schizophrenia. In order to avoid anxiety and guilt, the patient cannot will any act, but he may passively follow orders given by others, because the responsibility will not be his. Thus, if somebody tells a catatonic, "Show your tongue, I want to prick it with a pin," the catatonic may show his tongue in a very submissive way. This blind acceptance is due to the complete substitution of someone else's will for his own. Waxy flexibility or the retention of body positions, no matter how uncomfortable, in which the patient is passively put, can also be explained in this way. When the patient is put in a given position, the will or responsibility of someone else is involved. If he wants to change positions, he has to will the change, and that will engender anxiety or guilt.

Quite often the reverse seems to occur. The patient will resist the order, or will do the opposite. This is the phenomenon of negativism which has baffled many investigators. As we have learned from Richard and Sally, the resistance is due to the fact that often, even when the act is ordered by somebody else, the patient feels the responsibility for it. It is true that he is ordered to act, but he himself must will to move. Therefore he resists. Bleuler thought that one of the reasons for external negativism has to be found in the autistic withdrawal of the patient into his phantasies, which makes every influence acting from without a comparatively intolerable interruption (27, 30). According to this interpretation, the patient wants to be left alone or wants to be unaware of all stimuli emanating from the outside world, because they are unpleasant. This undoubtedly is the impression the observer receives: but, if we try to decatatonize early catatonics with injections of sodium amytal, we may convince ourselves that in many cases this interruption of stimuli from the external world does not take place, even if the patient wishes so. The patient who comes out of the stupor is able to give an accurate account of the events which occurred, or of the words which were spoken in his presence when he could not move or talk. This indicates that, in spite of appearances, the attention toward the external world is preserved and that only actions are blocked because only actions are willed. The phenomenon of negativism will be considered again further on in this section.

Formerly, psychiatrists used to say the most disturbing things about diagnoses and prognoses in the presence of catatonic patients, thinking that they could not pay any attention to what was said. Intravenous injections of sodium amytal have shown that in many cases the patients can. It is true, however, that in several instances, the attention of the patient is withdrawn from his surroundings since the patient cannot *will* to pay attention. In numerous other cases the catatonic pays attention to his surroundings, but his interpretation of the external world is unrealistic, and paleologic. This is particularly true in cases which present mixtures of catatonic and hebephrenic features. On the other hand, in the typical catatonic the perception of the external world is well preserved. Psychiatrists who have worked in institutions for many years know of several examples proving this to be so. We know that in the case of fire in hospitals, catatonics suddenly move, start to run or even help others. It is equally true that some others preserve their catatonic state and perish in the flames. Several years ago, I heard this small but significant episode; its authenticity has been guaranteed to me by a reputable psychiatrist. In a state hospital, resident psychiatrists, instead of attending to their duties, were playing cards, in the vicinity of a patient who had been in a complete mute catatonic stupor for many years. From a window the patient saw the director of the hospital coming toward that ward. He was reputed to be a strict man and the positions of the doctors would have been jeopardized had he caught them playing cards. All of a sudden, the patient shouted, "The director is coming." The doctors immediately stopped their game. From that moment on the patient resumed his catatonic silence, which he kept for many more years, possibly until his death. I did not witness this episode, but I believe it really happened. It is a remarkable episode, not because the patient was able to see the director from the window and infer the disastrous consequences for the doctors, but because under emotional stress, he was able to talk. That he was able to see the director and visualize a danger for the doctors, is not surprising to me. I have been convinced that the perception of the external environment is normal in many catatonics; at times it is even sharpened, because being unable to respond, they concentrate on the only process they are capable of, perceiving. Withdrawal, as a protection against unpleasant influences of the environment, is more typical of the hebephrenic. The catatonic withdrawal is a retreat from action and from will, rather than from the environment, but since the environment forces him to will, the catatonic may withdraw from it also.

The inability to act also covers any manifestation of emotion, so that quite often the observer gets the impression that the patient is apathetic. Occasionally, however, a little movement or sign discloses the emotional involvement which is present in some cases at least. I remember the case of a young man who had been hospitalized for many years in Pilgrim State Hospital. He was in a state of complete immobility, confined to bed, was wetting and soiling, and had to be tube-fed. Every time I was tube-feeding him tears would drop from his eyes. This only sign of his emotional life was enough to demonstrate that behind this armor of immobility he could still feel and suffer. It is possible, however, that especially in very pronounced cases, the patient is never aware of the fact that it is the fear of movement which immobilizes him. He may sink into the stupor and remain in it, without knowing the psychological processes which have determined it. Automatically, he may react to stimuli with inactivity. As the schizophrenic process proceeds, the patient bypasses the stage where his will has to be exercised and regresses to a lower, apparently more active stage, where he merely reacts in reflex or short-circuited ways which do not involve his will centers. Echolalia may be explained in terms of such a regression.

In less advanced cases, one clearly sees the involvement of the will. For instance, as an answer to an order, the patient starts a movement, but then stops, as if a counter-order had prevented him from completing the movement. Having decided to obey, he is then afraid to will the act involved, and he stops. At times there is a series of alternated opposite movements. For example, if one asks the patient to reach for an object, he starts the movement and then stops, many times in succession, giving the impression of performing a cog-wheel movement, similar to that observed in post-encephalitic patients affected by muscular rigidity. Incidentally, this resemblance to post-encephalitic is very superficial; the cog-wheel phenomenon in the catatonic has nothing to do with muscular tone, but has to do with an alternation of volition. For instance, in the case of a patient who reaches for an object, in the middle of the movement the patient becomes afraid of willing that act, decides not to perform the act and arrests his arm. But to decide not to perform the act is also a volition. The patient becomes afraid of it and starts to make the movement again. To do this is also a volition and he is again afraid. This series of attempted escapes from volition may go on for a long time; it is a horrifying experience, which only a few patients, like Richard, are able to remember and describe. Ferenczi, too, wrote that catatonia is really a cataclonia, a high-frequency alternation of activating and inhibitory impulses (77).

A mixture of obedience and disobedience often appears in the actions of catatonics. For instance, if we ask a patient to close his eyes, he may close them, and at the same time will turn his face in the opposite direction. More than once Bleuler has compared this resisting negativistic attitude of the catatonic to a sexual attitude, especially that of the woman who resists sexual overtures. He also feels that often the negativism of the catatonic has a sexual connotation. I am not convinced that this is true. It seems to me that a somewhat similar motivation causes the resistance in the catatonic and in the woman, fear of guilt versus a desire to act. In our culture sexual indulgence, especially in women, is often connected with guilt. The woman feels she must resist, not act, because if she does act, she will feel guilty. At the same time, she wishes to yield in order to gratify her sexual needs; therefore, there is an alternation of acceptance and resistance. At times, she puts on an act to convince her partner and herself that she cannot be considered responsible, inasmuch as she made some resistance. Many women enjoy phantasies of being raped. If they are raped, they have sexual gratification without the feeling of responsibility.

In our society unconscious feelings of guilt often induce acceptable ways of avoiding action. The hermit, the anchorite, the person who goes into a convent, all choose for themselves a life as deprived of action as possible. Some, though by no means all, of these persons want to avoid the guilt which would accompany their ordinary activities, especially the joyful ones. Often they remove their unconscious guilt, not only by escaping from actions, but also by indulging in ritual, that is, in sanctioned or sanctified actions. They do this for instance when they join religious orders. These people act as if they were condemning themselves to a metaphorical and partial catatonia, or to a social obsessive-compulsive psychoneurosis. Society treats those who have been found guilty similarly. By putting the culprits in jail, it limits their actions. An artificial and metaphorical catatonia is imposed on them. We remember that Richard, when he was over the catatonic attack, still wanted to escape from actions of life, by committing himself again to the state hospital. This fear of action of the catatonic at times becomes personified, projected externally and perceptualized in the form of voices, which tell the patient "no" when he is about to perform an act.

But how is it that the patient at times does not limit himself to avoidance of what he is supposed to do, but resists actively, and at times does the opposite? This active or willed disobedience is sometimes present in the normal person and in the negativistic child, as if the unwillingness to obey or to follow the order, would automatically engender an opposite action of resistance. I advance the hypothesis that the most primitive act of volition is a resistance, or a volition of resistance. In fact, before Homo Sapiens could acquire his choice of action, he was reacting automatically or reflexly to stimuli. His first act of volition was to resist this reflex response. We may thus enumerate the steps in the evolution of the function of will in this schema:

$$a \qquad\qquad b$$

reflex or automatic response $\rightarrow$ resistance to reflex response

$$c$$

or volition of resistance $\rightarrow$ volition with introjected guilt

$$d \qquad\qquad e$$

causality $\rightarrow$ volition with compliance to ritual $\rightarrow$ volition.

Ontogenetically, toilet training may be viewed as an example of the acquisition of volition of resistance.

In pathological cases there may be a return to states *a, b, c, d,* or to more than one of these stages at the same time. Of course, this is a very simplified schema, and many intermediate stages are omitted because they have not yet been differentiated. Probably in evolution these stages were hundreds of thousands of years apart from each other.

The patient who becomes increasingly anxious about his actions has the tendency to revert to the archaic state of introjected psychological causality. Before reverting to that stage he defends himself by resorting to compulsive, magical and ritual acts. At times, especially if there is no precipitation of events, the illness may be averted at this stage; if the anxiety increases, however, the patient is not able to establish compulsive defenses, and he sinks into a catatonic state.

It is not to be inferred that every obsessive-compulsive is potentially a catatonic. Some obsessive-compulsive symptoms are present in practically every human being as defenses against anxiety. There are infinite quantitative gradations from the normal to the catatonic. Many cases are definitely arrested at one of these numerous stages. Sudden and intense exacerbations occur in the person who is to become catatonic. If the process is very acute, a catatonic stupor may ensue without apparently having been preceded by a compulsive stage. There are undoubtedly many similarities between the obsessive-compulsive personality and that of the catatonic. The difficulty in making decisions, the occasional obstinacy in maintaining one's opinion, the going back and forth between two alternate dispositions or points of view such as aggressiveness and submissiveness, pleasing one's self or somebody else, dirt and cleanliness, order and disorder, the feeling of command coming from within, as contrasted with commands from outside, etc., are all obsessive-compulsive symptoms reminiscent of the catatonic negativism.

Fear of uncertainty (of the effect) is also a characteristic common to both catatonics and compulsives. Even a remote possibility that the dreaded event may occur arouses anxiety, as if that possibility might immediately materialize. For instance, the patient cannot feel *mathematically sure* that he will not become infected, if he does not wash his hands three times before eating. Many obsessive-compulsives actually become mathematicians in their search for that absolute certainty which allegedly is the only thing that can confer security. As was mentioned before, other obsessives become very religious and submerge themselves in ritual. The greater the fervor or the anxiety, the more extensive is the inclusion of ordinary acts in the ritual. Caro, a famous Talmudist of the sixteenth century, who experienced mystical hallucinations, wrote a book for religious Jews, the "Shulhan Aruk," or "Prepared Table," in which he examined every little act of life, and gave instructions on how to behave (Gordon, 116). He even gave instructions as to which shoe one should put on and lace first in the morning when first getting up (48). Several neurotics find a guide for their behavior in the study of numbers or astrology, as an escape from uncertainty. Many compulsive-obsessive patients would like advice from their therapists on what to do. They want to know what they are *supposed* to do in every circumstance. They want to follow a schedule, a routine. They would be happy if they could find a book, like Caro's, where all instructions are given. They dread *spontaneity,* which means, as the etymology of the word implies, acting according to one's will. Some of them feel guilty if they do what they wish to do; therefore, they never do what they wish, and they comply with authority. Other patients spend their lives going through the formality of situations without becoming at all involved in them. They become extremely conventional, or automatic, in order to escape the anxiety and the guilt of the spontaneous actions. The catatonic is much more afraid than the obsessive, because he is deprived of the ritual. The uncertainty of what may happen if he puts into effect the wrong volition, reduces him to immobility.

Bleuler (30) and other authors have found compulsive-obsessive behavior in patients who later became catatonic. It is equally true, however, that in many obsessive-compulsives who later become schizophrenic, the psychosis assumes a predominantly paranoid or hebephrenic sypmtomatology. The projected type of causality and other paleologic mechanisms play more prominent roles in their symptomatology. This raises the question of which patients are more apt to develop the catatonic type of schizophrenia. From the cases of Richard and Sally, and others which were not mentioned in this book, I am convinced that people who are apt to become catatonic are those who in their early childhood have been prevented from developing confidence in their own actions and reliance on their capability to will. The parents or parent substitutes have forced these patients either not to will or to follow parental decisions, so that when the patients had to make their own choice, they found themselves unable to act; if they acted, they were later criticized and made to feel guilty. In all types of schizophrenia, we find a struggle with the parents, but in catatonia this struggle is specifically connected with the actions and choices of the patient.

Of course, the fear of parental disapproval is not actually the same fear as the fear of action of the catatonic. The fear of action of the catatonic is much more intense, having acquired an archaic form; later it is disconnected from the fear of the authority, and it becomes fear of the action itself. Some patients develop for a certain period of time a mixed feeling of fear and power which we may call a feeling of *negative omnipotence*. They feel that if they move the whole world will collapse or all mankind will perish. Together with a feeling of cosmic power they have a feeling of cosmic responsibility. Finally, the fear of the action itself becomes unconscious, and is followed by an automatic state, in which the patient has entirely given up the function to will, and performs only automatic or reflex acts. Thus, one can conclude that the dynamic and the formal mechanisms very clearly are connected in catatonia.

Since 1863, when Kahlbaum differentiated catatonia, there have been numerous attempts to explain catatonia as manifestation of a primary physical disease of the brain (146, 147). Kahlbaum himself thought that catatonia was due to edema of the brain. The fact that the catatonic does not make movements in a normal way has been interpreted by some as a manifestation of a motor disorder, comparable to those found in neurological diseases. Some authors have tried to explain the syndrome as a disease of the cortical motor centers, others as a disease of the basal ganglia. The fact that post-encephalitic patients in their attitude, posture and lack of action, resemble catatonics very much has reinforced the belief that catatonia is primarily an organic disease. In 1921 DeJong began a series of investigations aimed at comparing the effects of bulbocapnine on animals with the symptomatology of human catatonia (59). DeJong and Baruk, as well as many other authors, found that when bulbocapnine is administered to animals, a clinical picture follows which is characterized by loss of motor initiative, maintenance of passively impressed postures, maintenance of posture against gravity, resistance to passive movements and variations of muscular forms (59-61).

I am not going to attempt a complete refutation of these organic theories of catatonia here. As far as the early theories are concerned, they have been confuted very well by Bleuler (30). As to bulbocapnine, Ferraro and Barrera, in a monograph on the subject, describe their experiments with cats and monkeys, showing the superficiality of the resemblance between catatonia and bulbocapnine intoxication (79). They found that the manifestations of bulbocapnine occur even in animals deprived of the whole cerebral cortex and have no psychic components whatsoever.

What has been described in this paragraph and in Chapter V, leaves no doubt that psychological causes determine the lack of action. Even a beginner realizes that a catatonic is not a paralyzed person. As a matter of fact, a catatonic may become extremely active, as during the period of excitement, or he may be alternately hypoactive and hyperactive. Painful events, like discussions about their complexes, or the presence of persons who arouse anxiety, aggravate the motor phenomena to a great extent. On the other hand, the presence of persons who have a reassuring quality, like the analyst, a nurse or a good friend may make the symptoms decrease or even disappear completely. The catatonic symptom is not primarily a *motor* phenomenon; it is a *will* phenomenon. It appears to be a motor phenomenon because, if the will does not permit movements, movements do not occur. However, this statement does not imply that the brain has nothing to do with catatonic phenomena. Without the cerebral cortex we have no catatonic phenomena, just as we have no voluntary actions; however, when those psychological factors which were mentioned are present, the cerebral cortex may be *used* in such a way that only catatonic symptoms, or predominantly catatonic symptoms, may result.

VI. Conception of Time

It is a faculty of the human being to remember the past, to take cognizance of the present, and to prospect about the future. Actually, the feelings and thoughts of the past and of the future are *present* thoughts and feelings. The only possible subjective or psychological tense is the present, but the human mind is able to transport to the present chronologically remote phenomena, thus permitting, in a symbolic way, the revival of the past and the anticipation of the future.

The ability to anticipate the distant future is one of the last achievements in evolution. Infrahuman animals do not possess this faculty. Experiments with delayed reactions have disclosed that even the highest species of mammals cannot keep future events in mind for more than a few minutes (123, 134). They can foresee only the very immediate future —that is, only the immediate reaction to a stimulus, or the outcome of their reaction to a stimulus, if the stimulus was present not longer than a few minutes previously. Prehuman species may be called organisms without a psychic tomorrow. Cattle go to the slaughterhouse without feelings of anxiety, being unable to foresee what is going to happen to them. In humans the ability to anticipate the distant future begins in about the second year of life. At that stage of development, the child becomes able to postpone immediate pleasure for some future gratification. In other words, it is when the ability to anticipate is developed that the "reality principle" originates.

Phylogenetically, anticipation of the distant future appeared at the primordial eras of humanity when man no longer limited his activity to cannibalism and hunting, which were related to immediate present necessities, but became interested in hoarding and, later, in agriculture, in order to provide for future needs. It was in this period that culture—that is, knowledge to be used in future times or to be transmitted to future generations—originated. A person who mentally was able to conceive only the present time would aim only toward what Sullivan calls "satisfaction." A person who is able to prospect the future as well, aims also toward what Sullivan calls "security."

In a paper published in 1947, I pointed out the importance of the role of this ability to prospect the future in the engendering of the type of anxiety which is due to lack of security.

For a more complete discussion of this problem, the reader is referred to that paper (9). I repeat here, however, some of the observations made. I pointed out that the neuroses experimentally produced in animals, are the result of the state of anxiety which is due to lack of satisfaction; they are not the much more complicated neuroses which involve the anxiety which is due to lack of security. Although the animal may remain neurotic or maladjusted after the experiment, the actual state of anxiety is determined by the *presence* of the external disturbing stimuli, or of their equivalents. In other words, the reaction of the animal is temporarily tied to the experimental stimulus; the fear of danger always involves the present time or the immediate future. On the other hand, in human anxiety there may be a temporal lapse between the anxiety-precipitating stimulus and the dreaded event, and the anxiety may last even when such an external stimulus is removed. Actually, in humans the external stimulus is replaced by an inner stimulus, which is symbolic of the external, is retained in the mind, and may even be unconscious. Anticipation of the future is thus impossible without the ability to symbolize.

In schizophrenia there is a tendency to abandon the faculty of anticipating the future; one finds in this condition what I have called "restriction of the psychotemporal field." The temporal orientation of the patient becomes gradually limited to the present time. Balken, in her study with the Thematic Apperception Test, found that the schizophrenic does not distinguish between past, present and future (14). According to her, the schizophrenic, in the attempt to "relieve the tension between the possible and the real," clings "desperately and without awareness to the present." In early schizophrenia, however, and especially in the paranoid type, the patient is still able to concern himself with past and future. Some delusions, especially with persecutory content, may involve the future rather than the present. The patient must be able to *foresee* the

conclusions of his reasoning, because it is the anticipated conclusion which retrospectively directs his train of thought. In
other words, in the process of demonstrating something, the
patient chooses only those possibilities which lead to the conclusion he has anticipated and wished. For instance, a 49-year-
old patient had the delusion that a certain man she knew was
going to divorce his wife and marry her. The wife of this man
was a respectable, attractive, blond young woman who had
just given birth to a baby. According to my patient, who had
an unconscious homosexual attachment for her, this woman
was ugly, had already undergone the menopause, and had
been a prostitute. How could the patient sustain her beliefs in
the face of such contradictory evidence? We shall not take into
consideration here the motivation of her thinking, that is, the
fact that unconsciously she wanted to reject her homosexual
desire. We are interested here only in the formal mechanism
of her delusional ideas. Consciously, the patient needed to
reach the conclusion that the man was going to divorce this
woman and marry her. She needed to believe that this woman
was unworthy of the love of this man. According to the patient,
therefore, the woman was extremely ugly, but being a prostitute, she had learned to dissemble her appearance, as all prostitutes do; she was a brunette, in fact, but had bleached her
hair. She had already undergone the menopause, but she had
been visiting a famous obstetrician who had given her hormone
therapy, so that she could conceive. As a matter of fact, the
patient saw this woman on the same street where this obstetrician resided. It is obvious that the patient could anticipate the
deductions of her thoughts, because it was the conclusion itself
(impossibility for the man to love that woman) which retrospectively directed and consequently distorted her reasoning.

It seems correct to assume, then, that well-organized delusions, such as those of the cited example, cannot exist without
the process of anticipation. The patient must be capable of

so-called seriatim functions (Morgan, 196). By seriatim functions is meant the organization or synthesis of skilled acts or thoughts into an orderly series. High species, like monkeys and apes, are capable of simple seriatim functions, but in men this ability is much more developed. The number of acts or thoughts which may occur in a given sequence may increase to a tremendous degree. Seriatim functions imply ability 1) to anticipate a goal and 2) to organize and synthesize acts or thoughts in a given temporal series.

In the beginning of schizophrenia, seriatim functions and ability to foresee the future are retained. The early paranoid who has delusions of persecution or of jealousy is able to foresee the future and direct his thoughts in logical, chronological patterns which lead to the foreseen delusional deductions. He retains a great emotional capacity in connection with his complexes, and at times is so apparently logical as to be considered lucid. Later he becomes less logical, less capable of organizing his thoughts in a logical series. The seriatim function disintegrates, and he is less able to foresee the future and the deductions of his reasoning; his delusions become related to the present time and not to the future, their content is not persecutory but more or less grandiose, and their emotional tone is shallower. Later his thinking presents definite scattering, his delusions are connected with the immediate present, and are of a definitely expansive type. "I *am* the Virgin Mary, I *am* the Emperor of China." He accepts his delusions as indisputable, immediate reality, no longer caring to demonstrate logically their validity. As a matter of fact, he would not even be able to attempt such a demonstration. Many authors have mentioned this shift of the type of delusions from persecutory in the initial stage of the illness to grandiose in more advanced stages. However, to my knowledge, the fact has been neglected that the delusions of grandeur are generally related to the present time, and are accepted by the patient without the necessity of an apparently logical explanation or deduction.

Occasionally, in advanced stages of the hebephrenic and paranoid types of schizophrenia, delusions seem to imply anticipation of the future, but it is not really so. For instance, a patient had the delusional idea that for her the calendar was always one day in advance. When for the rest of humanity it was Tuesday, February 13, 1946 for her it was Wednesday, February 14, 1946. This delusion is only superficially connected with anticipation of time, and has a symbolic meaning which is related to the present.

In dreams, too, the situation is lived in the present; we may remember past events, but we never project ourselves into the future. Although the dream may be the symbolic manifestation or fulfillment of a wish for a future event, the dreamt action is always in the present. The dreamer may worry about an imminent but not a distant danger. What is the purpose of this restriction to the present, that we find in dreams and, as a progressive tendency, in schizophrenia? Obviously it is the elimination of that anxiety which is due to lack of security. The patient who lives in the present and the dreamer may still experience anxiety, but only a less traumatic type of anxiety, the one which is connected with lack of satisfaction.

VII. Perceptualization of the Concept. Study of Hallucinations.

From the foregoing, the reader has certainly inferred that the person who thinks paleologically has the tendency to live in a world of perception rather than in a world of conception. The more paleologically a person thinks, the more deprived he becomes of concepts or of Plato's universals. His ideas become more and more related to specific instances, and are not concerned with classes, groups or categories. When abstract concepts are needed, they tend to be expressed in a concrete language often representing perceptual images. Numberless gradations are possible. With the progression of the pathologic process the ideational formations will contain more and more concrete elements, representing reality as it appears to the senses, rather than to the intellect. It has already been mentioned that when the connotation is lost, the denotation becomes much nearer to the perceptual level. Perceptual elements finally completely eliminate higher thought processes.

This process of perceptualization has its fullest expression in dreams and in hallucinations. As Freud and others have pointed out, the dream is just a translation of thoughts into visual images; thoughts become visual perceptions. In hallucinations they become perceptions involving every sense, but predominantly the auditory.

Although dreams as well as hallucinations must be included in the phenomena of "perceptualization of the concept," the following discussion will be concerned primarily with the latter, which are more pertinent to the major subject of this book. For a complete study of dreams, formal as well as dynamic, the reader is referred to the classical book by Freud, "Interpretation of Dreams" (96), and to the recent ones by Gutheil (122) and Fromm (101).

Even though I don't approve of the fact that in modern books of psychiatry no attempt whatsoever is made to interpret the important phenomenon of hallucinations from a point of view which is not exclusively one of motivation, I am not going to repeat here the numerous theories which have been formulated on this subject. The reader who is interested is referred to the book by Mourgue *Neurobiologie de l'hallucination* (198). In the following section only a few personal observations will be reported, with the hope that they may help to clarify this complicated phenomenon.

The symptom of hallucinations has to be studied in its three major characteristics: 1) *perceptualization of the concept,* 2) *projection to the external world of the inner experience,* and 3) *the incorrigibility of the experience.*

Hallucinations do not consist of ordinary, usual perceptions. Perceptions need for their occurrence stimulation of a sense from an external source and a recognition of the sensation.* Hallucinations consist of a process which is at a higher level than the perception. The stimulus which elicits them is an internal one and must be a mental process. This mental process, by engendering the hallucination, is regressing to the lower level of the perception. Many writers have for a long time debated and continue to debate the question of whether hallucinations are images which have acquired a special intensity and strength, or whether they are perceptions. Many people believe that they are nothing but intense images. However, the closer one examines patients, the more one becomes convinced that they actually experience perceptions. Patients do not think that they "hear voices" but they actually hear them, just as the dreamer does not think that he sees things, but actually sees them. The hallucinating person does not distinguish real voices from hallucinations.

---

* It may be useful to define what is meant by the terms sensation, perception and image, since these words have become obsolete in psychiatric books. By *sensation* is meant the conscious effect of a stimulus, when it acts upon one of our sense organs. Sensation is the first effect of the stimulus. It does not imply any recognition of the stimulus, that is any association with past experiences. Actually only new-born babies have sensations.

By *perception* is meant recognition and understanding of the sensation. For instance, when I see a book, not only do I see it, but know that I see it and know it is a book.

By *image* is meant an inner reproduction of sensations and perceptions, even when the stimuli which produce the latter are absent. The concept of image should not be confused with the concept of *engram*. With the latter term many neurologists designate a neuronal pattern of an acquired skilled act.

In the light of our general interpretation of the schizophrenic process, it is not difficult to understand hallucinations.
They are thoughts or images which use a mechanism of a lower
level of integration. Instead of using language or images, those
thoughts use mechanisms at the level of perception, which is
lower than the levels of verbal thought, and lower even than
the level of images. Images, stored in our memory, may be
used by hallucinations, but they are reproduced with the mechanism of perception.

As our thoughts at times descend from the Aristotelian to
the paleologic level, and within the paleologic level to more
or less primitive sublevels, so they may descend further to
the level of images and even to the level of perceptions. Hypnagogic hallucinations, which are phenomena occurring to
some people in the act of falling asleep, are often recognized
as images, that is, they are between the level of images and
that of perceptions. It seems useless, therefore, to continue to
argue as to whether hallucinations are intensified images or
perceptions. They are mental processes, usually occurring at
higher levels of integration, which use instead the mechanisms
of perceptions. In other words, they are perceptualized mental
processes.

The process which the patient follows when he regresses
from the abstract concept to the perceptualization of the
concept, may be represented in the following schematic way:

Abstract concept or connotation → Denotation → Denotation
by use of predicates or functions → Mental Images → Perceptions.

When we study the terminal stages of schizophrenia, we
shall see that the disintegrating process goes beyond the perceptual levels, and regresses even to the stage of sensation.
In evolution the opposite process took place, that is:

$$\overset{a}{\text{Sensation}} \to \overset{b}{\text{Perception}} \to \overset{c}{\text{Image}} \to \overset{d}{\text{Denotations by use of}}$$

$$\text{functions} \to \overset{e}{\text{Denotation}} \to \overset{f}{\text{Connotation.}}$$
$$\quad\text{(verbalization)} \quad \text{(verbalization)}$$

Verbalization is a process concomitant to *d, e, f,* and in specific instances may become even more important than *d, e, f.*

Images and hallucinations are elaborations of stored sensorial and perceptual material. Therefore, there cannot be images without present or past perceptions. For instance, if the dreamer thinks about himself, he sees himself in the dream as a concrete image or physical entity, not as an abstract concept symbolized by the pronoun I. However, since for anatomical reasons nobody can see his own face, the dreamer cannot recall the visual image of his face. This explains why the dreamer sees himself in the dream, but not his face. In dreams and hallucinations, the individual may perceive things which actually do not exist; in these cases, the images are made up, in a creative way, with elements which were actually perceived from the external world.

People who are deaf-mute from birth cannot experience auditory hallucinations. I have treated a schizophrenic deaf-mute who pretended that she was hearing people talking about her. Actually, by "hearing" she meant that she had the impression people were talking about her, as she inferred from the movements of their lips and from their general attitude. This patient was able to read and write; and her writing presented disconnected thoughts, and the other verbal characteristics found in schizophrenics who are not deaf-mutes.

I have no experience with schizophrenics who are congenitally blind, but I am inclined to believe that they cannot experience visual hallucinations. Gutheil writes that blind people, whose defect is congenital or acquired at an early age, dream with images derived from tactile and kinesthetic sensations. Kimmins, quoted by Gutheil (122), writes that children who have become blind before the age of five do not see in dreams, and that children who become blind after seven do "see" in their dreams (158).

The following question about both dreams and hallucinations may occur to the reader: If dreams and hallucinations are translations or regressions of thoughts to a perceptual level, how is it that in dreams and hallucinations the person not only hears and sees, but talks and thinks? This is due to the fact that there is no complete regression to the perceptual level. The concomitant occurrence of phenomena which belong to different mental levels is one of the most common characteristics of human psychopathology. Especially in schizophrenia, it produces a very bizarre clinical picture. In many cases, one may find symptoms belonging predominantly to one level, but a mixture always occurs. Thus a patient, for instance, may usually adopt the Aristotelian type of logic when he talks, but at times he may hallucinate, and therefore regress to a perceptual level. The voices he hears use a paleologic mode of thinking. It is this mixture, this splitting of the person at various levels, which is the most specific characteristic of schizophrenia, and which fully justifies its name (see page 14).

The picture of schizophrenia reminds one of those geological excavations where one does not see layers regularly overlapping other layers of more ancient origin, but where telluric movements have mixed the order, so that pieces of ancient layers appear at the surface and pieces of recent layers lie at the bottom. It is the painstaking job of the geologist mentally to place all the pieces in their original order. In the same way, the psychiatrist who is interested in formal mechanisms can refer to different levels the symptoms which the patient experiences at the same time.

The perceptualization of the concept is the most specific characteristic of hallucinations. Before this stage of complete perceptualization is reached, intermediate stages may be experienced. I have already mentioned hypnagogic hallucinations. Other intermediate stages occur frequently. For instance, an Italian patient who had two acute psychotic episodes, with delusions and hallucinations predominantly religious in content, experienced the following phenomena. Between the two psychotic episodes, when he was able to live outside the hospital and to attend to his work as a barber, he was hearing a voice inside himself expressing his thoughts. Every normal person can hear his own thoughts, because thoughts are generally expressed internally by auditory verbal images, but it was obvious from the description given by the patient that the perceptual quality of his thoughts was increased. He himself recognized that the voice was his own; as a matter of fact he knew that the voice was expressing his own thoughts in Italian, whereas the clients and other people around him were talking English. This phenomenon is very common in schizophrenics. Often the perceptual quality of the patient's thoughts is so pronounced that he is afraid that people around him will hear them. Since he has no control over the content of his thoughts, and they can be heard, he feels embarrassed. When the process is more advanced, he still recognizes that the thoughts are his own, but on account of their perceptual character, he feels that people are repeating them verbally. He has the impression that it is he who thinks, but that people around him pronounce the thoughts. They "steal" his ideas. These phenomena are generally called "écho de la pensée." When the process advances further, the patient does not recognize his thoughts as his own, and projects them completely to other people.

Another important point, which brings us back to a comparison with dreams, is the following: Why are hallucinations predominantly auditory perceptualizations and not visual ones as in dreams? We may advance only hypotheses on this interesting problem. The sense of vision originates very early in the phyletic scale. Even protozoas possess a rudimentary organ of vision (the eyespot in the flagellate Euglena). In fishes, the sense of vision already is very similar to that of men. This cannot be said for the sense of hearing. One has to go as high as the class of birds on the evolutionary scale, to find an organ similar to the human cochlea.

In dreams, when the most rest is desired, it is natural that only the more primitive sensory phenomena should occupy the major role. The tactile and olfactory senses are more primitive than the visual, but do not play such an important role in human symbolism. Of the important human senses, visual and auditory, the visual is the more primitive. Auditory images probably require more elaboration, which is not compatible with the state of sleep.

Another important fact may be that when the individual sleeps, all external visual perceptions are eliminated, and the centers which elaborate them are free for other activities. When the patient is awake and hallucinates, the visual centers are occupied by external perceptions. True, one may say that the auditory centers too are occupied by auditory external perceptions, but not in such a dominant manner. We know, for instance, that when an electroencephalogram is taken, the patient is asked to close his eyes because visual perceptions are very disturbing. Noises do not produce so much disturbance (Davis, 57, 58).

Auditory perceptions are less primitive than the visual and more apt to become used first when thought processes regress to a perceptual level. In addition, one's thoughts are generally experienced as an inner language, as a conversation with one's self, consisting of verbal auditory images. Some authors (Seitz and Mohlholm, 229) feel that auditory hallucinations are more frequent in people who have a predominantly visual form of imagery. The tests used to determine whether subjects have a predominantly visual or auditory imagery are not to be trusted entirely because they ignore the verbal representations which accompany the images, even visual. For instance, if the patient responds to the stimulus "ringing of the telephone" by saying, "I can imagine seeing it, but I can't hear it ring," he has a response using a visual image but at the same time internally he hears his thoughts, expressed by verbal auditory images, stating that he sees the phone. Auditory verbal images are, therefore, almost always present, even when they are accompanied by visual images. Because of the tremendous importance that language plays in human thinking, auditory images are almost always used in mental processes, even when visual images occupy the predominant role.

We come now to the second important characteristic of hallucinations: projection to the external world. This quality is present in dreams, too. In fact, the dreamer believes that the dream actually takes place outside of himself. We have seen that in those phenomena which precede regular hallucinations, at times, projection does not occur. For instance, patients may hear their own thoughts in almost a perceptual form, and yet they recognize that what they hear are their thoughts. Generally, however, hallucinations are projected to the external world.

The phenomenon of projection may also be interpreted in two ways, the dynamic and the formal. Dynamically, the individual projects, or experiences as not belonging to his own self, everything which is painful or which may cause anxiety, and which originated from others (see page 299). He wants to put distance between himself and the phenomenon which is experienced as unpleasant. Why he projects the voices as coming from certain other people will be discussed in connection with the projection of delusional ideas (pages 299–301).

Formally, one must remember that projection takes place

in the normal phenomenon of perception. Perception of an external stimulus actually takes place internally in our cortical centers. However, the perception is projected outside and is experienced as a reproduction of the external environment. We are aware of the stimuli hitting us from outside, but are not aware of the externalization of the perception into the outside world. This externalization coincides with what is known to us as a realistic status of the environment. Whether it is so, or whether the idealistic philosophers are correct in denying any external reality, is a problem which need not be discussed here. Now, this externalization or projection, which occurs normally in perception, occurs also in hallucinations. Inasmuch as the hallucination is experienced as a perception, the process of externalization is an implicit necessary concomitant characteristic.

We come now to the third characteristic of hallucinations: the incorrigibility of the experience or the inability of the patient who hallucinates to recognize that the hallucination is a false perception, having no foundation in reality. It is conceivable for us to imagine that if a normal person were to hallucinate, he would be able to realize, by testing himself in other ways, that the hallucination was false. This happens actually in the few non-psychotic persons who occasionally have hallucinations, but does not happen, as a rule, in the schizophrenic. For instance, a person I know experienced the following phenomenon: While he was preparing for an examination, for a few days prior to the test he was cramming in a furious way for days and nights. He had strong anxiety lest he not complete his preparation. In the town where he lived, there was a tower with a bell which would ring each hour on the hour. The day before the examination this person heard the bell ringing every ten minutes. He realized that the bell would not ring so often: he knew that it rang only each hour, and when he asked other people, he accepted as true the fact that they were not hearing the bell ring. He realized then that he was hallucinating, although he was not able to distinguish the hallucinated sound from the real one, and he understood that this phenomenon was due to his anxiety. He was afraid that the time would pass too quickly, and the day of the examination would arrive before he had finished his preparation.

Schizophrenics who are recovering start to doubt the reality of their hallucinations, in the same way that the dreamer in the process of waking up starts to realize that the dream was a dream. Generally however, the schizophrenic has no insight into the pathological nature of his hallucinations. This lack of insight is the repetition of what happens at higher levels in the field of logic. Again we have to invoke a dynamic as well as a formal mechanism. From a dynamic point of view, we know that the patient needs to believe the reality of the hallucination. From our study of the formal mechanisms we know that he interprets his own experiences with the means that he has at his own disposal. When he hallucinates, his thoughts regress to the perceptual level, and it is only with the means available at that level, that is, with the perceptions he experiences, that he evaluates what happens to him. The level to which he regresses predominates over the higher ones.

VIII. Disturbances of Association

The disturbances in thought processes which occur in schizophrenia extend beyond the loss of Aristotelian logic and the adoption of paleologic. They involve even the simple, normal associations of ideas, to such an extent that scattering of thoughts, dissociation, and word-salad are commonly observed. Although Bleuler has considered the disorder of association of ideas the most important symptom of schizophrenia, very little work has been done in America on this subject in the last few decades. This is largely a reflection of modern trends in psychology. An obsessive fear of so-called mental atomism has made many psychologists disregard this important aspect of mental life. Such as behaviorists have ignored the other important characteristic of mental life—consciousness—because the phenomenon cannot be understood at the present stage of our knowledge, for the same reasons many psychologists have completely disregarded the problem of association. Of course, there are several outstanding exceptions (Robinson, for instance, 221), but, as a rule, when one opens an American book of psychology, written in the last twenty years, one finds no mention of association of ideas. And yet there cannot be any doubt that ideas do associate. Maybe the problem is still completely obscure; maybe the term "association of ideas" is wrong and should not be used for the mental process which is involved; but the fact cannot be denied that this phenomenon exists and that it is one of the most important, perhaps the most important, of psychic life.

A two-minute observation can convince anyone that ideas do associate. I see my old grammar school and think of my childhood; I hear somebody mention the name of Beethoven, and I think of an acquaintance of mine who is a musician. I study my own thoughts or those of my friends, and I see that ideas do not occur at random, but that there is always a connection between them, no matter how petty and trivial this connection may be. It is because such power of association is so important and so general that we are so impressed and baffled by the schizophrenic, who seems to have lost it partially or totally.

Before we study the phenomenon in schizophrenia, let us examine very briefly how ideas associate in normal individuals.

When a person thinks logically, he organizes his thoughts according to a pattern or structure which leads toward an end or conclusion. If, however, he relaxes and lets his thoughts come up spontaneously, without exerting any selection or direction, ideas will come to him which seem to acquire consciousness for their own sake and not for any distant purpose. Conversation in casual social gatherings, often consists of thoughts occurring in this way. If we study these thoughts we see that even they follow one another according to certain rules. They do not come at random, but are determined rationally. We do not find irrationality, but psychological determinism. One idea is determined or caused by the occurrence of a previous one. The idea B, which follows the idea A, is associated in some way with A. It is because of this association that B may occur, and not because of chance.

What are the ways by which ideas associate? Although some authors have described or subdivided more types, ideas are generally considered as associating in two ways: by contiguity and by similarity.*

The *law of contiguity* states that when two mental processes have been active together or in immediate succession, one of them on recurring tends to elicit the recurrence of the other. For instance, if I think of a rose, I may think of its color or odor, or of the garden where I saw it; if I think of New York, I may think of the Empire State Building or of the Hudson River; if I think of fire, I may think of smoke, or of the danger of being burnt, etc.

The *law of similarity* states that if two mental representations resemble each other, that is, if they have one or more characteristics in common, the occurrence of one of them tends also to elicit the occurrence of the other. For instance, I think of the Empire State Building and I may think of the Eiffel Tower because they are both high constructions; I think of Beethoven and I may think of Brahms because they are both composers.

The *associative link*, that is, the element which makes two ideas associate is either the fact that they originally occurred

---

* Law of contrast is often added.

in the same place or at the same time or in succession or the fact that they have a quality in common. Using our own terminology (pages 204–205), we may state that two *ideas associate by contiguity if they have a common predicate of contiguity. Two ideas associate by the law of similarity if the associational link is a predicate of quality.*

In normal people there are also differences in the way ideas associate. As James described in his "Principles of Psychology," the association by similarity is the higher form of association, generally found in a larger percentage in gifted individuals (136). The association by contiguity is found in everybody, but occurs oftener in non-gifted individuals than in gifted ones.

In schizophrenia, we find a gamut of disturbances in association of ideas. The first disturbances, however, consist of the more frequent occurrence of ideas connected only by the laws of association. In non severe scattering of thoughts, we find that schizophrenics talk without logical direction; their thoughts are connected, one with the other, by the simple laws of association. The disturbance may be minimal and hardly noticeable; at other times the patient seems to wander here and there without purpose. The ideas, however, are still connected, but the lack of continuity reveals the extent of the mental disintegration, such as in the following passage from a letter of a schizophrenic patient:

> Dear Doctor Arieti,
>
> It Is Because I Am So Passionate That They Brought Me Here
>
> Doctor Webster Asked Me Why I Was Brought Here And I Couldn't Answer Without A Certain Hesitation, But Now I Know, I Know Now:
>
> I'm Too Passionate!
>
> That's Why I Can't Get A Job.
>
> You Had The Wrong Diagnosis

Take This For Instance:
   Look Up The Word Passions In The Encyclopedia
(A Masterpiece Of A Word) And In The Dictionaries.
Don't Get Cerebral Meningitis In Your Studies
   But You Will Find That There Is A Difference
Between The Passions of Jesus of Bethlehem And The
Passions Of Blue Beard
   Between The Passion Of Misplaced Sympathies And
The Passions Of Suicidal Thoughts.
   Are You Passionately In Sympathy With Your Great
Poet Dante, Doctor Arieti?
   And I Am In Passionate Admiration Of The Works
of Molière, The French Troubadour.
   And There Is The Passion Flower
And The Passion Plays Of Oberammergau.

The patient wants to convey the idea that she was hospitalized because she was too passionate. She is not mentally
sick. A wrong diagnosis was made. Soon, however, she becomes involved with the meanings of the word "passion" and
loses the main point. We see here that the laws of association
are respected, but that there is no logical or directed thinking,
and therefore no apparent purpose. This disturbance resembles
the flight of ideas which we find in manic patients. The resemblance, however, is only superficial. In the manic, the push
to talk is so strong that he has no time to think and cannot
adopt logical rules. In the schizophrenic, the lack of logic is
not due to this pressure, but to a withdrawal from logic. In
addition, in the flight of ideas of the manic, stimuli which elicit
associations come from the outside environment much more
frequently than in the schizophrenic. An object or color, an
event, in the immediate environment may lead to numerous
associations.
   When the schizophrenic process progresses, ideas still tend
to associate by similarity, but by a similarity which is con-

nected with the verbalization, rather than with the connotation. In other words, the *associational link is a predicate of verbal quality*. Two things or ideas are associated because they have the same phonetic or written symbols.

For instance, a patient liked to write the following lists of words on sheets of papers:

Why, y
See, sea, C

The patients quite often seem to forget the meanings of the word, and concentrate exclusively on the verbalization. They seem to have a predilection for phonetic similarity. Many of them devote time to writing prose or poems which seem very odd. No purposeful, logical or paleological thought appears, except occasionally. Ideas follow one another by the laws of association, or for the purpose of maintaining rhythm (verbal similarity). Stereotyped expressions associate easily, since repetition or identity is the highest degree of similarity.

The following poem was written by a patient, a hebephrenic woman, who was very regressed. She had pleasant delusions: for instance, she believed that she was growing feathers and becoming a bird, *"because"* she wanted to fly away from the hospital. She wrote me this poem when she heard that I was transferred to another division of the hospital:

Dear Dr. Arieti,

Brilliant to the sky,
Why you are far away
The spirit comes so nigh
While you are far away
Ah woe to the sad tiding
That you are not residing
Under the same roof
As our friends of the ebony hoof
Would take you out in flight

> And drive you quite aloof
> And would carry you in spite
> Of the fact that you are so light
> In your tender golden head
> Like a hollow round your head
> I'd send you a dozen horses
> Nay a gross
> Only to keep you awhile
> As extended as the Nile
> Happy in your bile
> Only you are far away
> And the mares are gray.

With the increase in occurrence of paleologic thought, there is a decrease in the number of associations by similarity, a process which occurs because the patient develops an increasing tendency to identify rather than to abstract. For instance, the normal person is able to place in one category, Hannibal, Julius Caesar and Napoleon, because he may abstract from each of these three subjects the quality of their being great military men (Arieti, 11). A person who thinks paleologically would be unable to abstract this quality from the whole of the subjects and would tend instead to identify Hannibal with Julius Caesar or with Napoleon, in agreement with the principle of Von Domarus. *Association by similarity has been replaced by identification by similarity.* Association by similarity, which requires ability to abstract, is an absolute prerequisite for Aristotelian logic. The paleologician gradually loses this ability, although he still retains the ability to associate by similarity of verbalization and by the law of contiguity. Finally, the necessity to identify is so great that he often has to substitute for A the thing which stands for A.

For instance, if you ask a patient, "What is the capital of France?" he may reply, "London." London and Paris are identified because they are both capitals. To the question "Where are you?" the patient may answer, "In a church." Churches and hospitals are identified because of many characteristics in common, such as being buildings for many people, or places where people are helped, etc. If the patient is asked the date of his birth, he gives a wrong date, but a date whose first two numbers are the same as those of the actual date. For example, a patient born in 1911 gave the date of birth as 1923, a patient born in 1917 gave the date of birth as 1988. Of course, even in these simple cases, the dynamic desire to deny reality or to make no contact with the examiner should not be overlooked.

When the schizophrenic process becomes even more advanced, a further complication occurs. *Not only ideas which might associate by similarity but also ideas which associate by contiguity are no longer just associated, but paleologically identified.* One idea or thing may be substituted for another, which occurred at the same time or place, or was learned at the same time or place, or which belongs to the same context.

For instance, a very regressed hebephrenic patient was asked the following question: "Who was the first president of the United States?" She replied, "White House." Although George Washington actually did not even live in the White House, White House had for her the same significance as George Washington. The idea of President of the United States was in her mind associated with White House. Each element of this context (any thing usually associated with presidents of the United States) had the same value as any other elements, and might have replaced any other element of the same context. At her level of regression one part of a context cannot be separated, or abstracted or distinguished any more from any other part of the same context or background. To associate George Washington with White House is a normal mental process which may occur to anyone, let's say, during a word-association test. The anomaly here is not that the two subjects, George Washington and White House, are associated, but that they are identified and substituted for one another.

It is therefore not surprising if the schizophrenic language appears to be fragmentary. When things are substituted for things which they resemble, or which are different parts of the same context or background, the result is incomprehensible. These tendencies to identify segments or fragments, which are usually only associated in large contexts, explain the so-called word-salad which has so far remained incomprehensible. It could be that what we call here "identification" of segments or fragments actually may not be identification or effort to identify so much as it may be the result of inability to separate or dissociate a part, or inability to distinguish any of the parts of a whole. For practical purposes, or from the point of view of the observer, there is an identification of all the parts of the whole with one another or with the whole.

Norman Cameron has studied the same phenomenon which he calls "metonymic distortion," pointing out the fact that the distortion consists of the use of an approximate but related term for the more precise definite term that normal adults would use (42). For instance, one of his patients said that he had "menu" three times a day instead of meals. Cameron describes this phenomenon very well when he writes that "the schizophrenic attributes a false equivalence to several terms or phrases which in the normal person might belong to the fringe of his conceptual structures." The patient strikes "not at the bull's eye" but at the periphery of the target. Cameron's formulations are important but tend to remain descriptive since they do not imply that the underlying process is the tendency toward progressive identification.

In some cases this tendency toward identification is progressing so rapidly that a word may come to replace or represent bigger and bigger contexts, so that finally the language of the patient is impoverished to the point of being reduced to relatively few words or stereotyped expressions. As Sullivan writes, in the stereotypy there is "an impractical concentration of meaning in the expression." (254). The same stereotypies mean many things, just as the crying of the baby does. In word-salad this impoverishment has not reached the point of reducing the language to a few words, but the elements of the sentences, being replaced for others in a unique selection, make up sequences of words which cannot be understood or are understood with great difficulty by a listener. It is debatable whether the patient himself understands what he is saying. This point will be examined when we shall discuss the therapeutic situation (see page 445).

Another phenomenon which Cameron has studied in advanced schizophrenia is what he calls "asyndetic thinking" (42–43). At the level of language behavior this disorder manifests itself as a juxtaposition of elements, without adequate linkage between them. It is to be mentioned here that such juxtapositions are identical with those which Freud has described in dreams. In my opinion there is not only a juxtaposition of elements but also a juxtaposition of meanings. Certain sentences are as confusing as photographic films which have been exposed several times. The superimposed images and meanings, however, have some connection in the mind of the patient. Often the word which, as we have mentioned, is representative of an enlarged context, is taken to represent another context of which it is also a part, and the two contexts become superimposed. Thus, for instance, a patient who uttered the following sentence "The house burned the cow" did not want to say only that her mother (the house) had cooked (burned) the meat (cow); she also wanted to convey the idea that the mother (house) was irritating and disturbing (burned) the patient who saw herself as submissive as a cow. The description of a general situation (mother-daughter relation) was superimposed on the description of a specific act (preparation of meal). Schizophrenic thought bristles with different planes of meaning and is, as I call it, *multifocal,* since it has to focus at the same time on different meanings with their different objective situations.

It should be noted here that something similar to some of the phenomena studied in this section occurs in another type of primitive thought, namely, magical thought. As Freud describes in "Tote n and Taboo," magic spreads by similarity and by contagion (99). Primitive people, for example, will make an image of someone who is hated, such as an enemy, and will then injure this effigy, believing that this enemy will be afflicted by a disease in the corresponding part of the body. On the other hand, if a person or a god is respected or loved the love may be manifested to his image. If the primitive people want rain, they resort to ritual and pantomimes in which they imitate rain, and the clouds and storm which produce it. This type of magic is based on the similarity between the performed action and the expected event. Frazer calls this type of magic imitative (83). There is also another important type of magic which is common in primitive cultures. If a person possesses anything which belongs to the enemy, such as his hair, nails, clothes, or even something which the enemy has simply touched, anything which he does to these things will happen to the enemy too. Here magic spreads by contagion or "contiguity." In mentioning these characteristics of magic, Freud is very much impressed by what Tylor considers the main characteristic of magic, "mistaking an ideal connection for a real one" (262). Freud states that magic spreads by similarity and contiguity, but since ideas do associate by similarity and contiguity, he thinks that the "madness" of the rules of magic must be explained by the dominance of association of ideas.

We are now in a position to go further. The "madness"

of magic does not consist in the association of certain ideas, like the idea of the effigy and of the person which it represents, or the idea of the clothes and the idea of the person to whom they belong. These associations are normal possibilities. The "madness" of magic consists of the *identification* of those things which should only be associated. At least their power or destiny, or function is identified. The effigy of a god has the same magic power of the god; the enemy, in a magic way, will suffer the same punishment as the cloth which belonged to him. It is as if magic, too, would follow Von Domarus' principle.

This tendency to identify what should only be associated is a characteristic of archaic thinking. We have seen that it first appears in schizophrenia as expression of paleologic thought, that is, of a thought which requires some logical organization. In magic, there is no *complete identification*, but only an identification of the power or outcome or function of two things, which should only be associated. In advanced schizophrenia, ideas which should be simply associated are completely identified. Thus, George Washington is identified with "White House." Of course, we are dealing with the same process which appears at different levels. What is the intimate nature of this process? We shall attempt to solve this problem when schizophrenia is re-examined from a general or synthetic point of view (See Chapter XIII).

IX. *Paleologic and Autism. Infantile Autism and Its Relation to Schizophrenia.*

In the previous sections of this chapter the terms autism and autistic have been purposely avoided, although they are commonly used in connection with schizophrenia. Hinsie and Shatsky, in their psychiatric dictionary, define autism as "a form of thinking, more or less genuinely, of a subjective character; if objective material enters, it is given subjective meaning and emphasis. Autism generally carries with it the thought that the material is derived from the individual himself, appearing in the nature of day-dreams, phantasies, delusions, hallucinations, etc. The content of thought, in other words, is largely endogenous. In classical instances of autistic thinking, such as occurs in schizophrenia, the unconscious sphere makes the largest contribution to autism." (127).

It is obvious that the terms autistic thought and paleologic thought are applied to the same phenomenon. Autism, however, is more of a descriptive term. In fact, Bleuler, who made the original contributions on autistic or dereistic thinking, limited himself to a description of it. Paleologic is more of a structural term; it means that autistic thought uses a paleological type of logic. Thus, both terms are useful; autism refers generally to a particular type of thinking; paleologic refers to the type of logic that is used in that type of thinking.

Of course, when definitions of autistic thought are formulated now, these should not be limited to a description, but should stress the fact that the main formal characteristic of this type of thinking is its foundation upon a non-Aristotelian logic, which has been designated as paleologic.

Bleuler spoke of the occurrence of this type of thinking not only in schizophrenia, but also in healthy adults "when the emotions obtain too great a significance," and in normal children during play activities (28). When children identify themselves with Superman, let us say, or the boogey man, or their parents, or when they play with toys, acting as if the toys were the things they represent, they seem to think paleologically. It is questionable, however, whether they really do so; children know that they play; they don't *believe* the reality of their games, they *make believe*. Undoubtedly, such a propensity for "make believe" is related to their facility to accept paleologic thinking, but to make believe is not proof of the necessity to think paleologically. It is a voluntary and playful reversion to paleologic thinking, just as that of the artist or of the person who makes humorous remarks (Arieti, 12).

Real autistic thought occurs in children at a very early age, when they think with paleological logic. (Several examples of this kind of thought were given on pages 197–199.) My ideas, however, about this type of thinking in children have changed somewhat since the time when I made my first observations. In fact, I am inclined to think now that the occurrence of autistic thought in young children is not a necessity, but only a propensity. Although even perfectly normal children may have autistic manifestations at the age of one and a half to three, the occurrence of such manifestations, even at that age, and their persistence afterwards, is much commoner in children who cannot relate well to the people with whom they live. If the child is well integrated, this propensity to autism is almost automatically overcome. If there are emotional difficulties between the child and the significant adults, autistic manifestations prevail. As will be discussed at greater length in Chapter XI, if anxiety-laden situations arise, which interfere with the process of socialization, this propensity of the child is enhanced to a pathological degree. Its most serious manifestations are found in that condition which Kanner has recently described and designated as "early infantile autism." Among the characteristics of children suffering from this condition, are excessive aloneness and the utterance of expressions which seem irrelevant or completely nonsensical. Kanner gives many examples of these expressions, which he calls "metaphorical" in the sense that they represent "figures of speech by means of which one thing is put for another which it only resembles" (150, 151). Kanner reports that the transfer of meaning in these expressions is accomplished in a variety of ways: a) through substitutive analogy, in which for example, bread basket becomes "home bakery"; b) through generalization or totum pro parte, in which "home bakery" becomes the term for every basket; c) through restrictions or pars pro toto —such as, when the number six is referred to as "hexagon."

If one recalls the discussion in sections II and III of this chapter, one can see that these examples given by Kanner represent typical paleologic expressions and may be re-interpreted in accordance with Von Domarus' principle, which implies substitutive analogy, generalization and restriction.

Kanner considers these children autistic and does not call them schizophrenics, in spite of certain similarities in thinking. Assisted by Kanner's contributions on this subject, I was able to recognize three cases which conformed with the description of "early infantile autism." A study of them enabled me to understand Kanner's reluctance to diagnose these cases as schizophrenics. They do present stereotyped utterances, neologisms and withdrawal. However, they do not present symptoms like delusions, hallucinations, ideas of reference, catatonia, etc., as reported in many descriptions of child schizophrenia, such as those given by De Sanctis (62), Potter (214), Bradley (36), and Kanner himself (149). In addition, and this is an important point, there was no evidence that these children had reached a normal or relatively normal adjustment after the age of two and one-half or three. On the contrary, it seems that since that age there had been some disturbance in their mental integration and especially in their process of socialization (see Chapter XI). A case reported by Betz indicates the same situation (24). In other words, it seems that there is no real schizophrenic regression in these children, but an inability to develop interpersonally beyond the level of one and one-half to two and one-half years of age. Instead, children who develop a schizophrenic syndrome, more or less similar to that found in adults, are able to integrate or socialize better after the third year of age and have already learned to use language normally before the mental disorder starts. It seems to me, however, that Kanner's patients must be considered psychotic, even if they are not considered schizophrenic. They do not correct, but entirely accept their autistic and paleologic ways of living. They remain, therefore, detached from reality, as schizophrenics do. In the long run they may become so similar to typical schizophrenics, as not to warrant a special classification. In Chapter XI, I shall return to this important subject of children suffering from "early infantile autism."

X. Paleologic and So-Called Primitive Thought

The difference between the concept of autism and that of paleologic thinking is even more obvious when one takes into consideration so-called "primitive thinking." We have already discussed several examples of thinking in primitive cultures, which indicate the frequent occurrence of a paleologic logic. And yet, primitive man cannot be called autistic; as a matter of fact, and here is the fundamental fact which has to be stressed, the opposite seems to be the case. The primitive, who may think paleologically, often does so not in order to be subjective and individualistic, but so that he may comply with the mores of his society. By using paleologic conceptions, he does not withdraw behind an autistic barrier, as the schizophrenic does, but, on the contrary, he becomes more intimately a part of his tribe.

The reference which I have made in previous works to the frequent instances in primitive cultures of paleologic thought, similar to that of the schizophrenic, has caused some criticism. It is the same kind of criticism which has been made of the works of Lévy-Bruhl, Storch, Werner, etc. Some of my concepts have been interpreted to imply the intellectual inferiority of certain non-Western peoples, a fact that many modern American anthropologists have convincingly disproved. Part of this criticism is deserved, since I did not adequately clarify this point. Although this book is concerned with a psychiatric problem, I shall not evade this important issue, which belongs more properly to the field of anthropology.

It seems to me irrefutable that paleologic thought per se must be considered inferior to the Aristotelian. It is much less reliable, it induces errors and the perpetuation of these errors, which could be avoided with Aristotelian thought. Unless we revise our philosophical concept of progress, we have to consider Aristotelian thought as being superior to the paleologic. The achievements in which humanity takes pride could not have been attained if the paleologic method of thought had been the prevalent one. The tendency of such thought to occur in early childhood, in a dream-state, and in pathological conditions, when our higher mental functions have not yet developed or cannot be used, seems to indicate irrefutably that it is a way of thinking which does not require our highest levels of integration. If we accept the evolutionary point of view in biology, and correspondingly a comparative developmental approach in psychology, we also have to accept the notion that intermediary stages once existed between some apes or ape-like species and the races of men who live today. Presumably these intermediary races of men thought paleologically. What has been said so far is not intended to imply that the non-Western peoples of today belong to these intermediary stages, in which thought is exclusively paleological. Such a blunder is inadmissible today. As a matter of fact, we know, for instance, that some of these races, like the African, are possibly of more ancient origin, and perhaps potentially superior to the white race. Then, one may ask, how is it that we find so many examples of paleologic thoughts in some of these non-white peoples? How is it that many examples of primitive thought given in this book are taken from non-Western peoples living today?

An important distinction must be made between the culture and the individual. An individual who belongs to one of these primitive cultures, if transposed to a Western culture, especially while still young, will completely lose the tendency to think paleologically. As a matter of fact, at close examination, anthropologists have noted that he is capable of thinking with Aristotelian logic in his own cultural environment, and in most instances actually does so. It is only when he wishes to comply with the mores of the culture, especially in situations which have a social significance—such as magic, religion, initiation rites, marriages, war, etc.—that he accepts paleologic conceptions.

Lévy-Bruhl, too, in speaking of "primitive" mentality in inferior *societies,* has been misunderstood. He wrote about paleological mentality only in social situations, not in the individual (170, 171). It is true that he considered some societies inferior, but only the societies, not the individual. Many anthropologists, as well as philosophers, like Cassirer, have overlooked this important distinction that Lévy-Bruhl made.

Thus, the point which I wish to make is as follows: the culture imposes paleologic conceptions on the individual, who is potentially capable of a higher way of thinking. The culture has retained patterns of thinking which belong to much earlier phases of evolution, and which have been transmitted with little or no modification.

Thus, in these primitive cultures of today, the propensity to think paleologically is not directly a psychological problem; it is a *cultural* one. It was only a psychological problem at a much earlier stage of evolution, maybe as long as 700,000 or 800,000 years ago, when, of necessity, man could think paleologically only. But why do some cultures retain so much paleologic thinking, even when the potentiality of the individual is beyond that stage? There is an intrinsic static quality in every culture, which has the tendency to transmit and therefore to perpetuate things as they are. In non-Western cultures, this tendency is much greater than in Western cultures. But even in our society, remnants of archaic ways of thinking which the individual alone can shake off, are maintained by the culture. An inhabitant of Mars would find many examples of paleologic thinking in the social, moral and religious mores of the Western man. But we don't need to think of an inhabitant from Mars; the non-Western man would be able to detect our paleologic ways better than he is able to discover his own. Paleologic thought has a tendency to perpetuate itself; the more abundant it is in a culture; the more difficult it is for the culture to get rid of it. Non-Western cultures indulge more in this type of thinking, and therefore cannot get rid of it so easily. For reasons which we cannot analyze here, Western culture has been quicker than the others to relinquish paleological modes.

This explanation also seems to clarify the question as to whether the study of culture is exclusively a psychological science or not. It seems to me that it is not. Culture is originally a psychological phenomenon in the same sense that mathematics, law, and the arts are. Culture originates in the minds of men, and cannot exist without the mind of man. However, mind and culture do not proceed with equal speed and although they interchange, and further each other's growth, the interchange is not equal. The bulk of culture is, in a certain way, the opposite of mathematics: It remains attached to certain primitive intellectual mechanisms, and often continues to act on the individual in accordance with these primitive mechanisms. At the same time, culture develops independently because of historical and geographical circumstances, which are not necessarily psychological in origin. When culture acts on the individual mind it becomes again a psychological subject. Thus culture originates and ends psychologically, but has an enormous intermediary life of its own. The beginning is psychological in a formal or psychostructural sense, that is, the culture starts as the application to the external world of the mental potentialities of man. The end is psychological in a dynamic sense. It acts as a powerful emotional and motivational force on the individual.

The importance of paleologic thought in the history of humanity has been underrated. One may wonder how these primitive races were able to survive or evolve into others if their actions were determined by a system of thinking which appears so unrealistic to us. There is no doubt that these races underwent a great struggle. Eventually the races which could not sufficiently overcome this type of thinking perished; those which evolved into a higher type of thinking did so at a slow rate and with tremendous difficulty. This conclusion can be conjectured from the following considerations. Modern anthropologists believe that the earliest human races appeared on this planet about a million years ago. Future researches may reveal that this figure is too conservative; at any rate, even if we accept this figure, the amazing fact is that, in spite of the existence of men for a million years, civilization originated only about 10,000 years ago, and the so-called historical period, of which we have more definite knowledge, only 5,000 years ago. The historical period includes only one-two hundredths of man's existence. If we compare the existence of man on earth to the life span of the individual, this period corresponds to just a few months.

The long delay in the development of civilization, of course, was due to the fact that men had to struggle hard for their own existence because of their paleological or unrealistic thinking. As we shall see in Chapter XI, this unrealistic thinking often made men more vulnerable than animals.

In addition, as we have already mentioned, paleologic thought tends to perpetuate the existing conditions. There are numerous substantiations for this allegation. For instance, Cro-Magnon men paleologically identified red powder with blood and therefore with life. They used to sprinkle the corpses of relatives with ochre in the hope that this color would restore them to life. It seems, from different excavations, that this practice persisted for at least 20,000 years, long after everyone should have been convinced of its futility.

An objection could be raised that such examples do not prove very much; they indicate only a quantitative and not a qualitative difference from certain equally absurd practices of Western man, which have been maintained for prolonged periods of time. It could also be pointed out that Cro-Magnons have left ample proof of their highly symbolic and Aristotelian thinking. These objections seem to be valid only because the examples that we must take from the material which is at our disposal, are recent examples. Cro-Magnon men lived about 70,000 years ago. They were already an evolved race, not much different from ours. Although the percentage of their paleologic thinking was bigger than ours and the persistence of such thinking longer, they were also capable of thinking logically. But what about the men who lived 500,000 or 900,000 years ago? What about Pithecanthropus Erectus and Paleoanthropus Heidelbergensis? Of course, we know so little about them, that we have to admit that much of our work is conjectural. On the other hand, one must remember that the anthropologists who exclude the possibility of an inferior type of thinking in very ancient races, take as proof of their allegations, examples from times which are, comparatively speaking, very recent.

It took man an extremely long time to free himself from this paleologic way of thinking, and to acquire a scientific attitude, which eventually led him to an Aristotelian interpretation of the world and to its subsequent mastery. Important remnants of the old system, however, survive in everybody's thinking today. But much more than remnants— actually all of the old mechanisms—have remained in one's unconscious, and are prepared to come back to the surface in the state of sleep and in pathological conditions, of which the most typical example is schizophrenia.

CHAPTER XI

The Retreat from Society

I. General Remarks. Discussion of Previous Contributions.

Now the most difficult part of the psychological structure of the schizophrenic process must be considered. We must try to interpret and understand those processes which make the patient retreat from society and live in a world of his own. Very little has been done on this subject. The textbooks give only a descriptive account of this withdrawal.

We shall also start with a description, and go on later to an interpretative attempt. It must be repeated here that the schizophrenic does not mingle freely, that he prefers to be by himself, and that any communication with another human being is a great effort for him. He prefers to replace with his inner experiences the actions which would require some kind of social situation. It is often said that the schizophrenic lives in a shell, that an autistic barrier separates him from others. He reduces communications to the minimum; if he is addressed, he resents even simple questions as intrusions into his own privacy. The patient lives a kind of private life which nobody, not even his roommate, his closest relative or his best friend can touch.

In every schizophrenic, to a more or less pronounced degree, there is an impairment of the ability to socialize, that is, to communicate with others and to share experiences with others. This impairment is even more pronounced than would seem from a superficial examination of the patient's behavior. For instance, in a state hospital where one sees many schizophrenics working together, one may get the impression that they actually cooperate and divide their labor in some kind of organized manner. Actually, the organization comes from a non-schizophrenic supervisor. It is true that the patients work together, but in a physical sense only, inasmuch as they work in the same place. Each one works independently. A group of schizophrenics in reality is not a group; it is a number of separate individuals. At first one gets the opposite impression; they are just a group, they have lost their individuality; they are just a bunch of schizophrenics, like a herd of cattle. This impression is far from the truth; they seem to have lost their individuality because they cannot communicate or transmit their individual feelings and ideas. If they talk, the formal characteristics of their utterances give the listener an impression of uniformity, which is only apparent. Their ability to share experiences is so disturbed that they cannot spontaneously initiate any plan with any other human being. There are exceptions: at times, friendships are possible between patients who are not too regressed or who are on the way to recovery. In many of these cases, however, one is a non-schizophrenic patient. Alcoholic and organic patients do not lose the ability to socialize as much as the schizophrenic does.

The extent of their inability to plan together or to share experiences is revealed in the following observation. During the second World War, when there was a serious shortage of man-power, the attendants at state hospitals were reduced to a minimum. The shortage in Pilgrim State Hospital was so acute that, at times, at certain hours during the night, one single attendant had to take care of several wards. Many patients, especially paranoids, often plan to escape. A single patient who tries to escape is easily overcome by the generally robust attendant. If two patients, however, were to cooperate they could easily overcome the attendant, grab his keys and escape. But even that degree of cooperation, between two people, is impossible for schizophrenics. Even a group of two, in the sense of two people planning and sharing common experiences, is impossible for them. That is why it was possible to keep patients from escaping even when the attendants were so few in number.

The amusing short story by Edgar Allan Poe, "The System of Doctor Tarr and Professor Fether," in which the staff of a private mental sanitarium is overcome and kept in captivity by a well-organized group of patients, is hardly believable. When we read in the newspapers that mental patients have rebelled or mutinied, we may easily conclude that these patients are psychopaths (generally detained as alleged criminally insane), not psychotics. Of course, a group of schizophrenics may also escape, when they are helped by non-schizophrenic persons. This ability to plan together and to share experiences is impaired even when the general intelligence of the patient is preserved.

What has been said so far is merely a description of this characteristic of schizophrenia. Now an attempt must be made to understand it. The explanation that the schizophrenic tries to cut all communications because he interprets anything coming from outside as hostile and unpleasant contains a great deal of truth, but can hardly account for all the facts. The schizophrenic is not a hermit, who withdraws from this unpleasant world. The hermit is potentially able to communicate and to share experiences, but not the schizophrenic. The patient undergoes a process of desocialization which, although motivated by the desire to withdraw from anxiety-ridden societal experiences, is something more than the actualization of this desire.

American psychiatrists, more than psychiatrists of other countries, have tried to interpret this phenomenon. This particular interest of American psychiatrists can be attributed to the special American intellectual climate. In a more or less direct way, American psychiatrists have been influenced by the philosophy of John Dewey and George Mead, who saw the human mind not as an isolated entity, but as something which is constantly being molded by society. According to Dewey and Mead, as a matter of fact, there would be no human mind without human society. The two American psychiatrists who made great contributions to the understanding of this process of socialization are Harry Stack Sullivan and Norman Cameron.

We have already discussed Sullivan's contribution at great length. We have seen how his whole concept of psychiatry is based on the process of socialization (see page 33). According to him, the self is created by the ensemble of the social relations that the child has with the significant adults in his life, by the reflected appraisal of these significant adults. If these interpersonal relations are unhealthy and create an excessive amount of anxiety, the psychological development is disturbed and the process of socialization is altered. This sequence of events may lead to schizophrenia.

Sullivan's concepts are of great value, but do not explain the whole problem. Although it is true that an altered relatedness to others in childhood may engender that other altered relatedness to others which we call schizophrenia, this interpretation does not explain the formal characteristics of this condition.

Norman Cameron thinks that, to a very large extent, the symbolic behavior of adults is socially derived (43, 44). Individuals with socially inadequate development progressively fail to maintain a level of intelligible communication. They have the tendency to separate themselves from their community, and to indulge in their own private thinking which does not require conformity to the thinking of others. Through a process of progressive desocialization, they replace the social language habits with personal, highly individual habits. In these people, the social community, which is a realistic interpretation of the interactions of the individuals with others, is replaced by the pseudo-community. This pseudo-community is a behavioral organization, which the patient has built up out of his distorted observations and inferences. Here he sees himself generally as the victim of some concerted action. Since the paranoid does not reveal his suspicions to others, the suspicions continue to build up and organize in the pseudo-community. When he finally voices his beliefs, they are already so established in rigid patterns of thinking that they cannot be removed. The negative response that he elicits in others, when he finally expresses his delusions, reinforces his belief that he is being persecuted. The autistic community, according to Cameron, is a behavioral organization consisting of imagination "in a fantasied context." The autistic community may be replaced by disorganization, which consists of fragmentary and chaotic behavior.

Cameron's formulations have the following merits:

1) They recognize the magnitude of the role society plays in abnormal behavior.
2) Not only do they give a good description of the progression of the disorder, but they explain how previous stages engender or favor the subsequent ones.
3) They recognize the importance that desocialization plays

in schizophrenia to a greater extent than other formulations.

On the other hand, they have shortcomings. From a dynamic point of view, Norman Cameron does not give an adequate account of the early experiences which interplay between parents and children, or of the importance that the feelings of the parents have in the process of socialization of the children. From a formal point of view, he describes but does not explain the characteristics of the autistic and disorganized behavior. As was mentioned before, the only thing which is explained is how the disorders favor a progression toward further disorganization.

The point of view advocated in this book is that the process of desocialization takes place because of a concomitant process of desymbolization. It is not enough to study the dynamics of the early interpersonal relations in the life history of the patient. These interpersonal relationships explain a great deal from a dynamic or motivational point of view; for therapeutic purposes nothing is more important than the study of these relationships. However, if we want to understand why the process of desocialization of the schizophrenic has its peculiar aspects, we have to study the process of socialization as it took place in the evolution of the human race from more primitive forms. Only a comparative developmental psychological approach may throw light on the subject. The high level of symbolic activity, of which the human mind is capable, would not have occurred without a human society. Human socialization and human symbolization are two phenomena, each of which cannot take place without the other.

Under the stress of the dynamic forces which operate in the schizophrenic, there is a tendency to lose the high levels of symbolization and socialization, which permit so much anxiety, and to regress to earlier stages of development. If we wish to understand properly what happens in schizophrenia, we must study these two processes as they evolved in the human species. This is a subject which involves excursion into other fields, such as semantics. Many readers may be reluctant to do so, but if psychiatry is to continue its expansion from the narrow limits of its early formulations, it has to take cognizance of the advances made in other fields which seem to be unrelated but actually are not. Some of the conceptions which are to be presented have been formulated under the influence of the writings of Giambattista Vico (263), George Mead (187), Ernst Cassirer (51) and Susanne Langer (165, 166). These authors have made penetrating studies, although they did not have the advantage of direct psychiatric observations.

II. Socialization and Symbolization from a Phylogenetic Point of View.

The processes of socialization and symbolization are quite complicated and need careful study. The author hopes to elaborate on them in another publication. Here, the fundamental facts about these processes will be reported, with a view toward a better understanding of schizophrenia.

The most outstanding capacity of the mind probably is its capacity to symbolize or to create symbols. From a very broad point of view, symbolization may be defined as *transformation* of *experiences*. Sense-data are not accepted by the mind as they are, but are taken to mean something else. The most primitive forms of symbolization are also present in animals; they begin in the phyletic scale as early as the conditioned reflex does, because they require something like the conditioned reflex.

Through repetition in the course of the experiment, the sound of a bell causes a dog to expect food and to secrete gastric juice. The sound of the bell becomes a *sign* of the forthcoming food. The bell is not food, and yet it indicates food. The sign thus stands for something else, which is present or about to be present in the total situation. It is part of a whole, which is selected to represent either the whole present situation or other parts of the present situation.

Men, too, use many signs. The physician sees a rash on the skin of the child and knows that this rash is the sign of chickenpox. But, more frequently, men use things which stand for something else, even when this something else is not present. When I say "George," the word "George" substitutes for the person George, when George is not present. Thus the word George is not necessarily a sign of the person George, but is oftener *a symbol* of the person George. People know it and know of each other that they know it.

Perhaps the greatest difference between the psychic functions of animals and men is that whereas animals are not capable of symbols, men are. The use of symbols expands our lives to an enormous degree. We may replace things with other things, to the nth degree. No human endeavor is conceivable without symbols. But the study of the expansions of the symbolic world is beyond the purpose of this book. The interested reader is referred to that excellent, thought-stimulating book by Langer, "Philosophy in a New Key" (165).

The problem to be considered here is the following: Why is the human mind capable of symbols? Is this ability due only to a more evolved nervous system or to some other concomitant and related factor? There is another necessary factor, the interpersonal process. Twenty dogs, who are conditioned to a bell, react to the sound of the bell individually, without any communication about the forthcoming food taking place among the dogs. Each dog reacts individually, his secretions of gastric juice being independent or, for practical purposes, almost independent of the secretions of the other dogs. But, if we mention the word George, and we all understand that we are talking about the person George, an agreement must have been reached between us. We all agree that the word George is a symbol of the person George. An interpersonal process has taken place, as a result of which the word "George" has become the symbol of the person George. Thus, verbal symbolization requires an interpersonal relationship. This description probably seems to be only an elaboration of the obvious, but what may seem extremely easy to us today was, on the contrary, one of the most dramatic, difficult and eventful steps in evolution, the change from the sign to the symbol.

What is the earliest or most primitive form of symbol of which the human mind is capable? It is a kind of preverbal symbolization which does not necessarily require an interpersonal process, the image. The image of my mother replaces my mother; the image of a hurricane reproduces the hurricane I once experienced. Although these images may be enriched tremendously by social relationships, they may exist even without them. They have peculiar characteristics. They are very private, individualistic, fleeting, flexible and mutable. Two persons never have the same image about the same object; the same person has different images of the same object in two different moments. Through images we live in our own private, individualistic world. It is a symbolic world, because it stands for an external world, and yet it is very close to sensation and perception, and therefore has a primitive emotional tone. This world is far from abstractions.

Do animals have images? This question is hard to answer; they probably do, especially images of an olfactory nature. They seem to dream, and if they dream, they must do so with some kind of images. However, animals do not seem to have the capacity to evoke or reproduce images when they want to, and, of course, they are incapable of expressing them to others.

Men, too, have great difficulty in communicating images. In the history of evolution, it was only when men acquired verbal symbols that they became capable of communicating their images. The process of socialization enables man to translate his inner private images into symbols which he can transmit to others. Without socialization, however, even his inner private images would be reduced to a minimum because most of his inner life is also determined by his relationships with other people. Social contacts stimulate symbols which may undergo a process of individual imagery, and then may be translated into more social symbols.

Let us now examine the transformation of the private image into a social symbol. The comparative psychologist, Kellogg, reports that his little chimpanzee, Gua, was so attached to him that whenever he left the house, she became very despondent (156). She would go into a tantrum of terror and grief. If, however, he gave her his coverall at the time of his departure, she seemed placated, showed no emotional displeasure, and carried the coverall around with her as a fetish. As Langer points out, this fact is extremely important. This is probably one of the first manifestations of high symbolization of which animals may be capable. The coverall represented the master. However, it was more than a symbol of the master; it replaced the master. It acquired the property that the master had, in that it would satisfy the ape emotionally just as he did. In other words, it was a symbol, but it was a symbol which was identified with the object it symbolized. Possibly the ape was able to evoke the image of his master at the sight of the coverall, or the coverall reproduced the image of the master plus coverall, or the ape really accepted the coverall not as a coverall, but as an emotional equivalent of his master. At the present stage of our knowledge it is impossible to be sure which of these possibilities is the correct one. If we follow our own terminology, we might say that

master and coverall were identified according to Von Domarus' principle.

Let us assume, theoretically, that at the same time that
Kellogg trained Gua, he had trained two other chimpanzees,
with potentialities similar to hers. When Kellogg would leave,
maybe the second chimpanzee would find comfort, not at the
sight of his coverall, but at the sight of one of his tools, let's
say. In fact, it is difficult to believe that the second chimpanzee
would have selected the coverall as a symbol of Kellogg.
Obviously there were some incidental events, specific in the
life of Gua, which caused her to choose the coverall as the
symbol of her master. For similar reasons, the second chimpanzee would be comforted at the sight of a tool, and the
third chimpanzee, let us say, at the sight of Kellogg's pipe.
Thus, we have three chimpanzees who use three different
things as symbols of the master. These symbols are private,
individual symbols which are valid only for the subject who
uses them. They are qualities, or parts of a whole, which they
symbolize. So the coverall, the tool and the pipe are parts of
whole situations. This form of symbolization follows Von
Domarus' principle; the symbol is not a social symbol. It is
valid only for one individual, since each individual uses a
different predicate (part-quality) as symbol of the object
which is symbolized.

Let us assume, again, a theoretical situation in which three
animals, higher than chimpanzees and lower than homo
sapiens, are together after the departure of their mother, for
example. One of the three ape-men children sees a stone
which is always used by the mother. Like Gua, he is sad at
the departure of his mother, but when he sees the stone he is
consoled. He is excited, makes a gesture with his hands, one
implying happiness, and emits the sound "ma-ma," similar to
the babbling of children. The other two ape-men children are
there, and in a sudden flash of illumination they understand

that the stone, the gesture with the hands and the sound "ma-ma" mean mother to the first child. A great event has happened in the world! The symbol which was individual is communicated to the second and third ape-man, and will mean the same thing to them as to the person who pronounced it. It becomes a verbal symbol, a social symbol, something which is shared, something which they have in common. From then on, when the first ape-man wants to express the idea of mother, he will use either the stone or that particular gesture of the hands or the sound "ma-ma." The others will respond to these signs as he does. By using them he will evoke in himself the same response that he evokes in others. The stone as a symbol of mother will originate fetish magic, so common in primitive people.

The gesture is a kind of language, which is still quite prevalent in primitive cultures, and has not completely disappeared even among Western men. Even today the movements of the hands stimulate the language centers. In fact, if the individual is right-handed, the language centers are in the left hemisphere, and they are in the right hemisphere if he is left-handed. Probably for this primitive ape-man the gesture language preceded or was more important than the verbal. For the sake of simplification we shall omit consideration of the fetish and the manual gesture, and concentrate on the verbal concomitant.

The first ape-man says "ma-ma" and the others understand "mother." They surrender their own individual symbols and accept "ma-ma" as a symbol of mother. Each of them, by saying "ma-ma" evokes in the other the same thing which he evokes in himself, or vice versa, he arouses in himself the same response that he arouses in the others. The symbol "ma-ma" eventually will replace the stone and the manual gesture.

The symbol "ma-ma" has a definite denotation: mother.

The concept "ma-ma" will have those syncretic qualities so well described by Werner (270). The symbol "ma-ma" will do other wonderful things. It will orient the mind of the ape-man to replace the image or visualization of mother with a verbal symbol. It will substitute for the individual fleeting images something which from this time on will be common to others and less temporary. Something which has a tendency to fade away is replaced by something else which has a definite form. It permits thinking of mother, not only in the present situation when mother is there, but also of a mother in the past, and a mother in the future. Thus the verbal symbol widens the horizon of the mind, which from now on will be able to reproduce the past and envisage the future. No longer will it be like the mind of animals, restricted to the present (see page 239).

By accepting the verbal sign, "ma-ma," the ape-men, however, have to give up many things: they have to give up their individual symbols; they have to repress the images which are so near to their sensations; and they have to lose part of the direct sensuous contact with the phenomenon. They gain acceptance in a social world which will multiply the symbols to an enormous degree.

To repeat, what has been described would not have occurred without a first interpersonal contact, as a result of which a symbol was grasped not only by the person who uttered it, but by at least one other living creature. When the first ape-man of our hypothetical example said "ma-ma" and meant mother, the symbol "ma-ma" was not yet language. It became language when the second ape-man interpreted it as a symbol of mother. The first ape-man, in turn, understood that the second ape-man had interpreted it as a symbol of mother. In other words, one ape-man could not have created even a rudimentary language of one word. At least two persons were necessary to make the transition from the level of private symbols to the level of verbal symbols.

There are several corroborations for these assertions. Children learn language, not only because they have the potentiality to learn it at a certain stage of their development, but also because they have interpersonal contacts. Deaf children do not learn how to talk, not because there is something wrong with their vocal equipment. In spite of their perfect neurological and laryngeal equipment, they become mute because they cannot receive the verbal symbols coming from other persons. Helen Keller, the amazing woman who has been blind and deaf since early childhood, in her autobiography, gives a very good description of her acquisition of verbal symbols in spite of her defects (155). As a cool stream of water flowed over one of her hands, her teacher spelled the word water into her hand, at first slowly, then rapidly. With a flashing thrill, Miss Keller realized that the letters w-a-t-e-r spelled on her hand meant that "wonderful cool something" *for her teacher;* and from then on, *for her too,* that "wonderful cool something" was represented by that combination of letters. Miss Keller describes the episode as a momentous experience. Now she had a medium through which she could communicate with other people. The barrier of isolation, which blindness and deafness had erected, could be demolished by her entrance into the level of verbal symbols, that is by the fact that an interpersonal contact with her teacher at the level of verbal symbolism, was made possible.

Children, who were abandoned in woods and were able to survive by fortuitous circumstances, without being taken care of by adults, never learned more than a rudimentary language, if they were found long after the age when a child usually starts to talk. The cases of Victor, Amala and Kamala are well known.

Before that wonderful experience with the water, Miss Keller had other kinds of symbols which were more primitive. For instance, she had signs. The fragrance of the flowers made her understand that she was in the garden. She also had images, made up mostly of kinesthetic, olfactory and gustatory elements. In addition, she had private symbols, since she was able to anticipate events. She said that she felt during this period as if invisible hands were holding her while she was making frantic efforts to free herself. Even before she was able to understand social symbols from her teacher, she had experienced emotional and social experiences with her parents and friends. However, no high social integration was possible until she acquired the use of verbal symbols.

To summarize the foregoing, there are four types of symbols:

1) Signs;
2) Images;
3) Private symbols, which from now on will be called *paleosymbols;*
4) Social (or verbal or common or communicable) symbols.

The signs we have in common with animals. The images are present in animals to a very rudimentary degree. If they exist in animals, they seem to be evoked only by external stimuli, not by internal ones, except possibly in the state of sleep. When the image is externalized, or when an external act of the individual or an object replaces the image, we have paleosymbols. The paleosymbols possibly exist in apes in a very rudimentary form, but are more characteristic of immediately pre-human races. The paleosymbols are understood only by the individual who produces them. The social symbols are exclusively human. They imply an initial process of socialization, and in turn they make social integration possible. A much higher degree of accuracy, predictability and verification becomes possible with them. A continuous expansion of social symbols has taken place since the acquisition of the first word. The history of humanity is the history of its social symbols. It is beyond the purpose of this book to give a detailed account of this process. It will be mentioned briefly however, that together with this process of expansion a process of abstraction and complex socialization occurred. Thus, the first words were specific for single objects, that is, denotation and connotation coincided. These first words had a strong tie with the images, especially physiognomic, or with the paleosymbols. They were so strongly connected with their denotation that they were confused with it, that is, the words were thought to be the things they symbolized. (See page 218.) At a higher level, a single word came to represent a class rather than a specific object. Mother meant any mother, not a single mother. Terms for abstract concepts were thus devised. These stages have been very well described by Werner (270).

At a much higher level of development, symbols were created which even transcended any ordinary class of objects. Thus, numbers stand for anything we want. The number 5 may represent five fingers, five names, five men, five feelings, etc. At a still higher level of development, algebraic symbols were created, which may represent any number. This process of increasing symbolization will continue with the future development of humanity. At the same time social relations became more and more complex; along with new symbols man acquires new roles: he is a man, a son, a father, a husband, a neighbor, a friend, an enemy, a buyer, a tax payer, a seller, and so on indefinitely. As socialization develops, man has to acquire an increasing number of roles, and with all of these he has to integrate at the same time that he has to remain the same person.

As was noted before, it is not the purpose of this book to follow the development of the processes of symbolization and socialization. Semantics and sociology deal with this subject. The emphasis here is on the interconnection between the two processes, on the fact that the one cannot exist without the other, just as in a certain way, the tapeworm cannot exist without the man, or a community of plants without pollinating insects and birds.

Another point, however, has to be mentioned which greatly complicates the situation. This is the overlapping of the levels of symbolization: Whenever a higher level is reached, the previous one does not cease to exist. These levels overlap in both directions, from the lower to the higher, and from the higher to the lower. The first direction is easily understood. Although man uses verbal symbols predominantly, he retains signs, as is evident when he looks at the clouds to see if it is going to rain. He has images, when he thinks about things which are not present, and also has paleosymbols, most of which are used, however, in his private phantasies, dreams, artistic productions and neurotic symptoms. The other direction in which the levels overlap is somewhat more complicated. For instance, although the process of socialization, with integrated social activities, could not have taken place without the acquisition of the fourth level, mental activities connected with social situations now invade the levels of the paleosymbols or private phantasies, the images and even the signs. An arrow indicating the direction of traffic on a street is a sign, but a highly socialized one. By far the majority of our images, phantasies, dreams, etc. involve social situations almost all of which could not have originated without the acquisition of the fourth level of symbolization. Man is a highly social animal, and this socializing attitude does not wish to be confined to the level at which it originated, but expands in both directions. When it moves toward more primitive levels, let us say, even to the level of signs, it should not be confused with those superficial social tendencies of which animals too are capable.

On the contrary, its expressions are always highly symbolized.

Thus far, we have emphasized the positive aspect of the evolution of the symbolic processes from the sign to the verbal symbol. We must, however, also consider the other aspect of the problem, that is, the potential danger that this process of the evolution of symbols constitutes. When an animal responds to a sign, as for example, when a cat responds to the odor of a mouse, he is a realist. The cat does not let his imagination confuse him. The odor is there; therefore, the mouse is there. At the level of signs, mistakes are difficult, unless artificial situations are devised by men to confuse the animal. Signs do not pretend to stand for something which is not there but are indicators of something which is there, or are seen as part of a whole which is there. At the level of signs, mental life is very limited, is narrowed to what is here at this moment, but mistakes are difficult.

At the level of images, the situation becomes more complicated. Images may stand for things which are not there. They attempt to reproduce a sensorial picture of what is absent, but memory is defective, and the individual's experiences interfere and tamper with the reproduction; the image is so fleeting that it cannot be reproduced twice in the same way, or be experienced by anybody except the person who has it, and it is strongly influenced by concomitant emotions. Consequently, it has a quality of indefiniteness; it is inaccurate and unverifiable.

In paleosymbols, the image may be substituted by an external object, gesture or a sound. But these externalizations are chosen arbitrarily by the individual. Therefore, they may lead to fatal errors. If the ape continues to react to the coverall as she reacted to the master, after the master dies, she may also die of starvation. The paleosymbols enlarge mental life, because they allow for the thinking of things which are not there, but are apt to lead to mistakes. The object which is taken as a symbol, or the manual gesture or the uttered sound, is not a reproduction of the thing which is symbolized. Furthermore, at the early stages of this level, the individual still has the tendency to confuse the paleosymbol with the object symbolized, or to see the paleosymbol as part of the symbolized situation, in the same way that the sign was. The paleosymbol is more definite than the image, but is also highly individual, subjective, emotionally-loaded and unverifiable. When the fourth level is reached, the paleosymbols invade the social life also. As a matter of fact, it would seem that every verbal symbol was a paleosymbol before it became a socialized or verbal symbol. The struggle that the individual had to undergo in evolving from the paleosymbol to the social symbol was no less strenuous than the struggle to evolve from the image to the paleosymbol. This struggle has not yet ended. We are still motivated by paleosymbols to a certain degree, though less and less. The struggle for survival which the primitive races had to undergo were the result of the mistakes to which these paleosymbols and their use in paleologic led. (See page 272).

Signs, images and paleosymbols permit the experience of fear, that is, an emotional reaction to the perception of an immediate actual danger. They also permit the experience of a certain type of anxiety, which may be called short-circuited anxiety, which is related to the fact that the individual is unable to react to two simultaneous confusing stimuli, or is unable to satisfy a need or to discharge the tension caused by his propensity to react when under the influence of a certain stimulus. Signs and images, however, do not allow for the experience of that form of anxiety, the most common in human beings, which is due to the anticipation of a future danger. Symbols, and to a much lesser degree, paleosymbols, are necessary for this form of anxiety (See page 239).

Consequently, one sees again the limitation of those researches which study psychopathological processes in animals with the purpose of elucidating the psychopathology of human beings. The psychopathology of animals is the psychopathology of signs, of the conditioned reflex, or of short-circuited anxiety. The psychopathology of human beings is predominantly a pathology of paleosymbols and symbols. Therefore, to study psychoneuroses or psychoses in animals would be the same as to study cerebellar dysfunctions in invertebrates. Invertebrates have no cerebellum. In saying this, the author is not denying the value of the experiments carried on by such people as Masserman (185), Mowrer (199) and others. These experiments do have value inasmuch as they illuminate basic processes of psychic life, as for instance, regression, instincts of preservation (reaction to fear), and anxiety caused by simultaneous conflicting stimuli or by inability to satisfy needs. These experiments, however, disclose only the pathological mechanisms at the level of signs, and we know that this level is the one least involved in human psychoneuroses and psychoses.

III. Socialization in the Individual. Desocialization in Schizophrenia. "Early Infantile Autism." Mechanisms of Projection.

Now that we have examined the processes of socialization and symbolization from a predominantly phylogenetic point of view, let us consider what happens ontogenetically in the normal individual, and finally in the person who becomes a schizophrenic. First of all, let us be reminded of one important thing, that for the purpose of simplification we have abstracted an artificial situation from a much broader context. That is, in connection with the process of socialization, we have discussed only the verbal symbols, and for the same sake of clarity, we shall continue to do so. However, it should always be remem-

bered that even before the acquisition of language, the child
has already acquired non-verbal social symbols of the highest
levels. Gestures, attitudes, actions, feelings, already have an
interpersonal meaning.

When the child is ready to learn language, he learns
that some of the sounds evoke a certain response in the
adults around him; he then learns to evoke in himself the
same response that these sounds elicit in others. Personal
babbling is given up and gradually is replaced by verbal
symbols. However, individual tendencies are strong at this
age. In many children there is that tendency, which is
generally called autistic, to name an object or a person with
a special sound that the child himself has invented. Parents
generally notice that certain sounds or words which are not
part of the official language are used by the child to mean
certain things. Thus, a child of a year and a half who used
to call water "br . . ." later transferred this verbalization from
water to milk.

These paleosymbols, used by young children, are either
created from the original babbling, or made up with badly
reproduced verbal symbols. Children, however, learn very
soon to repress these autistic or paleologic or paleosymbolic
activities, and adopt the social symbols learned from adults.
It must be noted that a strong autistic tendency, even in a very
young child, is a sign of some kind of disorder in his process
of socialization. (See also pages 264–268.) Children who use
a great many autistic expressions are children who cannot
integrate well socially. When one hears many autistic expressions in a child, one should look for some kind of difficulty
between the child and his parents, generally the mother. The
child is so unwilling to accept the symbols of the rejecting
mother that he resorts more than other children to his own
individual symbols.

Here is clearly illustrated the interconnection between the

dynamic and the formal mechanisms of the human mind. For a normal process of socialization, normal parent-children relations are necessary. It is the love, or the non-anxiety producing attitude of the parent which will encourage the process of socialization. The parent-child relationship is not only the first social act and the major impulse to further socialization, but it is also the stimulus to accept or to reject society. If the child is afraid of this first social act, he may be afraid of integrating socially with society at large, and his process of socialization may be retarded or disturbed or made impossible. There will be a greater tendency then to resort to private autistic activities. As a rule, it is because of negative emotional factors that the child resorts to mechanisms which otherwise are only potential, or present to a vestigial degree. Often, there is just a trace of autistic tendencies in happy children raised in a happy atmosphere.

In the process of assuming roles, which we have previously described, the normal child almost automatically accepts and considers these roles as his own. But these roles are attributed to him by his parents. For instance, when little George eats, he can say, "I eat," but if there is a disorder in his concept of himself, he thinks of himself as his parents see him and he will think, "You, George, eat." In other words, he has difficulty in incorporating attributes, feelings, points of view about himself which come from others. In the process of developing his self, the child has to acquire all these points of view of others about himself, and has to attribute them to himself. His self is a reflection of the feelings, thoughts and attitudes that the others have toward him. This development occurs only if the process of socialization takes place in normal circumstances, that is, if the child is not afraid to accept these reflections coming from others. If the parent rejects the child, there will be an interference with the acceptance of these reflections emanating from the parent; the development of the self will be hindered. It will be easier for George to think, "You, George, eat," than to think, "I, George, eat," because when he says "you, George, eat," he verbalizes an attitude of his mother which he has not accepted and therefore has not transformed into "I, George, eat." In other words, these social acquisitions which come from others and which, with the development of the self, become part of the self itself, have the tendency to remain separate from the self, whenever an emotional disturbance interferes with the process of normal socialization. This tendency generally occurs when the child is strongly rejected, and therefore he himself cannot accept the others. For this kind of disorder the rejection must be very severe; mild rejections are generally tolerated by the child.

This point has been very well illustrated in the cases of early infantile autism already referred to in this book, which Kanner has reported in the literature (149-151). Although Kanner has not attempted a dynamic or a structural interpretation, his data are very valuable, and his description of the syndrome is original and accurate. On page 266 we have mentioned the neologisms used by these children, and other expressions which, according to our definition, are paleosymbols and use a paleologic type of thinking. The whole symptomatology of these children cannot be repeated here, but some of the important findings will be added.

These children show an extreme disorder in their socialization. They are aloof, and detached, and do not want to have anything to do with people. They often eliminate people from their consciousness completely. For instance, Kanner mentioned, as a typical example, the fact that when one of these children was pricked, he showed fear of the *pin* but not of the person who pricked him. Comings and goings of the mother in the same room are not registered. Conversation does not arouse interest. The child does not look into anyone's face. He tries to eliminate any intrusion or any contact with any other human beings. But why? Although Kanner did not attempt any dynamic interpretations, he reported that the parents of these children were not warm-hearted. They were obsessive, cold and preoccupied with intellectual activities. In the three cases that I have seen I have been able to convince myself that the child was rejected, that the mother was so unable to give any warmth and tenderness that the child could not establish any positive emotional tie with her. The fear of the parents spread to other adults, and there was an attempt to cut all communications with human beings. There was, therefore, a dearth of verbal symbols, and a large number of paleosymbols. One of these children, during the examination, repeated in a stereotyped manner, "good-bye, good-bye, good-bye." He resented the examination and by saying "good-bye," he expressed the desire to leave.

Kanner has noted in the majority of his cases, and I have noted in two of the three cases I examined, that personal pronouns are repeated just as they are heard. If the child is told by his mother, "I will give you some soup," the child subsequently expresses the desire for the soup in exactly the same way. He speaks of himself as "you" and not too infrequently of the mother as "I." That is, he uses the same pronouns as his mother would use. This, of course, may be understood in relation to what was said before, that the child does not see those reflections coming from the adults around him, as related to his self. The "you" remains a "you" and is not transformed into "I"; it somehow remains a foreign body.

Some of those children who are mute, in spite of normal auditory and verbal apparatuses and normal intelligence, present in my opinion extreme cases of this emotionally determined disorder in socialization.

People who develop schizophrenia at an adult age, undoubtedly had difficulties during their childhood with their processes of symbolization and socialization. These difficulties, however, were overcome temporarily, and the autistic manifestations were repressed, in spite of the fact that they were more pronounced than normally. When the illness approaches and the patient regresses to a paleologic way of thinking, he has to use paleosymbols more and more, and he drops common symbols. By doing that, of course, he desocializes himself. Although he may still use common symbols, many of which have undergone a paleologic or private distortion, he is predominantly living at the paleosymbolic level. It is impossible for him to integrate socially, because he cannot use the common symbols of the society in which he lives. When we have taken into consideration common symbols, for the sake of simplification, we have considered only verbal symbols, but even gestures and motions are being desocialized by the schizophrenic, and they become mannerisms, grimaces, stereotyped movements, that is actions which society does not understand. The patient is no longer part of society, because a society is a symbolic integration of individuals, that is, a group of individuals who understand and organize and give roles to one another in accordance with common symbols.

I do not mean that the schizophrenic loses the understanding of the meaning which the society in which he lives gives to the common symbols. In several cases, especially when the illness is very advanced, this is actually the case, but it is not necessarily so. In the majority of cases the schizophrenic retains the intellectual understanding of these symbols, but they are emotionally remote to him; they are like foreign bodies, and do not arouse in him the strong reactions that his own paleosymbols do. Therefore, the schizophrenic, especially at the beginning of the illness, may still retain a capacity to socialize, or to check somehow the process of desocialization, but this will only be at the expense of a strenuous intellectual effort. Thus, we have that frequent picture of the schizophrenic who succeeds in partially relating to other people through his intellectual functions, but who is emotionally distant and desocialized.

Following one of the comparisons already used, the schizophrenic is not simply an anchorite. He is desocialized, not only because of his desire to escape from society like the anchorite, but also because he lives in a symbolic world which is not shared by any society. Perhaps he may be compared somewhat with a person who, in order to become an anchorite, inflicted some kind of sensory aphasia on himself.

The process of desocialization of the schizophrenic does not operate only in the sense of a loss of common symbols. There is also a tendency to reject, or to divest the self of those attitudes, roles and tendencies which become part of the self, and which were reflected from others. In other words, a great deal of what was introjected in the process of the development of the self, is not only rejected, but also projected, or given back to the persons who originally gave it to the self. An example will explain what I mean. The nagging, scolding attitude of the parent is originally introjected by the child, who will acquire a critical condemnatory attitude toward himself or what we have called the self image of the bad child (page 47). When the patient becomes psychotic, this attitude is projected, or given back to a parent-substitute, an authority, or a person paleologically conceived as a persecutor, because he seems to have one of the persecuting traits of the parent.

It seems to me that this explanation increases our present understanding of the mechanism of projection. Projection is not only an attributing of an idea to others; it is a giving back, a restitution of an unpleasant part of the self to the people who built that part of the self. That part of the self is given back, because it is unpleasant. The rest of the self is not going to accept it any longer. The person does not accept self-condemnation any longer as a part of the self; condemnation now comes from the persecutor. He does not hate himself anymore;

somebody else hates him. This mechanism is greatly complicated and made obscure by the fact that what is given back is not returned to the original givers, but to persons who symbolize them. Thus, paleologic mechanisms will transform, let us say, the condemnatory quality of a parent into the persecutory actions of a Nazi or an FBI agent.

This process could very easily be studied in a patient of mine, a 32-year-old man who developed mild psychotic episodes. When he was not psychotic, he presented a rather detached, shy, aloof, timid character. In his early childhood, he had the feeling that his parents had unjustly accused him. Later this feeling somehow changed into a deep feeling of self-accusation. He was the bad boy who was causing so much trouble to his parents. A feeling of guilt and inadequacy persisted in spite of the fact that he had acquired a predominantly detached personality. During the psychotic episodes these feelings of guilt, self-hatred and unworthiness disappeared. He had the idea, however, that agents of the FBI were after him, unjustly accusing him of having participated in subversive activities.

Some patients have the feeling that some alleged persecutors control their thoughts. Again, these alleged persecutors are symbolically the parents or the parent-substitutes who control the patient, forcing him to think, that is to view the world, as they wish, as opposed to the way the patient wishes to see it. On a concrete, almost perceptual level, the patient re-experiences what he experienced in his early life. Thus, in these cases, we may distinguish three successive periods:

1) First, the stage of introjection. The action or attitude of the parent is still external, actual, and is being introjected.
2) Second, the stage of assimilation. The child has accepted the attitude of the parent, which has become his own attitude toward himself. He accuses, hates or controls himself as the parents did.

3) Third, the stage of projection, or psychotic stage. The patient rejects and projects back to symbolic parents those attitudes toward himself that he now rejects.

This mechanism of projection may be viewed as the expression of a changing interpersonal relation between the I (the patient) and the *You*. In the first stage the *You* is the parent or parent-substitute; in the second stage the *You* has become that component of the patient himself, which may be called superego, if we adopt Freud's terminology, or the self-image of the bad child, if we follow the concepts expounded in the second part of this book. In the third stage the *You* is the persecutor.

The first stage, or the stage of introjection, is represented by the early period of life of the patient, when the uncanny experiences took place (see page 54). These uncanny experiences are repressed but continue to act on the patient during the second stage, by unconsciously motivating him toward awkward actions and toward distorted interpersonal relations. They participate in making the derogatory self-image much more pronounced and more difficult to tolerate. During the third stage the psychosis tries to eliminate this self-image.

An incomplete form of the above-mentioned mechanism is found in some neurotic, borderline and prepsychotic patients. In these cases the patient continues to accuse, hate, and disparage himself at the same time that he thinks that other people have the same feelings toward him. Thus, there is a partial projection to other people of the feelings which the patient nourishes toward himself, but there is no repudiation of this self-accusatory component of his psyche, that is of the self-image of the bad child. In these instances the mechanism of projection which is arrested before it reaches psychotic proportions consists of the fact that people in general are experienced as authorities and identified with the parents. It does not consist of a return to others of the derogatory self-image. In some of these cases the emotional disturbance to which the patient is subjected is terrific. The *You* is experienced both outside, in the external world, and inside, in the psyche of the patient. If the emotional pressure continues or increases, the patient may find relief only in a psychotic attack, which will remove *the internal You,* that is this unpleasant image of the self.

The fact that the schizophrenic acknowledges the existence of persecutors and enemies implies, one might say, that he makes contact with people and experiences some sort of social integration. That is true to a certain extent. The schizophrenic is capable of functioning at several levels at the same time. When he functions at a social level, it will be easier for him to do so if he sees only a disturbing, condemnatory society around him, because originally he had to adjust to an emotionally similar society in his childhood. In the process of projection he does not use mechanisms derived only from the social level, but also mechanism as low as the perceptualizations of the concepts. He hallucinates and hears the voices of the persecutors.

If I have been able to convey my thoughts, the relationship between what Kanner has so well described in early infantile autism, when the child says, "You want milk" and means "I want milk," and the schizophrenic who hears a voice saying, "You are a criminal," should be clear. In the case of the autistic child, he cannot transform something that he learns from his mother into a part of himself. It remains part of mother; mother would say, "You want milk." In the case of the schizophrenic, he no longer accepts the idea, "I am a bad boy"; a person symbolizing the one who originally attributed that feeling to the patient, is now saying, "You are a criminal." The original accusatory person has become a persecutor and the concept "bad boy" has become "you are a criminal," through paleological and paleosymbolic distortions. Only the presence of an extreme degree of anxiety would make this paleologic transformation possible. This paleologic transformation also has dynamic motivations. It will be easier for the patient to feel and discharge hostility towards these imaginary persecutors, or retaliate against them, than to feel hostility or retaliate against his own parents.

At the same time that the patient rejects these incorporated atttitudes from himself, by projecting them back, another process is taking place. The patient feels free to attribute to himself those attitudes and roles that he wished to give to himself in the past, but could not, because of the checking influence of the surrounding world. Those phantasies about himself which he had when he was young, but which had to be repressed or discarded because they were unrealistic in dealings with others, have the tendency to come back. Now they are accepted by the self, but these attitudes toward one's self are very rich in paleosymbols and use a paleological logic. The patient becomes a millionaire, a king, an inventor. Although these attitudes belong to the paleosymbolic level, they have been influenced to a large extent by the level of the common symbols, because without common symbols there would be no concepts of millionaires, kings, etc.

Nevertheless, it is possible to recognize that what occurs is an autochtonous or asocial expansion of the self (what some authors call a hypertrophy of the ego), which is due to the attributing to the self of attitudes and roles, which are originated by the self itself. These attributes are permitted to expand after the unpleasant attitudes, originally introjected from others, are rejected and projected. That is why the persecutory stage of the paranoid form of schizophrenia is often followed by a stage characterized by delusions of grandeur. At first, these attributes and roles the patient gives to himself show the influence of the common symbols, or, in other words, of the social level. However, the further he regresses from the social level, the more personal and bizarre these roles become.

The symptoms of cataclysmic catastrophe which many patients experience, like the feeling that the world has come to an end, must be considered as a subjective interpretation of expanding desocialization. Things which lose their meanings are, in a certain way, destroyed. At the same time those feelings of ecumenical influence which some patients experience, may be due to the attributing of subjective meanings to everything which surrounds the patient. Everything around becomes in meaning part of the patient, who consequently may feel he is expanding to a cosmic magnitude.

This implies, of course, that this process of desocialization may be arrested, or slowed down, or made more bearable by these restitution phenomena. Patients may remain indefinitely at a level of desocialization in which restitution phenomena are predominant. In many cases, however, the schizophrenic process progresses to a point where it is obvious that desocialization does not mean only enrichment with schizophrenic symptoms, but general impoverishment. As we have mentioned when we were discussing the overlapping of levels (page 290), many symptoms continue to exploit material belonging to levels from which the patient has predominantly withdrawn. Paleosymbols for instance are never pure expression of the paleologic level. When the patient says that she is the Virgin Mary she uses common symbols in a paleologic way. It is because paleosymbols are not pure, but retain remnants of the social level, that we are able to understand them. If it would not be so it would be almost impossible to understand schizophrenia. But as the illness progresses, even the invasion of social symbols at a paleosymbolic level decreases and the degree of the mental impoverishment of the patient manifests itself in its appalling grandeur. The more he divests himself of common symbols, the more difficult it is for the patient to take the roles of other people and the roles that he felt others assigned to him. This impoverishment reveals how much of man is actually made of social life. When what was obtained from others is eliminated man remains an insignificant residue of what he used to be.

Previously it was assumed that the more desocialized the patient is, the more he loses the benefits of his interchanges with society. This is true, but it is not all; he loses more than that. By desocializing he loses a great part of himself. This loss is compensated to a minimal degree by the individualistic restitution symptoms, but this compensation is inadequate and in many cases transitory. To be alone, as the schizophrenic is, does not mean only to be without others, but to be less of himself. The meaning of loneliness, as experienced even by normal people and by neurotics (a problem which has been psychiatrically approached for the first time by Fromm-Reichman [106]) may be fully understood, in my opinion, if we think of the tragic effect of desocialization in schizophrenia. Loneliness means fear of losing oneself partially or totally. This meaning reveals itself fully in the panoramic dimensions and in the intensity of the schizophrenic devastation; but the ghost of loneliness which haunts normal people too, may include, to a minimal degree, some of the qualities of these extreme and ultimate consequences.

This brings up another problem. The schizophrenic is *alone* in his world, but is he *lonely?* Recovered schizophrenics state that they felt terribly lonely when they were sick and there is no ground for thinking that this is a retrospective falsification. However, the fear of interpersonal relations is even stronger than loneliness. It is one of the major tasks of psychotherapy to make such fear less powerful than the desire to establish contacts with other human beings.

CHAPTER XII

The Retreat from Emotions

I. Emotional Impairment and Repression

At this point another important facet of the multifarious schizophrenic picture must be considered: the decrease or absence of affective manifestations. We shall begin again with descriptive notes.

The patient seems indifferent to his surroundings; no emotions appear on his face. He hears good news or bad news, and seems to react to them to a minimum degree or not at all. There is a great discrepancy or incongruity between the retention of his intellectual faculties and the loss of affective responses. At an advanced stage of the illness, he seems to have completely lost the capacity to feel. The picture is even more complicated. At times some affect is retained but appears inadequate or inappropriate. The patient is over-concerned about what may seem trivialities to the observer, whereas he may remain indifferent to something of the greatest importance. Even more amazing is the fact that patients who seem to have lost their capacity for affect, may regain it to a considerable extent, or entirely, for a brief period of time or permanently.

How can all of these manifestations be explained? The easiest way to explain them is by again invoking the mechanism of repression. The patient wants so much to avoid all these unpleasant feelings that he has to dissociate them from consciousness. In other words, the schizophrenic would react or continue to react as he did when he was a detached person, aloof and schizoid, except that he does it in an even more pronounced manner. The schizophrenic, like the schizoid, wants to deny the emotional impact of the external world, because it is too unbearable and irreconcilable with his inner world. All of this is true, but not enough. Again, we should not confuse the dynamic with the formal mechanisms, which occur at the same time. In the psychosis not only is there repression, but also there are distortions and transformations which automatically eliminate emotions as the normal person experiences them. I do not wish to imply here that there is a hard and fast difference between the mechanism of repression and detachment and that of distortion. They blend together and may be found in both neurotics and psychotics, though in different proportions.

The majority of authors and observers agree that in schizophrenia, not only is there less repression than in psychoneuroses, but the opposite often takes place. What is generally well repressed in the neurotic or the normal person, tends to come to the surface in this psychosis. The mechanisms of repression or of making things unconscious, do not seem to function too well in schizophrenia. The blunting of affect therefore, cannot be attributed solely to them. The reason why the mechanisms of repression do not function too well is that they would have too much work to do; too many unpleasant things would have to be repressed. The patient has tried to do so before becoming psychotic, but has failed. Now additional mechanisms are needed. Now the repressed emotions and ideas tend to come to the surface, in the form they originally had, or after having undergone distortion, that is, symbolic transformation. This symbolic transformation, of course, occurs in neuroses too, but not to the extent that it occurs in schizophrenia. In addition, in schizophrenia it involves the external world much more than in neuroses. As has already been mentioned and described numerous times, this transformation takes place by the adoption of archaic mental mechanisms.

But here another apparent paradox must strike the reader. We have repeatedly said that these archaic mechanisms, such as paleologic and paleosymbols, are much richer in emotional content than the usual mechanisms used by the normal person. Would it not then follow that the schizophrenic should be much more emotional than the normal person, whereas the opposite seems to occur? This problem, indeed, is complex and seems self-contradictory. I do not pretend to have found the final solution, but I dare to suggest some possibilities.

II. Relation Between Emotional Impairment and Desymbolization. The Individuality of the Schizophrenic Manifesting Itself as a Frustrated Artistic Propensity.

Lack of emotional responses is, to a great extent, implicit in the other mechanisms that we have already taken into consideration. When the patient loses his common symbols and therefore desocializes himself, it is impossible for him to have any emotional reaction to these common symbols. In other words, he does not *repress* the emotions; he cannot *experience* them. It is true that originally he did not want to experience them and therefore he repressed them, but in a second stage he desymbolizes himself, or transforms the common symbols into paleosymbols. Many conventional emotions or emotional reactions that society expects are lost, and are replaced by other emotions which appear bizarre and inappropriate to us, only because we cannot share them. The patient, however, does experience emotions when he uses paleosymbols. The following is just an approximate comparison. If a Western man went, let us say, into a Buddhist temple, while a religious ceremony was taking place, this man probably would watch the ceremony almost as an anthropologist would, that is, with some kind of cultural interest, but with emotional detachment. The other people in the temple, if they could forget that he was a Western man, would think that his emotional reactions were inappropriate. That man would not seem to be touched at all by the austerity and the holiness of the ceremony. He would not respond emotionally to their symbols. The schizophrenic is in a similar situation, or rather in a much worse one, because he has lost the ability to transport himself artificially into a set of values other than his own. However, when the patient is in his own symbolic world, he may react with very deep emotions. We have all noticed how distressed the patients really are by the alleged persecutors, and by hallucinations. Retention of these emotional responses is prognostically good, because it means that the patient has not regressed beyond a predominantly paleosymbolic level.

It is common experience, however, that the patient later seems to lose emotions even for the complexes in which he is paleosymbolically concerned. Persecutors and voices seem to leave him indifferent. As we mentioned before, this fact is even more difficult to understand because archaic mechanisms are supposed to be rich in emotional content.

The patient is not well integrated at the paleosymbolic level; in order to escape from the anxiety caused by this poor integration he will regress much more. This point will be explained in much more detail in Chapter XVIII, when we shall consider the mechanism of progressive regression.* At a certain stage of regression, paleosymbols remain the highest type of thinking for the patient. Progressively deprived of emotional symbols by taking refuge in lower and lower levels of integration, he becomes more and more incomprehensible to us.

The poor integration of the patient at a paleosymbolic or paleologic level is also disclosed by the study of his artistic activities, where he shows that he cannot use his poorly integrated paleosymbols efficiently. Both the normal artist and the schizophrenic are highly emotional and individualistic. It is this emotional and individualistic quality which predisposes them to artistic work. They use expressive media, like language, music, painting, etc. which do not faithfully reproduce what they observe or get from the external world. Through these expressions, they want the unique, creative, non-compliant part of their personality to emerge. Both the artist and the schizophrenic use archaic mechanisms, such as rhythms, alliteration, metaphors, images, paleosymbols, etc. However, there is a fundamental difference. The artist uses archaic mechanisms, but is able to integrate them, to blend them in the system of common social symbols, whereas the schizophrenic cannot. The artist would not be able to convey his new creative point of view to society, unless he also used a system of symbols which is more or less shared by the people to whom he conveys the message.

If my views are correct, artistic work is an adaptation of the original creative, individualistic experience to the set of symbols of society. Of course, this adaptation is not always carried out to the same degree. Imitative art cares much more about this adaptation than modern art. An adaptation, how-

---

* Lack of emotional expression which originate at a subcortical level will be discussed on page 428.

ever, is always necessary to a greater or lesser degree; otherwise the artistic work would remain incomprehensible.

For instance, a schizophrenic says, "Hang a hanger for
a kangeroo." We note the alliteration and the assonance in
this sentence, but the meaning is obscure. Benjamin Franklin
says, "If we don't hang together, we shall hang separately."
He uses a similar play of words, but is also able to convey a
meaning in a very original way. Franklin's pun is artistically
powerful. The repeated use of the word "hang" with different
meanings gives to the sentence a tone of strength, very appropriate to the intensity of the situation in which this sentence
was used, as well as a touch of healthy humor. The schizophrenic cannot integrate his archaic symbols, except maybe
at a level where only the pleasure of the assonance is sought.

What we have learned in the previous chapter about
desocialization will also help us to understand the differences
and the similarities between the artist and the schizophrenic.
The artist, as well as other creative persons, allows himself
to be alone and lonely, but only to a degree which facilitates
the emergence of his individuality, not to a degree which
necessitates actual desocialization. In another publication the
author hopes to illustrate more clearly esthetic theories which
have been conceived in studying psychiatric phenomena.

At this point we cannot omit the explanation of an apparent contradiction which may have puzzled the reader. The
reader might think: The author states that the schizophrenic
is extremely individualistic, does not want to accept the world
of his parents and therefore of his society, and wants to retain
his unique paleosymbols and his unique paleologic. Since he
describes the laws of paleologic and paleosymbols, which
apply to all paleologic or paleosymbolic thought, is not that
a contradiction? Is he not talking again of formality which
applies to all people regressed to a certain level, and not of
individuality, uniqueness? Is he not changing the universals

of Aristotelian logic and of the common symbols to the universals of paleologic and paleosymbols? How is that to be reconciled with the assumption of "uniqueness"?

Similar objection was made by Benedetto Croce to Giambattista Vico (56). Croce wrote that in his conclusions about the studies of ancient people, Vico had changed Plato's universals with "phantastic universals" (corresponding approximately to our paleologic universals). There is some truth in this allegation, since there cannot be any content without some kind of formal mechanism, and any kind of formal mechanism is subject to laws. Perhaps the works of the abstract painters come closest to being expressions of a content without form, but some form exists in their works too.

However, one could say without hesitation that one's originality and individuality, as far as the formal structure is concerned, is better expressed by archaic mechanisms, and for various reasons. First of all, there are many of them, corresponding to the various levels that humanity went through, and the schizophrenic and the artist may use any or several of them. Secondly, paleologic, to a great extent, is based on Von Domarus' principle. Now this principle is, or appears to our Aristotelian minds, as a principle or as a law; actually, it gives the most possible freedom to the individual. A subject may have an infinite number of predicates; it is up to the individuality of the person to select the predicate for the identification.

It is true that schizophrenics appear similar to us, and we are able to detect common symptoms in them. It is because of these common symptoms that we are able to recognize them. Actually their realm of originality exceeds by far that of the normal man. Paradoxically they seem similar to us because they are original, and because they don't use our methods of thinking. They are similar in their difference from us, as all Chinese may appear similar to white men. Being unable to understand the originality of the content of their expressions and actions, we tend to emphasize the frequent occurrence of the few formal mechanisms which we understand. Paradoxically, it is by adopting *universal* forms that the individuality of the patient, with its specific dynamic determinants, is allowed to emerge.

When the schizophrenic produces artistic works, his lack of integration is obvious. His works may have some similarity to works of modern artists, because the latter don't use common symbols as much as traditional artists, but the difference is important. No blendings of abstract concepts are visible in the work of the schizophrenic. The separate parts are put together, at times, in a sort of visual word-salad. Concepts are not reintegrated, but remain separate and inappropriate, as in the drawing reproduced in fig. 1, where athletic women have incongruously masculine physical characteristics. The desire to be a man or the feeling that these sporting women are like men, is awkwardly and unrealistically concretized in this picture, made by a hebephrenic woman. When this patient regressed further, her drawings became much more disorganized as in fig. 2, where profiles are hardly recognizable. The extreme uniqueness of the feelings and concepts of the patients is not corrected and is allowed to be represented in what appears to us a very bizarre manner. (See, for instance, figs. 3 and 4, drawings performed by a moderately regressed paranoid woman.)

CHAPTER XIII

The Schizophrenic Process. General Interpretation

In this part of the book we have considered several mechanisms by which the schizophrenic, in his attempt to avoid or to decrease anxiety, escapes from reality.

The mechanisms to which we have attached particular importance are the adoption of a special type of thinking called paleologic, the processes of desymbolization and desocialization, and the retreat from emotions. We have also examined the mechanism of escape from actions, especially in the catatonic, when introjected psychological causality was discussed. The process of limitation which occurs particularly in the simple type of schizophrenia was also mentioned briefly. Other mechanisms which as yet have not been noted, will be discussed in Part Four. Of course, it is not only possible, but certain, that other mechanisms have escaped the attention of the author. Other authors may differentiate other mechanisms or see the same mechanisms from another point of view. It may be correctly implied that this fragmentation of the schizophrenic psychopathology in different mechanisms is arbitrary and artificial. The various mechanisms which have been described and interpreted may be not just mutually dependent, but different expressions of the same basic process. In spite of this, it is not regrettable that the schizophrenic process had to be segmented in this way. In order for it to be understood as thoroughly as possible, in all its complicated aspects, there was no other way. At this point, however, we must ask ourselves the question: What is the basic process, if any, which manifests itself in so many different forms?

When we say "the basic process," we do not mean an organic process. The reader is reminded that, at this point, we are considering this matter exclusively from a psychological point of view. One may conclude that the schizophrenic process consists of impairment, in various degrees, of the ability to abstract. All the manifestations may be seen as a consequence of this impairment. For instance, let us again consider Von Domarus' principle. Why are two subjects identified when they have a predicate in common? It is only because of the inability to abstract or to separate that common predicate from the two subjects. The inability to abstract the common quality leads to the identification of the two subjects. In the process of abstraction a part or a quality is separated from the whole. In paleologic thinking this separation is not possible: the presence of the part evokes either the whole situation, or any other part of the situation. In a certain way, this process may explain mechanisms even as low as the simple conditioned reflex. The sound of the bell causes secretion of the gastric juice in the dog. The ringing of the bell has the same effect as the situation of which the ringing of the bell is just a part. In other words, the ringing of the bell produces the same effect that the situation "ringing of the bell plus presence of the food" engenders.

The paleologic level is higher than the level of the conditioned reflex, because an attempt is made not to reproduce the total situation, but to connect two different subjects from different contexts. The ability to make this attempt, although it implies a higher evolutionary level, leads to innumerable mistakes, which were not possible at the level of the conditioned reflex (level of the signs). The inability to abstract prevents the use of common symbols, which are nothing more than abstractions. The absence of abstractions thus prevents socialization and the experience of all those emotions which are connected with belonging to an integrated society. The lack of common symbols does not permit the patient to project himself into the future, and also handicaps him in his attempts to interpret reality with the principle of physical causality. To summarize, all the symptoms that we have described and explained in this part of the book may be reduced, in the final analysis, to impairment in a greater or lesser degree of what Goldstein calls the abstract attitude (112–114).

We may thus reach the following conclusion: Schizophrenia is a specific reaction to a severe state of anxiety, originating in childhood, reexperienced and increased in some later period of life. The specificity of this reaction consists in the *teleologic* or *motivational use* of a more or less advanced impairment of the abstract attitude.

Perhaps this is a relatively good definition of schizophrenia at this stage of our knowledge. However, I am sure that many readers will join the author in not being completely satisfied with it. It tends too much to give emphasis to the basic psychological process, and to minimize the important mechanisms which we have interpreted and which have really made us follow and feel the phenomena. In a certain way, it would be like saying that all the movements that we can study on earth are a more or less indirect influence of the force of gravity. That statement may be correct, but should not distract us from studying the specific movements, their interrelations and their laws. A good interpretation or definition of a basic psychological process must consider not only the negative aspect of the problem (in this case, the impairment of the abstract attitude) but also must attempt an explanation of the positive symptoms. For instance, by knowing only that there is an impairment of abstract attitude in schizophrenia, how could we understand the word-salad? How could we figure out why a patient said "White House" instead of George Washington?

The extreme state of anxiety and the teleologic impairment of the abstract attitude have a unique welding in schizophrenia. We have seen that the anxiety and its development in life tend to assume patterns which differ from those observed in psychoneuroses. On the other hand, the impairment of the abstract attitude found in schizophrenia differs from the impairment found in organic conditions. It differs first in the fact that it tends to be progressive. Why it tends to be progressive we shall study in Part IV of this book. Secondly it differs inasmuch as it is even more teleologic, that is, it *has the purposes of avoiding anxiety at the same time that it permits the uniqueness of the individual to emerge.* It is true that in organic cases, too, as Goldstein has demonstrated, the patient tries to avoid the anxiety of the catastrophic reaction. However, the catastrophic reaction is due to the anxiety caused by the limitations which derive from the organic impairment. In schizophrenia the threat is, or at least starts, as external or interpersonally engendered anxiety and limitations.

The other purposive characteristic is to make possible the emergence of the uniqueness of the individual. As Goldstein has written, the impairment of the abstract attitude of the schizophrenic is not only a return, more or less, to perceptual concreteness, as it is in organic cases, but in addition to that has the effect of introducing an originality of performance. The psychopath, too, through his symptomatology, emerges as an individual. However, for such an emergence he resorts to an *antisocial* pattern, whereas the schizophrenic resorts to an *asocial* one, that is, to one which requires a greater or lesser amount of desocialization. That individuality which the schizophrenic repressed when he succumbed to the malevolent influence of others is recaptured to a certain extent through the use of this impairment of the abstract attitude. To find himself again as an individual, he has to become psychotic.

PART FOUR

*A Longitudinal View
of Schizophrenia*

CHAPTER XIV

The First or Initial Stage

1. Introductory Remarks. Sequence of Early Substages. "Psychotic Insight." The Logical Reinforcement of the Paranoid.

In the previous sections of this book, schizophrenia has been examined from the point of view of its dynamics and of its formal psychological structure. We shall now study the psychosis from the point of view of its progression, meaning progression toward regression. Of the four outcomes of schizophrenia (recovery, improvement, arrest, regression), it is only the latter course which will be taken into consideration here. Although Kraepelin himself gave great significance to the progress of the illness, to such a point that all his concepts about this condition were influenced by it, this progression itself has not been studied longitudinally.

The difficulty in studying schizophrenia from a longitudinal point of view is implicit in the long duration of the illness. Many psychiatrists focus their attention on the initial stages, which respond better to any type of treatment. On the other hand, psychiatrists working in state hospitals do not see the prepsychotic or early psychotic stages. Meyer's longitudinal approach also is not complete inasmuch as it studies the patient from his birth to the onset of the psychosis, but does not study in detail the progression of the illness after its onset. Another difficulty in the longitudinal study of schizophrenia is its multiform clinical course, not comparable to that of any other known disease or condition. In fact, the same stage of regression which is reached by a patient in a period of a few days or weeks, may be reached by another patient in a period of over half a century. A third difficulty consists of the fact, so well known, that different levels of regression do not appear in any case in pure culture, any case presenting a mixture of several stages. It is only by artificial abstraction that we may reconstruct the individual stages.

Kraepelin spoke of progressive *deterioration*. Although he considered this characteristic of schizophrenia the fundamental one, he could not go beyond a descriptive approach, because he did not use the Freudian concept of *regression*. Therefore, he emphasized the type of symptomatology rather than the stage of the illness. It was more important for him to distinguish the three types, catatonic, hebephrenic and paranoid, than to attempt to individualize any stage. Later he added the simple type, after Bleuler. As was seen in the second and third parts of this book, these divisions in the four subtypes were accepted in the present study, not purely from a descriptive point of view, but also because they indicate the prevalence of specific dynamic and formal mechanisms. However, I feel that it is also important to divide the illness in four successive stages: the initial, the advanced, the preterminal, and the terminal. Therapeutically this distinction has no application at the present time and, from a prognostic point of view its value is limited, because, although it is ascertained that patients in the initial stage have a much better chance of recovery, it is also true that patients in the terminal stage of the illness may improve and recover in rare cases. The separate study of the different stages, however, may further clarify the intricacies of the disorder.

In this part of the book we shall accompany the patient from the initial stage of the overt psychosis to the terminal. As he progresses from one stage to the following, he will be seen less and less in an interpersonal context and more and more in isolation, wrapped in his own symptoms, within the walls of the psychiatric institution. Those interpersonal relations which were of so much significance when we studied the prepsychotic stages, lose importance when the patient succeeds in finding the path of progressive regression. The interpersonal relations of the past continue to act through the distortions they still engender, but the impact of new relations is diminishing progressively. That is not what we want, of course. If the few remaining interpersonal relations were studied and corrected, as done by Stanton and Schwartz (242, 243), or if the patients were exposed to a kind of "milieu therapy," as suggested by Rioch and Stanton (218), and to conditions as they exist in Chestnut Lodge Sanitarium, it would be much more difficult for many of them to follow the pattern described in this part of this book. The author hopes that one day the conditions described in Chapters XV, XVI, XVII will be things of the past, as the patients will not be allowed to go beyond the initial stage of the disorder. At the present time we must admit that these conditions occur, and that we must face and study them, in order to combat them more efficiently.

In this chapter we shall discuss only the initial stage of the disorder. How does the overt psychosis start? Of course, in numerous possible ways. In many cases, the beginning is slow, insidious and passes unnoticed. This is almost always the case in the simple type. On the other hand, in the other three types, the beginning may be either slow, acute, or very acute. We shall examine here only acute cases which lend themselves better to didactical purposes.

After a long period in which the patient tries by any available means to defend himself from his anxiety a period of panic follows. He is not able to cope with the situation any longer; he does not know what to do. This state of panic is precipitated at times by an apparently insignificant episode. I mention here the case of a veteran whom I saw only three times. He had great difficulty in readjusting to civilian life, and was uncertain as to whether he should reenlist in the army or not. He was engaged to be married, but had no position. At the end of the second session he felt that he did not want any more treatment, and I was not able to persuade him to continue, in spite of exerting some pressure. He felt that his only difficulty was the lack of an occupation and that once he found a job every difficulty in his life would be solved. One of the reasons given for discontinuing treatment was that he had to go out of town to visit wealthy and prominent relatives who probably would offer him a good position. There were no psychotic symptoms at this time. Three months later I received a telephone call from his wife. She said that the patient was very ill and that I must see him immediately. The patient and his wife came to my office. I saw the wife first, who gave me the following history. She and the patient had been married a month previously. His relatives had not kept their promises, but the patient had had several odd jobs, and everything seemed to be all right. Two days previously, the patient had secured a position as a bus driver. The very morning that she called me, her husband had had a minor accident; his bus had collided with a car. No one was hurt, but the car was damaged. The damage would probably amount to two or three hundred dollars. She said that since the time of the accident, which had occurred about seven hours previously, the patient had been excited, restless, and had talked non-sense. The night before, they had talked about their future plans and they had been very happy. The wife was pregnant, and they had been talking about the expected baby. According to the wife, the husband had shown no abnormality whatsoever. The trouble had started all of a sudden after the accident. When I saw the patient, he was restless and excited. He recognized that something very important was disturbing him, but he was not able to say what it was. During the interview my phone rang twice. Each time he thought that some people were calling me concerning him. They must be after him. They must know where he is. Because he heard the voice of a woman at the end of the line, he assumed that it was the voice of his aunt. She was talking to me about him. He did not know what was happening. Everything was confused, strange and moving. The following are some of his productions, taken verbatim: "The world is going very fast; it keeps spinning on an axe, but keeps going. If the people of the world are going a little faster, they try to go with the world, and they shouldn't. It is my desperate opinion that the people are rushing slowly and slowly and when they reach a certain point they start to realize that they are going fast or slow, and they cannot be judges of the world as it is spinning. The world has changed, is going fast, keeps going, going. I couldn't keep up with it."

I recommended immediate hospitalization. The patient was hospitalized in a Veterans Hospital, received shock therapy, and I heard later that he had made a seemingly complete recovery. Since I had seen this patient only three times, I was not in a position to make a complete dynamic evaluation of the case. Possibly any other anxiety-producing incident would have precipitated the psychosis at this point in the life of the patient. After returning from the Army, he had made an attempt to adjust to civilian life. The old personal difficulties, which were not manifested as long as he was in the Army, made this adjustment not an easy one. At the same time that his difficulties increased, the demands made on him complicated the situation. He felt that as soon as possible he should marry the girl to whom he had been engaged for a long time and who had waited for his return. His relatives disappointed him, and his dependency on them was frustrated. Finally, he secured a good position as a bus driver, and two days later had an accident. He realized that he would lose his position, and this realization reinforced his deep feeling of worthlessness. Whether he unconsciously provoked the accident, we are not in a position to say; of course, such a possibility exists. After the accident he broke down. The accident was to him the proof of his inherent inadequacy, especially since he gave so much importance to having a job. Almost all his security was precariously founded on his having a position. Now nobody would have any confidence in him. The relatives were right in not trusting him with a job. He was hopeless; he was not able to keep pace with life.

This case shows how a simple event may induce or unchain a psychosis, when the ground is ready for it, of course. Since we know so little about this patient, we cannot understand the fundamental issue, that is, why he was so vulnerable that even the accident, in itself not at all a serious one, was capable of eliciting a major mental disorder. In order to understand the vulnerability of this patient we would have to know his detailed life history. This case is nevertheless valuable for didactical purposes, because it shows that a few hours after the clear-cut onset of the acute attack, the schizophrenic symptoms were already very pronounced. The patient's thoughts were disorganized. He saw the world in a different way, going fast, so fast that he could not cope with its movements. The abstract feeling of inadequacy was concretized in his not being able, in a physical sense, to keep up with the movements of the world. The accident with the car probably provided the idea of the movement. Ideas of reference were already in full swing and paranoid concepts were developing. He already saw things in a different, confusing way, and was making an attempt to reinterpret reality.

Less acute onsets occur when the patient feels unable to satisfy excessive compulsions and falls into a state of panic. Another possible subacute onset is characterized by the realization on the part of the patient that lately something has been happening to him. He is confused, disturbed, and afraid that he is becoming insane. It is almost as if he were fighting against this tendency to become mentally ill. A little later he is afraid that people will recognize that he is becoming insane. Subsequently, he cannot resist the break any longer, and he gives vent to full-fledged psychotic symptoms. Often, very early after the psychotic break, he is still confused, and does not understand things clearly. At times he feels that people are acting out a play to confuse him. The world becomes a big stage. This feeling that the world is a stage, experienced by the early schizophrenic who gets worse, is almost the opposite of a feeling that many manic-depressive patients experience when they get better. The manic-depressive who is recovering often feels that he really has not been so sick, but that he himself (not the surrounding world) has been acting in order to appear sick.

The schizophrenic in the midst of the confusion may have something like a sudden flash of insight. All of a sudden he understands things. His confusion is at least partially eliminated because he accepts his psychotic interpretation of the world.

The following case clearly illustrates the initial substages of the illness. I saw this patient just once for a check-up about five years after he had recovered from an acute attack. At the time of my examination, he seemed to have made a

satisfactory adjustment, he was happy, and he did not seem
to remember anything about the acute episode that he had
experienced while he was in military service. The adjustment,
satisfactory in every area which was considered, made me feel
very optimistic from a prognostic point of view.

The history of this patient revealed that while he was in
the service, after he had made attempts to be discharged on
the basis of hardship for the family, he had developed an
acute episode characterized by hallucinations and delusions.
He misidentified people and felt that through television "they"
were keeping track of his movements. He had somatic complaints and was argumentative. He received a course of electric shock treatments, developed amnesia for the episode, and
made an apparently complete recovery. A few days after the
onset of the psychosis, he had written a letter to his family,
which described the beginning of his attack very well. Here
are some excerpts from his letter:

". . . . I entered the hospital and was admitted in Ward
1 for feet trouble, or better to cure a "wart" as they call
it on my right foot. Well, to my surprise on the tenth
day that I spent there the doctor made such a grim to
me, that it finally dawned on me that I was there not for
feet but for mental observation, the feet must have been
just an excuse of which I was ignorant until then. When
I discovered that, my first thought was to get out of the
place; finally on the 12th day I was allowed to leave and
it was Saturday. As I got out, the first breath of air that
I inhaled made me feel as though I came out of a prison.
At any rate, while waiting for the bus two fellows that I
knew . . . picked me up and brought me to my squadron
. . . they left me in front of my barrack and left; looking
up, I saw that everybody was dressed and were going to
the ramp on parade . . . I sat waiting for the parade to be
over. When they finally came back my first thought was
to go to the orderly room to ask about a furlough which

I had been waiting from week to week. The next thing
I remember at 12 o'clock I had to report on the line for
duty which I did. There, to my surprise I felt out of
place, fellows spoke to me but it didn't make much
sense to me. I remember I got a splitting headache, at
that time all the aeroplanes were gone cross country,
there were very few left on the line. I went back to my
squadron all puzzled and yet I was unable to figure it
out.

The following day I went back on the line. They put
me to work, but to my amazement I realized that I had
forgotten to do the simplest things on an engine. Everybody looked at me with some sort of sneeer. Then I was
asked to stand fire guard on a plane; a certain sergeant
. . . asked for a loan of $5 and another fellow asked for
a loan of $2 to whom I gave. At night I heard lots of
planes warming up engines on the ramp, everything
seemed to be very noisy, cars coming and going and
motorcycles. Everything in my surroundings seemed very
strange, it just didn't make any sense. I used to go to
the general hall almost afraid of everything. In the
barrack one evening I heard some real beautiful music
which I enjoyed very much, yet to my eyes everybody
didn't seem very friendly.

The following morning I was made room orderly,
cleaned all the barrack downstairs and upstairs; for some
reason I knew that everybody thought I was crazy, I sat
on the stoop and tried very hard to hold myself from
crying, I cleaned the barrack extra just to show them I
wasn't crazy and that I was as normal as others.

One night or perhaps in the early morning I felt as
though my brain came back to me, it felt like little par-
ticles of sand going back in its place. The airplanes were
still going on the ramp and I began to think. I try to find
out what it was all about. All of a sudden I thought that
the two extremes, too much quiet in the hospital and too
much noise on the line, were the cause of it all. I got

dressed and I went right back to the hospital and tell them what my trouble was. There to my surprise they didn't pay much attention to my saying and I went back to the squadron. On the way to the hall I thought some more and having in mind the expression of the doctor in the hospital, that noise of the aeroplanes which I don't think had ever heard before, it stroke my mind that it was no longer an accident but had been done purposely. I remembered this sergeant . . . ask me on the line if I wanted a discharge; well, then I put 2 and 2 together and I no longer thought but knew that the reason for the entire affair was just for that. In reality I was always preoccupied about home, my wife and child although they were in my father's house, yet that thought of me being in the army while many other married men were out really discomforted me. I wished I was out myself . . . .

Then I found myself in Room #6; here too I heard lots of noise, my mind has been on and off; I got to the point where I believed in many things, autos coming and going, birds, especially one to signify my wife, another to signify my penis, etc., etc., etc. Here I have seen my father and mother and two sisters, seen my wife twice; once on Oct. 12 a date which I shall not forget; my mind wasn't my own and I didn't even move to meet her. From room #6 I was moved in back of the ward, then I had a fight with a sergeant and am presently under guard."

This letter remains an accurate document of the sequence of the events at the beginning of the psychosis. The fact that in this letter the distortions are not pronounced makes the understanding of the early development of the psychosis easier. Being in the armed forces apparently caused the patient a great deal of apprehension, and reinforced his anxiety. He had made attempts to be discharged, and had not succeeded.

Of course, we do not have any preceding history of the patient and therefore we do not know why he should be so vulnerable. For reasons which have not been determined, he could not adjust; the anxiety became intolerable and overwhelmed his defenses, and he became psychotic. His letter describes very well the dream-like atmosphere of the first few days of the attack. It reminds one of Kafka's novels.

During these first few days things started to appear funny, peculiar, confused, dream-like to him. When he reported for duty, after being discharged from the ward, he felt out of place; what people said made no sense, and they seemed to look at him in a sneering manner. Everything seemed changed, everybody was unfriendly; he was afraid, and felt that people thought he was insane.

After this first impression of confusion, bizarreness, and apprehension, the patient progressed to another stage. He felt that his brain was "coming back" to him. Things which were happening were no longer accidental, but had been done *purposely*. He put "two and two" together and everything became clear to him. The feeling of being insane was discarded; he acquired, as in a flash, what I call "psychotic insight." In his system of reference, everything became understandable. He was able to fit things together.

Thus, we have seen a sequence of stages: first, a period of intense anxiety and panic; second, a period of confusion, when everything seems strange and crazy; and third, a period of psychotic insight. When this psychotic insight occurs, the external world is understood according to a new system of thinking, which, of course, follows the motivational trends of the patient. Often when this psychotic insight occurs, *the patient experiences a feeling of being exceptionally lucid*. He feels that he never has thought as clearly and effectively as he is doing now. Such an impression is occasionally conveyed to the layman.

In the catatonic type of schizophrenia, the period of psychotic insight is replaced by the catatonic state.

After this very beginning of the psychosis, the usual symptoms of schizophrenia flourish: hallucinations, delusions, ideas of reference, catatonic posture, etc. These symptoms will not be described here. We shall limit ourselves to some general comments on the directions that symptoms may take. The patient has now lost the battle for the supremacy of his consciousness and logical thinking. If he follows the catatonic pattern it is because he is overwhelmed by fear of actions. If he follows the hebephrenic path, he is swayed by the unconscious forces which will make him resort to paleologic thinking. If he selects the paranoid way, it is because he mobilizes the remaining conscious and logical forces in the service of his unconscious. That is, he will use the logical forces to corroborate and to sustain feelings and ideas which are emotionally determined and paleologically conceived. When only the logical thinking is obvious and not the paleological, we have that picture which Kraepelin called paranoia. Inasmuch as some paleologic thinking is almost always present, a paranoid rather than a paranoiac picture is generally observed. In paranoia no archaic mechanisms appear; the real emotional motivation is being repressed and masqueraded by an extremely well elaborated logical defence. The paranoiac resorts to logic rather than to primitive mechanisms; he resorts to a faulty logic too, however, because he makes the fundamental error of assuming for truth what is only a possibility. He selects only those possibilities which fit into his system of preconceived ideas; then he tries to demonstrate the validity of his preconceived ideas, with the support of the possibilities he selects. This vicious circle soon generates delusional thinking, at times, of tremendous proportions. In the well-systematized paranoid, both the logical and paleological systems or, if we prefer the orthodox Freudian terminology, both the ego and the id are at the service of the psychosis.

This *logical reinforcement* of delusional and paleological material at times reaches fantastic heights. Even in the beginning of the illness, the patient tries to give a logical appearance to phenomena which he experiences and which he himself recognizes as illogical. If he hears voices and does not know how the voices may reach him, he tries to explain the phenomenon by believing that hidden radios or loud speakers transmit the messages. Hidden dictaphones or "wired" rooms record everything he says, does, or even thinks. In past centuries, when these modern inventions did not exist, psychotics explained their hallucinatory phenomena in terms of magic, sorcery, spiritism, etc., or, in other words, in terms which could have been acceptable in those days. In the hebephrenic type this need for apparent logicality is absent or greatly diminished. The patient accepts the delusional material without being concerned with the demonstration of its validity.

The fundamental characteristic of this stage of schizophrenia, of any type, is that the patient has not as yet reached a state of equilibrium in spite of his symptoms. The symptomatology may change, not only toward more or less regression, but also from one of the four major types to another. Thus, occasionally we see sequences of this kind occurring. A patient who, in the beginning of the psychosis, has a paranoid symptomatology, may all of a sudden change into a catatonic state. Subsequently he may become decatatonized, and exhibit paranoid symptoms again. These changes indicate that the patient searches every possible pattern in order to escape anxiety. The search, however, is for pathological mechanisms, and unless fortunate circumstances take place, these changes are not necessarily hopeful signs.

In many patients, but especially in paranoids, the symptoms are such as to elicit unfavorable reactions in others, which, in turn, will increase the anxiety of the patient. A vicious circle is thus established.

II. Prognostic Criteria

It is during the initial stage of the illness that the problem of prognosis acquires particular significance. In fact, although remissions are possible and occur at any stage of the illness, the chance of recovery or remission is much greater if the patient has not gone beyond the first stage.

The course of each case is unpredictable; no one can be absolutely sure of what pattern a given patient will choose. However, it has been found that a certain group of symptoms and factors tend to occur more frequently in patients who recover and that other symptoms and factors tend to occur in patients who get worse instead. It is therefore useful to examine certain characteristics of the initial stage which have a prognostic significance.

Conscious anxiety is an important symptom. The fact that no stability has been reached and that anxiety has not been eliminated, in spite of the presence of the psychosis, may be a positive sign, inasmuch as it invites the patient to leave this state and to go back to reality, especially under the effect of treatment. On the other hand, it may induce the patient to go into a state of deeper regression. If the paranoiac and the paranoid are very anxious, they will mobilize more and more logical and paleological mechanisms to convince themselves of their new "reality." The hebephrenic will become more and more grandiose and disconnected, the catatonic more and more immobile. When the paranoid, forced by his anxiety, uses an increasing number of logical defences, he may remain at this initial stage for a long period of time, possibly for the rest of his life.

Fig. 1: Drawing made by a female hebephrenic patient. Athletic women have masculine physical traits.

Fig. 2: Another drawing by the same patient, at a much more advanced stage of regression. The disorganization is so marked that the profiles are hardly recognizable.

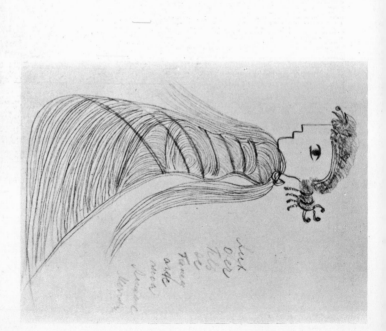

Figs. 3 and 4: Drawings made by a moderately regressed paranoid woman. The individuality of feelings and concepts is represented in a bizarre manner.

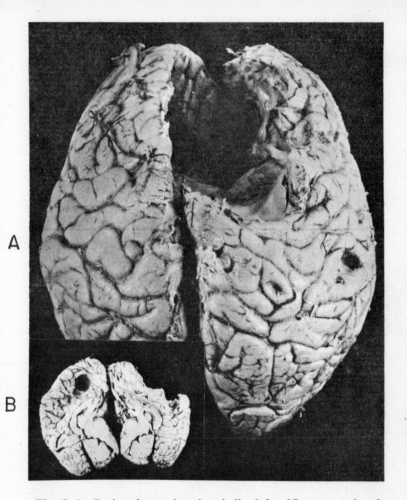

A

B

Fig. 5 a): Brain of a patient hospitalized for 27 years under the diagnosis of the hebephrenic type of dementia praecox. The brain is seen dorsally after a huge encapsulated fibroblastic meningioma and a small one have been removed. The larger tumor had replaced most of the right frontal lobe and, to a lesser degree, the left frontal lobe.

b): The same brain after the hemispheres have been separated. Notice the extension of the destruction of the normal tissue in the right hemisphere. The tumor extended from the right hemisphere toward the left frontal lobe, producing there a well-defined cavity.

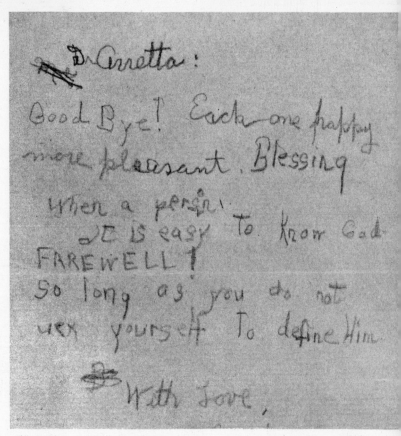

Fig. 6: Letter of a patient suffering from motor aphasia, after being shot in the left hemisphere. Notice the similarity to schizophrenic word-salad.

Thus, anxiety may work in two ways. But without anxiety, no improvement is possible. Of course, we should not confuse the decrease in anxiety due to improvement, with the decrease in anxiety due to progression of the illness. The latter is accompanied by more and more detachment from reality, whereas the opposite occurs in the former.

A general attitude of defiance or compliance is also another important prognostic characteristic. If the patient is compliant toward therapists and nurses, the chances of his recovery are much greater than if he is defiant (Seitz, 228). This is particularly true about the paranoid. The patient who defies the therapist, and wants to demonstrate, at any cost, the veracity of his allegations, and is uncooperative and unwilling to submit to the suggestions of the therapist, has a more guarded prognosis. He wastes his energies in the fight to retain his psychosis. He will use more and more logical reinforcement.

The general affective condition is also important. The more depressed the patient is, the better is the prognosis. At times the depression is so marked that the syndrome is called schizo-affective, or a differential diagnosis from manic-depressive psychosis is difficult to determine. The schizophrenic depression, however, is not necessarily accompanied by a conscious feeling of unworthiness. The more adequate or richer the affective behavior is, the better is the prognosis.

A state of hopelessness, not accompanied by congruous depression, is an ominous prognostic sign.

The content of the delusional or hallucinatory material has important prognostic value. The more the patient projects toward others and exonerates himself, the more severe is the psychosis. If, on the other hand, he believes that he is persecuted because he is somehow guilty or responsible, the prognosis is better. The prognosis is much better if the delusions concern feelings of guilt and responsibility. But here again the diagnosis may be uncertain, wavering between schizophrenia and manic-depressive psychosis, or it may be what several authors call a schizo-affective psychosis. At times, the differential characteristics are difficult to evaluate, as for example when the delusions follow a schizophrenic pattern and the depression and the feeling of guilt present a manic-depressive picture. The following example is typical of this combination. I consider it common also because in my practice I have encountered three or four similar cases, almost identical, even as to the minor details.

The patient was a thirty-two-year-old chemist, Catholic, the youngest of five children. After the death of his father, which occurred when he was three, he was raised in an orphan asylum, where he stayed until puberty. He was a very shy, submissive person, fearful of authority, who gained some kind of security through intellectual achievements. In his youth he had been too shy to date girls; occasionally he would visit a prostitute. At the age of thirty, he met a rather energetic woman who became interested in him and persuaded him to marry her. It is doubtful whether he ever loved her. He considered her physically unattractive and domineering. On the other hand, she was the only woman who had ever paid any attention to him. Two years after the marriage, the wife became sick with a rather serious arthritic disorder, which made her appear even more unattractive to him. One day the patient was sent by his firm to a distant city on a business commission. While he was sitting in the lobby of his hotel, he was approached by a prostitute who asked him whether he would like to have her come to his room. He agreed. They had intercourse, after which he promptly dismissed her. After she left, he started to worry. She had had a funny look on her face. Maybe she was sick. Maybe she had infected him. He became so disturbed that he returned to New York City sooner than he had planned. He visited his physician to find out whether he could detect any sign of infection. The physician did not find any pathology. A few days later the patient thought he saw some peculiar spots on his penis. This time he was sure he had syphilis. He visited two or three specialists who reassured him that he had no venereal disease. A blood Wassermann was taken and was found to be negative. Two weeks later he noticed some peculiar pimples on his wife's face, and he also heard that a neighbor's child, whom he had caressed on the street a few days before, was sick in bed. He became convinced that he had infected his wife and this child with syphilis. He also noticed that the workers in his firm showed some peculiar pimples on their faces, and he was almost sure that he had spread the infection to the whole company. He was not absolutely sure of all his apprehensions, but "almost" sure, and he tried to rationalize his anxiety. For instance, every two weeks he would take a new blood Wassermann. Although all of them were negative, he was not sure that he was not syphilitic. He had read in a book that the Wassermann reaction is accurate only in 98% of the cases. After all, he might belong to that 2%, which shows inaccurate results. He was very depressed and felt extremely guilty. He connected several events with his delusions. For instance, he had read in the paper that two or three people had committed suicide. All of these people lived in a part of New York City which was crossed by a subway line which he used to take. He thought that maybe he had infected these people by touching them or using the same seats. These people had contracted syphilis from him, and consequently had committed suicide. He was very depressed, and so preoccupied with these thoughts that he had to stop working. He was seen by several psychiatrists, who differed as to the diagnosis. Two-thirds of the group who had seen him emphasized the delusional system, and favored the diagnosis of schizophrenia. One-third pointed out that the patient was very depressed, that he had strong feelings of guilt, and that the delusions were not projected, but somehow introjected, as for example his feelings of responsibility for the increase in the number of suicides. They felt that the depression was congruous with the tremendous feeling of guilt, and favored the diagnosis of the depressed type of manic-depressive type of psychosis. The patient had two or three psychotherapeutic sessions during which the hostility for his wife came to the fore. But the awareness of this hostility increased his feelings of guilt also. Since it was not possible to arrange a psychotherapeutic treatment, the majority of physicians who examined him recommended shock treatment. After the first treatment, a striking symptomatic improvement was noted. The delusions seemed to have lost their strength, and after the fourth or fifth grand mal seizure, the patient seemed free of all delusions. This apparently excellent response to electric shock confirmed the opinions of those who had diagnosed the case as one of manic-depressive psychosis. Two years later, however, the patient manifested open symptoms again. His mother had died of a cerebral hemorrhage, and again he thought that she had died because he had infected her with syphilis. A person who worked in the same firm also had died of apoplexy, and the patient felt responsible for his death too. I could not treat the patient, and I don't know what has become of him. Unfortunately, this case could not be explored or treated dynamically, in spite of the excellent possibilities. It has been briefly reported here as an example of the fact that delusions of guilt have a better prognosis and a better response to any type of treatment, at least as far as the single attack is concerned.

There are, however, other delusions connected with guilt and responsibility, which do not have a good prognostic meaning. They are seen in the hebephrenic type of schizophrenia especially. For instance, a patient felt that if he went swimming in a pool or in the ocean, he would impregnate all the women who were in the water. Therefore he did not go, since he did not want to be responsible. This patient had been told by his mother that he had been responsible for all her sicknesses which had started from the time she was pregnant with him. Her "being pregnant with him" had symbolically become his act of "impregnating mother" and it aroused feelings of guilt. He did not want to repeat his original sin. By thinking of his own original sin, however, he magnified his power; he had the power to impregnate many women, and in a psychotic way, he compensated for the inferiority feeling which his mother had engendered.

Hebephrenics and catatonics, at times, feel that they are or that they may become responsible for all the evils of the world. In these delusions, the feeling of power is more obvious than the feeling of guilt, which may not be apparent (see also page 236).

If the delusions involve members of the family, such as the spouse or the parents, generally there is an arrest of the illness, or very slow regresison, but the probability of final recovery, without recurrences, is not enhanced or reduced.

The state of insight has important prognostic value. Opinions differ on this point, mainly because the word "insight" has been given several meanings. The "psychotic insight," which was described on page 331, has a negative prognostic value. The more the patient feels that he understands what is behind the strange things which happen to him, the more unfavorable is the prognosis.

The insight which the patient may have about the symbolic meaning of his symptoms generally has a negative prognostic value. The repressive forces are all destroyed and the patient is in immediate contact with the sources of his disturbances. Of course, an exception is the symbolic insight, which is acquired through treatment, because in this case the anxiety is also progressively removed.

The insight, by which is meant one's awareness of being

sick, is, on the other hand, a good prognostic sign. It is reminiscent of the insight that the dreamer has when he is about to wake up from a dream, and realizes that what he experienced was a dream, not a reality. This type of insight has a particularly good prognostic value, if it occurs after a period in which it was absent.

There are also patients who are generally in a borderline condition with occasional outbreaks of transitory psychotic symptoms. These patients are usually aware that they are sick; at times, they go as far as to diagnose themselves as cases of schizophrenia or dementia praecox. In this case, the insight does not have a good prognostic value as far as complete recovery is concerned; however, it somehow seems to indicate that the process of regression is prevented or at least slowed up.

The ability to pretend, or to lie, is a good prognostic sign. Delusional life is reality for a patient, not pretension. When he is questioned about his delusions, he cannot deny them, or lie about their existence, even when he knows that admitting them will have an unfavorable result, such as the rejection of his demand for discharge from the hospital. He cannot lie or pretend, because he cannot shift to an imaginary assumption. The denial of delusions, which are so real to him, requires a power to abstract or to shift to a set of facts which from his point of view are unreal. At times, when he knows that admitting his truth would mean being kept in the hospital, he will try to be as evasive and defensive as possible, but he will not actually lie. When the patient is able to lie about his delusions, he is in the process of recovery. He will not have to lie for a long time, because the delusions will soon disappear.

This inability of the schizophrenic to lie should not be confused with the inability to lie which certain obsessive-compulsive patients present. The latter cannot lie, not because they cannot shift to an imaginary assumption, but because they feel compelled to tell the truth in order to ward off guilt and anxiety.

The *onset* of the illness is prognostically important. The more acute the onset is, the more favorable is the prognosis. The prognosis is favorable because the immediate precipitating factors in these cases are more important than in less acute cases. The underlying historical factors can be compensated for again, if the anxiety about the immediate precipitating factor is removed. This rule is not constant. Every psychiatrist has observed very acute cases which did not recover or improve.

Finally, *the acceptance of one's illness, or resignation to being sick* has an ominous prognostic meaning. However, this trait belongs more properly to the second or advanced stage of schizophrenia. Other prognostic criteria have been considered by Rennie in an accurate statistical analysis of one hundred cases of schizophrenia who recovered (216).

III. Atypical Forms of Schizophrenia

Before concluding this chapter on the first or initial stage of schizophrenia, it may be helpful to mention some of the atypical forms of this condition. In fact, it is during the first stage that diagnostic problems present themselves.

In the second part of this book those relatively rare forms were mentioned, which are called folie à deux and à trois, (page 141), and that form which I have called externalized psychosis (page 142).

Some other atypical forms which should be noted are: schizo-affective psychosis, schizophrenia in childhood, schizophrenia in old age, schizophrenia complicating neurological disease, and propfschizophrenia, or schizophrenia accompanying mental deficiency.

Schizo-affective psychosis is a term that certain authors

apply to cases which present a symptomatology characterized by both schizophrenic and manic-depressive features. A case of this type was described on page 336. In my experience, in the long run, most of these cases prove to be suffering from typical schizophrenia.

Child schizophrenia was first described by Sante De Sanctis, who called it Dementia Praecocissima (62). Since then, many important studies of this condition have been made, such as those of Potter (214), Mahler (182), Bender (20), Despert (63) and Clardy (54). Since the author of this book has had so little experience with child schizophrenia, he prefers not to write at all about this subject, and refers the reader to the works of the above-mentioned authors.

Schizophrenia in old age presents a baffling problem. Many psychiatrists exclude such a possibility, since they feel that a relatively young age is necessary for the occurrence of this psychosis. Young age, however, does not seem as important as Kraepelin thought. Statistics show that the age of the onset of schizophrenia is always advancing. This finding may be due to the fact that many cases which were diagnosed in the past as suffering from paraphrenia, paranoid conditions, paranoia, paranoid type of involutional psychosis, alcoholic psychosis, etc., are now being recognized more and more as cases of schizophrenia.

Many psychotic pictures occurring in old age present a paranoid symptomatology characterized by delusions of persecution. (The patient is poisoned, robbed, deprived of his property, etc.) If these patients were younger, there would be no doubt in classifying them as cases of the paranoid type of schizophrenia. However, many feel that old age is a very important factor in these cases. These patients were able to avoid the psychosis throughout their lives; their defenses were not broken until the changes due to old age occurred. Therefore, many psychiatrists prefer to diagnose these cases as suffering from the paranoid type of senile psychosis. The problem is still debatable. If we study the history of these patients, we discover that they have made only a limited adjustment throughout their lives. Most of them have had suspicious, withdrawn personalities. A great many of them never married. Somehow, they managed to escape an acute breakdown until old age occurred. Old age presents new problems of adjustment, at the same time that it produces lesions in the nervous system, which make the person less responsive to the new demands of adjustment. Deterioration and regression are much slower in these paranoid forms than in the typical cases of senile psychosis. Impairment of orientation, memory, recall, intelligence, etc. is much less marked, and in certain cases not appreciable.

In addition to these paranoid cases characterized by delusions of persecution, there are other cases who present delusions of grandeurs, or delusions and hallucinations, with very bizarre content, which somehow seem to bring comfort rather than grief to the patient. Thus I remember a man almost seventy years old, of the African race, not regressed or deteriorated, who imagined that a beautiful Chinese woman was visiting him every night. He had vivid, visual hallucinations. A woman who became sick after the age of sixty-five had phantastic delusions of transformation into animals. She also felt that she was the Queen of Hungary and that the hospital was her royal palace. These senile pictures generally resemble those found in the second stage of schizophrenia. I feel that for a very long time schizophrenia was present at a latent stage in these patients, and that it became manifest when old age occurred. Whereas in the paranoid persecutory type (or paranoid type of senile psychosis) there was only a prepsychotic maladjustment, in the last mentioned cases there was greater pathology prior to the occurrence of the overt symptoms.

Schizophrenia accompanying neurological disease is also a baffling problem for those psychiatrists who are mainly interested in diagnostic and pathogenetic problems. Every psychiatrist has seen several cases with a schizophrenic symptomatology, showing the typical serology of general paresis. Are these, cases of general paresis which have a schizophrenic-like symptomatology or cases of schizophrenia superimposed on a general paresis? This picture of general paresis with a schizophrenic symptomatology has become more frequent in the United States since the expansive type of general paresis which used to be very common, has become a rarity in the last few decades.

Several cases of Huntington chorea start with paranoid pictures. In the beginning their choreiform movements may be mistaken for mannerisms and grimaces, and the diagnosis of schizophrenia is made. I have seen paranoid pictures also in cerebellar atrophy, multiple sclerosis, muscular distrophies, and in many cases of post-encephalitic conditions.

In pernicious anemia, all kinds of psychiatric syndromes have been reported (Bowman, 34), but in my experience paranoid conditions are the most frequent. (Ferraro, Arieti and English, 78).

Brain tumors, especially in the frontal lobes, may show a schizophrenic symptomatology. Fig. 5 shows the brain of a patient after a huge encapsulated fibroblastic meningioma has been removed. This patient, diagnosed as hebephrenic schizophrenia, had been in the hospital for twenty-seven years. She lived a vegetative existence. Prior to her hospitalization, she had complained of headache and had had two epileptic seizures. These symptoms were ignored, because when she entered the hospital she showed schizophrenic symptoms, and no neurological signs whatsoever. In the twenty-seven years of hospital life, no epileptic seizure was observed. She appeared to be a typical regressed hebephrenic.

These cases of misdiagnosed brain tumors are becoming

rarer and rarer, because the history of seizures and headache prompt physicians to order electroencephalograms, X-ray studies, and possibly pneumoencephalograms, even in the presence of an apparent schizophrenic symptomatology. These diagnostic methods did not exist at the time the last mentioned patient was admitted to the hospital.

In neurological conditions which paralyze the patient, such as cerebral vascular accidents, occasionally a catatonic syndrome is superimposed. We have thus an unusual combination: the neurological paralysis is covered by the catatonic symptomatology.

These cases, where a schizophrenic or schizophrenic-like symptomatology accompanies a neurological condition, are generally classified as psychoses with chronic brain diseases. At least, this is the tendency in the state hospitals of New York. Of course, the importance of the neurological disease cannot be dismissed. We must say, however, that in many instances, the neurological disease greatly increases the anxiety of the patient on account of its crippling effects, and unchains even a small propensity toward a schizophrenic psychosis. Psychotherapy at the beginning of the neurological disease may prevent the psychosis.

Schizophrenia also occurs in a small minority of mental defectives. This combination is generally called *"propfschizophrenia."* Generally, the mental defect protects the patient from those situations which engender schizophrenia. In certain cases, however, especially when the mental deficiency is not too pronounced, paranoid episodes with delusions and hallucinations may occur. Generally these episodes have a short duration, but they may be followed by slow regression.

The previously assumed incompatibility between schizophrenia and epilepsy (incidentally, an assumption which led Von Meduna to the introduction of convulsive shock treatment) seems disproved, as several cases have been reported of this rather unusual combination of the two conditions.

CHAPTER XV

The Second or Advanced Stage

The second or advanced stage of schizophrenia is reached when the patient seems to have accepted his illness. Anxiety is no longer so easily observed. Outbursts are less frequent. The delusions and the hallucinations have lost a great many of their unpleasant qualities; often the patients like to hear "the voices" which bring them comfort. At least, they no longer seem to be disturbed by them. Persecutory trends have lost their strength, and no effort is made to support them with pseudo-logical arguments. Often the persecutory delusions have been replaced by delusions of grandeur. (See page 242). The thinking is much more disconnected. It presents almost exclusively paleologic mechanisms, or even more primitive processes, like word-salad.

The patients are less active and have a tendency to stereotype all their activities or to reduce them to a mere routine. Hospitalized patients repeat the same things every day with little variation. They sit in the same place in similar postures, and talk in the same way. They seem to avoid more and more any unpredictable situation or any spontaneous response. Life becomes increasingly monotonous. As a rule, however, the patients do not seem to be bothered very much. They may resent hospitalization, but express the resentment without vehemence or animation. Although their lives become nar-, rower and narrower, they do not seem to be bored. As a matter of fact, they never yawn. Boredom is an emotional state of which they do not seem capable. Boredom would produce anxiety.

Catatonics in the second stage, however, are a little more active. Waxy flexibility is often replaced by stereotyped minimal activity. The patients are less rigid and allow themselves to perform some movements. It seems almost as if at this stage, the four types of schizophrenia (simple, paranoid, hebephrenic and catatonic) have acquired a much more similar symptomatology. At this stage it may be difficult to differentiate a paranoid from a hebephrenic. Paranoids, however, reach this stage much later than hebephrenics. In many instances they remain indefinitely at the first stage.

As was noted before, at this stage the patients seem to have no anxiety. As a matter of fact, they seem contented, and when they harbor grandiose delusions, they seem proud of themselves. They seem to have achieved what they have wanted, that is, they seem to have acquired self-esteem and to have removed anxiety. Now a very important question, which has not only theoretical value but practical value as well, because it is related to therapeutic procedures, is the following. Is it really true that the patients have acquired self-esteem and removed anxiety? We have seen that in the first stage also the same attempt to remove anxiety was made by accepting psychotic mechanisms. We have also seen, however, that in the first stage, even at a superficial symptomatological level, anxiety was still observed.

Once the patients have selected the path of schizophrenic

desocialization, they tend to continue to follow that path. The process of desocialization is like quicksand; in most cases, it actually increases the anxiety of patients especially when they feel pressured to resocialize, but find themselves deprived of the necessary tools.

At the second stage of schizophrenia, anxiety is not seen. One could say that the illness has been a good transformer, has transformed anxiety into psychotic symptoms. Theoretically, however, we have to assume that anxiety is still there, at least potentially, to perpetuate the illness. In fact, if there were no anxiety, the patients would tend to recover. That is what happens in some cases; but in the majority of cases the ghost of anxiety is still there, even if not observed. Any tendency toward normalization must reactivate anxiety, and the patients therefore maintain the psychotic symptoms. Actually, any attempt toward recovery, even the slightest one, must produce great anxiety, because by becoming psychotic, the patients have given up many of the means (powers of abstraction, etc.) which equipped them to fulfill social demands. They are in a situation similar to the one described by Goldstein in organic cerebral cases (112–114). The patients are afraid to go into a "catastrophic reaction"; their tendency, therefore, is to do the opposite, to follow the path toward more stereotyped activity and desocialization. Any anxiety-producing demands may push them further toward regression.

The situation is a vicious circle. What should be a defense actually, in the majority of cases, makes the patients more helpless and vulnerable, a circumstance similar to that which occurs in some organic diseases. For instance, in pulmonary tuberculosis, the fibrous tissue, which the organism develops to defend itself against the infection, actually limits the pulmonary tissue, and decreases the vital capacity of the patient.

The symptoms of the second stage of schizophrenia will not be described here. The old textbooks of psychiatry, and especially Kraepelin's monograph, give accurate descriptions of this stage of the illness. All of the classic symptoms are seen at this stage, which is the richest in clinical symptomatology.

Some questions, however, must be asked at this point. To what extent is this simplification of habits and reduction of all activities to a mere routine determined by hospital life? It cannot be denied that institutional life offers little opportunity for spontaneity. Some patients prefer to stay in the hospital, even when the absence of active symptoms induces their physicians to discharge them. They don't want to go back to the world, where they have to face anxiety-ridden situations again (which they may symbolize and experience concretely as persecutions).

On the other hand, one may say that by removing most opportunities for spontaneity, hospital life plays the game of the illness. That individuality which the patient has tried to retain against superior forces in his family and his society may be entirely submerged in the organization of the mental hospital. In other words, does hospitalization enhance regression? How can hospital life be organized so that anxiety situations will be removed without the patients being pushed toward regression?

Many studies have to be carried out before these questions can be answered. The effect of confinement per se has to be studied. Comparisons should be made between the effects of confinement on psychotics and on persons who are restrained for other reasons, such as prisoners and patients suffering from totally disabling physical infirmities.

CHAPTER XVI

*The Third or Preterminal State. The Hoarding
and Self-Decorating Habits*

Whereas the first stage of schizophrenia has been intensely studied by many psychiatrists from a dynamic point of view, and the second stage has been studied in great detail by the early descriptive authors, the third and fourth stages have been relatively neglected.

This neglect, even by those authors who limit their studies to a description of the symptoms, may seem difficult to understand, since almost the majority of patients who are in these stages are hospitalized. The classical symptoms of schizophrenia, however, are no longer prominent at these stages, so that many observers may have felt that the patients did not present symptoms worth reporting. They have described these patients as approximating more and more a vegetative existence, and a state of "idiocy." Very little more than these generalities is mentioned in the literature. The result is that even from a simple, descriptive point of view, relatively little is known about these patients.

When I was working in Pilgrim State Hospital, I had an opportunity to study these very regressed patients, and I felt that such study could eventually reveal important information. As I reported in a previous contribution, I gave the name "preterminal" to a stage which is rather difficult to delimit or to differentiate (8). This stage occurs generally from 5 to 15 years after the beginning of the illness, but may occur sooner or later.

In this phase of the illness, hallucinations and delusions have disappeared or cannot be elicited. In some cases they are still present, but are completely disorganized and deprived of any apparent emotional charge. The patients present severe disintegration of thought processes, so that their ideas are conveyed to the examiner with great difficulty.

In this stage, it is difficult to distinguish a catatonic from a paranoid. It seems that the different types converge towards one another during this stage even more than during the second stage. Although all the types of schizophrenia may pass through the preterminal stage, in a large group of cases belonging to this phase we find a predominance of patients previously diagnosed as affected by the paranoid type. This preponderance may be due to the fact that paranoid patients remain at this level a longer time or even indefinitely without regressing further. Hebephrenics and catatonics, on the other hand, regress sooner to the terminal stage.

The reason that patients of the four types seem more alike during this phase is that most of the obvious symptoms have disappeared. On account of the absence of many symptoms, these patients are at times discharged from the hospital, if a suitable non-demanding environment is found. They manifest what Lewis calls "improvement by regression" (174). It would seem as if in these cases the illness has really been able to achieve its purpose. A little more than the most superficial examination, however, reveals that these patients are very sick. Not only is the impairment of their thinking very marked, but they also present peculiar habits, which are typical of this stage.

These habits are numerous but probably many of them have escaped the notice of observers. Often, in fact, institutionalized patients learn to conceal them very well. Examples of some habits are picking of the skin, pulling out of hair, and performance of rhythmic movements. Particular attention will be given in this chapter to two habits which, in the opinion of the writer, are the most common, the hoarding and the self-decorating habits.

The habit of hoarding consists of the practice of collecting a more or less large number of objects, generally of limited size and generally of no practical use. The objects which, in the course of my investigation, were found to have been hoarded by the patients were papers of any kind—old letters, toilet paper, pages of newspapers, etc.—pieces of wood, stones, leaves, sticks, soap, spoons, strings, rags, hairpins, old toothbrushes, wires, cups, feathers, cores of fruit, stale food, feces, hair, pencils, pens, combs, small boxes, cardboards, etc. One patient used to carry a large number of teaspoons grabbed in the dining room and hidden in her bosom until she was discovered. Another patient had collected a large number of her own feces and still another had collected 117 prune pits in a stocking. Another patient preferred to hoard her daily ration of food rather than eat it. She eventually had to be tube fed. Less regressed patients, whose habits have been developed more recently, may collect objects which have some symbolic or actual use, like letters, pictures, recent papers. However, their subsequent behavior discloses that they do not collect these things with the purpose of using them, but just for the sake of collecting them. Not only do they not use these objects, but they start to hoard others which have no use whatsoever. Some patients start to develop this habit by collecting and wrapping objects of the same kind in separate bundles. Later, however, they no longer continue to divide them and keep them separately according to their kind, but put them all together.

The patients collect these objects in their pockets, in bags or boxes, in their stockings or socks, and not infrequently in their shoes. Female patients very often hide them in their bosom or in other parts of their body. Many carry the entire collection with them, always as if it were an important part of their person. Others collect the objects under their beds, pillows, or other relatively hidden spaces. Some patients put paper and other objects wherever they can find a hole. A patient had made a hole in the lining of a mattress and had put into it an enormous quantity of toilet paper and other trash.

When the patients become more regressed and approach the terminal stage, they start to use the cavities of their own bodies as deposits for the hoarded material. Male patients frequently deposit small objects in their external auditory canals or in their nasal cavities. Female patients resort to their vaginas. In my series, seven patients had the habit of placing objects in their vaginas. One of them had put into her vagina a small metal cup, two handles of teaspoons, several small pieces of soap, and a little rag, at the time when this practice was discovered. A patient used to hoard small objects in her oral cavity, but did not eat them. During her meals she would remove the objects and put them back in her mouth afterwards. In a few cases, the patients had resorted to their somatic cavities only when they were deprived of their bags or pocketbooks.

In the opinion of the writer, this hoarding habit is extremely frequent among regressed patients, but the extent of its incidence cannot be easily evaluated, because nurses and attendants try to prevent it. In fact, if the patients were permitted to hoard as many things as they were inclined to, such a large quantity of garbage and trash would collect in the hospital wards as to interfere with their hygienic management. The repression of this tendency is a real problem of administrative psychiatry.

Although I have observed and studied this habit in patients of both sexes, I was able to do statistical investigations only in female services. I collected a series of 64 patients presenting this habit, although for the reasons mentioned above, the actual number of patients having the hoarding tendency probably could have been many times as large. Forty-eight, or 75% of the patients were diagnosed as cases of schizophrenia. The other 16, or 25%, were diagnosed as follows: Involutional psychosis, Paranoid Type—1, Paranoid Condition—2, Manic Depressive Psychosis—4, Alcoholic Psychosis, Paranoid Type—1, Cerebral Arteriosclerosis—3, Psychosis due to Epilepsy—4, General Paresis—1. Such variety of psychiatric entities denies the specificity of this habit. It could be that, at least in some of these 16 cases, the initial diagnosis, made many years previously, had not been the correct one. In fact, at the time of this investigation their condition, at a clinical level, was in no way different from that of an advanced schizophrenic regression. I am inclined to think, however, that the hoarding habit is not pathognomonic of advanced schizophrenia, but that it may be found in all the conditions which bring about a state of regression. As a matter of fact, several years after I had reported the original investigation of this habit in schizophrenia, I observed similar, although much less pronounced, hoarding tendencies in several very old nonpsychiatric patients, institutionalized in a home for the aged. The fact remains, however, that schizophrenia is the most common condition which brings about a regression to the level of the hoarding habit.

Within the schizophrenic group, 29 patients or 60.42%

were of the paranoid type, 9 or 18.75% were hebephrenic, 7 or 14.58% catatonic, 2 or 4.16% were of the simple type, and 1 or 2.08% of the mixed types. The group of paranoid patients is by far the largest and becomes even more outstanding if we add to it the other 4 patients diagnosed as paranoid but not schizophrenic (Involutional Psychosis, Paranoid Type; Alcoholic Psychosis, Paranoid Type and Paranoid Condition).

In addition to the statistical and diagnostic importance of the hoarding habit, there remains the problem of the psychological significance of this tendency. Attempts to obtain information directly from the patients have been unsuccessful. The majority did not answer inquiries, but reacted by smiling in an apparently incongruous manner. Several gave evasive replies. Only a few attempted to give a logical explanation. The patient who had filled the mattress with toilet paper said that she had done it so as to be ready in case she developed a diarrhea. Another patient replied, "I use what God has given me." It appears to the writer, however, that such practices give a certain amount of pleasure to the patients. As a matter of fact, when they are deprived of their collections, they are obviously displeased, sometimes resistive to these hygienic steps and resentful of them. They are not as resentful as one would expect, however, considering the constancy and apparent zeal which they often show in this collecting tendency. It is hard to estimate whether relatively more pleasure is derived from the act of collecting or from keeping the collection; probably pleasure is derived from both of these actions.

Textbooks of psychiatry do not mention this habit which is common in advanced schizophrenia. However, occasional instances have been reported in the literature. For example, Staerke described a paranoid patient who had the habit of collecting corks (241) and Abraham reported the case of a psychotic patient who used to collect stones (1).

In the orthodox psychoanalytic literature, the habit of

collecting is interpreted as an expression of the anal character. Abraham and Jones (137) have described the same hoarding habit in neurotics presenting anal traits. In these cases, however, the habit occurs in a much less accentuated and bizarre form than I have observed in the preterminal stage of schizophrenia. Abraham describes persons who "collect bits of paper, old envelopes, worn-out pens and similar things, and cannot get rid of these possessions for long periods of time." (1).

I have no objection to calling this habit anal, if the use of such a word is for the sake of common understanding. However, in my opinion, this habit has nothing to do with the anus or with sexual pleasure. I am inclined to think instead that it is a primitive or archaic habit, which is found at a certain level of mental integration. This level corresponds in phylogenesis to the stage when human beings cease to be interested only in the present, that is, in activities connected with immediate needs, such as finding food and eating it immediately. (See page 239). When "Homo" became "Sapiens," he started to think and worry about his future needs and collected food in order to prevent famine. Anthropologists have often reported that primitive people used to hoard food in holes made in the earth. Man abandons the most primitive state of savagery when he becomes a food gatherer. In the schizophrenic, however, the habit seems inappropriate, like a shallow or sham reproduction of the utilitarian activity of the habit of the primitive. The schizophrenic seems to hoard in order to possess; the objects he collects have no intrinsic value; they are valuable only inasmuch as they are possessed by the patient. The patient seems almost to have a desire to incorporate them, to make them part of his own person, and puts them in his mouth, nostrils, vagina, anus, etc.

The ability to retain feces, in spite of the urge to defecate, may require a level of mental integration which corresponds to the level of the hoarding habit; it is viewed here simply as a function of a certain level of development. In some cultures, or in some environments, for social or individual reasons, the activities of this level of development may be emphatically retained, and emphatically transmitted to the individual. At any rate, whatever interpretation one gives to this hoarding tendency (libido at anal stage, primitive level of integration, cultural or interpersonal influence, or a mixture of all these interpretations), the fact remains that this tendency is a non-pathognomonic manifestation of advanced schizophrenic regression.

Another habit which recurs especially at this stage of regression is the self-decorating habit. As a rule it is observed in patients slightly less regressed than those presenting the hoarding habit, who are at what may be considered the beginning of the preterminal stage. Though in my experience this habit has been observed to be less common by far than the hoarding habit, it is generally better known, because it meets the eyes more easily. For reasons which I was unable to determine, but which make one think of complementary social factors, I observed this habit more frequently in patients of African races. The habit consists of the primitive use of small objects or stains for decoration of one's body. Pieces of paper and rags are cut into several bands, and bracelets, rings, necklaces and belts are made with them. Many, predominantly female patients, paint their faces in a conspicuous, ridiculous manner. Many patients of both sexes adorn themselves by placing buttons, stamps, small boxes, corks, or coins on their chests.

The same objects which are hoarded by other more regressed patients are sought by these patients and are valued only for decorative purposes. It is therefore possible, though by no means proved, that the self-decorating habit is also connected with the hoarding habit.

A normal person cannot see any decorative value in this

practice, which appears not only inartistic but often disfiguring and ridiculous. Such is obviously not the impression of the patient. Although he seems apathetic to his environment, he is interested in decorating his body. When he is asked why he decorates himself in such a manner he often denies any decorative purposes. A female patient said that she used paper bracelets "to cover her own arms." Another one replied that she used rag-made necklaces "to tie her neck." These practices, which probably, in a certain way, express the most primitive artistic manifestations, should not be confused with other artistic activities of schizophrenics. Patients at an advanced stage of schizophrenia, but not yet at the preterminal stage, often display considerable artistic ability. (See pages 311–313). Although their works show formal characteristics of schizophrenic distortions, the examiner is able to recognize in them a certain artistic value. It is more difficult to find this value in the activities occurring at this stage, though these activities too may be considered artistic expressions.

Anthropology teaches, in fact, that similar self-decoration is probably due to a most primitive artistic tendency. Bracelets, necklaces, and other small objects were commonly used by both sexes during the paleolithic period. The practice of painting the body was also common among the cave dwellers (MacCurdy, 179).

But what are the meaning and purpose of this practice? Desire to increase the sexual appeal, self-satisfaction in producing the artistic objects, or esthetic admiration of one's self? In schizophrenics this habit seemingly does not have any practical or social purposes, but possibly it offers a certain kind of satisfaction through the making of the ornamental objects or through self-admiration.

By analogy, one might be tempted to interpret art, as originating, not for utilitarian purposes, but exclusively for the pleasure of the artist. Some interesting observations reported by Boas would seem to corroborate this point of view (31). This anthropologist noted that the rawhide boxes of the Sauk and Fox Indians were made of a piece of hide which was carefully and skilfully ornamented according to a definite plan. When the boxes were made, the hide was folded and the pattern, which had required so much work, was completely lost. This author gives other examples to illustrate that when materials, originally made with patterns, were used for practical purposes, the patterns were disregarded. He reaches the conclusion that the previous work seems to be done only for the satisfaction of the maker.

Although my observations would lead to similar interpretation, I think it would be hazardous to reach such a conclusion from my findings on schizophrenics. The fact that a habit has no obvious environmental value in schizophrenics, does not prove at all that its equivalents at a phylogenetic or ontogenetic level had no social value. The schizophrenic process engenders a resurgence of primitive habits, which often appears to us a shallow or an exclusively formal reproduction of what happened in ontogenesis and phylogenesis. These habits seem worthless to us, because they do not have the same utilitarian purpose that they had originally. It is an error on the part of the observer to look for the same purpose. However, these habits must indeed have a purpose. Even the schizophrenic, in spite of his withdrawal, has a need for activity. No matter how regressed he is, he needs some feeling of power which is more or less gratified by actions and performances. He tends to act, therefore, and in the easiest possible way, in a manner which does not bring about anxiety. He tends to act in accordance with the mechanisms which correspond to the level or levels to which he has regressed.

I am sure that other primitive habits of the preterminal stage have escaped my attention. Perhaps the nurses and attendants who are in closer contact with these patients would be in a better position to describe them than physicians. It is to be hoped that in the near future some nurses will publish their daily experiences and observations with these very regressed patients.

As far as the hoarding and the self-decorating habits are concerned, they will be examined again, and their interpretation will be continued after the description of the terminal stage.

CHAPTER XVII

The Fourth or Terminal Stage

I. Primitive Oral Habits and Their Interpretation

We have come now to the fourth or last stage of schizophrenia. At this stage a new set of phenomena occurs. Some of the symptoms appear no longer as psychological in nature, but neurological. It seems almost as if we have reached a stage where psychology and neurology coalesce. The indefinite quality of some of the symptoms leaves ample space for speculation and makes their study difficult.

How and when does this last stage start? It is well known that decreased activity is one of the most common characteristics of progressing schizophrenia, though not a constant one. This motor reduction often interferes with the dietary requirements of the patient to such a point as to bring about a state of malnutrition, anemia and, occasionally, avitaminosis. This inactivity, which is a part of the schizophrenic withdrawal, is noted throughout the long years of progressing regression, interrupted only by occasional and transitory partial remissions. In patients who continue to regress indefinitely, however, a more or less sudden increase in motor activity is noted at a certain point. As a rule such an increase is not transitory but lasts for the lifetime of the patient, or until a physical illness neutralizes its effects. It is when this partial increase of motor activity takes place that what I call the terminal stage begins.

In the patients whom I observed and whose clinical records I studied, the terminal stage started any time from seven to forty years after the onset of the illness, but it probably may start even sooner, or later. The increase in activity is only relative, since the patients somehow remain underactive in comparison with normal subjects. Their actions, which are now more numerous, appear sharply reactive or impulsive; they are reactive to certain habitual situations, which will be taken into consideration shortly, or impulsive, inasmuch as they appear to be due to sudden internal stimulation. The patients may be impulsively destructive, assaultive, and much more violent than previously. At this stage of the illness they do not seem able to experience hallucinations or to elaborate delusions. Their verbal expressions are either completely absent or reduced to a few disconnected utterances.

The most striking changes, however, are noted in the dining room. The patients who had always eaten so little as to have reduced themselves to a state of malnutrition now seem to have a voracious appetite (bulimia) and often gain a considerable amount of weight. The nurses often report that these patients have the habit of stealing food. In reality, closer observation reveals that the concept of stealing is not implied in the actions of these patients. They cannot prevent themselves from grabbing food at the sight of it, so that they are better termed *food grabbers*.

Observations in the dining room reveal other interesting habits. A few of these patients show preference for certain foods. No matter how many kinds of food are in the dish, they always grasp and eat the preferred food first. They do not alternate the various kinds, as normal adults do, but only when they have entirely finished the preferred food do they start to eat the others. Similarly, if they show several degrees of preference, they first eat the food which is the first choice; when this is finished, they eat the second choice, and so on. If there are desserts, these are generally eaten before anything else. It seems that the patients are obliged to react first to stronger stimuli. The preference for a certain food is not shown by all patients who are food grabbers. On the other hand, such preference is maintained only for a brief period after the acquisition of the food-grabbing habit. After this period the patients seem to eat with avidity any kind of food. *Whatever belongs in the category of edibility elicits equal and prompt reaction.* Another characteristic which is often observed is the extreme rapidity with which these patients eat (tachyphagia). In a few minutes these food grabbers may finish the rations of several patients, if they are not prevented from doing so. Often they do not leave any remnants of food in the dish but clean the plate with the tongue.

The patients may remain indefinitely at this stage which is characterized by the food-grabbing habit, but the majority progress more or less rapidly to a more advanced stage, characterized chiefly by what I have termed the habit of "placing into mouth." At this stage the category of edibility is no longer respected. Whereas the patients had previously distinguished themselves for grabbing food and food only, now they manifest the habit of grabbing every small object and putting it into the mouth, paying no attention at all to the edible or nonedible nature of it. If they are not restrained, these patients pick up crumbs, cockroaches, stones, rags, paper, wood, clothes, pencils, and leaves from the floor and put them into the mouth. Generally they eat these things; occasionally they swallow them with great risk. Many patients, however, limit themselves to chewing these nonedible objects and finally reject them. When they eat or swallow dangerous materials, such as an ink well or a teaspoon, they are erroneously considered suicidal. Closer observation reveals, however, that the idea of suicide is not implied in the action. They simply react to a visual stimulus by grasping the object and putting it into the mouth. They act as if they were coerced to react in this way. It is as though they were especially attracted by small, three-dimensional stimuli, which seem to be distinguished from the background more distinctly than usual.

On the autopsy tables of state hospitals it is a relatively common experience to find spoons, stones, pieces of scrap iron, wood, paper, cores, etc., in the stomachs or intestines of patients who were affected by the most advanced stages of schizophrenia.

As a typical example, the case of A.R. will be mentioned briefly. This patient entered Pilgrim State Hospital in October 1933 at the age of 32. On admission he had delusions and hallucinations but was fairly well preserved. The diagnosis of dementia praecox, paranoid type, was then made. Subsequently he showed a steady downhill progression in his mental condition. He became negativistic, mute, manneristic and idle. He had the habit of wetting and soiling, and required a great deal of supervision. On frequent occasions it was necessary to tube-feed him. He did not show any interest in his surroundings, appearing completely withdrawn and living an almost vegetative existence. In the dining room, however, he showed some interest, grabbing food and eating in a ravenous manner. On December 31, 1939 he died of acute intestinal obstruction. At autopsy 14 spoon handles were found in his colon, 2 spoon handles and a suspender clasp were found in his stomach. In the terminal ileum there was a rolled piece of shirt collar which was the cause of the obstruction. The collection of foreign bodies found in the stomach of this patient is very modest in comparison with that found in many other patients.

The grasping and ingestion of the objects may be accomplished by a quick movement, as a prompt reaction to a visual stimulus, or by a slow movement, apparently not accompanied by any emotional coloring. If the patients are under some mechanical restraint, they may try to reach the objects directly with their mouths.

It is also not rare to see some patients grasping their own feces, chewing them and eating them, at times with great pleasure and satisfaction (coprophagia). These coprophagic patients may put everything indiscriminately into their mouths and incidentally their own feces, but this situation is rather exceptional. As a rule, they show a marked discrimination in putting into their mouths specifically their own feces. Other patients often smear themselves with their own excrements.

Are these habits only manifestations of a silly, purposeless behavior of demented patients or are they determined by deeper causes? I feel that the latter viewpoint is correct, and that a genetic approach may help explain these habits.

In fact, it is possible to interpret them not as newly-acquired habits but as behavior manifestations of lower levels of integration. The food-grabbing habit reminds one of what is generally observed in cats, dogs, monkeys, and other animals. The animal is coerced to react to the food, at the sight of it. The food does not stand for itself but is what Werner calls a "thing of action" (270). It is a "signal thing," the sight of which leads immediately to a fixed action (Werner). The animal cannot delay the reaction or channel the impulse into longer integrative circuits. Similarly, other habits previously described disclose the same syncretic characteristics encountered in more primitive organizations. It is well known that when monkeys, dogs, cats and other animals are given different items of food at the same time, they eat first the preferred food (for instance, meat in the case of the dog, or banana in the case of monkeys), and only when the entire portion of the preferred food is finished do they start to eat the other foods. They cannot alternate the various kinds but are coerced first to react to the strongest stimulus. Also, a three-and-a-half to four-year-old child, if not prevented, eats first the preferred food, and only when he has finished it does he eat the others.

When the patients become even sicker, this integration of the stimuli is even more primitive, so that they react to edible and nonedible objects in the same way, by grasping them and putting them into the mouth. The category of edibility is no longer respected.

This habit of regressed psychotics has some points in common with what is generally observed in children, approximately from six months to two years of age. When confronted by objects of a certain size, children of this age grasp these objects and attempt to put them into the mouth. There is no discrimination made between edible and nonedible objects; the baby places in his mouth anything that comes within his reach and licks, sucks or eats it.

"If the object is too heavy or cannot be grasped with the hand . . . the infant brings his mouth close to the object and licks or, in the case of clothing or bibs or blankets, sucks at it" (Kanner, 149). Rugs, cotton, leaves, worms, wool, wood, stones and paper are eaten or at least put into the mouth. "The objects eaten are the objects accessible; accessibility and not 'craving' or 'appetite' governs their selection" (Kanner, 149). All parents have observed this particular behavior when their children have reached this age and attribute it erroneously to various causes. Most of the time they attribute it to incipient teething or to increased appetite. Generally the people in charge of the child remove the object from the child's mouth with their own hands, fearing it may be swallowed. But the child, if let alone, will test the object and often reject it if it is not edible or if it has an unpleasant taste. Only relatively seldom is the object swallowed, with serious consequences. It seems almost as if taste discrimination, or at least oral discrimination by means of the sensory properties of the oral cavity, supersedes the visual one. In pathological conditions this habit persists up to the third and even fourth year and is erroneously called perverted appetite or pica.

In a series of papers issued in 1937, 1938 and 1939, Klüver and Bucy described interesting observations on trained monkeys after the extirpation of both temporal lobes (159–161). The extirpation included Brodmann's areas, 22, 21, 20, the area 19 being left untouched. The removal of both lobes constantly caused typical manifestations, whereas the ablation of only one lobe or of an entire lobe and a part of the other did not bring about characteristic results.

The authors found that the monkeys, after this surgical treatment, showed an irresistible tendency to grasp anything within reach. They placed the grasped object in the mouth, bit it, touched it to the lips and finally ate it, if edible. If inedible, the object was rejected. All objects, edible or not, were grasped indiscriminately. Every operated monkey manifested this particular type of reaction, environmental changes having apparently no influence at all. It seemed as if all previous learning had no influence whatsoever on their behavior. As a matter of fact, the established reactions to visual and weight differences were superseded by the constant grasping and putting-into-mouth reaction (called by the authors "oral tendencies"). In addition, it seemed to the observers as if the animal were "acting under the influence of some compulsory or irresistible impulse. The monkey behaves as if forced to react to objects . . . in the environmental stimulus constellation." It seemed to be dominated by only one tendency, namely, the tendency to contact every object as quickly as possible, any visual object immediately leading, whenever possible, to a motor response.

A different kind of forced ingestion of inedible objects is reported in another field of investigation. Members of primitive tribes are in the habit of eating some inedible substances (geophagy). They are almost forced to eat these objects since they cannot avoid eating them when they see them. This habit is highly discriminatory for a certain substance in a given tribe but retains almost a compulsory characteristic.

The above-mentioned examples, taken from different fields of investigation, have some features in common, namely, the picking up of objects from the immediate environment and the placing of them in the oral cavity, with no discrimination as to their nature and no consideration of the fact that they are not edible. These actions, in all the cited instances, have a more or less compulsory characteristic.

It could be objected that such similarities are only apparent or very superficial, and that we ourselves disclose paleologic thinking in connecting these various instances. Somebody else could emphasize the differences in the situations taken as examples. On the other hand, the differences may be due to various factors acting contemporaneously with the common factor which may be an expression of a certain level of development. The differences could be explained without difficulty. The precise execution of movements of the monkey in contrast with the lower and less accurate movements of the child may be attributed to the fact that whereas voluntary movements have not yet been well acquired by the child, whose central nervous system is not yet completely myelinized, they have been acquired by the monkey.

Unlike the child, the bitemporal monkey of Klüver and Bucy can indefatigably continue to grasp every object, to react repetitiously in this way to every visual stimulus. This reaction is probably due to the fact that the damage or the lack of cerebral areas causes the animal's hyperactivity or the state of "being forced by the stimulus," similar to that which is observed in human cases with extensive cerebral defects (Goldstein). The highly discriminatory geophagic habit of certain tribes may be one of few vestiges of a much more primitive level. The fact that regressed schizophrenics presenting the described behavior grasp objects not in such number and not with such rapidity as the Klüver and Bucy monkey, or not at every opportunity, as the child, may be explained if we take into consideration the other aspects of the schizophrenic picture. The volitional and emotional impairment of the schizophrenic may be responsible for such difference.

Klüver and Bucy give an interesting preliminary interpretation of some behavior characteristics of their bitemporal monkeys, in considering the latter as "psychically blind." Since in their tendency to approach their mouths and place all objects in them "without hesitation" the animals show no discrimination, no preference for food or for learned reactions, and no ability to concentrate on particular objects, the authors consider these monkeys to be psychically blind. The present writer has not the advantage of the valuable direct observations of the authors, but if he has understood correctly, Klüver and Bucy come to the "psychic blindness" or visual agnosia conclusion in view of the fact that the animal which has undergone the removal of both temporal lobes, grasps and uses each object indiscriminately, even though it had learned before the operation to distinguish the objects and use them discriminately. But is that behavior really due to "psychic blindness" or to that "compulsory or irresistible impulse" which forces the monkey, as well as the child, and at times the regressed schizophrenic, to grasp any object within reach? We also must direct our attention to the fact that the ability to appreciate differences in lightness, size, shape, distance, position and movement is not reported to be impaired in these monkeys. Therefore, we can reach the conclusion that the only bodies which are not "recognized" are the bodies with a definite, sharp three-dimensional shape. Although the forced placing-into-mouth reaction of these monkeys is not explained by assuming the presence of visual agnosia, it cannot be disproved that the monkeys are really in a certain way psychically blind. As a matter of fact, in a certain sense even the child of one or two years of age may be considered partially psychically blind. The visual stimuli often do not lead the child to recognize the objects; his visual perceptions are still partially agnostic. By means of the mouth, more than by his eyes, the one-year-old child explores what is still unknown to him. Werner states: "The mouth is the primitive means of knowing objects, that is, in a literal sense, through the grasping of the objects. The spatial knowledge of an object results from a sucking in of the thing through the mouth and a consequent tactual discovery and incorporation." (270). However, the child apparently grasps the objects and puts them into his mouth not in order to know them, but under a certain kind of primitive impulse. It happens that in doing so he starts to know the objects and this behavior has beneficial results for him. The demented schizophrenic in the terminal stage of regression may also be considered, in a certain way, partially psychically blind because the visual stimuli of the objects do not elicit cognitive and affective associations concerning their inedibility and the relative danger of putting them into his mouth and eating them. However, the possibility must be taken into consideration that he is conscious of the inedible qualities of these objects, but that he cannot inhibit the impulse to grasp them. Such a possibility cannot be ruled out. We may, however, advance the hypothesis that this behavior of children, bitemporal monkeys and regressed schizophrenics is a primitive way of reacting, which is characteristic of a certain level of development and is inhibited or transformed by higher centers. In other words, we may be dealing with one of those responses in which a short-circuiting takes place between the functions of reception and those of reaction instead of the usual response with participation of the higher centers. These reactions are intermediate between reflexes and voluntary acts, having some characteristics of compulsory acts. The "placing-into-mouth" reaction seems to belong to a much lower level than the archaic mechanisms described in other chapters, but seems to be at a higher level than for instance the grasp reflex, found in infants of one to three months and in adults with lesions of the frontal lobes, although the grasp reflex does not always appear as a true reflex but frequently as a prehension attitude implying some voluntary action. Schilder, however, considers the taking of objects into the mouth "at least as primitive as grasping." (225). This placing-into-mouth reaction is apparently not caused by any agnosia but seems to belong coincidentally to a level at which high apperceptions elaborating visual stimuli are not yet possible. This primitive reaction may have its early origins even in low vertebrates. It may have some connection with the feeding response of amphibians, reptiles and birds, animals in which the temporal lobe is represented only by the hippocampal area. Although its main purpose in phylogenesis is to contact food, it certainly is also a means of recognizing objects, especially for those animals whose visual centers have not reached a high degree of development.

Taking into consideration the coprophagic habit, the fact is worthy of mention, that such behavior is usual in healthy apes. To my knowledge this fact has not yet been reported in relation to psychiatric implications. In the Laboratory of Primate Biology of Yale University, directed by Dr. Yerkes, the writer had the opportunity to observe the frequency of such a habit in the chimpanzees kept in captivity. In one of his publications, Yerkes states that the causes, controls and prevention of coprophagy among captive chimpanzees have been searched carefully but with discouraging results (277). He feels that the hypothesis that coprophagy is induced by dietary deficiency finds no support in the inquiries conducted in his laboratories and concludes that this behavior is determined by complex underlying factors.

Köhler had previously described such peculiar behavior of primates (162). He reported that out of the many chimpanzees studied by him only one did not indulge in coprophagy. He states that the habit of smearing themselves with excrements is also frequent among chimpanzees. Such habits have not been observed in healthy monkeys. In mental patients this behavior is observed especially among catatonics and hebephrenics. Although it is a sign of advanced regression, it is not as malignant as the "oral tendency" described here, probably belonging to a less primitive level. As a matter of fact, catatonics, who have eaten feces or smeared themselves, occasionally gain a temporary remission (Chrzanowski, 53) or even an apparently complete recovery (personal observations).

II. Perceptual Alterations and Their Interpretation

The patients may remain indefinitely at a level characterized chiefly by the oral habits described above, or may progress to a more advanced phase which is characterized by apparent sensory alterations.

On account of the lack of cooperation and communicability of these patients, such alterations cannot be studied with the usual neurologic technic, but much stronger stimuli, not ordinarily used, or observation of the patient's reaction in certain special situations must be employed. Therefore only gross alterations are reported here, and no claim to accuracy is made.

It seems as though the patients who have reached this stage are insensitive to pain. They appear analgesic not only to pinprick but to much more painful stimuli. When they are in need of surgical intervention and require sutures in such sensitive regions as the lips, face, skull or hands, they act as though they cannot feel anything, even in the absence of any anesthetic procedure. I have many times sutured wounds caused by their violent and assaultive behavior, without eliciting any sign of pain or resistance.. Other patients seem to feel some pain, but far less than normal persons would. Only exceptionally is there a local withdrawal. The same anesthesia is noted for temperature. The patient may hold a piece of ice in his hands without showing any reaction. Pieces of ice may also be placed over the breast, abdomen or other sensitive regions without eliciting any reaction or defensive movement. Such patients also appear insensitive when the flame of a candle is passed rapidly over the skin. They may sit near the radiator, and if they are not moved, they may continue to stay there even when, as a result of close contact, they are burned. This state of insensitivity is, in my opinion, one of the chief causes of the large number of burns occurring in wards in which regressed schizophrenic patients live.

One may be induced to interpret this lack of responsiveness to pain and temperature stimuli not as true anesthesia but as an expression either of catatonic inactivity or of a certain kind of "inner negativism." Repeated observations, however, have led me to the conclusion that such an interpretation is not valid. Patients who show anesthesia for pain or temperature stimuli are not, as a rule, inactive; on the contrary, they show the aforementioned relative increase in activity, which, together with the apparent anesthesia, is responsible for numerous accidents. The possibility that these patients do not react to dangerous sensations on account of inner negativism in my opinion is also untenable because many such patients do not show other signs of negativism. The phenomenon of negativism, although not absent at this stage of the illness, is much more commonly observed in patients who have reached a less advanced stage. On the other hand, the possibility that pain and temperature sensations are perceived, but that only the affective components of such perceptions are lost, must be taken into consideration and will be discussed later. In a small number of patients this apparent anesthesia or hypesthesia for pain and temperature stimuli is only transitory. Even patients who have been insensitive to heat for several months to some extent may reacquire capacity to perceive pain or temperature sensations or both. Occasionally, striking changes occur at brief intervals. However, I have the impression that some degree of hypesthesia is always retained. Partial hypesthesia is also found in many patients who have not yet reached the terminal stage. Tactile perception does not seem impaired in these patients. Tendon and superficial reflexes are not only present but often increased. The corneal reflexes are also present. On the other hand, many, but not all, of the patients who present anesthesia for pain and temperature stimuli seem also to have lost the sensation of taste. When they are given bitter radishes or teaspoons of sugar, salt, pepper or quinine, they do not show any pleasant or unpleasant reaction. They do not spit out the unpleasant substances as quickly as possible, as do control mentally defective persons or deteriorated patients with organic disease, but continue to eat the entire dose without hesitation. Some of them seem to recognize salt but do not object to pepper or quinine. Others react mildly to quinine but not to pepper or salt.

In contrast to this lack of reactivity to pain, temperature

and taste stimuli is the normal reaction to strong olfactory stimuli. Patients who do not react at all to such stimuli as flames, pieces of ice and suturing, react in a normal way when they smell such things as ammonia and strong vinegar. They withdraw quickly from the stimulus, with manifest displeasure. Such a reaction strikes the observer, inasmuch as many other strong stimuli from other sensory fields do not bring about any response, or bring about only a mild reaction. It seems as though the phylogenetically ancient olfactory sense can better resist the schizophrenic process. However, the schizophrenic patient does not seem to make use of these olfactory sensations as well as he can, probably on account of his general withdrawal.

The aforementioned phases of the terminal stage (phases characterized by the food-grabbing habit, the "placing into mouth" habit, apparent anesthesia for pain, temperature and taste sensation, and preponderance of the olfactory sense, respectively) do not always occur in the order given. A large number of patients, especially, but not exclusively, those of the paranoid type, remain indefinitely at a less advanced stage. In others two stages of the illness overlap. For instance, a few patients who have the food-grabbing habit may retain the capacity to hallucinate. Other food grabbers may already have anesthesia for pain and temperature stimuli, and so on. However, the order described is the one in which I have most commonly observed appearance of the symptoms. Occasionally a patient may improve and return to a less advanced stage. Intravenous injections of sodium amytal do not produce any perceptible change in the picture of the terminal stage of schizophrenia.

Although statistical conclusions are premature and difficult on account of this overlapping of symptoms, I have the impression that the number of patients presenting the habit of grabbing food or of placing objects in the mouth is large in services for patients at the terminal stages. The number of patients presenting some hypesthesia for pain, temperature and taste sensations is also large. On the contrary, patients presenting absolute anesthesia for pain and temperature sensations are relatively few.

Several authors have reported altered perception of pain in cases of early catatonia, and Bender and Schilder have discussed this subject in relation to the capacity to acquire conditioned reflexes (21). In my experience, the hypesthesia found in patients with early catatonia is generally not so severe as that observed in patients who have reached the terminal stage, and often is not detected if, instead of pinprick, one uses stronger stimuli. Anesthesia for temperature and taste stimuli is even more rare in patients with early catatonia and is not comparable to that encountered in very regressed patients, with conditions originally diagnosed as various types of dementia praecox. However, the possibility is not denied that the nature of the phenomenon may be the same. In many of the textbooks of psychiatry no mention is made of this analgesia encountered in some deteriorated schizophrenics. Bleuler, however, reported that an analgesia, sometimes quite complete, occurs in schizophrenia not too rarely. He stated that this anesthesia is responsible for the fact that the patients readily injure themselves (29).

In agreement with the observations of Bender and Schilder on patients with early catatonia, I am inclined to believe that the real sensation of pain and temperature is not lost in patients in the terminal stage. The fact that the corneal reflexes are always retained may be a proof of it. However, these patients seem to be unaware of the painful and thermic stimuli and do not show any emotional reaction to them. They seem to be unable to perceive the stimuli. In other words, the rough sensation may be present but remains isolated and is not elaborated to the perception level. The patients are unable to recognize the emotional and cognitive value of the termic and painful stimuli and therefore are unaware of the possible dangers which they at times imply. For this reason they often hurt themselves. These patients, for all practical purposes, have agnosia and may be compared to persons with sensorial aphasia who hear spoken language without understanding it.

Is this loss of nociceptive perception only an exaggeration of the general schizophrenic emotional indifference? Probably the cause of these derangements is the same, but for all practical purposes these patients are better described as having agnosia and may be termed "psychically analgesic," and not apathetic only. They fail to perceive pain and temperature sensation, not only from an emotional but from a cognitive point of view. That is the reason that they so often hurt themselves if they are not under constant supervision. At present it is a controversial problem whether these phenomena are due to loss of emotional capacity or to loss of perception of pain and temperature sensation. The relation between emotional indifference and agnosia has been taken into consideration by von Monakow and Mourgue, who observed impairment of emotions in aphasic persons (267, 268). The same authors considered the possibility that asymbolia may be due to disturbances in the affective sphere.*

The fact that taste perception is often lost or impaired in these analgesic patients and that the olfactory perceptions are preserved instead is also thought-stimulating. The association of taste and pain asymbolias points to the conclusion that taste should be included among the general somatic sensations, as investigations by Boernstein (32, 33) and by Shenkin

---

* The recent findings by Penfield and Rasmussen prove that pain and temperature sensations are retained even when the whole cortical areas which supersede these sensations are removed (208). These findings make even more difficult to interpret the pain and temperature anesthesia of the schizophrenic. (See page 431 for a hypothetical explanation.)

and Lewey (236) seem to prove. The striking survival of smell perceptions, which are phylogenetically very old, may induce one to think that the archipallium is less affected than the neopallium by the schizophrenic process. The olfactory sense, which is the dominant sense in lower vertebrates, in some regressed schizophrenic patients seems to reacquire a position of predominance among the senses, not because of increased acuity but because of impairment of perceptions of stimuli coming from other sensory fields. However, contrary to what is found in lower vertebrates, these schizophrenic patients do not take advantage of the olfactory sense as they could. It is interesting to observe that the sense of smell in schizophrenic patients is not involved even in short-circuiting reactions, whereas it was involved in the monkeys of Klüver and Bucy.

CHAPTER XVIII

Recapitulation and Interpretation of Schizophrenic Regression

In the previous chapters of Part IV, we have seen the long and multiform course of schizophrenia, from the initial to the terminal stages. We shall try now to recapitulate what we have reported in detail and to interpret the factors which in many cases make this regression unavoidable.

We have seen how an uncoped-with state of anxiety and vulnerability, whose roots are to be found in early childhood, makes the patient enter the first stage of the illness. In the first stage he exploits a potentiality for using archaic mechanisms which are dormant in every human being. The patient resorts to them when any other method of decreasing anxiety and maintaining his own individuality has failed. In the first stage the patient is still struggling between the world of reality and the world of his symptoms. He is not completely regressed to any particular level, and is still experiencing anxiety.

In the second stage, this fight between reality and illness is over. There is no apparent emotional turmoil. One feels that the patient has more completely regressed to a lower archaic level. Paleologic thinking and desocialization are predominant. The patient seems to have accepted his illness; but the illness does not seem to have accepted the patient at this stage, and seems to require further regression. How is this to be explained?

Throughout this book it has been maintained that when the dynamic factors compel the patient to develop schizophrenic symptoms, there is a regression. However, the patient, with rare exceptions, does not *integrate* at a lower level. He cannot. Biologically, psychologically and socially he is not fit to integrate at a level which is not originally his own. What he will undergo is a *regression,* but not an *integration* at a lower level. Perhaps an example from biology will clarify this issue. Lower animals, who do not have a cerebral cortex, are integrated at a non-cortical level of development. For their kind of life, they do not require a cerebral cortex. But a higher animal without a cerebral cortex does not function like a healthy animal of a non-cortical species. He is in a pathological condition, because his whole organism, each part of it, was integrated at a level which required the cerebral cortex.

No matter how much the schizophrenic regresses, he cannot become a healthy infant, he cannot become a pre-sapiens man, he cannot become a chimpanzee. Children, ancient men, apes are totally integrated at their respective levels; the schizophrenic will never be. He will not even be able to exploit the reduced potentialities of the levels to which he regresses. For instance, we have seen that when in the terminal stage, many sensory perceptions are impaired, the patient cannot exploit the ancient olfactory sense as much as he potentially should be able to, because his total organism, like the organism of every man, is not organized for the prominence of this sense. In other instances, it is true that he will repeat compulsively actions and habits of the levels to which he regresses, such as the hoarding habit, or placing into mouth habit, etc. These habits, however, have lost their original purposeful meaning, and are not integrated with the rest of the life of the patient. No matter how much the patient regresses, he will always be disintegrated. This process of disintegration is enhanced by another phenomenon which, as we have seen, occurs repeatedly. This phenomenon consists of the fact that when a higher level is out of function or does not function properly, several lower levels are disinhibited at the same time and interfere with one another.* The schizophrenic patient is thus obliged to operate at several levels at the same time. This adds to the confusion, and increases the disequilibirum and the disintegration. But disintegration is not a state which nature accepts. Then how does the patient defend himself from it? With further regression. The same mechanism is repeated all over again.

The patient has reached the third state of regression when his voluntary life is so much obliterated that certain primitive habits acquire prominence. The habit which was given particular importance in my research is the habit of hoarding objects. When the patient regresses further, he shows a tendency not only to collect these objects, but to make them become part of himself by putting them in the natural cavities of his body (vagina, mouth, anus, auditory canals, etc.). When he regresses further and reaches the terminal stage, he does not grasp the objects any longer for the purpose of collecting them, but in order to ingest them. He places them indiscriminately in his mouth, no matter whether they are edible or not. Examining these phenomena in a longitudinal section, one is induced to believe that one habit is just a continuation or transformation of the other; first, the objects are

---

* The disinhibition of lower levels seems to involve only cortical levels. As a matter of fact in some cases the indications are that in schizophrenia there is an increased inhibition of subcortical levels. (See page 430.)

collected, then an attempt is made to incorporate part of them, finally they are totally incorporated, by ingestion. We have here a bizarre reproduction in reverse of phenomena which occurred in phylogenesis. Low species grasp, or pick up only what they eat or use right away. Very primitive men are also exclusively interested in activities which have an immediate goal. (See page 239). Later they become interested in future needs and collect objects. (See page 356). The newborn baby is concerned with activities which involve his mouth; only much later will he become interested not in ingesting objects but in collecting them.

At the terminal stage of the illness many patients also show those quasi-neurological alterations that we have described in the previous chapter. These alterations indicate a regression to a level where even many of our common perceptions do not exist. At this level the organism is able to experience some sensations, only when they are deprived of perceptual elaborations.

From the preterminal to the terminal stages there is a progressive decrease of the processes involving apperceptions and perceptions. The actions of the patient are responses less and less mediated, and more and more primitive, almost like reflexes. Finally, it seems as if some of the sensory stimuli are not even perceived or recognized, although they are experienced as sensations. Are these perceptual alterations a further step of teleologic regression, the final unique outcome of a progressive self-perpetuating regression? It would seem so. The patient seems compelled to escape even from perceptions and he functions like a person suffering from psychic agnosia.

What is the relation between the reported observations on regressed schizophrenics and the libido theory promulgated by Freud? The oral tendencies seem to be manifestations of what Freud calls the oral stage and the hoarding tendencies seem to be manifestations of what Freud calls the anal stage.

Although I have already dealt with this matter in other parts of this book, the problem needs more discussion at this point. The Freudian theory of regression appears to me fully acceptable. There seems to be no doubt that the schizophrenic regresses to lower levels. However, I do not think that the regression is caused by what is implied in the libido theory. The phenomena observed in the schizophrenics are not due to an arrest of sexual energy, but to an attempted return to lower levels of integration. Not the sexual energy only, but the stage of the whole biological development is involved.

The oral tendencies of the new-born infant are biologically determined. As Clara Thompson puts it, the newborn infant is chiefly a mouth (258). At birth the most mature part of the cortex is that which presides over the functions of the oral cavity. Erotic pleasure, if it exists at all, is incidental. The pleasure that the baby and the regressed schizophrenic attain with their oral tendencies seems to be a general pleasure derived from the ability to do what they have the potentiality of doing at that specific level.

The collecting habit, considered by orthodox Freudians as an anal habit, is also biologically determined, although reinforced by cultural attitudes. The desire to collect without incorporating the objects, requires a much more differentiated neurological apparatus. It requires, among other things, the ability to anticipate the future (page 356). The perceptual alterations described in the previous chapter are also difficult to explain with the libido theory.

Summarizing, it seems to me that all these manifestations, among which are those which are called anal and oral, are symptomatic, not of an arrested sexuality only, but of lower levels of integration which have lower psychological and, at times, neurological organizations. At each of these levels, when they appeared originally in phylogenesis, a mature sexual development could be reached; but when regression occurs,

sexuality cannot integrate well to lower levels, for the reasons
which have been mentioned in this chapter.

At this point, we may again attempt a definition of schizophrenia, which takes into consideration the regression. *Schizophrenia is a specific reaction to an extreme state of anxiety,
originating in childhood, and reactivated later in life by
psychological factors. The specific reaction consists of the
adoption of archaic mental mechanisms, which belong to
lower levels of integration. Inasmuch as the result is a regression to, but not an integration at lower levels, a disequilibrium
is engendered which causes further regression, at times to
levels even lower than the one in which certain perceptions
are possible.*

PART FIVE

The Psychosomatic Aspect
of Schizophrenia

CHAPTER XIX

Introductory Remarks

Many psychiatrists today continue to think that schizophrenia is based on a primary organic pathology. Diametrically opposite is the attitude of those researchers who, in categorical terms, assert that there is no organic change in this psychosis. The organic pathology which is occasionally found, according to them is not related to the schizophrenic process but is purely coincidental.

Indeed, the thousands of articles written on the somatic changes in schizophrenia have not thrown much light on this condition. However, one cannot say that there are no somatic changes in schizophrenia. To deny them would be to doubt the laborious works of honest workers and to blind ourselves to facts, just because we do not want to see them. In fairness to those who deny organic changes in schizophrenia, we must say that the majority of these exclusively psychologically-oriented workers deal with schizophrenics in relatively early stages of the illness, and that they have very little experience with patients who have been sick for ten, twenty or more years. But it is in the latter that organic changes are more likely to be found. These findings, some of which will be reviewed in this part of the book, have not been consistent, and their interpretation is difficult.

In my opinion, the findings do not prove that schizophrenia is primarily an organic condition, but rather the opposite, that is, that the psychological changes produce alterations of the somatic functions. These altered somatic functions in turn may produce even organic pathology in certain cases. In other words, the psychosomatic effects that we find in neuroses may be found in psychoses also. I see no reason why it should not be so. In addition, some somatic changes may be compensatory mechanisms or reactions to other changes. A chain of altered functions, leading to clear-cut anatomical pathology, may be engendered.

The author has not engaged in studies designed to find organic changes in the soma of schizophrenics, nor has he read all the works written by other authors on this subject. In fact, the number of such articles is so great that it is almost impossible to become acquainted with all of them. Lewis (173) and Bellak (18) have each reviewed most of the works written in one decade. The present author has selected for review a few of those which seemed to him the most important contributions.

The somatic changes will be discussed under three headings: 1) The cardiovascular changes; 2) The endocrine changes; 3) Metabolic and various other changes. These findings will be reinterpreted according to the above-mentioned psychosomatic concept. For reports on the other somatic changes, the reader is referred to more complete works on this subject, and especially to the paper by MacKenzie Shattock (253). Although I disagree with some of his conclusions, I greatly admire his highly scholarly paper, a real mine of information. Another important work, especially for the study of the gastro-intestinal apparatus and the reticulo-endothelial system in schizophrenia, is the one by Buscaino (37).

Some of my personal studies about the functional changes involving the nervous system have already been mentioned (pages 372–378). The role of the central nervous system in schizophrenia will be studied in Chapter XXI and given prominent consideration. This is an unusual procedure. In fact, the central nervous system, which occupies the first role in organic psychiatric studies, receives the least consideration in psychosomatic research. This seems unjustifiable to me and caused only by a fear of neurology which psychodynamic psychiatrists have acquired. If psychological stimuli produce functional or organic disorders in practically every organ of the soma, there is no reason why they should not be able to affect the nervous system, too, which is more directly under their influence.

Finally, a chapter will be devoted to the study of the autonomic nervous system and its central control in schizophrenia.

CHAPTER XX

Somatic Changes in Schizophrenia

I. The Cardiovascular Apparatus

The prevalent opinion of the authors who have studied this subject is that the blood pressure of schizophrenics is generally lower than that of the general population of similar age. Freeman, Hosking and Sleeper found in a series of 180 patients that the average systolic pressure was 104.5 mm. Hg. and the diastolic was 54.5 (86). These values were much lower than those found in medical students examined as control cases. The highest values were found in paranoids and the lowest in catatonics. Rheingold too has found the blood pressure of 129 schizophrenics in an early stage of their illness, to be lower than that of the general population (life insurance applicants) (217). Shattock has compared the blood pressure of "refractory" patients to those of socialized patients (235). He found that the average systolic pressure of 46 refractory schizophrenics was 118 mm Hg., and that of 32 socialized schizophrenics 131.5 mm Hg. The paranoid patients in each of the two groups had the highest blood pressures. Gottlieb and several other authors have found a close correlation between the systolic and diastolic pressure in schizophrenics (118). Some authors (Cameron and Jellinek, 41) have found a rise of blood pressure in clinical remission after insulin treatment. Farral and Vassaf have noted even an increase in the size of the heart after this treatment (69).

Nolan Lewis, in his well-known study on the constitutional factors in Dementia Praecox, found a hypoplastic cardiovascular system in schizophrenics who came to autopsy (172). He made it clear, however, that such hypoplastic condition was not found in paranoids. Hypertrophy of the heart was never found, even in presence of valvular lesions.

Finkelman and Haffron found the volume of circulating blood in 39 schizophrenics to be diminished, in comparison to that of manic-depressive patients (82). The intracranial blood flow has been studied by numerous authors, but so discordant are the findings that no conclusion is possible. Perhaps it is safe to say that no important deviation from normal values has been obtained in the intracranial flow of schizophrenics.

Another alteration which has interested many authors is the exaggerated tendency towards vasoconstriction found in all vessels from capillaries to large arteries. Abramson found excessive vasoconstriction in the vessels of schizophrenics exposed to cold temperatures (2). He found improvement in the blood circulation after insulin treatment. Jung and Carmichael (145), Minski (195), and others have found vasomotor disturbances leading to cyanosis. Some authors felt that the vasoconstriction was an exaggerated reaction to cold temperatures and inactivity (Stern, 245). Others, on the other hand, feel that there is a permanent vasoconstriction in the vessels of patients, especially catatonics.

Shattock (235), who has studied intensely the vascular conditions of schizophrenics, found the following:

1) At room temperature, 62–65 F. (16.7–18.3 C.) cyanosis of the extremities, especially of the feet, was present in 43% of 220 female psychotics and in only 5% of 300 male psychotics.

2) At room temperature, 62 F. (16.7 C.) the average temperature of the hands and feet of 30 female schizophrenics was significantly lower than that of 30 female affective psychotics.

3) There was no relation between cyanosis of the extremities and advancing age.

4) There was imperfect correlation between cyanosis and inactivity.

5) The effect of posture on the circulation of cyanosed extremities was shown by diminution of cyanosis after raising of the feet.

6) Temporary relief of cyanosis was obtained by any means which brings about vasodilation, like vasodilator drugs, etc.

7) The brachial, radial, dorsalis pedis of 28 female schizophrenics who suffered from peripheral cyanosis were found to be contracted and pulseless, but these vessels were normal after vasodilation had been obtained.

Summarizing, we may state that the four main alterations found in the cardiovascular apparatus of schizophrenics are 1) decrease in the size of the heart; 2) decrease in the volume of the blood flow; 3) decrease in systematic blood pressure; 4) exaggerated tendency to vasoconstriction and resulting diminished blood supply.

The whole circulatory system of many schizophrenics seem hypoplastic or at least in a state of diminished functionality. How are these findings to be interpreted? Do they indicate a congenital cardiovascular hypoplasia of the pre-schizophrenic, who, on account of this hypoplasia, will be predisposed to schizophrenia? Or are these findings not a pre-disposition or cause of schizophrenia, but rather one of the results or of the many by-products of this condition? In interpreting these findings, we have to take into consideration the following points:

1) These findings are not constant. Although it is true that the average blood pressure of a large number of schizo-phrenics is lower than the blood pressure of a correspond-ing number of people taken from the general population, the individual schizophrenic does not necessarily have a low blood pressure. In other words, low blood pressure, or hypoplasia of the heart, or other vascular alterations, are not present in each case of schizophrenia, or necessary for the diagnosis of schizophrenia. In the initial stage of the illness, the cardiovascular alterations are, by far, less frequent.

2) The fact that several authors have found these symptoms, including the hypoplasia of the heart, diminishing or dis-appearing at remission, seems a strong indication that these symptoms are functional, not based on a congenital defect.

3) The schizophrenic makes relatively few demands on his circulatory system, which consequently is less active than that of a normal person. First of all, the physical activities of the schizophrenic are very much reduced.* Even though he may have transitory periods of excitement, restlessness, and impulsive behavior, his activity as a whole is very much decreased. Secondly, he does not discharge his anxiety or other emotional states through his cardiovas-

---

* A lowering of blood pressure which is found in many tubercular patients who are confined to bed or compelled to rest, may also be partially due to inactivity.

cular system any longer. The psychological stimuli of external or internal origin, which produce variations in the blood pressure of the normal person, do not affect the schizophrenic very much. Sociological factors, which complicate our modern society more and more, have an effect on the vascular system. High blood pressure and arteriosclerosis are much rarer in Negroes who live in Africa than in Negroes who live in the United States. The schizophrenic becomes less perceptive to the sociopsychological stimuli which act on the cardiovascular system, or finds other mechanisms of response to them. Paranoid patients, who remain better socialized and more active than the other schizophrenics, maintain a higher blood pressure. Again, it is the paranoid mental condition which allows better functioning of the cardiovascular system. It is not a more efficient cardiovascular system which predisposes the individual to the paranoid type, rather than to the simple, hebephrenic and catatonic types.

4) Some authors, like Lewis, have been impressed by the fact that even in cases with valvular lesions, hypertrophy of the heart was not observed. Again, I think that, although the heart was diseased, the diminished demands made on it made a compensatory hypertrophy unnecessary. Even without this compensatory hypertrophy, the schizophrenic would supply sufficient blood to his organs; however, if his heart suddenly were requested to work more efficiently, as in the sudden outbreak of an acute infective condition, the patient might succumb. General practitioners occasionally find unusual combinations of diseases which show an uncommon course in the clinical picture. For instance, if a patient with a sick heart, in danger of decompensation, is also affected by a crippling arthritis, which reduces the activities of the patient to a very minimum, his heart may not decompensate for a long time, or only when an

acute infection occurs. The same situation may occur in schizophrenia.

5) The low blood pressure and the diminished activity make the patient more vulnerable to low temperatures. The vasoconstriction which is found in many schizophrenics seems to have the main purpose of preventing dispersion of heat. If a normal person is exposed to a cold environment, he will try to warm up by moving, doing exercises, eating, grinding his teeth, etc. The regressed schizophrenic does not increase his activities which, on the contrary, remain very few. If he is in a catatonic state, he may not move at all. Thus a compensatory mechanism, which does not require a voluntary act, occurs. Vessels constrict, and cyanosis may ensue. Cyanosis is found more frequently in women than in men, because in our society certain parts of the female body, such as arms and legs, are more exposed than those of men. This fact holds true even for patients in mental institutions.

Another factor increases the constriction of the vessels, especially in catatonics. The postures, which they maintain at times for whole days, one day after another, activate anti-gravity vasoconstrictor mechanisms. Without these mechanisms, edema due to blood stasis would be very frequent. Edemas of the ankles and feet are common in catatonics who maintain postures in a standing position, but would be much more frequent if these vasoconstrictor mechanisms were not present. We cannot minimize the importance of motor activity for a good blood circulation. The fact that marked vasoconstriction is found in patients who are at times restless and destructive does not invalidate this interpretation. First of all, as mentioned before, although these patients may be episodically hyperactive, they are, as a whole, hypoactive. Secondly, autonomous mechanisms which have originated during long periods of inactivity may continue to function, sometimes even if such inactivity decreases, because the cardiovascular system may not become quickly adjusted to the new demands. It has to use the old mechanisms. The vasoconstriction obviously has an additional compensatory function, namely, to raise the blood pressure. It may seem strange that the blood pressure of the schizophrenic is so low, notwithstanding the vasoconstriction. The obvious conclusion is that the blood pressure would be even lower, without this vasoconstriction. Such low blood pressure, although tolerable in normal circumstances, cannot be tolerated by the body when the temperature is low.

6) We do not imply with the foregoing that this relative hypofunctionality of the cardiovascular system is directly due only to inactivity or to diminished cardiovascular responsiveness to emotions. Another mechanism has to be taken into consideration, which is involved either directly or through the mechanisms already mentioned. This is an altered functionality of the autonomic nervous system which regulates the cardiovascular system. But, as we shall mention in Chapter XXII, we feel that this altered functionality of the autonomic nervous system is also psychosomatic in origin.

II. The Endocrine Glands

Great etiological significance has been attributed to the endocrine system in the etiology of schizophrenia. This occurred in an era when endocrinology was making great advances.

Many cases of schizophrenia presenting varied endocrinologic disorders have been described, and each time with the implication that the mental disease may be in a state of causal relationship with the endocrinopathy. A visit to a large mental hospital would be sufficient to point out that the number of endocrine disorders is not much larger among schizophrenics than in the general population, and that an occasional endocrinopathy should be considered an accidental concomitant finding.

In my clinical experience with ambulatory schizophrenics I have not found a high percentage of any typical endocrine syndrome. In some large state hospitals one finds a slightly larger percentage of adolescent schizophrenics who are dysplastic than would be expected from the general population. In a large hospital one sees also a considerable number of cases of marked obesity in hebephrenic girls, and of the adolescent type of dystrophia adiposo-genitalis (Frohlich's syndrome) in both boys and girls who are affected by the simple type of schizophrenia. It is possible that these endocrine disorders have crippled the patients not only physically but also psychologically, have increased their anxiety and made them more susceptible to the psychosis.

Now that the enthusiasm for endocrinology in psychiatric circles has passed, it seems universally agreed that no classical endocrinological syndrome can be considered responsible for schizophrenia. The possibility remains that another endocrine disorder, not manifesting itself with the usual symptoms, may be incriminated eventually. Many researches have been carried out with the purpose of investigating this possibility.

The thyroid gland, for example, has been studied by many. Witte, who studied a series of 815 patients, was unable to confirm the high percentage of thyroid atrophy that other authors had found (276). He observed, however, a tendency to accumulate colloid, a characteristic indicative of moderate functional hypothyroidism. In a minority of patients, Hoskins found a triad of symptoms: low oxygen consumption rate, secondary anemia, and scanty, nitrogen-low urine (133). This minority of patients generally responded favorably to thyroid medication.

Pathology of the adrenal glands has also been suggested, especially since the catatonic picture, with asthenia, low blood pressure, low oxygen consumption and anemia, reminds one of Addison's disease. Hoskin's therapeutic experiments, however, failed to show any improvement in patients under adrenalin medication.

That the adrenal glands may be implicated was also suggested by Selye's recent studies (230, 231). According to him, any stressful condition engenders a syndrome consisting of 1) acute gastro-intestinal ulcers; 2) adreno-cortical stimulation, evidenced by hyperemia and discharge of secretory granules from the adrenal cortex; and 3) thymico-lymphatic involution, accompanied by characteristic hematologic changes (lymphopenia, eosinopenia and polymorphonuclear leucocytosis). Later Selye found that the stressing situation acts upon the body directly and indirectly through the pituitary and adrenal glands. Through some "unknown pathway" the stressing stimulus travels from the directly injured area of the body to the anterior pituitary. This gland, after being stimulated, secretes ACTH hormone which, in turn, stimulates the adrenal cortex to discharge corticoid hormones. Some of these corticoids are prophlogistic, that is, they enhance the inflammatory potentiality by stimulating the proliferative ability and the reactivity of the connective tissue. Other corticoids are antiphlogistic, inasmuch as they inhibit the production of granulomatous tissue and other facets of the inflammatory process. The total of these non-specific reactions is what Selye called the "general adaptation syndrome."

Many authors have observed a dysfunction of the adaptation syndrome in schizophrenia. According to Pincus and

Hoagland, schizophrenics respond to "stress" differently from normal persons (213). The ingenious experiments of these two investigators prove that if the patients are given adreno-cortical extracts, their responses to stress are not considerably different from those of normal control subjects. On the other hand, if the patients are given high doses of ACTH, their responses to stress are by far inferior to those of control subjects. The authors conclude that the adrenal cortices of the patients are not adequately stimulated by ACTH. ACTH may be produced normally in the schizophrenic; it is the adrenal cortex which does not respond. Although these authors do not think that this lack of response is the one and only "cause" of the psychosis, they think that it may be one of a number of important factors that are involved. Pincus and Hoagland have worked on patients who had an average duration of hospitalization of 2½ years. Gildea (quoted by Pincus and Hoagland) found an abnormal adaptation reaction in chronic patients, but not in early patients (213). Also Parson, Gildea and others obtained data different from those of Pincus and Hoagland (207). They found that psychotic subjects respond to epinephrine in the same way that the controls do. The degree of lymphocytopenia was practically the same as in the control subjects. Electroshock produced a degree of lymphocytopenia similar to that obtained after epinephrine. Since lymphocytopenia following stress is dependent upon a normal pituitary-adrenal system, Parsons and collaborators conclude that this functional system is not impaired in schizophrenics. On the other hand, the same authors found that psychotic patients, both manic depressive and schizophrenic, do not respond to psychological stress with lymphocytophenia or hyperglycemia. In this respect, they do differ from normal subjects. The findings obtained by the authors mentioned and by others are such that no definite conclusion is possible. They all seem to agree on one thing: Psychological stress does not produce a normal general adaptation reaction in the schizophrenic.

This result is easy to understand because the psychological stressing stimulus may not be perceived as stressing by the schizophrenic. Therefore, it may never reach the pituitary gland or, if it reaches the pituitary gland, it may have lost a great deal of stressing power. But even if the stimulus is physiological or chemical and not psychological, it must travel from the injured part of the body to the pituitary gland, and it probably travels not humorally but through the nervous system. Now, as we shall see in Chapter XXII, the psychological states of the schizophrenic may indirectly alter or delay or weaken even the non-psychological functions of the nervous system, so that the stressing stimulus may have lost power when it reaches the pituitary gland. If the pituitary gland is stimulated, however, the adrenal gland should be stimulated in turn because here the interstimulation is not through the nervous system, but humorally, namely, through the ACTH hormones. Pincus and Hoagland, however, found that when patients were administered a standard 25 mgm. dose of ACTH, they responded much less intensely than normal subjects (213). They concluded that the adrenal cortex of schizophrenics is much less responsive than that of normal subjects. Actually, the mechanism is more complicated than that, as Pincus and Hoagland themselves admit, because the stimulated adrenal glands also secrete hormones, which again act on the pituitary gland and perhaps on the central nervous system.

Some authors have considered the pituitary gland as being directly involved in the etiology of schizophrenia, but the evidence so far has not been convincing. More importance has been attributed to the sexual glands, especially since sexual maladjustment is one of the symptoms of the disorder.

Mott reported a more or less advanced atrophy of the testicles in all cases of schizophrenia, and a complete arrest of spermatogenesis in the majority of them (197). Hemphill, Reiss and Taylor confirmed these findings in biopsy specimens from patients who did not belong to the paranoid type (124, 125). They saw that in the males the atrophy was limited to the seminiferous tubules and speculated that what was at fault was probably a gonadotropic hormone from the anterior lobe of the pituitary gland. Miss Morse criticized Mott's work (quoted in 126). She felt that the changes found in the glands of the patients might have resulted from causes unrelated to schizophrenia. For instance, the age of the patient, the state of nutrition, the nature and duration of the terminal illness are all factors which influence the histologic condition of the endocrine glands. Miss Forster, a pupil of Mott, confirmed her teacher's findings (quoted in 126). She noticed signs of early involution in the ovaries of schizophrenic women who had reached the age of thirty.

Menstrual disorders, especially prolongation of the interval and amenorrhea, are very common in schizophrenic women and well known to all psychiatrists. Ripley and Papanicolaou investigated the menstrual cycle of patients with studies of vaginal smears (220). They found in both schizophrenic and affective disorders a greater irregularity than in a comparable normal group. A tendency to a delay, a weakened expression, or a complete temporary suppression of the follicular reaction were found by these authors. They also frequently noticed prolongation of the menstrual interval and amenorrhea. All of these alterations were interpreted as the result of a hindered growth of the ovarian follicles. Ripley and Papanicoloau also found a correlation between the severity of the illness and the degree of abnormality of the menstrual cycle. An improvement in the psychological symptomatology was usually accompanied by a return to a more normal menstrual function.

The authors could not ascertain the existence of an etiological relationship.

How is one to interpret these reports on the endocrine system in schizophrenia? Although nothing has been definitely ascertained, one may nevertheless attempt to formulate some conclusions and hypotheses with the probability that they may be correct.

1) An etiological relationship, proving that schizophrenia is engendered by an endocrine disorder, has not been demonstrated. On the contrary, the more we know about the syndromes caused by dysfunction of the endocrine glands, the more we depart from this assumption.

2) It seems fairly well established that in the majority of cases of schizophrenia, especially in the chronic cases, there is a diminished functionality of the endocrine system. At this stage of our knowledge, it is difficult to determine whether this diminished functionality is due to decrease in the production of hormones, or to the decreased responsiveness to them. This point has been well emphasized by Hoskins.

3) The authors who believe in the organic nature of schizophrenia have seen in this diminished functionality of the endocrine system another proof that their assumption is valid. The writer joins those authors who view this diminished functionality of the endocrine system as another psychosomatic disorder of schizophrenia. According to this interpretation, the psychological picture of schizophrenia directly or indirectly diminishes the amount of stimulation to which the endocrine system is subjected; the resulting diminished functionality in turn engenders in the organism unusual functional compensatory mechanisms and eventually even organic damages, such as fibrosis of the testicles.

It is appropriate at this point to mention an ingenious work of Roizin, which deserves great attention (222). Roizin worked with roosters which were experimentally blinded and fed artificially. In comparison with control cases, he found very marked atrophy of the testicles of the blind rooster, although the general weight was not considerably diminished. (At the end of the experiment the average total weight of control cases was 1.250 gm., and the weight of the testicles 8.40 gm. In the blinded animals the total weight was 1.100 gm., and the weight of the testicles 0.320 gm.)

Roizin's findings may be interpreted as indicating that lack of sensory stimulation was producing the atrophy or impairment of growth of the testicles. Something similar may occur in human beings. Blindness in men would not produce atrophy of the testicles, because men may become stimulated by other sensory organs, or by inner images and thoughts. In many cases of schizophrenia, however, this inner or external stimulation is defective. It is important to add that testicular alterations have not been found in paranoid patients, who are in better contact with external reality than hebephrenics and catatonics. (Hemphill 124, Hemphill, Reiss, Taylor 125).

4) Here too we must repeat what we have mentioned in connection with the cardiovascular system. The diminished functionality of the endocrine system in schizophrenia is not necessarily directly related to the decrease in stimulation to which the endocrine system is subjected on account of the psychological picture of the psychosis. An altered functionality of the autonomic nervous system, which controls the endocrine glands, may be responsible, even totally, for this hypofunctionality. But again, as we shall see in Chapter XXII, we feel that this altered functionality of the autonomic nervous system is psychosomatic in nature.

III. Metabolic and Various Other Changes

Numerous metabolic changes have been described in schizophrenia. Many authors have proven in a convincing manner that in many schizophrenics there is a deficiency in the intake of oxygen. (Hoskins 131, 132). Several explanations have been given: for instance, that the blood of the patient leaves the lungs in an undersaturated condition; or, that the tissues fail to absorb an adequate quantity of oxygen; or, that the sluggishness or hypoplasia of the circulatory system does not permit an adequate oxygen supply. Other authors have tried to correlate this low consumption of oxygen with hormonic changes (Gornall, Eglitis and others, 117). Here again one may repeat what has been said in relation to the circulatory system. Is the low intake of oxygen what compels the schizophrenic toward low activity? Are the psychological manifestations of schizophrenia similar to those described by McFarland (180) in state of oxygen deprivation? Or is the opposite true, that is, that the psychological condition of schizophrenia, with its withdrawal characteristics, reduces the oxygen requirements of the patient?

The carbohydrate metabolism in schizophrenia has also been studied by numerous authors. The reader who is interested in this subject is referred again to the excellent review by Shattock (235). Shattock states that many of the reports have been contradicted by other authors; however, the following three findings have seldom been disputed: 1) the presence of a normal fasting blood-sugar curve; 2) a tendency to sustained hyperglycemia in early or acute cases; 3) a normal intravenous glucose tolerance test in many patients who, instead, had showed prolonged hyperglycemia after oral administration of glucose. Although these findings are undisputed, their interpretation is very controversial. Lack of hyperglycemia during emotional states will be examined again on page 427.

Many other metabolic studies have been done in schizophrenics, from the determination of enzymes of the brain (Ashby, 13) to the study of the mineral constituents of blood cells (Katzenelbogen and Snyder, 154). No conclusion could be drawn, except the one drawn by Bellak and Wilson who, commenting on the biochemical studies on schizophrenics, wrote, "Their only consistent difference from normals lies in the greater variability of values for almost any factor investigated." (19).

Without resorting to laboratory tests, other apparently simple physical findings in schizophrenia impress the clinician. First of all there is the well known fact that most schizophrenics belong to the asthenic constitutional type. It is common knowledge that Kretschmer attributed a great significance to this particular constitution in the etiology of schizophrenia (164). Every psychiatrist has found a considerable percentage of schizophrenics who do not belong to this constitutional type. However, the fact remains that the majority do.

Here again, one could ask: Is the so-called introvert or detached personality, which is found in many preschizophrenics, a result of the asthenic constitution? Or can the asthenic constitution in a certain way be the result of the personality? Every clinician has seen, with changes in character and age, changes also in the physical appearance of the person. The dreaming, introverted adolescent, who finally succeeds in integrating well in life, has the tendency to acquire a more athletic constitution. The schizophrenic who recovers is less asthenic. The asthenic constitution may be the result of a certain kind of withdrawal from actions. More investigations are necessary to elucidate this problem.

Another finding which many psychiatrists have noted is

the frequent, although by no means constant, fact that many schizophrenics seem younger than their age. The organically-minded psychiatrists may see in this another proof of the arrested physical development of the schizophrenic. One must consider other possibilities. The withdrawal from activities spares many organs from wear and tear, and preserves the asthenic constitution, which generally confers a juvenile appearance. Furthermore, the lack of mimic play in the face of the patients, which is due to decrease in emotional responsiveness, gives an almost juvenile impression. Many post-encephalitics also appear younger than their age, on account of their mask-like faces.

Many observers think that schizophrenics have an odd look or expression in their eyes. In the depressed type of manic-depressive psychosis, a characteristic sign has been described. The inner third of the upper lid is contracted upward and a little backwards, changing the arch into an angle. This fold is called Veraguth's fold, from the name of the author who described it. (See fig. 7B.)

According to my own observations, a small minority of schizophrenics and borderline patients present a different peculiarity. In normal subjects, the upper eyelid covers the upper part of the iris; its edge is between the pupil and the outer circumference of the iris, but nearer to the pupil than to the outer border of the iris. (Fig. 7A.) In a minority of schizophrenic and borderline patients the edge of the eyelid instead is more distant from the pupil and most of the upper iris is uncovered. In certain cases the eyelid may be at the level of the sclera and may leave the whole iris uncovered. This sign is not constant, and in my opinion is only part of a frequent mimical expression of the schizophrenic, which shows a mixture of withdrawal and bewilderment. (Figs. 7C and D). It is less pronounced than the eye signs found in thyroid diseases.

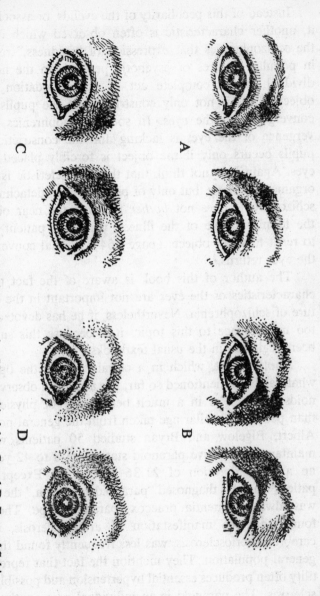

FIG. 7: A. Normal eyes. B. Eyes of depressed patient, showing Veraguth's fold. C and D. Eyes of Schizophrenics. Explanation in the text (page 406).

Instead of this peculiarity of the eyelids, or associated with it, another characteristic is often observed which confers to the schizophrenics that expression of "madness," reproduced in popular pictures of psychotic persons. In the normal individual in the complete act of accommodation for near objects there is not only constriction of the pupils but also convergence of the eyes. In some schizophrenics this convergence of the eyes is lacking and the constriction of the pupils occurs only if the object is forcibly placed near the eyes. Again I do not think that this characteristic is a sign of organic pathology, but only of psychological detachment. The schizophrenic does not *bother* focusing for near objects. In the terminal stage of the illness, when the patient is forced to react to small objects (page 364), normal convergence of the eyes returns.

The author of this book is aware of the fact that these characteristics of the eyes are not important in the total picture of schizophrenia. Nevertheless, if he has devoted perhaps too much space to this topic, it is because this subject has been neglected in the usual textbooks.

Another fact, which in a certain way is the opposite of what has been mentioned so far, has also been observed. Paranoids seem to be in a much better state of physical health than people of similar age taken from the general population. Alpert, Bigelow and Bryan studied 50 patients who have maintained an active paranoid state from 8 to 42 years, with an average duration of 21.36 years (4). Except for one patient who was diagnosed "paranoid condition," the diagnosis was always dementia praecox, paranoid type. The authors found that the manifestation of arteriosclerosis, including cerebral arteriosclerosis, was less frequently found than in the general population. They mention the fact that repressed hostility often produces essential hypertension and possibly arteriosclerosis. The paranoid is an individual who continually acts out his hostilities, and gives expression to his conflicts, as contrasted with the person who represses and develops tension. The authors do not draw any definite conclusions. However, their excellent work, which they call "preliminary report," should stimulate further research. Incidentally, it is common knowledge that paranoids tend to deteriorate less than other patients, when they reach old age. Their sensorium is much better preserved. However, when they finally do show signs of arteriosclerosis, their mental condition improves. They are less resentful, and less concerned with their delusions.

CHAPTER XXI

Theoretical Considerations About the Role of the Central Nervous System in Schizophrenia

The role of the central nervous system in schizophrenia is a very controversial subject. As we know, a primary pathology of the central nervous system is advocated by the majority of authors who consider schizophrenia an organic disease. According to them, schizophrenia is a neuropathological disease like multiple sclerosis, or rather, like general paresis, because it involves the functions of the cerebral hemispheres predominantly. The fact that no pathology has been demonstrated is no proof for these authors that such pathology does not exist, but rather that our present methods of investigation are not capable of revealing it. Biochemical alterations affecting the brain at a "molecular level" and not detectable with histologic stains, are suggested. We know that even authors such as Jung and Sullivan, who are by and large psychogenically oriented, have not excluded the possibility that schizophrenia may be caused by organic pathology of the central nervous system.

In this chapter, a different approach will be followed. We

shall not start by speculating on the possibility of a primary pathology of the nervous system, but rather, ask ourselves what parts of the nervous system are functionally involved in the schizophrenic symptomatology. In other words, we shall consider not what parts of the nervous system are diseased, but what parts are functioning when a patient has ideas of reference, thinks paleologically, hallucinates, etc. Then we shall try to understand what type of coordination of the functions of these parts of the central nervous system is involved, or in a certain sense, *forced* by the schizophrenic syndrome.

The author is aware of the fact that the concepts expressed in this chapter cannot be fully proven at the present stage of our knowledge. He presents them not as final conclusions, but as working hypotheses, aiming to stimulate further research toward a closer integration of the psychological and the neurological.

This matter will be discussed in elementary terms. Physicians and other readers who may be disturbed by the simplicity of the discussion, should be reminded that this subject has led to a great deal of misunderstanding, and that therefore we should not be afraid of using too clear or simple language.

Let us start, therefore, with the most elementary question. Is there any doubt that in schizophrenia the central nervous system is involved, in the sense that many of the symptoms are mediated or produced by the nervous system, although not necessarily because of an organic pathology of the nervous system? Of course not. For instance, it is obvious that the patient would not have delusions, or a bizarre way of thinking, if he did not have a brain. The central nervous system is as necessary for the production of these symptoms, as it is necessary for the production of mental processes in the normal man. We may go further and say that at least most of the schizophrenic symptoms are produced in the cerebral cortex.

Here again, from a theoretical point of view, we do not exclude the possibility of an extra-cortical pathology. Someone, let us say, may conceive that some pathology of the diencephalon is responsible for schizophrenia. Even in this case, however, symptoms such as delusions, hallucinations, etc., must be recognized as cortical phenomena, which would occur only when the diencephalon is in a pathological condition. Most of the schizophrenic phenomena involve the functioning of the patient in a social and symbolic world; they affect his thinking and his planned actions, and all of these activities require cortical centers. The schizophrenic symptoms require the function of the cerebral cortex, independently of whether the cortex is healthy or diseased.

Let us now examine what parts of the cortex relate to those functions which mediate schizophrenic symptoms in the primary or early stage of the illness. Starting with the frontal lobe, we shall proceed by eliminating the areas which are not involved. It is obvious that the area pyramidalis (Broadman area 4, in the pre-central convolution) is not involved in the symptoms, I mean in the pathological aspect of the symptoms. A delusion may require the patient to move, and therefore may need the function of the pyramidal area, but the movement as a motor phenomenon is not pathological *per se*. The strip region, located immediately anterior to the pyramidal cortex, is also to be excluded, because it is related to the tone of the muscles. The broad premotor area 6 is not involved since it is connected with the execution of movements. The extrapyramidal cortex (areas 8 and 9) is not involved, since no extrapyramidal disturbance is found in schizophrenia. The area better defined as 8 α β δ according to Foerster revision, is not involved either, since the movements of the eyes are not impaired, in a neurological sense. Broca's area is not involved since the patient speaks well, from a motor point of view.

One may conclude then that that part of the frontal lobes

extending posteriorly from the extrapyramidal areas to the central sulcus is not necessarily involved in the symptoms of early schizophrenia. What remains, then, of the frontal lobe is the great prefrontal association area (see fig. 8).

Now we shall consider the parietal lobe. The postcentral, the supramarginal and the angular gyri, as well as the inferior part of the superior parietal lobule supersede various types of sensations, stereognosis included. The supramarginal gyrus is concerned with pain perception and the angular gyrus is needed for the recognition of visual verbal symbols. Since these functions are not involved there remains a little area of the parietal lobe that may play a role in schizophrenia. This is an ill-defined region which includes small contiguous parts of Broadman's areas 7, 19, 39 and 40.

If we now consider the temporal lobe, we have to exclude the auditory area, the Werniche zone, and the music center. It is true that the patient hallucinates, but it is also true that the content of the hallucinations must originate at levels higher than the primary auditory centers. What is left, then, of the temporal lobe is part of the middle and inferior temporal gyrus.

The hippocampal gyrus and the uncus, as well as the cingulate gyrus, may be involved. This part of the brain will be considered later.

As far as the occipital lobe is concerned, here again we have to exclude all visual centers. The early schizophrenic is neither blind, nor psychically blind. The only remaining part on the occipital lobe is part of area 19.

Summarizing, we may state that the cortical areas, whose functions, whether motor, sensory or symbolic, are well known today, do not seem to be involved in determining schizophrenic phenomena in the early stages of the psychosis. These phenomena therefore must be a function of the areas which are left. Again I must emphasize the fact that I do not imply at all that these remaining areas are in a pathological condition. I do not believe that, but I do believe that symptoms of *psychogenic* origin at a physiological level must be constructed in these areas.

The regions which have not been excluded may roughly be divided into three large areas. One of them is the so-called archipallium and mesopallium, including the rhinencephalon, the hippocampus, the cingulate gyrus and possibly the posterior orbital gyri. Today, this large area is considered to be related to the mechanism of emotions. For theoretical considerations which will be disclosed later, I think that this area is not *primarily* involved, but only *secondarily*.

Two other areas are left: one is the area usually called prefrontal, and the other is an area which occupies a central undefined region, in the temporal, occipital and parietal lobes. (Fig. 8) We shall call these two areas the PF (prefrontal) area, and the TOP area (from *T*emporal, *O*ccipital, *P*arietal). These areas are the great association areas, where the highest psychic functions presumably take place. Those two areas are also called the silent areas of the brain, because their function is not easily discerned, and because lesions there, especially unilateral lesions, do not necessarily result in definite clinical symptomatology. These are also the areas which are the last to appear in phylogenesis. Even in apes and in extinct races of men, such as Pithecanthropus Erectus, they are undeveloped or underdeveloped. In addition, they correspond, not exactly, but with great approximation, to those areas which Flechsig found to be the last to myelinize. These are the areas where neurology and psychology coalesce.

First, let us take into consideration the posterior of these areas, the one which we have called the TOP area. This area may be viewed as the point of convergence or as the central part of a much larger area consisting of the whole temporal, occipital, and parietal lobes. This larger area may be con-

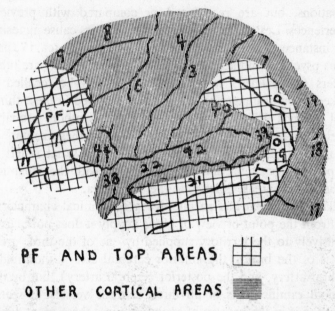

PF AND TOP AREAS

OTHER CORTICAL AREAS

Fig. 8: Left cerebral hemisphere showing extension of PF and TOP areas. Explanation in the text (page 414).

sidered as the great receptive area, where stimuli coming from the external world receive various levels of elaboration. We cannot understand the functions of the TOP area without reconsidering the whole of the temporal, parietal and occipital areas.

The calcarine area, part of the first temporal convolution, and the post central gyrus have been called the arrival platforms (Orton, 205) because stimuli from the external world arrive there and are transformed into visual, auditory or other sensations. For instance, a lesion in the calcarine region (area 17) causes blindness. The stimuli are then elaborated, in areas adjacent to the arrival platforms, up to the level of perceptions; that is, the stimuli are not experienced merely as sensations, but are recognized or compared with previous experiences. Lesions in these secondary centers cause agnosias. For instance, a lesion in area 18, contiguous to area 17, produces psychic blindness. Contiguous to these centers are other centers (third level) where past stimuli may be recalled or evoked. Mental images resort to material stored in these third-level centers. What we have called paleosymbols probably develop in areas immediately contiguous to these centers of the third level, after associating with others. What is left of the parietal, occipital and temporal lobes, with the exception of the speech areas, belongs to the TOP area.

The TOP area has an interesting anatomical characteristic. From the point of view of blood supply it does not belong exclusively to the territory supplied by one of the three great vessels of the brain (the anterior cerebral artery, the middle cerebral artery, and the posterior cerebral artery), but by the terminal ramifications of all three of these vessels. It seems almost as if in the process of evolution these three great arteries had to stretch or prolong their terminal branches in order to cover this last arrived area.

In the TOP area probably numerous other levels of elaboration take place. Stimuli, passed through the first, second, and third levels, are associated and elaborated to high symbolic levels. It is after the level of paleosymbols (page 288) that stimuli from the external world are elaborated at a social level. Higher symbolization goes together with socialization; close association between the TOP area and the centers of language is therefore necessary. The TOP area and the centers of language are probably developed at the same time, at least in the sense of acquiring functional specificity. Once the verbal symbols are acquired, the TOP area may go much further in elaboration and development. From the point of view of myelinization, the language centers seem to be more ancient than the TOP area. This could make one think that language is needed before higher symbolization and socialization are possible. However, as was said above, the TOP area is ill-defined; its external part probably includes at least part of areas where visualization and paleosymbols occur, prior to the acquisition of language.

In all probability, impulses reverberate continuously in these two areas (language centers and TOP area), and the increase in symbolization and socialization necessitates the contemporary development of both. Through the corpus callosum, both hemispheres are involved. Millions and millions of associations occur in these areas, where a progressive change from the sensation to the highest abstract conception takes place. Only some of the associations which are put into activity by a stimulus become conscious; others, which probably occur at the same time but involve shorter circuits, remain unconscious or at the marginal field of consciousness.

There is no doubt that the functions which occur in the TOP area are functions which are pathologically involved in schizophrenia. In schizophrenia, there is a gradual return from the abstract to the concrete, from highly socialized symbols to paleosymbols, from high conceptual constructions to sensorial perceptions, and finally from perceptions to sensations. In other words, there is a reluctance to use the most central parts of the TOP area, the parts which, phylogenetically speaking, have been the last to develop. Finally, when the illness progresses, there is a tendency to abolish almost entirely the functions of the TOP area and to use only the residual parts of the temporal, parietal and occipital lobes.

Now, once more, I state that I do not imply at all that the TOP area has some kind of organic pathology; on the contrary, I feel that the psychological conditions of the patient compel him to avoid those high symbolic functions which perpetuate or increase his anxiety and to descend, in a protective way, to less elevated functions which do not arouse so much anxiety. Many of these symbolic functions which arouse anxiety take place in the TOP area. The schizophrenic, therefore, more and more avoids the use of the TOP area. By eliminating the TOP area, however, he does not return as a well-integrated individual to a lower level of integration. All the nervous areas, in the process of evolution, have continuously readjusted themselves by new associations every time a new area has been developed. The whole nervous system, and especially the cortex, may be in a state of maladjustment when the TOP area is in a state of decreased functionality. Eventually, even atrophy of the TOP area and others which are associated with it, may occur.

We have taken the TOP area into consideration first, but the prefrontal area, too, is involved in schizophrenia, even at an earlier stage than the TOP area. We know, from neurophysiology, that the prefrontal areas, after using the data obtained from the temporal, occipital and parietal lobes, permit planned thinking in a sequence of logical processes, and make possible anticipation of the distant future. The PF area is in a state of continuous collaboration with the TOP area; it is doubtful that without the PF elaboration of the data, the highest levels of abstraction of the symbols could be reached. Now, it is obvious that the psychological processes occurring in the PF area are those capable of evoking the greatest amount of anxiety.* The schizophrenic will gradually avoid these processes. He may resort to more primitive psychological processes, which require shorter circuits; he gradually abandons the Aristotelian way of thinking, becomes less and less involved in abstract thinking. What has been said about the

---

* Greenblatt and Solomon also feel that frontal lobe circuits must be conceived as sustaining *emotional tension* in psychotic individuals. These authors correctly state that this tension causes a disorganization of personality functions in the psychotic and a deterioration in social adaptation (120, 121).

TOP area may be repeated here. When the schizophrenic abandons the highest, long-circuiting processes, he does not automatically become adjusted to lower levels of integrations which use less of the frontal lobes. Incidentally, that, in my opinion, is what psychosurgery tries to achieve. (See page 486). The patient becomes not adjusted, but maladjusted to a lower level, and symptoms occur. Not only will he not use logic, but he will use paleologic. Not only will he be unable to formulate a very highly abstract concept, but the concept will express itself in a paleologic and perceptual way. In Hughlings Jackson's language, negative and positive symptoms will occur. With relatively few exceptions (page 351), an adaptation at a lower level will not take place, because, as we have seen in Part IV, self-perpetuating mechanisms of progressive regression will be unchained.

So far, we have taken into consideration only the schizophrenic at an early stage of the illness. The patient at the terminal stage, as described in Chapter XVII, must also be reconsidered. At that stage, it should be remembered, the schizophrenic seems to lose the perception of various sensations; he acts as if he were psychically blind, to a large extent, and he has those oral tendencies which have been described in monkeys after ablation of both temporal lobes. We may think that the area of reduced functionality now not only extends to the TOP area, but includes the whole of areas 2, 5, 40, 39, 19, 18 and possibly 22, 38. As far as the PF area is concerned, its functionality must be almost completely eliminated since, as we have discussed on page 371, the activities of patients at this last stage, are very primitive, stereotyped and almost as simple as reflexes. In the frontal lobes visceral centers, which are contiguous to the highest psychic areas, have been described. When they do not receive associations any longer, some alteration in their functionality is to be expected, as we shall see in Chapter XXII.

Why is the area of reduced functionality extended so much in the terminal stage? We have seen how any return to a lower level produces not an equilibrium, but a condition from which the patient still has the tendency to escape. (See page 381.) This means that the tendency to reduce the functionality of certain areas will persist and will involve other cortical areas, finally even the perceptual centers.

Since the beginning of his illness, the schizophrenic has tended toward a sort of life which required shorter and shorter cerebral circuits. First he tends to reduce the functions of the areas which are the last to appear in phylogenesis and the last to myelinize in ontogenesis. These areas are probably not completely myelinized in childhood.

The prolonged childhood characteristic of the human race, in comparison with the shorter period of parental dependency occurring in other species, is due to the appearance of the cortical centers which make the life of the human child much more difficult to integrate and in need of others. The human child's higher psychic centers at the same time equip him for the experience of long-circuited anxiety. This increased dependency on others or, in other words, this absolute need for interpersonal relations, may bring about the anxiety which, if not coped with by other defense mechanisms, may induce schizophrenia. Schizophrenia, on the other hand, attempts to make the nervous system return to a functional level at which long-circuited anxiety cannot be experienced. In order to avoid anxiety, the schizophrenic will use his cortex as little as possible, and will thus resemble an organic case, as Goldstein has emphasized many times.

This similarity to organic cases is more pronounced than is generally assumed. For instance, in fig. 6, a letter of a patient is reproduced. The content of this letter resembles schizophrenic word-salad. Actually, the letter was written by a non-psychotic patient suffering from motor aphasia. She was a young woman who had been shot by her irate husband. The bullet damaged her Broca's area and surrounding regions. She was not able to talk, but understood simple spoken language. She was relearning how to write, but could not find the right words. This letter was written to me on my last day of service at Pilgrim State Hospital. The patient, who knew I was leaving, wanted to say farewell and thank me. In the letter, however, she seems to express ideas different from, or even the opposite of those which she wanted to express. The result is something similar to word-salad. The difficulty may be the same one which the regressed schizophrenic presents. Each part of a mental context is equivalent to another; the patient is unable to pick up the right part. An organic patient, who replies to the question, "What city is the capital of France," with "La Marseillaise," probably uses the same mental process as that of the schizophrenic who replied "White House" to the question, "Who was the first president of the United States?"

Another point must be considered. Is there a possibility of a neurophysiological explanation for the impairment of emotions in schizophrenia? Our knowledge about the neurophysiology of emotions is so limited that we are still forced to speculate. Human emotions, I feel, also must be originated in or stimulated by cortical processes. It is the expression of the emotions and the perception of the bodily changes accompanying the emotions which require lower centers.

When I am saddened by the news that a friend of mine has died, I do not experience anything similar to being cut by a knife. It is true that my emotional reactions may have a manifestation which includes a sensation similar to that of being cut by a knife, or something else according to my individual experiences, but my emotional reactions include much more than that. I had to understand the news, I had to evoke the memory of my friend, I had to visualize what his death would imply. All these mental processes require high cortical

functions. The emotion *per se* may be elaborated in the archipallium or in the hypothalamus, or even lower centers. There
is no doubt that the externalized manifestations of the emotions are at least partially integrated in the hypothalamus, but
only after the nervous excitement has passed through higher
centers.

One may think that in schizophrenia there is an altered
functionality of the archipallium whose important participation in the mechanism of emotion has recently been recognized. One may even suppose that this altered functionality of
the archipallium is the original cause of this mental condition.
At the present stage of our knowledge, we are not in a position
to deny such a possibility. Such a possibility seems to me,
however, improbable. It is my belief that schizophrenia involves first the functions of the centers which are the last to
appear in phylogenesis. The archipallium, instead, is the most
ancient part of the cortex. A *primary* dysfunction of the archipallium in schizophrenia, if demonstrated, would compel us
to abandon all our genetic theories. At the present stage of
our knowledge, the writer is much more inclined to believe
in an altered functionality of the archipallium, which is *secondary* to the psychogenic hypofunctionality of other cortical
areas. If we follow again Hughlings Jackson's principles, a
hypofunctionality of neopallic areas should be accompanied
by a release and hyperfunctionality of the archipallium.

How is this release of the archipallium manifested in
schizophrenia? We cannot answer this question adequately,
since we know so little about this part of the brain which, to
paraphrase Le Gros Clark (167), has been for so long neglected by neurologists as a piece of old furniture to be rele-
gated to the cellar. Although in man the neopallium has come
to great prominence, the archipallium has readjusted itself to
the evolutionary changes and, having abandoned the olfactory

functions, must have assumed a different role. How this hypothetical release of the archipallium could manifest itself in
schizophrenia will be taken into consideration in the next
chapter.

Let us try to summarize now the points we have considered
and reach some conclusions, in view of other neurological
concepts.

In a teleologic attempt to escape from anxiety, the schizophrenic avoids those psychological functions which require
the highest cortical centers, those which have been last to
develop. There is, therefore, a functional or psychosomatic
hypofunctionality of the highest cortical areas (PF and TOP
areas). At the same time that these cortical areas are in a
state of functional hypoactivity, the functions of lower cortical
areas acquire prominence. Hughlings Jackson's concepts are
correct in relation to schizophrenia too. This syndrome presents negative symptoms, caused by hypofunctionality of highest levels, and positive symptoms, caused by the prominence
of released lower centers. The hypofunctionality of certain
areas must also alter associations or nervous connections with
distant or neighboring areas. What results is a functional
diaschisis, similar to the one described by Von Monakow in
organic cases.

Another important fact is what, in neurological terms, may
be called *dysencephalization,* or a process opposite or almost
opposite to the so-called *encephalization of function.* By the
latter term, neurologists mean the fact that in the evolution of
the central nervous system from lower to higher species, many
functions, the centers of which lie in more caudal and less
evolved parts of the central nervous system, shift brainward
or toward higher centers (Fulton, 107). In schizophrenia, the
opposite seems to take place. For instance, abstract concepts
of higher levels use lower auditory perceptual centers and

become auditory hallucinations. One may thus think that schizophrenia is accompanied by the following neurological processes, which are of *psychosomatic origin*:

1) Hypofunctionality of certain cortical areas;
2) Diaschisis;
3) Relative prominence of lower centers;
4) Dysencephalization.

The last one may prove to be the most characteristic.

CHAPTER XXII

The Autonomic Nervous System and Its
Central Control in Schizophrenia

I. Defective Response of the Autonomic Nervous System to "internal environment"

Ernesto Lugaro, a well-known Italian psychiatrist, whose influence was felt even in English-speaking countries at a time when the positivistic schools had the lead in the field of psychiatry, wrote that the somatic symptoms of dementia praecox, be they spontaneous or induced, may be all interpreted as a disturbance of the vegetative nervous system (177, 178).

A prominent American neuroanatomist, the late Stephen W. Ranson, in a private letter written to Hoskins shortly before his death, expressed the belief that the best place to seek a solution of schizophrenia is in the hypothalamus, one of the organs of central control of the autonomic nervous system (133).

These statements, coming from such prominent sources, contain some truth, but, according to this author, are liable to lead to confusion, if they are interpreted as indicating that the *original* cause of schizophrenia is to be found in a pathology of the autonomic nervous system or of its central control.

A psychiatrist who devotes himself to the psychodynamic study of schizophrenia has enough grounds to convince himself that the symptoms of this condition have developed as a result of altered interpersonal relations and of emotional conflicts, leading to altered symbolization and progressive desocialization. Schizophrenic processes require, as we have seen in the previous chapter, the function of high cortical neopallic centers. They could not occur without them. Although, at the present fragmentary stage of our knowledge, such possibility cannot be excluded from the point of view of strict logic, it is highly improbable that the disorder starts with a pathology of phylogenetically ancient structures as those of the peripheral autonomic nervous system and of its diencephalic control.

That every somatic symptom of schizophrenia has a great deal to do with the autonomic nervous system cannot be denied. One could also state that every somatic function of the normal person has a great deal to do with the autonomic nervous system, and he would be equally correct. The deep psychological disturbances occurring in schizophrenia affect adversely every manifestation of the life of the patient; it is natural that repercussions of these disturbances involve the autonomic nervous system too.

These repercussions in the autonomic nervous system are engendered by two mechanisms. The first mechanism is very simple and directly related to psychological factors. We have seen many occurrences of it in Chapter XX. The psychological picture of schizophrenia, with decreased emotional responsiveness, diminished stimulation of any kind, and hypoactivity, determines a decreased stimulation of the autonomic nervous system. We have seen that some characteristics of the cardiovascular system, endocrine apparatus and other organs in schizophrenia, may be interpreted in this way. We are not going to repeat here those findings. We must recognize, however, that this mechanism does not explain sufficiently the inadequacy of the autonomic nervous system in the psychosis.

This inadequacy is seen in defective homeostatic reactions. As we know on account of the contribution of Cannon and his school, the organism aims to maintain a constant environment, that is, constant physico-chemical conditions (46). If these conditions are changed by anoxia, hypoglycemia, hemorrhage, cold, fever, or administration of many drugs, many responses of the autonomic nervous system are engendered which tend to restore the organism to normality. Various authors have found that this restoration is defective in schizophrenia. For instance, Freeman and Carmichael, as well as many others, have found that schizophrenic patients have less cardiovascular response to intravenously injected epinephrine than normal subjects do (85). Altman, Pratt, and Cotton also found altered cardiovascular responses to mecholyl (acetyl-beta-methylcholine) in schizophrenics (5). Meco found that the rise in temperature, as a reaction to different thermogenic substances, mainly foreign proteins, is much less pronounced in schizophrenic patients than in control subjects (188). Freeman studied the effects of dinitrophenol in schizophrenics and found that their reactions in skin temperature, insensible perspiration rate and oxygen consumption was considerably less marked than in control subjects (84).

Several authors have also found that ascertained psychological excitement does not produce an adequate sympathetic-adrenal discharge in the psychotic. Thus psychotic patients, examined during intense emotional display, did not show hyperglycemia as, instead, normal people do. (Bowman and Kasanin, 35, Gildea and coworkers, 110, Whitehorn, 274).

A much larger number of findings, reported by various authors, could be mentioned. Some of these findings have already been described in connection with the pituitary-adrenal system (page 399). Inasmuch as this is not a book intended primarily for the physiologist, we prefer to refer the reader who is interested in this subject to the stimulating book by Gellhorn (109). For our purpose it was sufficient to indicate here that there seems to be increasing evidence that the autonomic nervous system is in a state of hypoactivity or disfunction in at least the majority of cases of schizophrenia. Although a certain lack of responsiveness is due to the decreased psychological stimulation, this obviously cannot be the only mechanism. In fact the organism of the schizophrenic reacts deficiently to conditions of altered internal environment. The ability to react to these conditions is related to the central control of the autonomic nervous system, especially to the hypothalamus. We have to examine then the possibility of an altered functionality of the hypothalamus. This will be done in the following section.

II. Hypofunctionality of the Hypothalamus. Inadequate Expression of Emotions

As we have discussed in the previous section, there seems to be no doubt that the hypothalamus, and probably other cerebral centers which supersede the visceral functions, are in a state of hypofunctionality in schizophrenia. This hypofunctionality of the autonomic nervous system may also explain the decrease in the somatic manifestations of emotions which is noticed in this psychosis.

At this point it may be pertinent to remember that the role the hypothalamus plays in emotional life was stressed by Cannon, when he refuted the James-Lange theory of emotion (45, 47). According to him, hypothalamic stimulation produces two discharges, one upward and one downward. The one directed upward, toward cortical centers, would determine the nature of the emotional *experience*. The downward discharge would *express* the emotions with patterns of somatic and autonomic behavior.

In spite of its improvement over the James-Lange theory, Cannon's theory does not give adequate importance to the cortical mechanisms which are necessary for the experience of emotion. Emotions in humans take place in forms of high symbolization, and visceral or somatic participation is not their predominant feature. We have discussed several times that highly complicated emotions cannot arise in human beings if the latter were not provided with TOP and PF areas (page 422). These areas permit those symbolic and anticipatory mental processes and those neural long-circuits which mediate the greatest amount of emotions. The archipallium, as accumulating experimental evidence indicates (108, 109, 167, 206), has a great deal to do with the experience of the emotional quality of these processes which originate in neopallic areas. Obviously reverberating processes between archipallium and neopallium are always occurring. Certain structures of the archipallium may exert certain modulating or controlling influences, similar, in a certain way, to the functions of the cerebellum over the movements.

Papez's theory of emotions, invoking a circuit consisting of the hypothalamus, the anterior thalamic nuclei, the gyrus cinguli, the hippocampus and their interconnections, seem much nearer to the truth than previous theories (206). The interrelation, however, between these ancient parts of the brain which Papez has taken into consideration and the neopallium must be stressed.

In accordance with Jackson's principles, we may now postulate a chain of causes and effects which may explain what happens to the hypothalamus and other autonomic centers in schizophrenia.

We have seen that in schizophrenia there is a progressive

reduction of the functions of neopallic areas. In my opinion this reduction is functional, or psychosomatic, and reversible. It is forced by psychological processes for the purpose of avoiding the neopallic patterns, which are needed in those highly symbolic processes which determine great anxiety. This reduction of neopallic areas in its turn may engender a release of the more ancient archipallic centers. At first, one would think that the release of the archipallium would increase the emotionality of the patient, but we have to remember that with the term archipallium we include many structures representing possible different sublevels, and that their specific action in the experience of emotions is unknown. At any rate, the release of the archipallium will increase the inhibitory power which this part of the brain exerts over lower structures, like the hypothalamus. This inhibition of the hypothalamus may explain the hypofunctionality of the autonomic nervous system, as far as homeostatic reactions are concerned, as well as the decrease in somatic and visceral expressions of those emotions which are still experienced in schizophrenia, in spite of the neopallic-symbolic disintegration.

The interesting study by Bard and Mountcastle may support this point of view (15). These authors found that removal of the neocortex produces a state of placidity in cats. Anger or sham rage never occur. Nociceptive stimuli elicit mild responses. If these animals are subjected to ablation of the gyrus cinguli or to various parts of the rhinencephalon they become angry and ferocious. These experiments suggest that the rhinencephalon restrains the hypothalamus. This action is opposed to the one exerted by the neocortex; in fact, removal of the cortex increases the inhibitory effect of the rhinencephalon.

Incidentally, the rhinencephalon may exert a restraining influence not only over the hypothalamus, but also on the thalamus, possibly through some hypothalamic-thalamic con-

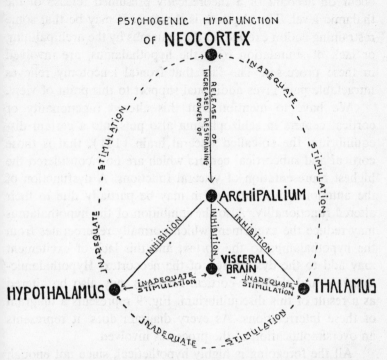

FIG. 9: Diagram illustrating the relations between the neocortex, the archipallium and the hypothalamus in schizophrenia. Explanation in the text (page 430).

nections. We have seen that in the terminal stage of schizophrenia pain and temperature perceptions are decreased or abolished (page 377). We have interpreted this phenomenon as a consequence of some possible psychosomatic dysfunction of the parietal cortex. Penfield and Rasmussen have on the other hand found that pain and temperature are experienced in humans at a thalamic level, when the cortical areas are removed (208). In the terminal stage of schizophrenia an increased ability to experience pain and temperature should occur on account of a theoretically presumed release of the thalamic level. The opposite is the case. It may be that some restraining action exerted on the thalamus by the archipallium, or lack of stimulation from the hypothalamus, are involved in these processes. The fact that frontal leucotomy relieves intractable pain gives additional support to this point of view.

We have to mention that this altered functionality of cortical centers in schizophrenia also puts into a certain disequilibrium the so-called visceral brain (181), that is those cortical and subcortical centers which are now considered the highest representation of visceral functions. A dysfunction of the autonomic nervous system may be partially due to their altered functionality. Also the inhibition of the hypothalamus may reduce the excitement which normally reverberates from the hypothalamus to the cortex, and this lack of excitement may add to the dysfunction of the neocortex. Hypothalamic-thalamic and thalamic-cortical relations may also be altered as a result of this disequilibrium. Fig. 9 represents a diagram of these interrelations. As every diagram does, it represents an oversimplification of the processes involved.

All the foregoing is highly hypothetical, since not enough neurophysiological evidence is available to support these views. However, even if all the ideas expressed in this chapter will have to be reexamined or abandoned, this thinking will not have been fruitless, provided the fundamental concept will survive that psychogenic factors may unchain a sequence of altered functionality of brain processes, involving even structures like the centers of the autonomic nervous system, which are not *directly* exposed to psychological stimulation.

PART SIX

Treatment of Schizophrenia

CHAPTER XXIII

Psychotherapy of Schizophrenia

I. Goals of Psychotherapy

At the present time two main types of therapy are administered to schizophrenics: physical therapy of various kinds, such as shock treatments, psychosurgery, etc., and psychotherapy. Whereas for the past fifteen years physical therapies have been preferred by the largest number of psychiatrists, an awakening of interest in the psychotherapy of schizophrenia has occurred recently and many favorable reports about this type of treatment have been presented. Pioneers in this field have been Sullivan, Federn, Fromm-Reichmann, Rosen, as well as a large number of less important contributors.

This chapter will describe a technique of psychotherapy which discloses the influence of Fromm-Reichmann's writings (102–105). However, several other sources, including what the author has learned from nurses and attendants who were successful in their dealings with schizophrenic patients, have contributed to the formulation of this technique.

Psychotherapy of schizophrenia, as the author conceives

it, aims at the following results. First, in an atmosphere of devoted acceptance, trust, and effort to "reach" him, the patient retrains himself to establish communication with others and to relinquish his specific, individualistic ways of living. Second, with increase in ability to communicate, especially with the therapist, the patient gains insight into the genetic and dynamic nature of his difficulties. Third, through various coordinated efforts, the patient gains self-esteem.

The therapy will be successful only if all these three goals are achieved. Pursuit of only one or two of these goals, as advocated by other therapists, in my opinion is not enough. The attempts to attain these goals, of course, are made concomitantly, as they are often included in the same therapeutic procedure: However, for didactical purposes, we shall take into consideration separately first, the technique of the therapeutic session; then the feelings and general attitude of the therapist; third, the general participation in the patient's life and the assignment of tasks. Precautionary measures and contraindications to psychotherapy then will be discussed.

An attempt will be made to give a down-to-earth description of the technique, but no detailed reference to any particular case will be given in this section of this book. For individual cases the reader is referred especially to the second part of this book and, to a lesser degree, to all the other sections. The reader should always remember, however, that each patient is in a certain sense unique and requires an individual technique, which no book can adequately illustrate.

The technique presented here applies to patients who may be treated ambulatorily, but may be applied also to hospitalized patients, provided some variations and important additions are made. For these important additions the reader is referred to the excellent works by Stanton and Schwartz on the effect of the hospital as a milieu therapy (242, 243) and also to the informative article by Rioch and Stanton, in which the literature and the problems involved in this type of therapy are reviewed (218).

The nature of this field is such that not enough experience can be gained by a single therapist. Each case is so time-consuming that the number of cases treated by a therapist is relatively small, and therefore the experience that each therapist can obtain is limited. I have concentrated my efforts on the patients who do not require hospitalization.

I feel that with psychoanalytically oriented psychotherapy a conspicuous number of patients may reintegrate socially, even without hospitalization. From my own cases, I am not in a position to state whether or not one can obtain permanent cures. Not enough time has elapsed since I started to treat psychotics with this method. Such a concept as cure, however, is difficult to apply even to neuroses. I do feel that in many schizophrenics, a degree of adjustment superior to the pre-psychotic level can be reached with this type of therapy.

II. *The Therapeutic Session*

The first problem in psychotherapy is, of course, how to direct the therapeutic session.

First of all, should the patient use the couch? In my own experience, I have found that the couch should be avoided, at least during the first stage of the treatment. The patient is very much in need of closeness, even in a physical sense, and no additional obstacles should interfere with the attempt to reestablish contact. Furthermore, if the schizophrenic patient does not see the therapist, his tendency toward archaic ways of thinking may almost make him feel that the therapist is not present. One patient who used the couch at the beginning of treatment felt that I was not there, that he was hearing my "disembodied voice." Sechehaye, too, reports that her patient had the need to see her; when the patient could not see the therapist, she felt that the therapist was not there (227). This feeling is reminiscent of children who close their eyes when they want to make things disappear (Fenichel, 75). On the other hand, the patient may find it unbearable to look at the therapist's face, and should not be required to do so, if he does not wish to. As a matter of fact this matter should not even be discussed at the beginning of treatment. Some patients go to the extent of closing their eyes during the session or of turning the face in a diametrically opposite direction. These manners should not necessarily be interpreted by the therapist as a rejection of the treatment, but as methods used by the patient to reduce to a more tolerable degree the frightening aspect of the interpersonal contact. The patient should be allowed to face in any direction he wants. I have found that in the majority of the cases, it is best to sit next to the patient.

How does one start to conduct a session with a psychotic patient? Naturally, the technique has to vary according to the patient. We cannot treat a mute catatonic as we treat a verbose paranoid. If the catatonic is mute, no attempt should be made to force him to talk. To do so would be disastrous for the treatment. The therapist should take the initiative and talk to him. The conversation should be a pleasant one, and should consist of neutral topics, that is, of subjects which will not increase the anxiety of the patient. This may be difficult to do, and many mistakes are possible, because the catatonic spreads or generalizes his anxiety to a tremendous number of things. (See page 126). At any rate, more important than the topic of these talks is the general attitude of the therapist, as will be discussed in more detail later. *The patient must feel that a benevolent, sincere effort is being made to reach him, with no demand being made on him.* At times, even these one-way talks irritate the patient because he feels that they are just one-way talks or monologues and not real communications. The patient discloses his displeasure by withdrawing further.

In these cases the therapist must be willing to respect the patient's desire for silence, without showing any discomfort or anxiety about it. A state of silence or of non-verbal communication will then be *shared*.

More difficult than with catatonics is the beginning of treatment with hebephrenics and paranoids, who are able but unwilling to verbalize. Here the tendency of the young therapist, especially if trained in a state hospital, is to approach the patient with many questions, in an attempt to make him talk. This attempt is understandable, because there are many things that the therapist would like to know, and the therapist also tends to feel that if the patient is under pressure he will finally talk. However, from the point of view of therapy, this method should be discarded. Each question is experienced by the schizophrenic as an imposition, or an intrusion into his private life, and will increase his anxiety, his hostility and his desire to desocialize. In certain respects, the schizophrenic is like a young child. When a stranger visits a family, and in greeting their young child, asks him questions, he will not be accepted by the child, because the child feels that the stranger wants something from him. But later on, when the stranger is not a stranger any longer, if he asks questions that the child is capable of answering, the response will be favorable; contact will be made. The schizophrenic, too, in a later stage, will be glad to answer questions which do not require an effort.

In the beginning, however, no questions should be asked, because every question implies an effort. This technique seems very easy, but it is actually very difficult to follow, because the therapist feels compelled to ask questions. He feels that for diagnostic and legal purposes some questions must be asked. For example, in state hospitals, the physician must ask questions which, if necessary, will prove in court that the patient is psychotic and legally detained. Whatever the diagnostic and legal requirements are, this procedure is not indicated from a therapeutic standpoint. Generally, the best procedure is to have a physician conduct a general mental examination which involves some questioning. Then the patient should be referred for therapy to another psychiatrist who will follow the procedure described here. The data collected by the diagnosing psychiatrist should be used by the therapist-psychiatrist, as much as possible, to remedy his paradoxical position in which there is so much he has to know and so much he may lose or spoil if he tries to obtain the information directly from the patient. Concomitant treatment of another member of the family may partially help this situation, as we have seen on page 86.

Even the diagnostic interview with the first psychiatrist should not be too disturbing or inquiring. If the patient says, "They are persecuting me," the psychiatrist has to refrain from asking the patient who the persecutors are. The patient often does not name them, but uses the pronoun "they." Also, if he says that he *knows* that "they" are persecuting him, that there is "something funny going on," the therapist has an urge to ask him how he knows that there is something funny going on, and what this funny thing is. These questions are actually therapeutically destructive. In many early cases, the patient actually does not know the answers. He himself does not know who the persecutors are or what the strange feeling is. What he experiences are only vague feelings, and questions of this type may actually help him crystallize into concrete images or persons, feelings which as yet have not become well-defined delusions or ideas of reference. If the therapist has patience, later on he will understand where this feeling of persecution comes from, and why the patient has the need to externalize with delusions a vague feeling of hostility which the patient feels has been directed toward him.

If we don't ask questions, then what do we do? As was mentioned in relation to catatonics, in the beginning the therapist takes the initiative and talks in a pleasant manner about neutral subjects. Sometimes, I look at an art book with the patient, and take the initiative in discussing the pictures in plain language. These pictures should *not* lead easily to identification, as those of the Thematic Apperception Test do. They should not arouse anxiety. At the very beginning of treatment, when the patient's suspiciousness and distrust are very pronounced, he should leave the session with the feeling that he has been given something, not with the feeling that something, even diagnostic information, has been taken from him. When the patient has gained some security in contact with the therapist, he will talk more and more, and eventually will even talk about his problems and give the therapist some historical material. At times, this material is collected only after an extremely long period, because of the patient's distrust and difficulties in communicating. However, if the therapist is familiar with the dynamic factors of schizophrenia, such as were discussed in the second part of this book, he is prepared to expect certain things, and is therefore aided in recognizing and interpreting these factors. The difficulties in understanding schizophrenic language and thought may also be overcome to a certain extent, if the therapist is familiar with the mechanisms which were discussed in the third part of this book.

We are not going to illustrate here applications of what has been expounded in part II and part III, as these applications will appear self-evident, once they are well understood by the therapist. It cannot be emphasized enough, however, that, as far as the psychodynamic mechanisms are concerned, not too infrequently one encounters a set of unusual circumstances, never described before. The therapist must always be prepared for such a possibility. In spite of his familiarity with the formal mechanisms described in the third part of this book, the therapist will find much material totally obscure in certain cases, on account of their extreme individuality and unpredictability. I am thinking especially of the productions of several paranoids and hebephrenics, who are very talkative, in spite of advanced regression. Their talk consists so much of word-salad, that the therapist who attempts to treat them does not know how to start and is bound to feel discouraged.

The fact that the patient wants to talk is an encouraging sign; even if his talk seems incomprehensible, he still has the need to communicate and this need may facilitate the treatment. The therapist should listen patiently; he should not pretend that he understands because the patient detects any pretension, but should maintain a benevolent attitude and manifest a desire to communicate even in a non-verbal manner (see page 452). If the therapist is willing to listen to the patient for a long time, he will be surprised to find out that even the word-salad will become more comprehensible. The therapist will detect that some themes recur often and that the patient's talk follows certain patterns. Finally, some preoccupations of the patient with certain things will become evident and will offer important clues. The therapist will grasp the general feeling tone of what the patient says even if he does not grasp the content. The general frame of reference or the "cosmology" of the patient will be indented.

But again, we must add, that what is asked of the therapist is much more than it seems. Many therapists, especially those who have almost exclusive experience with psychoneurotics, are unable to endure a talk which makes no sense to them for a long period of time. The terror of lack of communication may be experienced by the therapist much more than by the patient. The therapist may experience anxiety throughout the interview, which makes him wish to terminate the session. This menacing feeling is experienced in two disturbing ways, as threat of nothingness, and threat of meaningfulness. It is experienced as threat of nothingness when the therapist finds himself inclined to accept temporarily the convenient idea that there is no content in what the patient says, that it is just nonsense. But this idea undermines his therapeutic intentions and revolts his feelings of human solidarity. Threat of meaningfulness is experienced by the therapist inasmuch as he senses that there is a meaning, a meaning which escapes him. When he finally feels that he grasps this meaning, he may not be able to repeat it. In fact, I myself and many therapists with whom I have worked, have at times felt that we had grasped the meaning of what the patient wanted to say, but we could not repeat it to ourselves with our language, or communicate it to others in meetings or during supervisory hours. We felt that the report to the supervisor would be inaccurate and the instructions received would therefore be erroneous.

This grasping of the ineffable meaning may be considered intuitional on the part of the therapist, an intuition which cannot be shared. Since I am reluctant to use the word intuition, I prefer to say that in these cases, in order to break the schizophrenic barrier and reach the patient, the therapist has succeeded in sharing the state of desocialization and individualism of the patient. There has been no real intuition, but an unusual kind of communication at a non-verbal level, or a primordial verbal communication, something which perhaps may be compared to the esthetic communication that the artist establishes with the observer of his work of art, or something similar to the primordial effects that paleosymbols must have produced on people when they became social symbols. (See page 285). The inability to communicate the meaning to others is due to the fact that, in order to make contact with the patient, the therapists had to share his state of impaired communication and his incommunicable unique feeling. This, of course, happens in a minority of cases. Most of the time we are able to make an approximately accurate translation in our own language.

The therapist may have several other feelings of doubt in treating the patient. Has the patient preserved the ability to understand our common language and does he understand the therapist? Does the patient understand himself when he speaks in a word-salad? It seems to me that most schizophrenics retain the ability to understand us, at least potentially. If the non-verbal communication to which we have referred and the general feeling in the therapeutic situation are such as to put the patient in a receptive attitude, he is certainly capable of understanding us. This receptive attitude may not be established for a long time, but in certain cases may be obtained even during the first interview. Let us remember that the schizophrenic maintains his potential capacity to resume higher levels of integration and therefore high levels of communication whenever these are not accompanied by anxiety. This is demonstrated by the following observation, made by almost every therapist. A regressed hebephrenic may seem unable to understand the therapist at all during an unsuccessful session, even when the latter speaks in the most concrete language. However, when the therapist tells the patient that the session is ended, the patient rises and goes away, thus showing that he understood the meaning of this sentence. It seems almost as if the patient had allowed himself to be touched verbally by what he understood as implying a decrease in anxiety (avoidance of the unpleasant session).

Often the problem is not at all one of understanding our common language, but of misunderstanding. In other words, the personal problems of the patients make them give special meanings to what we say. That is true in different degrees for all patients, from the preserved paranoid to the regressed hebephrenic.

This impairment in exchange of meanings, which is always more or less present although the patient retains a potential ability to resume understanding of our language, is partially compensated by the fact that the patient has increased his sensitivity to non-verbal communication, that is, to the feeling tone or to the atmospheric quality of the session. The reader should notice that we stated that the patient has increased his *sensitivity* and not his understanding, because, although it is true that he may sense or recognize this feeling tone much better than a normal person does, it is also true that in many instances he attaches to it an egocentric and grossly inappropriate meaning, even if this meaning contains a grain of truth. (See page 464).

\ As to the problem of whether the patient understands himself when he speaks in a very disconnected manner, as for instance, in word-salad, the matter is controversial. The patient himself must suffer from his inability to inhibit lower cortical levels, as we have discussed on page 381. We have compared some of his productions to photographic films which have been exposed several times. The patient must be disturbed by this impairment as much as the listener is, just as the aphasic is disturbed by his own defect. The schizophrenic in a vague way is aware of what he wants to say, and he is also aware of the fact that he wishes to communicate. He experiences several feelings at the same time, as well as a desire to communicate several things at the same time, even if he is not able to formulate verbally these concommitant desires, either to himself or to the listener. The therapist may help him to understand his own productions.

Here again one is reminded of what happens in the field of art. Some modern painters have expressed the experience that when they paint they have only a dim awareness of their feelings and that they know only with a certain approximation what they are going to paint or express. At times, even when the painting is finished, they do not know what they wanted to represent. It is from the reactions that these paintings will evoke in people that the artists discover what they themselves felt and wanted to express. In the same way the schizophrenic patient may understand better his verbal productions if he is helped by the therapist, that is, when the latter is able verbally or non-verbally to communicate to him that a specific meaning has been conveyed and a given reaction has been engendered.

It is important for the therapist to be aware of his anxiety about these difficulties in communication and to be able to cope with this problem if he wants to work with regressed schizophrenics. In fact, as we shall mention again later, the patient will perceive this anxiety immediately.

It is obvious that when the impairment in communication is very pronounced, the therapeutic sessions must be very frequent, at least once or twice a day. Of course, the number of sessions varies according to the individual patient. Some will do well even with as little as three sessions a week.

In the majority of schizophrenic patients free association should not be encouraged since it enhances the already pronounced tendency toward scattering of thoughts. However, in patients who are only mildly psychotic, with no signs of regressions, free association may be useful in certain instances. With verbose, well-systematized paranoids we may face a different problem. These patients may speak exclusively about their delusional complexes. In these cases I feel that some pressure has to be exerted on the patients. They should be encouraged to talk about something else. An indirect attempt should be made to make them see that there is something else besides their persecutors in the world; in other words, an effort should be made to circumvent their delusions. This should be done, not in order to repress the complexes, which would be impossible, but rather to enable the patients to increase their ties in the world. At the beginning, the patients' peculiar contacts with the environment are established only through their delusions. If the therapist, with his general attitude, which will be discussed later, is able to make the patients enlarge their interests, a great victory will have been achieved. In many cases of well-systematized paranoiacs and paranoids this is impossible. They remain fanatically and exclusively interested in their complexes and refuse to talk about anything else. They want only to prove to the therapist, as though to a judge, that their suspicions are well-founded. Of course, it is useless to enter into any arguments with the patients. It is also inadvisable to pretend to accept their delusions or hallucinations, with a few exceptions, to be mentioned later. Tower, in a very interesting paper, has emphasized the desirability that the therapist remain non-involved in the delusions of the patients (261). Fromm-Reichmann recommends telling patients that the therapist does not hear or see what the patient hears or sees (105). They should investigate together the reasons for the difference in their experience. In many cases where the delusional material cannot be circumvented, ambulatory treatment is not useful or feasible, and hospitalization becomes necessary.

As was noted before, at a certain stage of therapy, the physician will be able to collect data and to formulate certain problems of the patient in his own mind, and reach some understanding of the dynamic factors.

Should interpretation be given? Here again we have to distinguish between interpretations of the individual symptoms and interpretations of the general dynamic factors, although the two are closely related. As Fromm-Reichmann has pointed out, interpretations of the symptoms in many cases are not necessary. Often the patient is much more aware of the meaning of the symptom than the therapist is, although he has lost insight into his general condition. Frequent interpretations, such as some authors like Rosen (223, 244) advocate, in my opinion, *are not an indispensable requirement* in all cases, and the whole process of recovery should not be attributed to them. However, they are very useful in many cases. For example, non-regressed paranoids are often not aware at all of the meaning of their symptoms, and interpretations are necessary when these patients are ready to accept them. Thus, I found it very useful to explain to some paranoids, in language which they could understand, that the feeling of persecution is a re-externalization of the hostile feeling which they experienced in early childhood (see page 299). I was also successful in explaining to them that the feeling which they experienced of having their thoughts controlled by an external force is a reactivation or a concrete representation of the feeling which they had in early childhood, that their thoughts were being crushed or controlled by those of the dominant adults.

Also often successful was the interpretation given to the patient of his own negativistic or ambivalent attitude when this was explained as a persistence of the original oscillation between the parental wishes and his own. Powdermaker (215), in her therapeutic efforts, stresses this important point which was also discussed in this book (page 125), especially in connection with catatonics. Another point which I found useful to explain at an advanced stage of treatment, was the fact that the fulfillment of a wish, or the enjoyment of any satisfaction, was accompanied by strong guilt feelings, and that therefore, satisfactions were almost automatically followed by reexacerbation of symptoms. It was explained that the guilt feelings were due to the fact that the patient was still clinging to the idea that it was bad to satisfy his own wishes in disregard of the parental prohibitions. Sechehaye also has stressed this point (227). Before such interpretations can be given, the patients must be ready to accept them, as a result of having themselves given the historical background which made these interpretations possible. At times a partial interpretation of some symptoms, like the explanation of them in reference to current events only and not to early experiences, is more harmful than useful. For instance, if the feeling of being persecuted is recognized by the patient only as a projection of his own hostility for the alleged persecutor, he may be afraid of his newly discovered hostility. Some patients who had gained partial insight have stated that they preferred the feelings of being persecuted rather than experiencing their own hostile and aggressive feelings toward other people. Rather than endure their own aggressive tendencies these patients may actually stimulate the return of the psychotic symptoms. If, on the other hand, the symptom is interpreted totally as a forced, although distorted, reproduction of a situation that existed in childhood, there will be much less fear of immediate hostility toward others.

Interpretation of the general genetic dynamic factors should be given when the patient is receptive to them. Although he may be aware of many of these factors, he has somehow lost the ability to put things together, and he needs the help of the therapist. No effective reintegration is possible without a clear and ordinate understanding of the general genetic factors. In the beginning of treatment, instead of complete interpretation, the therapist may offer what has been called by Semrad an "appropriate comment" (232). By appropriate comment is meant a brief commentary on current material or relevant past material to clarify certain issues, or to relate, in a preliminary manner, things which to the patient did not appear to be related.

Some authors attribute almost the whole success of the therapy to the interpretations. Beck reported that in one case treated by him for a total of 30 weekly sessions over a period of eight months, he was able to obtain the disappearance of symptoms when he interpreted to the patient the fact that his delusions were based on identification with his father and on the phenomenon of borrowed guilt* (17). Rosen, too, relies to a large extent on a method of interpretation, which Federn has called "direct analytic therapy" (223). He showers the patient with direct interpretations, uses what he thinks is the language of the patient's unconscious, and, as Federn says, participates in the psychotic reality (71). I am more inclined to think that Rosen's successes are due to that wonderful general attitude which he is able to assume toward the psychotic (see page 453).

Another method of participation in the psychotic reality is the method of symbolic realization, devised by Sechehaye (227). She succeeded in entering in the symbolic world of her patient (a girl whom she treated for a period of over 10 years) and lived in it with her, rather than interpreting the symbols directly. The patient was not isolated any longer, and under the maternal, affective influence of Madame Sechehaye, was able to reintegrate.

III. Feelings and General Attitude of the Therapist

A large percentage of authors, including the present writer, feels that even more important than the technique of the sessions, as a verbal communication, is the general attitude and the feeling of the therapist toward the patient. This topic requires considerable study, since many authors have written about it from divergent points of view.

One of the first things that the therapist should analyze

---

* This interpretation does not seem complete to me. In Beck's paper it is not sufficiently explained why the patient had such a strong need to borrow his father's guilt. Such need must have been a derivative of his relationship to his mother, for whom he had "buried hostility." The role which his mother played is not adequately explained. I feel that Beck's success was due to his interest and empathy for the patient, and to the fact that, to use his own words, he was able "to perceive the patient's needs and to deal with them in a flexible way."

when he has just started treatment is his own feeling for the patient. If he experiences a strong feeling of empathy and interest, the chances are that he will be able to make significant contact with the patient. If, instead, he has the feeling that he is bored, or irritated, or that his patience is strained, for example, when the patient is evasive, a therapeutically significant contact will be difficult to make. Efforts of the therapist to combat or to conceal these feelings are generally of no value, since the patient will sense them anyhow. The schizophrenic personality and the schizophrenic symptomatology are such as to arouse hostility very easily in people, and, of course, in the therapist also. If at the beginning of the treatment the therapist has a feeling of hostility, or even a feeling of non-acceptance for the patient, any attempted treatment will be doomed to failure.

The treatment will be more successful if the therapist has a positive feeling of empathy for the patient. As Eissler has emphasized, these feelings are generally experienced at the first contact with the patient (65). If, at the very beginning of treatment, the patient somehow feels that he was able to convey a message to the therapist, or that the therapist was able to reach him without any pressure having been exerted, or any demand having been made, a great deal will have been accomplished.

The kind of feeling, positive or negative, that the therapist will have for the patient will depend not only on the patient's personality and psychological problems, but also on the therapist's personality and problems. If the therapist has been analyzed, he is in a better position to determine what the characteristics are in certain patients, which make him react in a negative way. If the analysis has not been successful in removing these tendencies, he should avoid treating patients who have the problems to which he reacts negatively. On the other hand, some very individualistic attitudes of the therapist, which are based on the therapist's own psychological problems, may be not at all harmful but beneficial to the treatment. For instance, Eissler feels that his childhood fantasy of wanting to rescue people was reactivated when he tried to save schizophrenics from the shock treatment, which he considered "a great danger," (65). Eissler thinks that the therapist must be moved and stirred; therapeutic failure must be unacceptable to him, "the whole gamut of emotionality must be at his quick command. . . . he should believe in his own omnipotence." What Eissler means probably is that the therapist should be as omnipotent in his own eyes as he is in the patient's eyes (see page 457).

What has been said so far has involved only the feeling of the therapist for the patient. We will now examine the general attitude of the therapist in a more active role, an attitude which may be manifested at a non-verbal level. In my experience, I found that this general attitude as a rule should be one of acceptance, warmth, kindness and consideration. The expression, the gesture, and the voice of the analyst should convey those feelings to the patient, particularly when the patient was exposed to overt, unconcealed hostility in his early life. However, there are important exceptions. If the parents of the patient had the appearance of being warm, kind and considerate, at the same time that their more subtle behavior discharged hostility onto the patient, warmth, even when it comes from the analyst, may scare the patient. He is afraid that sooner or later, he will again be badly disappointed, as he was by his parents. It is natural that he be suspicious and afraid. In this case, the therapist should maintain a reserved attitude until he feels that the patient trusts him. What is fundamental is that the patient must derive from the general attitude of the therapist the feeling that the latter is sincere in his attempts and therefore trustworthy. The therapist must never be caught in any act which will make the patient distrust him; he should always remember that it is because the patient distrusted first his parents and later society that he needs to maintain his isolation. The therapist should never pretend to offer love or friendship to the patient, when in reality he feels differently toward him. One is reminded of the patient quoted by Fromm-Reichmann, who said to the young analyst who had professed friendship during the first interview, "How can you say we are friends? We hardly know each other" (105). However, no matter whether the analyst is overtly warm or reserved, he must be consistent, convincing, intensely interested, and, as Betz writes, communicate to the patient his strength, his fairness and his kindness (25). Rosen feels that in the treatment of schizophrenics, the counter-transference must be similar to the feelings that a good parent would have for a highly disturbed child (224). Rosen expresses the idea extremely well when he says that the therapist must identify with the unhappy patient, as the good parent identifies with the unhappy child, and be so disturbed by the unhappiness of the patient that he himself cannot rest until the patient (child) is again at peace. The patient will unconsciously perceive this feeling. Rosen thinks that the therapist must make up for the tremendous deficit of love which the patient experienced in his early life.

It is often very difficult to maintain this general attitude if the therapist does not know how to handle the hostility of the patient. In many cases the handling of the hostility is the major therapeutic difficulty. The establishment of closeness between therapist and patient at times engenders this hostility. The patient cannot stand too much closeness; he fears that rejection after so much closeness will be more painful, and he wants to be the one who rejects and hurts. Whenever possible, the therapist must clarify these vague feelings to the patient, adducing the factors in his life which confirm this interpretation.

Hostility accompanies every case of schizophrenia, but is

disguised in several forms. As Bychowski points out, it may assume the form of extreme passivity, because every act is a potential act of hostility of which the patient himself is afraid (39). It may also assume the form of projection, "He hates me" instead of "I hate him." In his symbolic representation, the patient is correct in feeling "he hates me"; he is aware now of the hostility which once was really directed towards him. However, this hostility now comes, not from the person who originally hated the patient, but from an imaginary substitute. Also the hostility which the patient sees in this substitute is not a reproduction of the original hostility, but a distortion of it. (See page 300). Whenever possible, one should explain to the patient that the hostility is misdirected, and that he is acting as if situations which have long since disappeared were still in existence. Hostile manifestations are often only tests which the patient uses to probe the therapist. If the feeling of trust is maintained, the hostility will decrease, but it is very difficult to maintain this trust since the patient is extremely suspicious and sensitive and sees signs of rejection at any moment. Fromm-Reichmann mentions a patient who went into a catatonic stupor twice when the hour of her appointment was changed. A patient of mine, also a catatonic, went into a tantrum because I answered the telephone during a session.

When it has proven to be impossible to handle the hostility, the therapist may allow another person to be present at the interview. The patient will not resent this person as an intruder, if he understands that this is being done to protect him too from the expression of his own hostility.

The atmosphere of kindness and warmth that we have described above should not degenerate into one of over-solicitousness or become a smothering attitude. Although the patient needs as much care and understanding as a baby does, he should not be babied, since that part of him which is still adult, in spite of the illness, would resent this treatment. This over-solicitousness would be experienced by the patient in the same way as he once experienced that destructive anxiety of the parent, which did not permit him to take little risks, like going bicycling or ice-skating, and which, under the pretense of concern and love, undermined his self-esteem.

At this point, we have to take into consideration another aspect of the patient-therapist relationship, which presents itself in several cases. Several patients, and, in my experience, especially those whose symptomatology is more one of withdrawal than of projection, tend to consider the therapist as an omniscient, all-powerful person, on whom they want to depend entirely. Lidz and Lidz, who in a concise, excellent paper have discussed this aspect of therapy, feel that these patients had mothers who had an intense need to sustain in their children a parasitical attitude (175). A symbiotic relationship between mother and child was thus developed. The child did not live in his own right but as an appendage of mother. The reader will remember that similar problems were discussed in detail in part II of this book. My emphasis, however, was slightly different from that of Lidz and Lidz. In my opinion a decrease in self-esteem, due to the patient's realization that he always does what mother considers wrong, accompanies in several cases the belief that mother always does everything right. She must be omniscient and omnipotent, as the patient thought she was, when he was a baby. He should not do things, but let her do them. As a matter of fact, that is what mother desires. The patient tends to establish not a symbiotic relation, but a parasitic one, one reminiscent of the fetus completely taken care of by the mother. But here, in several cases, restitution phenomena determine those feelings of altered relatedness, so well described by Lidz and Lidz. The patient feels not that he is a parasite but that he is in a symbiotic relation. In simple words, he feels that he is extremely important to mother; mother could not live without him. In addition, he believes that if mother does not allow him to do things, it is not because she is bad, but because she is good. He makes efforts to preserve the good image of the mother and to repress her bad image (see page 48). Certain attitudes of the mother, which are reassuring, are magnified, and the others, which are anxiety-arousing, are completely obliterated.

In the therapeutic relation, the patient may tend to resume this symbiotic attitude. This tendency may be useful only at the very beginning of treatment, when every means must be exploited to make contact with the patient, but will be harmful later if it is not combated. As Lidz and Lidz indicate, the patient must soon realize that the relationship with the therapist is not just a repetition of the symbiotic bond, but a new type of close relationship: this other person can *care* for him, rather than just take *care* of him. The patient must feel and recognize that the therapist is motivated by an interest in helping him for his own sake, and not for some personal ulterior motive.

Lidz and Lidz feel that this symbiotic need may be so strong as to require a change of therapist. In the opinion of this writer, this change seldom will be necessary, if strong efforts have been made to combat it, from a relatively early stage of therapy. If the treatment is to be successful, it must appear to the patient much more than a repetition of the symbiosis. He must soon realize that the therapist is not the parent and permits a gradual expansion of the patient's personality as a separate entity. Whenever possible, the patient should be reminded of the differences between the therapeutic situation and the old ties. The differences rather than the similarities between the two situations, must be emphasized.

The strong need to maintain the stultifying dependency will appear in different forms, but this need should always be explored. For instance, the patient may be afraid of his own improvement. When the patient looks at this progress with a feeling of achievement he may be afraid that he will not be able to remain so independent, and at the same time, he may long for the old dependent (symbiotic) attitude. The dangerous fascination that the old dependent attitude has for him should be explained.

\The patient may insist that the successful therapist is omniscient and omnipotent. For instance, one of my patients during the tenth month of treatment, told me, "The most tragic day for me will be the day when I discover that you make a mistake. My parents, my husband, every human being, I expect to make mistakes, but not you." I immediately tried to dislodge this belief, by assuring her that I make mistakes, that I make them every day, and that often I catch myself in the process of making them. I also told her that I had made mistakes even in her treatment, and that yet she had improved. From that day on, she began to accept me on a more realistic plane. She did not continue to think that her recovery was based on my extraordinary powers. I suppose a patient may at times be almost hypnotized into a state of remission, by believing in the magical powers of the analyst, but I wonder whether such a remission would last.

Actually, these phantasies of the patient are pathological ways to regain self-esteem. At the beginning of therapy, the patient I have just mentioned felt that since I had such superhuman ability, I was the only person who knew that she was a good girl and, therefore, the only person who could appreciate her.

\ Even in fairy tales, the person who is helped by the magic supernatural being is a person who believes he deserves to be helped, a person, therefore, who has not lost his self-esteem. When the patient is made to feel that he is accepted by the therapist, in spite of the fact that the latter has no magical powers, real progress is made.

Another patient of mine was very disturbed when he

heard from me that I had to take a few days off because I had to undergo a tonsillectomy. He was particularly disturbed by the fact that I needed another doctor to treat me and operate on me. In his phantasies about me I appeared self-curative. How could it be that I needed another doctor? If a physical illness were to strike the patient would I be able to cure him? For two or three days he woke up at night with anxiety feelings, thinking that I would not be able to take care of him if something happened to him. Eventually, the patient was reassured when he saw that I resumed his treatment as before, after I myself had been treated by other doctors.

Another belief which the schizophrenic often holds (and the neurotic too, at times) is that the doctor knows all the answers to the problems discussed, but withholds them from the patient, either capriciously or because he feels that the patient, in a certain sense, has not grown up sufficiently. This, too, is a resurgence of a belief that little children have about the surrounding adults, who at times are really too secretive about certain matters. When the child grows up in a normal environment, he sooner or later accepts the fact that the parents cannot answer all the questions, all the "whys," because they themselves don't know the answers. The schizophrenic, however, returns to the previous level, in which belief in the omniscience of the adults still prevails. Again, the therapist should interpret this mechanism to the patient and should show him that the therapist's inability to answer all questions is a characteristic of human nature and not necessarily a handicap. In the process of improving, the patient himself will be able to answer many of his own questions; others he will answer in cooperation with the therapist; some he will never answer, and yet nothing bad will result.

Another attitude which the schizophrenic holds much oftener than the neurotic is that he is the unique interest of the therapist. The therapist cannot possibly be as interested in the other patients as he is in him. I suggested a raise in the fee of a schizophrenic patient, who was able to secure a remunerative employment, after I had been treating him for a year at a reduced fee. The patient was furiously insulted and almost interrupted the treatment. His faith in me was vacillating; I was treating him for money, and not because I had any interest in him. When I explained to him that by intending to raise the fee, I was acknowledging his growth, and the fact that he no longer required special conditions, he was able to accept my suggestion.

Another practical problem which presents itself in connection with this strong symbiotic need of the patient is how to prepare him for the vacation time of the therapist. Especially if the vacation time occurs just a few months after the beginning of treatment, the patient may experience a strong feeling of panic at the idea of being left alone. If he is a catatonic, he may actually relapse into a stupor. The situation may reactivate the patient's strong feelings of being rejected, and direct attempts to convince him that this is not the case are futile. In many instances, the therapist may avoid these complications by preparing the patient far in advance for this brief separation. He should be told a few months previously that the physician has made plans for a vacation, and that he should expect a few weeks interruption in treatment. In many cases, especially if the treatment is still at a preliminary stage, some ties have to be maintained even during the vacation time. The patient should be told that he may write to the analyst, or that if an emergency arises, he may even telephone him. In my experience, I have found that patients very seldom avail themselves of these concessions; on the other hand, they feel reassured. In the cases where the help of a therapeutic assistant is needed (see page 468), this difficulty is partially removed by arranging different vacation times for the therapist and for the therapeutic assistant.

Wexler is an author who advocates the adoption of a general attitude different from the one suggested by this writer for the therapist of schizophrenic patients (271). Wexler views the schizophrenic disorganization as the result of a primitive, archaic and devastatingly punitive superego, in the presence of urgent instinctual demands. According to him, this archaic superego is nothing more than the internalized parental figures, "the ghosts of the past." I have no objection to this dynamic interpretation of schizophrenia. The reader knows that it largely concurs with what was described in Part II of this volume. Wexler, however, feels that this dynamic mechanism indicates that the therapist should assume superego roles. He feels that the therapist should be harsh and strict, forbid sexual thoughts and feelings, and have a generally repressing attitude. He also has quoted Nunberg, who attributed his patient's improvement to his submission to the strong, authoritarian analyst and to his belief in the analyst's magical power (204). I definitely agree with Fromm-Reichmann that the analyst should try to have the patient see him in the opposite way, that is, not on an "authoritarian pedestal." I do not deny the irrefutable fact that Wexler and Nunberg obtained great success with the patients they reported, but I am not sure that the good results obtained were due to the reasons mentioned by those authors.

Tyrannical parental authority prevented a normal development in the schizophrenic. By submitting to his tyrannical parents, the patient was not able to build that amount of self-esteem which is necessary to face the difficulties of life. On the other hand, by submitting to an authoritarian and harsh therapist, Wexler's patient apparently was able to reestablish her self-esteem and to improve. She was confident that by submitting she would obtain approval and affection from the analyst. Wexler succeeded in conveying to the patient the feeling that she could trust him, even if he was tyrannical and strict. In my opinion that was the fundamental point. In his case, in order to convey this feeling of being trusted, Wexler had to resort to assuming a strict authoritarian role. It could be that the analysts who successfully assume this strict superego role have a type of personality which conveys this feeling of trust, especially in the adoption of that role. If an analyst is successful in adopting the superego role, he does not have to contend with the guilt feelings that a permissive attitude may engender in the patient at the beginning of treatment.

Wexler and other authors stress the point that the therapeutic situation must be very similar to the old genetic situation. It seems to me that most of the improvement is due to the differences in the two situations, not to the similarities. The apparent similarity perhaps helps the treatment in the beginning, but the patient must sense the difference in the underlying feeling, in order to improve. I have found it useful to interpret this to the patient, too, at an advanced stage of treatment (see page 472). The same is true for the neurotic. Is a good transference just a repetition of what happened earlier between the parent and the patient? The present writer fully agrees with Janet Rioch that the therapeutic transference must expand, not repeat, the original experience, and must open new vistas, which will permit the growth of the patient (219). As a matter of fact, it is one of the constant aims of therapy to help the patients lose distortions arising from the tendency to repeat the old situation.

Mann, Menzer and Standish have made an interesting study of the attitudes in the therapist which have led to the deterioration of the therapeutic relationship, in the psychotherapy of functional psychoses (184). They found that the therapist is not directed by conscious motivation in the choice of patients. The therapist tends to choose patients with problems similar to his own, and thus may reactivate his own conflicts, so that he may respond with "emotional flight" or with retaliation. By "emotional flight" the authors mean an unrealistic attitude of the therapist which will not permit the patient to discuss feelings related to the therapist's conflict. This unrealistic attitude of the therapist was generally brought about by the excessive demands of the patients, demands which the therapist could not or did not want to fulfill. The demands which were made on the therapists were sexual demands or permission to go home.

In my own experience, I have found that one demand of the patient which may disturb the feelings of the therapist is the request that the therapist accept the delusional system, or a delusional idea of the patient. Especially well-preserved, fanatic paranoids like to put the therapist on the spot with this type of demand. In my opinion, it is better not to yield to this pressure of the patient. Rosen reports instead that in treating certain patients the therapist must accept their psychotic reality; he must act as if he accepts the fact that they are Moses, Christ, Napoleon, etc. (224). In my experience with a few cases where I tried this technique, I did not find it good. We must remember that there is always a part of the patient, no matter how little it is, which does not accept the psychosis. In treatment we have to rely a great deal on that part. As has been mentioned several times, we must maintain the trust of the patient at any cost, and sooner or later he will realize whether or not the therapist means what he says or not. He will develop contempt for the therapist if he acts as if he believes what even a part of the patient himself does not believe. I do not doubt, however, that if the therapist is able to identify with the patient to such a point as to share his psychotic experiences emotionally with him, this technique may be useful. This identification, however, is very difficult to accomplish. I have used the technique of allegedly accepting the patient's psychotic reality, only for reasons of expediency and very reluctantly, when there was no other way to avoid violence or to make preparations for hospitalization. A therapist who is inclined to feel guilty if he does not fulfill the delusional demands of the patient, or one who lets himself be intimidated easily by the aggressive tendencies of the patient, should not treat defiant paranoids. He will do much better with catatonics and hebephrenics.

Semrad, Menzer, Mann, and Standish made another study of the doctor-patient relationship in the psychotherapy of psychotic patients (233). They found that the libidinal and aggressive tendencies of the patients were "so intense as to mobilize immediate anxiety through the reawakening of the doctor's repressed infantile aggressive and libidinal problems." The reawakening of these problems in the doctor led to interference with the psychotherapeutic task.

There is no doubt that one of the greatest difficulties encountered in treating psychotics is the intensity of the relationship with the therapist which is required. This intensity is apt to bring the therapist's problems to the surface, at times with unexpected violence. As Mary White wrote, in discussing the above-mentioned paper of Semrad and his co-workers, the psychotic gives the physician a prolonged opportunity to learn about himself (272).

Several of my psychotic patients have been able to detect in me certain feelings and moods, at times when even I was not aware of them. This has been observed by practically everybody who has practised psychotherapy with psychotics.

If the patients detect an unpleasant mood in the therapist, the latter should not deny it, but admit it, together with the information that such a mood has nothing to do with them. Clara Thompson reports that disturbances in the analyst's life and the admittance of such disturbances to the patient may have a favorable effect on the analysis (260). Feigenbaum, during a session with a paranoid, received by telephone the news that a close friend had suddenly died (73). His reaction to the sad news brought about a human response from the patient, whose analysis from that time on took a turn for the better. Clara Thompson reported the reaction of a schizophrenic patient at her grief for the death of her analyst and teacher, Ferenczi (257). Her sorrow convinced the patient more than anything else that she was not a cold person as the rest of the world had been.

If the therapist does not explain these unhappy feelings to the patients, patients may misinterpret them. They tend to react as young children do when they see their parents worried or unhappy. An egocentric distortion makes them feel that the unpleasant feeling is related to them. They react in accordance with this interpretation, that is, with a feeling of being rejected or with detachment.

In what we have just mentioned, we have another illustration of that perplexing and mixed picture that the schizophrenic presents: on the one hand, he is very sensitive and capable of seeing through a situation and seeing the truth, even more so than a normal person; on the other hand, what he does with what he sees is so distorted that it will increase, rather than decrease his difficulties. The increased sensitivity of the patient is explained by his early history (page 54) and the increased awareness of his own feelings is explained by the process of desocialization (page 303). We should not forget, however, that the process of desocialization engenders concomitant distortions. In some psychiatric circles, the amazement produced by the discovery of the increased power of "seeing through" of the schizophrenic, has made enthusiastic therapists forget the negative side of this quality. This enthusiasm is obviously a reaction to the previous psychiatric pessimistic and descriptive attitudes. The fact remains that the schizophrenic cannot be considered indeed only a person of great feeling and understanding; he is a much more complicated creature. He adds a great deal of misunderstanding to what he keenly understands.

Incidentally, in my experience, I have found that this ability to see through a situation appears not only in full-fledged schizophrenics but also in several prepsychotic stormy personalities. Schizoid personalities, on the other hand, do not manifest this characteristic prior to their break with reality.

IV. General Participation in Patient's Life and Assignment of Tasks. Use of Therapeutic Assistant

As we have already mentioned, a great part of the reintegration of the patient will consist of the building up of his self-esteem. As a matter of fact, it is only if he feels that his self-esteem is being rebuilt that the patient will continue the treatment. The threat that many patients, including psychoneurotics, see in psychoanalytically oriented therapy, is nothing else but a fear that this treatment will decrease, rather than increase, their self-esteem. This fear is particularly pronounced in schizophrenics because actually almost every interpersonal relation they have had has produced an injury to their self-esteem. It is the purpose of the therapist to help the patient not only to dispel this fear but to increase his confidence in himself. The therapist will be able to do that not only by conveying to him the feelings which have been described in the previous sections, but also by showing him, at a practical, concrete level, that he, the therapist, believes that the patient is capable of participating in life activities, is able to perform certain activities, wants to perform them and find a role in the structure of society.

This requires the therapist's participation in the whole life of the patient. The treatment of schizophrenics cannot consist only of the sessions; much more is involved. Rosen went to the extent of shopping with the patients (223). He spent 10 hours daily with some patients. Sechehaye, too, spent practically the whole day with her only patient (227). The patient must feel that the therapist, like a parent-substitute, shares all the events of his life. As we mentioned before, there is a tendency to return to a condition of early childhood, but here again, it is the difference, and not the similarity with the early situation, which is important. Although the new parent-substitute participates in the whole life of the patient, he does not stultify the growth of the patient, who is allowed to take his own initiative whenever possible. The patient also wants tasks to be given to him, and demands to be made on him, contrary to the way he felt at the beginning of the treatment. To a certain extent, it is by fulfilling these tasks that the patient will gain in self-evaluation. I learned this technique when I was working in Pilgrim State Hospital. At that time I noticed that the rate of discharge of schizophrenic patients was much higher in certain wards than in others. This was happening in so-called "back buildings" for chronic patients where no physical or psychotherapeutic treatment was given. I soon came to the realization that the high rate of discharge was a consequence of the way certain nurses treated the patients. These female nurses offered the patients an image of a good mother, by appearing warm, strong and kind. The patients responded to this atmosphere of consistent warmth by becoming more active. The nurse or the female attendant then would give the patient tasks, which the patient was certainly able to perform and would then praise the patient, who felt an incentive to do more. The patient felt that she deserved the praise of the nurse, and in this way her self-esteem increased. Inasmuch as in wartime there was a serious shortage of employees, the nurses naturally had a tendency to show affection for those patients who would help. This affection, however, did not seem to the patients to have strings attached to it, as original parental affection did. The difference was due to several factors:

1) The assignments were not out of proportion to the capa-

bilities of the patient. The patient was asked to do what could reasonably be expected of her, and therefore her insecurity was not increased.

2) The patient would definitely and consistently get some kind of approval or preferential treatment, which increased her self-esteem. The work, therefore, was seen primarily not as an exploitation on the part of the nurse, but as a method of improving oneself.

To summarize, what I think was happening was that the nurse, a very maternal person, not at all hostile but love-inspiring, with her general attitude was able to remobilize the patient. Once the patient was made to move as a result of this attitude, she became involved in a method of increasing her self-esteem. Of course, not all patients responded to this atmosphere, but a fairly good number did. Unfortunately, since I worked predominantly in female services, I noticed this happening only to female patients. I am not unwilling to assume, however, that the same thing may happen to male patients, especially if they are in contact with very understanding "maternal," even male nurses. I am inclined to believe that many so-called spontaneous recoveries which occur in the back buildings of state hospitals are due to the beneficial effects of the interpersonal relationships with nurses or attendants.

But coming back to our ambulatory patients, we have to take their wishes into consideration when we assign tasks. They will be more willing to do what they like. It is useful to remember that schizophrenics, more frequently than average persons, have artistic inclinations (page 310). Some of my patients, during treatment, started to study painting, music or classical dancing, with considerable success, in spite of adult age. These artistic expressions, if examined by the therapist, will reveal what is going on inside the patient.

However, the therapist should avoid giving the patient the impression that his works are appreciated for their diagnostic value.

As mentioned before, even one single patient requires much attention; at times one person must be at the continuous and exclusive disposal of the patient. It is obvious that the therapist alone cannot do this job. As I have described in Part II of this book, whenever possible, I have resorted to the help of another person, whom I called the therapeutic assistant. The therapeutic assistant stays with the patient during the day, except, of course, for the time of the session. She cooperates with the patient in the fulfillment of the assignments, and to a large extent, she must duplicate that general attitude which we have described for the therapist.

In my opinion, the work of the therapeutic assistant is essential in the majority of cases. First of all, it is too precarious or dangerous to entrust the treatment of such fragile and dependent patients as schizophrenics, to one person only. If, for some unexpected reasons, the therapist must discontinue treatment, the patient should not feel that everything is lost. Secondly, at least two useful interpersonal relationships are needed in most cases for a healthy reintegration and socialization. We should not forget that even in the original situations, generally there are two persons, the two parents, who help the child to grow. It is difficult for one person only to supply the patient with all that he needs. Thirdly, it is a physical impossibility for the therapist, in the economic structure of our society, to devote so much time to one patient.

The therapeutic assistant not only should create a warm general atmosphere of acceptance, but should help the patient to share feelings again and do things together with another person. The therapeutic assistant should always be there, near the patient, as a person on whom the patient may depend whenever he wants to; he should provide what I call *concrete availability*. By this I mean that the patient must be able to rely on him, not as an image of a distant potential or magic helper, but as a person who is there in physical proximity.

It is a good practice to use as therapeutic assistants, persons who have been analyzed; however, in my opinion, well-adjusted persons with warm, irradiating personalities have done this work very well, even if they had not undergone analysis. I had started to use therapeutic assistants long before I read Federn's papers. I was pleased to read that he had advocated the same thing, the use of a "helper" (70, 72). In some cases, Federn used as a helper, Miss Gertrude Schwing, a nurse whom he had analyzed. Gertrude Schwing was very successful and later published her significant book on her work with schizophrenics (226).

Rosen, in his work, has been assisted by two nurses, who had previously suffered from schizophrenia, and who had recovered as the result of his treatment. I have not as yet been helped by former patients, but I see the potential advantages of such a possibility. I have generally used young psychologists or social workers. Nurses who have not been exposed to dynamic psychiatry are generally not good as therapeutic assistants, unless they have those personality qualities which were mentioned above and which are not due to their training. It is to be foreseen, however, that nurses trained in interpersonal relations, in accordance with the ideas expressed by Peplau in her excellent book (209), will provide very valuable therapeutic assistants.

At this point, it must be mentioned that if the patient is helped by a therapeutic assistant, he may become involved in one of those triangular social processes, first described by Stanton and Schwartz (242, 243). I have seen them occur a few times in my ambulatory patients, although not with that intensity with which they occur in hospitalized patients. If the patient feels that there is a non-expressed disagreement be-

tween the therapist and the therapeutic assistant about his
own treatment, or between the therapist or therapeutic assistant and a parent, he is bound to become disturbed. This
disturbance is relatively mild, since the patient generally feels
that the therapist is on his side in disagreements between therapist and therapeutic assistant, or that the therapeutic assistant
is on his side, when the latter disagrees with the parent. When
the problem is openly discussed or an agreement is reached,
the disturbance tends to disappear. Incidentally, the disturbance may have something to do with the reactivation of the
feeling which the patient used to have in his childhood, that
he was the cause of the victim of the dissension which existed
between his parents.

Federn wrote that the helper may be even a relative or a
friend (70, 72). In my opinion, a relative, especially a close
relative such as a parent or the spouse, is not a good helper,
because he is too much involved in the emotional problems
of the patient. Even if the relative who acts as an assistant
has been analyzed and has overcome his own emotional problems, the patient's problems in connection with this person
will make the task a very difficult one. I have encountered a
few cases where the husband wanted to act as a therapeutic
assistant, but these attempts were not successful. The patients
tended to resume a symbiotic relationship with their husbands. They tended to become passive bodies which had to
be taken care of completely. Of course, in these cases, the
hostility for the husbands was given this opportunity to express itself.

As mentioned before, analysis of relatives may help indirectly, both because we obtain additional information about
the background of the patient and also because the attitude of
the relative toward the patient may change (see page 87).
Changes in the family situation may be very useful, and the

therapist must investigate all the possibilities for such changes. Often it is better for the patient not to live with his own family, where many disturbing feelings originate. The unconscious or conscious hostility of the relatives may still block the efforts of the therapist if the patient lives with his own family. Although in a foster home or in family care, situations may arise which the patient will emotionally identify with those which took place in his own family, it will be easier for him to discuss these new situations and to understand them in treatment.

V. Advanced Stage of Treatment

All of these factors—the transference and countertransference, the interpretations, the general attitude and the sharing of experiences with the therapeutic assistant, the changes in the environment, the possible analysis of relatives,—will coordinate in the process of reintegration.

One of the difficulties encountered at a later stage of treatment is the fear of improvement, as mentioned before. The patient has to be made aware that he improves for his own sake and not for the sake of pleasing anyone else. Contrary to his belief, the improvement will make him freer, not more dependent, not more obligated to others. In the process of reasserting himself, he may re-experience that feeling which tormented him in his pre-psychotic stage, when he thought that *to be himself meant to be queer,* and that therefore it was better for him to conform and to be as others wanted him to be. Actually, this feeling will not last a long time after its return, because the patient is learning to accept himself as he is and to have respect for his own feelings and his judgment. The reflected appraisals of the therapist and of the therapeutic assistant have built his self-esteem to a large extent and have helped him to find himself or to build his sense of self-identification. Criticisms are no longer experienced as total rebuffs.

Tendencies to resort to archaic forms of thinking must now be fully interpreted. The process by which the patient tends to confuse similarity with identity may be explained. Also, the fact that when a situation has a characteristic of his childhood, the patient tends to react as he did then must be clarified. This tendency has to be explained in relation to the emotional overtone on account of which the mentioned confusion occurs.

Whenever the therapist feels that the patient is ready for a decrease in the number of sessions, this step should be taken. The patient generally dislikes a reduction in treatment, because of his dependency, which may remain great, in spite of the improvement. The opposite may also happen. The patient may want to terminate therapy too quickly. If he does so, he usually does not want to contact the therapist any more, because the latter reminds him of a period of his life which he wants to forget. Even when he is recovered, he is not strong enough to be reminded of the psychotic episode without being hurt. Federn, too, has mentioned this apparent ingratitude of the patient for the analyst (70, 72). To be reminded of a psychotic state, and to be asked questions about it, may precipitate a relapse. According to Federn, the patient is intuitively right in avoiding his former analyst.

The patient develops similar feelings for the therapeutic assistants. Whenever several therapeutic assistants were used in successive stages of the treatment, the patient felt uncomfortable when he met again the assistant who had helped him at an earlier stage of treatment. The patient is eager to show his improvement to the former assistant, and at the same time is almost ashamed of it. He is almost tempted to slip back to the stage in which he was when he was working with that assistant. In addition, the former therapeutic assistant often almost automatically makes the mistake of treating the patient as she used to, as if she were unwilling or unable to acknowledge the improvement.

At an advanced stage of treatment, the patient may become distressed by typical neurotic symptoms. Rosen also has mentioned this common occurrence (224). One of the compulsions commonly found, especially in former catatonics, is the compelling necessity to do everything best and to avoid mistakes. The patient must buy the best suit, must go to the best doctor, must read numerous times what he writes for fear of having made mistakes, etc. These symptoms are easy to explain if we remember the underlying psychodynamic mechanisms. The protection of inactivity is no longer available, but the patient still wants to please mother and avoid mistakes, or identify himself with mother and do what is best. The "power" to avoid the mistake is searched also as proof of the ability to fight a now and then reemerging feeling of powerlessness. If the patient is able to avoid the mistake or to obtain the best results, he has power; he does not need to feel hopeless or to go back to the state of withdrawal.

In recovering schizophrenics, often we must try not only to interpret the symptoms, but also to suppress them. By suppressing, I mean creating situations in which these symptoms are not likely to occur, and vice versa, avoiding situations where they may easily occur. For instance, if the patient has the tendency to indulge in rituals when he is alone, he should not be left alone. Psychosomatic symptoms, such as palpitations, pseudo-heart attacks, also occur frequently. They are generally transient, and it is best not to devote much therapeutic time to them.

VI. Precautionary Measures

It is obvious that the treatment of a psychotic individual, especially ambulatory treatment, presents a certain risk. The risks are generally exaggerated. As far as I know, episodes of violence have been very rare. However, they have occurred, and no precautionary measure that we know of today can be absolutely sure of safeguarding the therapist or the patient from these episodes. Usually, common sense and the feeling of the therapist are more than sufficient. If the therapist feels that the patient is dangerous and more anti-social than asocial, he should not treat him outside of a hospital. Also, whenever the danger of suicide exists, either the patient should be hospitalized or the relatives should be notified that very close supervision is needed.

If the therapist feels that he is afraid of the patient, he should try to find out why he is afraid. Often the personal problems of the therapist, more than the actual actions of the patient, engender such fear. If the therapist is under analysis or supervision, he should discuss this fear with his own analyst or supervisor. If he is not under analysis or supervision, he may discuss the matter with a competent colleague. As we mentioned before, the treatment of some schizophrenics is bound to elicit in the therapist a disturbing counter-transference. A colleague, by being less emotionally involved, is able at times to help the exhausted therapist. However, if in spite of this help, the therapist continues to be afraid of the patient, he should not treat him. The patient senses this fear, and becomes more hostile toward himself, because he feels that he is so bad as to cause fear even in the therapist. He may also become more resentful toward the therapist and really burst into acts of violence.

At times, during treatment, the patient may become worse and require hospitalization. Whenever possible, the patient should be told the truth by the therapist, and be reassured that the treatment will be continued while he is in the hospital. Sometimes, however, the situation is out of the hands of the therapist, because the patient, generally a defiant paranoid, refuses hospitalization. The family should be informed of the situation. In a minority of unfortunate cases, the patient is so hostile and openly or potentially dangerous, that he cannot even be told by the therapist that he needs hospitalization. Here, too, special arrangements have to be made with the family.

A situation from which the therapist must protect himself is the possible accusation of having sexual relations with the patient. Sexual intentions are often attributed to the analyst, even by neurotic patients. However, with neurotics, this is not a serious problem. It is easy to discuss these feelings and to interpret them. The situation is much more complicated with a psychotic, who, in his tendency to concretize ideas, does not speak of intentions of the therapist, but of real acts. Since the nature of the therapy is such that it does not allow for the presence of a nurse or an attendant during the session, the physician must master the situation in other ways. First of all, the young therapist is warned against taking these accusations too seriously. He should not put himself in a position of defense, but whenever possible, he should interpret these sexual feelings to the patient, as he would do with a neurotic patient. Generally, the psychotic patient who does not dare to have feelings of closeness, has to distort anything resembling them. As Sullivan would say, "in a malevolent way," he transforms his own longing for closeness or the analyst's warm attitude into sexual acts initiated by the analyst. The therapist should take notes, reporting the expressions of these accusations, not out of context, but in an account of the session which is as complete as possible. In the proper context these ideas will appear delusional to everybody and can be used if the paranoid patient, who cannot stand closeness with the therapist, interrupts treatment, and makes legal charges against him. A phonograph record of the session would be very useful. As was mentioned before, the presence of a witness when the patient has the feeling that the therapist uses him or her sexually is not recommended. In a certain respect, this recommendation is contrary to what has been suggested in cases of uncontrollable hostility.

If the paranoid patient feels that the therapist wants to abuse her sexually, the presence of another person may reinforce her belief. A young resident was attempting psychotherapy on a hospitalized antagonistic paranoid who soon accused him of some kind of sexual activity when he was alone with her in the office. The doctor asked an attendant to be present at the subsequent interviews. Such procedure did not dispel the ideas of the patient, but reinforced them. According to her, the therapist, now having a paid witness on his side, could really do whatever he wanted with her. She really believed that sexual affairs were taking place, even in the presence of the attendant. The resident then assumed a disparaging, contemptuous attitude, after which these sexual phantasies disappeared, because there was no longer any fear of closeness. The rapport was lost, however, and treatment had to be discontinued.

If the patient who harbors such ideas is a minor, and if interpretations have not been successful, the therapist should inform the relatives of the existence of such ideas, and advise treatment with a therapist of the same sex. One should not forget that the relatives are emotionally disturbed people, and that in their unconscious desire to interrupt the treatment and hurt the patient, they are bound to believe the patient's allegations, if they have not been informed by the therapist in advance. Revelation of such ideas to the relatives may be harmful as far as the treatment is concerned, but after all, we cannot expect the therapist to be a masochist who does not want to protect himself.

I have not read or heard of actual physical sexual attacks being made by psychotic patients on therapists.* Homosexual desires generally manifest themselves in symbolic forms. Declarations of love toward the therapist of the opposite sex are not rare, especially in paranoids who express these feelings in a bizarre, generally harmless manner. These erotic feelings are different from the usual transference feelings of neurotics, inasmuch as they are more overt and are more obviously a form of resistance to the treatment. They generally, although not always, indicate that the treatment is experienced as an attempt to decrease the patient's self-esteem. By lavishing love on the therapist the patient tries to protect himself from this alleged attempt. If the therapist would yield and have sexual relations with the patient, that fact would be proof to the patient of the therapist's acceptance of him. Incidentally, similar feelings, expressed openly by some psychotic patients, for the parents of the opposite sex, seem to me often to indicate the same thing. Physical love is a concrete symbolization of what is really wanted: love and reassurance.

VII. Contraindications

The contraindications to psychoanalytically oriented therapy with schizophrenics are not based on any theoretical premise, but on the fact that therapists have not yet learned to cope with certain situations in certain cases. For instance, when the therapist is confronted with a very acute schizophrenic process, at times he feels almost overwhelmed by the precipitous sequence of events. The patient is rapidly led to disintegration by increasing anxiety. In such cases, the ther-

---

* Sexual attacks toward nurses and attendants have occasionally occurred.

apist not only may find himself unable to cope with the anxiety of the patient, but he actually may increase it, even if he makes every effort to use the most refined technique. In these cases it seems as if the anxiety of the patient has the tendency to spread to any kind of interpersonal relationship, including the one with the therapist. No doubt, the more we know about the psychotherapeutic process, the more we shall learn how to eliminate the factors in the therapeutic situation which may increase anxiety in the patient. As a matter of fact, as we have seen in this chapter, we have already succeeded in doing this in a large number of cases. We have also seen how important the personality of the therapist is in this respect. However, the fact remains that in many rapidly disintegrating cases, psychotherapy, as we are able to practice it today, is not useful. These cases, unfortunately, still represent a considerable percentage of all cases of schizophrenia. I do not mean to imply that all rapidly disintegrating cases do not respond to psychotherapy. As a matter of fact, many do, especially patients who rapidly lapse into catatonic stupor. The rapid precipitation of events should never discourage the therapist, and a trial period of psychotherapy should always be undertaken before the patient is referred for other types of treatment.

The second contraindication to continuation of psychotherapy is the inability of several therapists to make any kind of contact with the same patient, even if he is not disintegrating as rapidly as those just described. For reasons which are not completely clear at present, some patients remain totally impervious. The therapist "feels" that he is not going to "reach" the patient. This may be due to the therapist's problems, as we have seen. However, if several therapists have made attempts, with the same results, the probability is that the patient's need to desocialize is such that our present psychotherapeutic techniques will not be able to arrest such a need. It is then the physician's duty to try another type of treatment.

VIII. Conclusions

Although these notes on the psychotherapy of schizophrenia are by no means definite or complete, they are sufficient to offer some ideas of the technique and its difficulties. Nothing can replace experience. The reader must realize that this treatment is very complicated and requires much more from the therapist in emotional investment, time, and sacrifice, than the treatment of neurotics.

Several authors consider the treatment of schizophrenia more an art than a science. This is true, not only because our knowledge of it is very limited, relatively speaking, and therefore has not as yet passed the tests of a scientific procedure, but because, as we have already seen a few times, this treatment confronts the therapist with very individualistic manifestations which require from him, in addition to all the other therapeutic attitudes, some kind of esthetic-like participation.

CHAPTER XXIV

Some Comments on the Physical Therapies
of Schizophrenia

This chapter is not intended to be a repetition or a summary of the many works written on the techniques of psychiatric physical therapies. Many authors, who have devoted themselves mainly to this subject, have written excellent books on their findings. The reader is referred to the book by Kalinowsky and Hoch on the technique of shock therapy (148); to the books by Freeman and Watts (87), and by Mettler (189), for psychosurgery; and to Fiamberti's work on acetylcholine treatment (81).

This chapter will be a critical discussion only of the indications and therapeutic mechanisms of the two major types of treatment, shock treatment and psychosurgery.

I. Shock Treatment

Shock treatment, in the two forms of insulin coma and electric convulsions, is the method most widely used today for the therapy of schizophrenia. Metrazol treatment has been replaced almost completely by the electric method.

In the opinion of the author shock therapy is only a symptomatic treatment. The patient may lose his overt symptomatology, but the basic psychopathological factors remain unchanged, unless the treatment is accompanied by psychotherapy, or by changes in the environment of the patient. Fortunately, environmental changes may occur, since the drastic nature of shock treatment often acts as a catalyst on the emotional attitudes of the relatives toward the patient. The majority of cases which after shock therapy are discharged from hospitals as cured, are in reality only freed of symptoms. The fact that patients have lost delusions and hallucinations and other apparent symptoms does not mean that they are cured. If these patients who are discharged were to be probed by more psychodynamically oriented procedures (a measure which I do not recommend unless sustained by regular prolonged psychotherapy), the incompleteness and fragility of their improvement would manifest themselves.

In spite of these negative aspects shock treatment should by no means be removed from our armamentarium. It is still useful in several cases. The reasons for my apparently inconsistent attitude are simple ones which must be faced with equanimity and in a realistic spirit by those who advocate psychotherapeutic methods as I do:

1) Psychotherapy, even at the present stage of psychiatric development, can be available only to an infinitesimal minority of patients.

2) Psychotherapy, even in the hands of the most experienced, does not work in every case (see page 478).

3) There are cases which are extremely urgent on account of the concomitant occurrence of a physical illness. In these cases some results have to be quickly effected, and

one cannot afford to wait for the long, time-consuming therapeutic procedure.

4) Symptomatic treatment cannot be condemned when something better is not available. For example, x-ray treatment may be an unsatisfactory, symptomatic treatment for malignant neoplasms, but in many instances it is the only treatment which may be given.

Another point which should be considered, because it has been a subject of concern for many who advocate the exclusive use of psychotherapeutic methods, is the question of whether shock treatment can hurt the patient physically or psychologically. *Primum non nocere* has been one of the first therapeutic concepts since ancient times. It seems to me that this concern has been exaggerated. Complications such as fractures are no more common than complications, let us say, after general surgery. The treatment, however, does produce a change in the nervous system. Some writers have found severe histologic alterations, especially in the case of insulin treatment (Ferraro and Jervis, 80), while instead, others have found irreversible cell damage *only* when the animals died in coma, or when unusually high doses of units were injected over a long period of time. (Accornero, 3, Weil, Liebert and Heilbrunn, 269).

As far as the convulsive treatment is concerned, both metrazol and electric, the works of many authors (Winkelman and Moore, 275, Arieti, 6, Cerletti and Bini, 52, Globus and co-workers, 111, etc.) seem to have made evident that the produced changes are all *reversible,* unless an unusual quantity of treatment is given for a prolonged period of time. From the histologic studies, it is to be deduced that the nervous tissue returns to a normal condition not too long after treatment.

If physical hazards do not exist or are minimal when proper therapy is given, then the objections of many authors must concern possible psychological harm. Eissler speaks of "the great danger" he saw in shock therapy, and of his great efforts to save patients from it (65). Many psychiatrists, among whom are people whom I greatly admire and respect, and from whom I have learned a great deal, go so far as to feel that the practice of shock treatment is the expression of some hostility of the therapist, or of the desire to get rid of the patient, or a remnant of the medieval concept which held that it was good to punish the "possessed" mental patient. These feelings and ideas to me seem far-fetched and unduly dramatic. I do admit that therapists who do not succeed with psychotherapy, may have the desire to remove the patient from the psychotherapeutic situation, and refer him to shock therapy. With a few exceptions, which involve personal problems of the therapist, I do not feel that patients recommended for shock therapy are being punished. This may actually be the concept of the patients. There is no more hostility or desire to punish in instituting shock therapy than there is in doing surgery on a patient who needs it. I feel, as a rule, that the selection of shock treatment is the expression, not of hostility, but of the organic leaning of the psychiatrist. This leaning may be valid or not, but it need not be an expression or a rationalization of hostility.

But let us go back to the psychological harm that the treatment may produce. Usually it is assumed that the patient feels that finally he has been punished or "castrated." From the cases of schizophrenia which I have treated psychotherapeutically after shock treatment, I cannot reach that conclusion. The feeling of having been punished is more frequently encountered in manic-depressive or involutional patients who have been treated with convulsive therapies.

The other psychological objection is based on the fact that the shock treatment does not eradicate the causes but represses them. This statement about shock treatment is correct; it was implicit in the statement that this therapy is only symptomatic. But if, in many patients, it is impossible to eradicate the causes of the disorder, it is of some value at least to repress the asocial and antisocial symptoms. Incidentally, even certain forms of psychotherapy, like that of Federn,* aim at a symptomatic repression of the id (70, 72).

Generally, after shock therapy, the patient is able to return to society; he will no longer be a public charge, and although his functions may be curtailed, he may be able to live some kind of limited social life. In many fortunate cases, where the dramatic succession of events (acute attack → hospitalization → institution of shock treatment) have acted as catalytic agents on the environmental forces, the results may be much more than a removal of the immediate symptoms.

How is shock treatment capable of producing its symptomatic therapeutic effects? Here the field is still open to the realm of speculation. Gordon, in an interesting short paper, lists no less than fifty theories which have been advanced to explain the effect of shock treatment (115). Twenty-seven of them are somatogenic theories and twenty-three are psychogenic. At the present stage of our knowledge it is difficult to ascertain which one or which combination of them is valid. In spite of the fact that shock treatment acts as a psychological catalyst on the relatives of the patient, and in spite of the fact that I consider schizophrenia a psychogenic condition, I am inclined to believe that shock treatment has a predominantly physiological action, not a psychological one. Although the improvement may be partially due to the fact that the patient receives some kind of care, obviously it cannot be due only to the fact of being treated, irrespectively of the nature of the treatment. Past physical treatments, like hormone therapy, did not produce any effect on schizophrenics. The symptomatic

---

* I do not believe that Federn obtained a repression of the id exclusively, although he interpreted his treatment as aiming at that goal.

improvement is also not due to the fact that patients become more accessible to psychotherapy. Although it is true that they become more accessible to psychotherapy, I have seen hundreds of patients, discharged from hospitals after shock treatment free of overt symptoms, even though they did not receive any kind of psychotherapy.

I share with many others the theory that the improvement is a consequence of the reversible histologic alterations produced in the central nervous system, particularly in the frontal lobes. These alterations engender that transient clinical picture of organic disorder, characterized by impairment of memory and confusion. In order for the patient to experience that kind of anxiety which produces a psychosis, the two cortical areas which were mentioned on page 414, must be capable of functioning adequately. If those areas, and especially the prefrontal region, are in an altered condition, no long-circuited anxiety is possible. There is loss of memory of the conflicts, or if the conflicts are remembered, they are incapable of eliciting anxiety. By the time the reversible alterations have disappeared, the patient may have reoriented his life, or his life may have been reoriented for him, or the acute, precipitating factors may have disappeared, so that there may be no recurrence of the symptoms. But if these factors have not changed, sooner or later there will be a relapse. The chief objection to this theory is the following. Why isn't shock treatment effective in psychoneuroses? After all, we know that in psychoneuroses, too, anxiety is the basic factor. The transient damage produced in the frontal lobe by shock treatment is not enough to prevent that degree of anxiety which is necessary to engender a neurosis. In other words, according to this theory, to elicit the anxiety which causes a psychosis, a higher degree of functionality is necessary than for the development of the anxiety which leads to psychoneuroses. We have already learned that in order to become psychotic, the patient must have cortical centers which will permit him to experience long circuiting anxiety, that is, cortical centers which will permit him to live in a symbolic and interpersonal world.

Shock treatment thus seems to operate by putting the patient artificially on a lower level, where it will be easier for him to integrate. We have seen that the illness itself attempts to do so. However, with relatively few exceptions (see page 351), the illness fails in its teleologic attempts, because, although it pushes the patient to lower levels, it does not give him the ability to integrate, but on the contrary puts in motion a mechanism of self-perpetuating and progressive regression. The shock treatment is successful if the patient, with the help of others, can manage to reach some kind of solid integration before the conflicts come back; so that he will be able then to repress them or to find some kind of modus vivendi with them. Shock treatment, like all organic cerebral traumata, does not unchain a progressive regression.

That the effect of shock treatment on the autonomic nervous system should not be considered responsible for the improvement of the psychological symptoms, is implicit in what was expounded in Chapters XXI and XXII.

II. Psychosurgery

The discussion of psychosurgery will be even briefer. Here the attitude of conditional acceptance, which was held for shock treatments, does not exist. The mode of action of psychosurgery is possibly fundamentally the same as the one described for shock therapy. Damage is caused to the nervous system, so that it will not be able to produce most of the anxiety which permits the psychotic symptoms. The big difference between psychosurgery and shock treatments, however, is that whereas the changes caused by the shocks are reversible, the damage produced by surgery is permanent.

For the rest of his life the patient will not be able to use the coordinated function of his cerebral centers.

The principle of psychosurgery is the same principle which inspires other neurosurgical procedures. For instance, in order to eliminate the involuntary movements of post-encephalitic Parkinsonian patients, cortical tracts are cut. No cortical impulses, therefore, can produce the pathological movements by acting on other centers. There is an important difference, however: we know that the neurological changes of the encephalitics are permanent; it is a physical impossibility for them to reacquire the normal functions of the extrapyramidal centers which are diseased. In the schizophrenic, instead the damage is not necessarily permanent: it has an external, interpersonal origin, which, although it may change the functions of the cerebral centers, does not change the histologic structure.* We cannot feel authorized, therefore, to barter a permanent damage for one which is not.

The authors who advocate psychosurgery try to reassure us by stating that only patients who have lost any chance of recovery are treated with this method. But when has a schizophrenic patient completely lost all his chances? In addition, it could be that new methods, or additional opportunities in the future, will increase his possibilities of recovery. By doing surgery on him, we give up all hope. We share the pessimism and hopelessness of the patient. We are ready to make him more docile, but less human, without any possibility of redemption.

---

* With the exception of a possible cortical atrophy of certain areas after decades of illness.

BIBLIOGRAPHY

1. ABRAHAM, K. The Psychosexual Differences between Hysteria and Dementia Praecox. In *Selected Papers on Psychoanalysis*. Hogarth Press, London, 1927.
2. ABRAMSON, D. I. *Vascular Responses in the Extremities of Man in Health and Disease*. University of Chicago Press, 1944.
3. ACCORNERO, F. L'istopatologia del sistema nervoso centrale nello shock insulinico. Riv. di. pat, nerv. 53:1, 1939.
4. ALPERT, H. S., BIGELOW, N. J. T., and BRYAN, L. L. Central Arteriosclerosis in the Paranoid State. Psychiatric Quarterly, 21:305, 1947.
5. ALTMAN, L. L., PRATT, D., and COTTON, J. Cardiovascular response to acetyl-beta-methylcholine (mecholyl) in mental disorders. J. N. and M. Disease 97:296, 1943.
6. ARIETI, S. Histopathologic changes in Experimental Metrazol Convulsions in Monkeys. Am. J. Psychiat. 98:70, 1941.
7. ARIETI, S. The "Placing-into-Mouth" and Coprophagic Habits, J. N. and M. Disease, 102:307, 1945.
8. ARIETI, S. Primitive Habits in the Preterminal Stage of Schizophrenia. J. N. and M. Disease, 102:367, 1945.
9. ARIETI, S. The Processes of Expectation and Anticipation. Their Genetic Development, Neural Basis and Role in Psychopathology. J. N. and M. Disease, 100:471, 1947.
10. ARIETI, S. Special Logic of Schizophrenic and Other Types of Autistic Thought. Psychiatry, XI:325, 1948.
11. ARIETI, S. Primitive Intellectual Mechanisms in Psychopathological Conditions. Study of the Archaic Ego. Am. J. Psychotherapy 4:4, 1950.

12. ARIETI, S. New Views on the Psychology and Psychopathology of Wit and of the Comic. Psychiatry, 13:43, 1950.

13. ASHBY, W. Psychoses and the Quantitative Distribution of Enzymes. Quoted by Bellak and Willson, J. N. and M. Disease, 105:1, 1947.

14. BALKEN, E. R. A Delineation of Schizophrenic Language and Thought in a Test of Imagination. J. Psychol., 16: 239, 1943.

15. BARD, P., and MOUNTCASTLE, V. B. Some Forebrain Mechanisms Involved in the Expression of Rage with Special Reference to Suppression of Angry Behavior. Research Publ., A. Nerv. and Ment. Dis. 27:362, 1947.

16. BAYNES, H. G. *Mythology of the Soul. A Research into the Unconscious from Schizophrenic Dreams and Drawings.* Methuen & Co., Ltd., London, 1949.

17. BECK, A. Successful Outpatient Psychotherapy of a Chronic Schizophrenic with a Delusion Based on Borrowed Guilt. Psychiatry, 15:305, 1952.

18. BELLAK, L. *Dementia Praecox. The Past Decade's Work and Present Status: A Review and Evaluation.* Grune & Stratton, New York, 1948.

19. BELLAK, L. and WILLSON, E. On the Etiology of Dementia Praecox, J. N. and M. Disease, 105:1, 1947.

20. BENDER, L. Childhood Schizophrenia. Am. J. Orthopsychiat., 17:40, 1947.

21. BENDER, L. and SCHILDER, P. Unconditioned and Conditioned Reactions to Pain in Schizophrenia. Am. J. Psychiat., 10:365, 1930.

22. BENEDICT, R. *Patterns of Culture.* Houghton, Mifflin Co. New York, 1934.

23. BENJAMIN, J. D. A Method for Distinguishing and Evaluating Formal Thinking Disorders in Schizophrenia. In *Language and Thought in Schizophrenia: Collected Papers,* edited by Kasanin, J. S., University of California Press, 1944.

24. BETZ, B. J. A Study of Tactics for Resolving the Autistic

Barrier in the Psychotherapy of the Schizophrenic Personality. Am. J. Psychiat., 104:267, 1947.

25. BETZ, B. Strategic Conditions in the Psychotherapy of Persons with Schizophrenia. Am. J. Psychiat., 107:203, 1950.

26. BINI, L. and BAZZI, T. *La Schizofrenia. Nosografie e Teorie Generali*. Abruzzini, Roma, 1949.

27. BLEULER, E. *The Theory of Schizophrenic Negativism*. Nervous and Mental Disease Monograph Series, n.11, New York, 1912.

28. BLEULER, E. Autistic Thinking. Am. J. Insanity, 69: 873, 1913.

29. BLEULER, E. *Textbook of Psychiatry*, translated by A. A. Brill, The Macmillan Co., New York, 1924.

30. BLEULER, E. *Dementia Praecox or the Group of Schizophrenias*. Translated by Joseph Ziskin. International University Press, New York, 1950.

31. BOAS, F. *Primitive Art*. H. Aschehong & Co., Oslo, 1927.

32. BOERNSTEIN, W. S. Cortical Representation of Taste in Man and Monkey: 1) Functional and Anatomical Relations of Taste, Olfaction and Somatic Sensibility. Yale J. Biol. & Med., 12:719, 1940.

33. BOERNSTEIN, W. S. Cortical Representation of Taste in Man and Monkey: 2) The Localization of the Cortical Taste Area in Man and a Method for Measuring Impairment of Taste in Man. Yale J. Biol. & Med., 13:133, 1940.

34. BOWMAN, K. M. Psychoses with Pernicious Anemia. Am. J. of Psych., 92:372, 1935.

35. BOWMAN, K. M. and KASANIN, J. The sugar content of the blood in emotional states. Arch. Neurol. & psych. 21:342, 1929.

36. BRADLEY, C. *Schizophrenia in Childhood*. Macmillan & Co., New York, 1941.

37. BUSCAINO, V. M. Patologia extraneurale della schizofrenia. Fegato, Tubo digerente, sistema reticolo endoteliale. Acta Neurologica 8:1, 1953.

38. BYCHOWSKI, G. Physiology of Schizophrenic Thinking. J. N. and M. Disease, 98:368, 1943.

39. BYCHOWSKI, G. *Psychotherapy of Psychosis*. Grune & Stratton, New York, 1952.

40. CAMERON, D. C. Heat Production and Heat Control in Schizophrenic Reaction. Arch. Neurol. Psychiat., 32:704, 1934.

41. CAMERON, D. C. and JELLINEK, E. M. Physiological Studies in Insulin Treatment of Acute Schizophrenia; Pulse Rate and Blood Pressure. Endocrinol. 25:100, 1939.

42. CAMERON, N. Reasoning, Regression and Communication in Schizophrenics. Psychological Monographs 50, n. 1, 1938.

43. CAMERON, N. *The Psychology of Behavior Disorders. A Biosocial Interpretation*. H. Mifflin Co., Riverside Press, Cambridge, 1947.

44. CAMERON, N. and MAGARET, A. *Behavior Pathology*. H. Mifflin Co., Riverside Press, Cambridge, 1951.

45. CANNON, W. B. The James-Lange Theory of Emotions: A critical examination and an alternative theory. Am. J. Psychol. 39:106, 1927.

46. CANNON, W. B. Organization for physiological homeostasis. Physiol. Rev. 9:399, 1929.

47. CANNON, W. B. Again the James-Lange and the Thalamic Theories of emotion. Psychol. Rev. 38:281, 1931.

48. CARO, J. *Shulhan Aruk*. Orach Chazim, Konigsberg, 1862.

49. CAROTHERS, J. C. A Study of Mental Derangement in Africans. J. Ment. Sci., 93:548, 1947.

50. CAROTHERS, J. C. Frontal Lobe Function and the African. J. Ment. Sci., 97:12, 1951.

51. CASSIRER, E. *Language and Myth*. Translated by S. K. Langer, Harper & Bros., N. Y. 1946.

52. CERLETTI, V. and BINI, L. Le Alterazioni Istopatologiche del Sistema Nervoso nell' elettroshock. Riv. Sper. di Freniat., 64:2, 1940.

53. CHRZANOWSKI, G. Contrasting Responses to Electric Shock Therapy in Clinically Similar Catatonics. Psychiatr. Quart., 17:282, 1943.

54. CLARDY, E. R. A Study of the Development and Course of Schizophrenia in Children. Psychiat. Quart., 25:81, 1951.

55. COHEN, M. B. Review of *The Contributions of Harry Stack Sullivan,* by Mullahy (202) Psychiatry 15:339, 1952.

56. CROCE, B. *La Filosofia di Giambattista Vico.* Laterza, Bari, 1947.

57. DAVIS, P. A. Effects of Acoustic Stimuli on the Waking Human Brain. J. Neurophysiol., 2:494, 1939.

58. DAVIS, P. A. The Electrical Response of the Human Brain to Auditori Stimuli. Am. J. Physiol., 126:475, 1939.

59. DEJONG, H. Veber Bulbocapninkatalepsie. Klinische Wochenschr., 1:684, 1922.

60. DEJONG, H. and BARUK, H. Pathogenie du Syndrome Catatonique. Encéphale, 25:97, 1930.

61. DEJONG, H. and BARUK, H. La Catatonie Experimentale par la Bulbocapnine; Etude Physiologique et Clinique. Masson, Paris, 1930.

62. DE SANCTIS, S. *Neuropsichiatria Infantile. Patologia e Diagnostica.* S. Lattes & Co., Turin, 1925.

63. DESPERT, L. Thinking and Motility Disorder in a Schizophrenic Child. Psychiat. Quart., 15:522, 1941.

64. DEUTSCH, H. *Psychology of Women,* Vols. I and II. Grune & Stratton, New York, 1945.

65. EISSLER, K. R. Remarks on the Psychoanalysis of Schizophrenia. In Brody and Redlick. *Psychotherapy with Schizophrenics.* International University Press, New York, 1952.

66. ENGLISH, O. S. and PEARSON, G. H. J. *Common Neuroses of Children and Adults.* W. W. Norton, New York, 1937.

67. ERIKSON, E. H. Problems of Infancy and Early Childhood. *Cyclopedia of Medicine, Surgery, and Specialties.* F. A. Davis Co., 1940.

68. FARIS, R. E. L. and DUNHAM, H. W. *Mental Disorders in Urban Areas. An Ecological Study of Schizophrenia and Other Psychoses.* University of Chicago Press, 1939.

69. FARRELL, M. J. and VASSAF, F. Observations on the Effect of Insulin Shock Therapy in Schizophrenia. Arch. Neurol. Psychiat., 43:784, 1940.

70. FEDERN, P. Psychoanalysis of Psychoses. I. Errors and How to Avoid Them. II. Transference. Psychiat. Quart., 17:3, 17, 246, 1943.

71. FEDERN, P. Discussion of Rosen's Paper. Psychiatr. Quart., 21:23, 1947.

72. FEDERN, P. *Ego Psychology and the Psychoses.* Basic Books, New York, 1952.

73. FEIGENBAUM, D. Analysis of a case of Paranoia Persecutoria, Structure and Cure. Psa. Rev. 17:159, 1930.

74. FELIX, R. H. and KRAMER, M. Extent of the Problem of Mental Disorders. Annals American and Political Social Science, 286:5, 1953.

75. FENICHEL, O. *The Psychoanalytic Theory of Neurosis.* W. W. Norton, New York, 1945.

76. FERENCZI, S. Stages in the Development of the Sense of Reality. In Ferenczi, S., *Sex in Psychoanalysis,* Basic Books, New York, 1950.

77. FERENCZI, S. Some Clinical Observations on Paranoia and Paraphrenia. In Ferenczi, S., *Sex in Psychoanalysis,* Basic Books, New York, 1950.

78. FERRARO, A., ARIETI, S., and ENGLISH, W. H. Cerebral Changes in the Course of Pernicious Anemia and Their Relationship to Psychic Symptoms. Jour. of Neuropath. & Experim. Neur., 4:217, 1945.

79. FERRARO, A. and BARRERA, S. E. *Experimental Catalepsy.* State Hospital Press, Utica, N. Y., 1932.

80. FERRARO, A., and JERVIS, G. A. Brain Pathology in Four Cases of Schizophrenia Treated with Insulin. Psychiat. Quart., 13:419, 1939.

81. FIAMBERTI, A. M. L'Acetilcolina Nelle Sindromi Schizofreniche. Riv. di Pat. Nerv., 66:1, 1946.

82. FINKELMAN, I. and HAFFRON, D. Observations on Circulating Blood Volume in Schizophrenia, Manic-Depressive Psychosis, Epilepsy, Involutional Psychosis and Mental Deficiency. Am. J. Psychiat. 93:917, 1937.

83. FRAZER, J. G. The Magic Art, quoted by Freud in *Basic Writings of Sigmund Freud,* Modern Library, New York, 1938.

84. FREEMAN, H. Heat-Regulatory Mechanisms in Normal and in Schizophrenic Subjects (under Basal Conditions and After the Administration of Dinitrophenol). Arch. Neurol. & Psychiat., 43:456, 1940.

85. FREEMAN, H. and CARMICHAEL, H. T. A Pharmacodynamic Investigation of the Autonomic Nervous System in Schizophrenia. I. Effect of Intravenous Injections of Epinephrine on the Blood Pressure and Pulse Rate. Arch. Neurol. & Psychiat., 33:342, 1935.

86. FREEMAN, H., HOSKINS, R. G. and SLEEPER, F. H. Blood Pressure in Schizophrenia. Arch. Neur. & Psychiat., 27:333, 1932.

87. FREEMAN, W. and WATTS, J. W. *Psychosurgery.* Charles C. Thomas, Springfield, 1942.

88. FREUD, S. The Defence Neuro-Psychoses. Neurologisches Zentralblatt, v. 10 & 11, 1894. Reprinted in *Collected Papers,* 1:59.

89. FREUD, S. Further Remarks on the Defence Neuro-Psychoses. Neurologisches Zentralblatt, Oct. 1896, n. 10. Reprinted in *Collected Papers,* 1:155.

90. FREUD, S. Psycho-Analytic Notes Upon An Autobiographical Account of A Case of Paranoia (Dementia Paranoides). Jahrbuch fur psychoanalytische und psychopathologische Forschungen, III, 1911. Reprinted in *Collected Papers,* III: 387.

91. FREUD, S. On Narcissism: An Introduction. Jahrbuch, VI, 1914. Reprinted in *Collected Papers,* IV:30.

92. FREUD, S. *The Ego and the Id.* Hogarth Press, London, 1947.

93. FREUD, S. Neurosis and Psychosis. Zeitschrift, Vol. 10, 1924. Reprinted in *Collected Papers,* II:250.

94. FREUD, S. The Loss of Reality in Neurosis and Psychosis, 1924. In *Collected Papers,* II:277.

95. FREUD, S. *A General Introduction to Psychoanalysis.* New York, Garden City Publishing Company, 1938.

96. FREUD, S. The Interpretation of Dreams, in *The Basic Writings of Sigmund Freud.* Modern Library, New York, 1938.

97. FREUD, S. Psychopathology of Everyday Life, in *The Basic Writings of Sigmund Freud.* Modern Library, New York, 1938.

98. FREUD, S. Wit and Its Relation to the Unconscious, in *The Basic Writings of Sigmund Freud.* Modern Library, New York, 1938.

99. FREUD, S. Totem and Taboo, in *The Basic Writings of Sigmund Freud.* Modern Library, New York, 1938.

100. FREUD, S. *Collected Papers, Vol. I, II, III, IV, V.* The International Psychoanalytical Press, New York, London, Vienna, 1946.

101. FROMM, E. *The Forgotten Language.* Rinehart & Co., Inc., New York, 1951.

102. FROMM-REICHMANN, F. Transference Problems in Schizophrenia. The Psychoana. Quart., 8:412, 1939.

103. FROMM-REICHMANN, F. Notes on the development of Treatment of Schizophrenia by Psychoanalytic Psychotherapy. Psychiatry, XI:3, 1948.

104. FROMM-REICHMANN, F. *Principles of Intensive Psychotherapy.* University of Chicago Press, 1950.

105. FROMM-REICHMANN, F. Some aspects of Psychoanalytic Psychotherapy with Schizophrenics. In Brody and Redlich: *Psychotherapy with Schizophrenics,* International Universities Press, New York, 1952.

106. FROMM-REICHMANN, F. Lecture on "Loneliness," given at Hunter College, under the auspices of William Alanson White Institute on Oct. 6, 1953.

107. FULTON, J. F. *Physiology of the Nervous System.* Eds., Oxford University Press, New York, 1943.

108. FULTON, J. F. *Frontal Lobotomy and Affective Behavior.* New York, Norton, 1951.

109. GELLHORN, E. *Physiological Foundations of Neurology and Psychiatry*. Minneapolis, University of Minnesota Press, 1953.

110. GILDEA, E. F., MAILHOUSE, V. L., and MORRIS, D. P. The relationship between various emotional disturbances and the sugar content of the blood. Am. J. Psychiat. 92:115, 1935.

111. GLOBUS, J. H., HARREVELD, A. VAN, and WIERSMAN, C. A. G. The Influence of Electric Current Application on the Structure of the Brain of Dogs. J. Neuropath. & Experim. Neurol., 2:263, 1943.

112. GOLDSTEIN, K. The Modification of Behavior Consequent to Central Lesions. Psychiat. Quart., 10:586, 1936.

113. GOLDSTEIN, K. The Significance of Psychological Research in Schizophrenia. J. N. and M. Disease, 97:261, 1943.

114. GOLDSTEIN, K. *Language and Language Disturbances*. Grune and Stratton, New York, 1948.

115. GORDON, H. L. Fifty Shock Therapy Theories. The Mil. Surgeon, 103:397, 1948.

116. GORDON, H. L. *The Maggid of Caro*. Pardes Publishing House, New York, 1949.

117. GORNALL, A. G., EGLITIS, B., MILLER, A., STOKES, A. B. and DEWAN, J. G. Long-Term Clinical and Metabolic Observations in Periodic Catatonia. An application of the Kinetic Method of Research in Three Schizophrenic Patients. Amer. J. of Psych. 109:584, 1953.

118. GOTTLIEB, J. S. Relationship of the Systolic to the Diastolic Blood Pressure in Schizophrenia. The Effect of Environmental Temperature. Arch. Neurol. & Psychiat., 35:1256, 1936.

119. GRALNICK, A. Folie à Deux. The Psychosis of Association. Psychiat. Quart., Part I, 16:230, 1942, Part II, 16:491, 1942.

120. GREENBLATT, M. and SOLOMON, H. C. *Frontal Lobes and Schizophrenia*. New York, Springer Publishing Co., 1953.

121. GREENBLATT, M. and SOLOMON, H. C. Concerning a Theory of Frontal Lobe Functioning. in Greenblatt and Solomon: *Frontal Lobes and Schizophrenia* (120).

122. GUTHEIL, E. A. *The Handbook of Dream Analysis*. Liverwright, New York, 1951.

123. HARLOW, H. F., WEHLING, H., and MASLOW, A. H. Comparative Behavior of Primates: Delayed Reaction Tests on Primates. J. Comp. Psychol., 12:13, 1932.

124. HEMPHILL, R. E. Significance of atrophy of testis in schizophrenia. J. Ment. Sc. 90:696, 1944.

125. HEMPHILL, R. E., REISS, M., and TAYLOR, A. L. A Study of the Histology of the Testis in Schizophrenia and Other Mental Disorders. J. Ment. Sci., 90:681, 1944.

126. HENDERSON, D. K. and GILLESPIE, R. D. *A Text-Book of Psychiatry*. Oxford, New York, 1941.

127. HINSIE, L. E. and SHATZKY, J. *Psychiatric Dictionary*. Oxford, New York, 1950.

128. HOCH, P. and POLATIN, P. Pseudoneurotic forms of schizophrenia. Psychiatric Quarterly, 23:248, 1949.

129. HORNEY, K. *The Neurotic Personality of Our Time*. Norton, New York, 1937.

130. HORNEY, K. *Our Inner Conflicts*. Norton, New York, 1943.

131. HOSKINS, R. G. Oxygen Consumption (Basal Metabolic Rate) in Schizophrenia. II. Distribution in Two Hundred and Fourteen Cases. Arch. Neurol. & Psychiat., 28:1346, 1932.

132. HOSKINS, R. G. Oxygen Metabolism in Schizophrenia. Arch. Neurol. & Psychiat., 38:1261, 1937.

133. HOSKINS, R. G. *The Biology of Schizophrenia*. Norton, New York, 1946.

134. HUNTER, W. S. The Delayed Reaction in Animals and Children. Behavior Monographs, 2:86, 1013.

135. JACKSON, J. H. *Selected Writings*. Hodder and Stoughton, London, 1932.

136. JAMES, W. *The Principles of Psychology*. Dover Publications, 1950.

137. JONES, E. *Papers on Psychoanalysis*. Wood, New York, 1913.

138. JUNG, C. G. The Association Method. Amer. J. Psychol. 21:219, 1910.

139. JUNG, C. G. *Studies in Word Association.* Heinemann, London, 1918.

140. JUNG, C. G. The Content of the Psychoses, in *Collected Papers on Analytical Psychology.* London, Tindal & Cose, 1917.

141. JUNG, C. G. A contribution to the Study of Psychological Types. In *Collected Papers on Analytical Psychology,* Bailliere, Tindall & Cox, London, 1920.

142. JUNG, C. G. *Psychology of the Unconscious.* Transl. by B. M. Hinkle, Moffat, Yard, New York, 1921.

143. JUNG, C. G. *The Psychology of Dementia Praecox.* Nerv. and Ment. Disease Monograph Series, New York, n. 3, 1936.

144. JUNG, C. G. On the Psychogenesis of Schizophrenia. Lecture Given at the Section of Psychiatry of the Royal Society of Medicine, London, 1939. J. of Mental Sci., 85:999, 1939.

145. JUNG, R. and CARMICHAEL, E. A. Uber Vasomotorische Reaktionen und Wärmerregulation im Katatonischin Stupor. Arch. f. Psychiat., 107:300, 1937.

146. KAHLBAUM, K. L. *Die Katatonie oder das Spannungsirresein.* Hirschwald, Berlin, 1874.

147. KAHLBAUM, K. L. *Gruppierung der Psychischen Krankheiten.* Kafemann, Danzig, 1863.

148. KALINOWSKY, L. B. and HOCH, P. H. *Shock Treatments and Other Somatic Procedures in Psychiatry.* Grune & Stratton, New York, 1946.

149. KANNER, L. *Child Psychiatry.* C. C. Thomas, Springfield, Ill., 1942.

150. KANNER, L. Early Infantile Autism. J. Pediat., 25:211, 1944.

151. KANNER, L. Irrelevant and Metaphorical Language in Early Infantile Autism. Am. J. Psychiat., 103:242, 1946.

152. KASANIN, J. S. The Disturbance of Conceptual Thinking in Schizophrenia. In Kasanin (ed.) *Language and Thought in Schizophrenia: Collected Papers.* Univ. of Calif. Press, 1944.

153. KASANIN, J. S. Developmental Roots of Schizophrenia. Am. J. Psychiat., 101:770, 1945.

154. KATZENELBOGEN, S. and SNYDER, R. Mineral Constituents in Blood Serum and Cells of Schizophrenic Patients. Arch. Neurol. & Psychiat., 13:321, 1933.

155. KELLER, H. *The Story of My Life*. Doubleday & Co., New York, 1951.

156. KELLOGG, W. N. and KELLOGG, L. A. *The Ape and the Child*. McGraw-Hill, New York, 1933. Quoted by Susanne Langer.

157. KELSEN, H. *Society and Nature. A Sociological Inquiry*. Univ. of Chicago Press, 1943.

158. KIMMINS, C. W. *Children's Dreams*. Allen & Unwin Ltd., London, 1937.

159. KLUVER, H. and BUCY, P. C. "Psychic Blindness" and Other Symptoms Following Bilateral Temporal Lobectomy in Rhesus Monkeys. Am. J. Physiol. 119:352, 1937.

160. KLUVER, H. and BUCY, P. C. An Analysis of Certain Effects of Bilateral Temporal Lobectomy in the Rhesus Monkey with Special Reference to "Psychic Blindness." J. Psychol., 5:33, 1938.

161. KLUVER, H. and BUCY, P. C. Preliminary Analysis of Functions of the Temporal Lobes in Monkeys. Arch. Neurol. & Psychiat., 42:972, 1939.

162. KOHLER, W. *The Mentality of Apes*. Harcourt, Brace, New York, 1925.

163. KRAEPELIN, E. *Dementia Praecox and Paraphrenia* (from 8th German Ed.) Livingston, Edinburgh, 1925.

164. KRETSCHMER, E. *A Text-Book of Medical Psychology*. Transl. by E. B. Strauss. Oxford, London, 1934.

165. LANGER, S. H. *Philosophy in a New Key*. Harvard Univ. Press, 1942.

166. LANGER, S. K. On Cassirer's Theory of Language and Myth. In *The Philosophy of Ernst Cassirer*. Library of Living Philosophers, Evanston, 1949.

167. LE GROS CLARK, W. E. Ignorances in the Anatomical Field.

in Tanner, J. M.: *Prospects in Psychiatry Research*. Oxford, Blackwell Scientific Publications, 1953.

168. LEVIN, M. On the Causation of Mental Symptoms. J. Mental Sci., 82:1, 1938.

169. LEVIN, M. Misunderstanding of the Pathogenesis of Schizophrenia, Arising from the Concept of "Splitting." Amer. J. Psychiat., 94:877, 1938.

170. LÉVY-BRUHL, L. *Les Fonctions Mentales dans les Societées Inferieures*. Alcan, Paris, 1910.

171. LÉVY-BRUHL, L. *La Mentalité Primitive*. Alcan, Paris, 1922.

172. LEWIS, N. D. C. *The Constitutional Factors in Dementia Praecox*. Nervous and Mental Dis. Publ. Co., New York, 1923.

173. LEWIS, N. D. C. *Research in Dementia Praecox*. The National Comm. for Mental Hygiene, New York, 1936.

174. LEWIS, N. D. C. Unpublished Lecture. Inter-State Hospital Meeting, Oct. 1944.

175. LIDZ, R. W. and LIDZ, T. Therapeutic Considerations Arising from the Intense Symbiotic Needs of Schizophrenic Patients. In Brody and Redlich, *Psychotherapy with Schizophrenics*. Internat. Univ. Press, New York, 1952.

176. LIEF, A. *The Commonsense Psychiatry of Dr. Adolf Meyer*. Fifty-Two Selected Papers. McGraw-Hill, New York, 1948.

177. LUGARO, E. *Modern Problems in Psychiatry*. Manchester University Press, Manchester, 1909.

178. LUGARO, E. Sul mecchanismo delle azioni nervose. Riv. Pat. Nerv. & Ment. 29:26, 1924, (quoted by Fiamberti, 81).

179. MACCURDY, G. G. *Human Origins. A Manual of Prehistory*. Vol. I. D. Appleton Co., New York, 1926.

180. MCFARLAND, R. A. The Psychological Effects of Oxygen Deprivation (Anoxemia) on Human Behavior. Arch. Psychol. 22: Monograph 145, 1932.

181. MACLEAN, P. D. Psychosomatic disease and the "visceral brain." Recent developments bearing on the Papez theory of emotion. Psychosom. Med. 11:338, 1949.

182. MAHLER, M., ROSS, J. R. JR., DeFRIES, Z. Clinical Studies in Benign and Malignant Cases of Childhood Psychosis (Schizophrenic-like). Am. J. Orthopsychiat., 19:295, 1949.

183. MALZBERG, B. *Social and Biological Aspects of Mental Disease*. State Hospitals Press, Utica, 1940.

184. MANN, J., MENZER, D., STANDISH, C. Psychotherapy of Psychoses: Some Attitudes in the Therapist Influencing the Course of Treatment. *Psychiatry*, 13:17, 1950.

185. MASSERMAN, J. *Behavior and Neurosis*. Univ. of Chicago Press, 1943.

186. MAYER-GROSS, W. Psychopathology of Delusions. History Classification and Present State of the Problem from the Clinical Point of View. in Morel, *Psychopathologie des Délires*. Hermann & Co., Paris, 1950.

187. MEAD, G. H. *Mind, Self and Society*. Univ. of Chicago Press, 1934.

188. MECO, O. L'esistenza e l'interpretazione di una scarsità di reazione piretica nei dementi precoci. Riv. Pat. Nerv. e Ment., 44, 677, 1934.

189. METTLER, F. A. *Psychosurgical Problems*. Blakiston, Philadelphia, 1952.

190. MEYER, A. The Role of Habit Disorganizations. From a paper read before the New York Psychiatric Society, Jan. 3, 1905; Nervous and Mental Disease Monograph Series, No. 9, Studies in Psychiatry, 1:95, 1912. Reprinted in Lief, A., (176).

191. MEYER, A. Fundamental Conceptions of Dementia Praecox. Brit. Med. Jour., 2:757, 1906. Reprinted in Lief, A., (176).

192. MEYER, A. The Dynamic Interpretation of Dementia Praecox. Amer. J. of Psychol., 21:385, 1910. Reprinted in Lief, A., (176).

193. MEYER, A. Substitutive Activity and Reaction Types. Nerv. and Ment. Dis. Mono. Series No. 9, Studies in Psychiatry, 1:155, 1912. Reprinted in Lief, A., (176).

194. MEYER, A., JELLIFFE, S. E., HOCH, A. *Dementia Praecox, A Monograph*. Gorham Press, Boston, 1911.

195. MINSKI, L. Note on Some Vasomotor Disturbances in Schizophrenia. J. Ment. Sci., 83:434, 1937.

196. MORGAN, C. T. *Physiological Psychology*. McGraw-Hill, New York, 1943.

197. MOTT, . Normal and Morbid Conditions of the Testes from Birth to Old Age in One Hundred Asylum and Hospital Cases. Brit. Med. Jour., Nov. 22, 29, Dec. 6, 1919.

198. MOURGUE, R. *Neurobiologie de l'Hallucination*. Lamertin, Bruxelles, 1932.

199. MOWRER, O. H. An Experimental Analogue of "Regression" with Incidental Observations on "Reaction Formations." J. Abnorm. & Social Psychol., 35:56, 1946.

200. MULLAHY, P. *Oedipus Myth and Complex*. Hermitage Press, New York, 1948.

201. MULLAHY, P. *A Study of Interpersonal Relations*. Hermitage Press, New York, 1949.

202. MULLAHY, P. *The Contributions of Harry Stack Sullivan*. Hermitage House, New York, 1952.

203. MURPHY, G. and CATTELL, E. Sullivan and Field Theory. In Mullahy (202).

204. NUNBERG, H. The Course of the Libidinal Conflict in a Case of Schizophrenia. In *Practice and Theory of Psychoanalysis*. New York, Nervous and Mental Disease Monographs, No. 74, 1948.

205. ORTON, S. T. The Three Levels of Cortical Elaboration in Relation to Certain Psychiatric Symptoms. Am. J. of Psych., 8:647, 1929.

206. PAPEZ, J. W. A proposed mechanism of emotion. Arch. Neurol. & Psychiat., 38:725, 1937.

207. PARSONS, E. H., GILDEA, E. F., RONZONI, E., HULBERT, S. Z. Comparative Lymphocytic and Biochemical Responses of Patients with Schizophrenia and Affective Disorders to Electroshock, Insulin Shock and Epinephrine. Am. J. of Psychiat., 105:573, 1949.

208. PENFIELD, W., and RASMUSSEN, T. *The Cerebral Cortex of Man*. New York, Macmillan Co., 1952.

209. PEPLAU, H. E. *Interpersonal Relations in Nursing.* G. P. Putnam's Sons, New York, 1952.

210. PIAGET, J. *The Child's Conception of the World.* Routledge & Kegan Paul, London, 1929.

211. PIAGET, J. *The Child's Conception of Physical Causality.* Kegan, Trench, Trubner, London, 1930.

212. PIAGET, J. *The Language and Thought of the Child.* Routledge & Kegan Paul, London, 1948.

213. PINCUS, G. and HOAGLAND, H. Adrenal Cortical Responses to Stress in Normal Men and in Those with Personality Disorders. Part I, Some Stress Responses in Normal and Psychotic Subjects. Part II, Analysis of the Pituitary-Adrenal Mechanism in Man. Amer. J. Psychiat., 100:641, 1950.

214. POTTER, H. W. Schizophrenia in Children. Am. J. Psychiat., 12:1253, 1933.

215. POWDERMAKER, F. Concepts found Useful in Treatment of Schizoid and Ambulatory Schizophrenic Patients. Psychiatry, 15:61, 1952.

216. RENNIE, T. A. C. Analysis of One Hundred Cases of Schizophrenia with Recovery. Arch. Neur. and Psych., 46:197, 1941.

217. RHEINGOLD, J. C. Autonomic Integration in Schizophrenia; Autonomic Status Determined Statistically, Thyroid Factor, and Possible Thyroid-Hypo-Thalamus Mechanism. Psychosom. Med. 1:397, 1939.

218. RIOCH, D. McK. and STANTON, A. H. Milieu Therapy, Psychiatry, 16:65, 1953.

219. RIOCH, J. The Transference Phenomenon in Psychoanalytic Therapy, Psychiatry 6:147, 1943. Reprinted in Mullahy, P., *A Study of Interpersonal Relations.* Hermitage Press, New York, 1949.

220. RIPLEY, H. S. and PAPANICOLAOU, G. N. Menstrual Cycle

with Vaginal Smear Studies in Schizophrenia. Am. J. Psychiat., 98:567, 1942.

221. ROBINSON, E. S. *Association Theory Today.* Century Co., New York, 1932.

222. ROIZIN, L. Organi di Senso Quali Generatori di Riflessi Neuro-endocrino-vegetativi della Regione Diencefalo-ipofisaria. Rassegna di Neurologia Vegetativa, 1:338, 1938.

223. ROSEN, J. N. The Treatment of Schizophrenic Psychosis by Direct Analytic Therapy. Psych. Quart., 2:3, 1947.

224. ROSEN, J. N. *Direct Analysis. Selected Papers.* Grune & Stratton, New York, 1953.

225. SCHILDER, P. *Brain and Personality.* Nerv. & Ment. Dis. Publ. Co., New York, 1931.

226. SCHWING, G. Ein Weg Zur Seele des Geisteskranken. Rascher Verlag, Zurich, 1940.

227. SECHEHAYE, M. A. *Symbolic Realization. A New Method of Psychotherapy Applied to a Case of Schizophrenia.* Internat. Univ. Press, New York, 1951.

228. SEITZ, P. F. A Dynamic Factor Correlated with the Prognosis in Paranoid Schizophrenia. Arch. Neur. & Psych., 65:604, 1951.

229. SEITZ, P. F. & MOLHOLM, H. B. Relations of Mental Imagery to Hallucinations. Arch. Neur. & Psych., 57:469, 1947.

230. SELYE, H. Stress (The Physiology and Pathology of Exposure to Systemic Stress). Acta Med. Publ. Montreal, 1950.

231. SELYE, H. *The Story of the Adaptation Syndrome.* Acta Med. Publ. Montreal, 1952.

232. SEMRAD, E. J. Discussion of Dr. Frank's paper. In Brody and Redlich, *Psychotherapy with Schizophrenics.* Internat. Univ. Press, New York, 1952.

233. SEMRAD, E. V., MENZER, D., MANN, J., STANDISH, C. A Study of the Doctor-Patient Relationship in Psychotherapy of Psychotic Patients. Psychiatry, 15:377, 1952.

234. SERIEUX and CAPGRAS. Quoted by Mayer-Gross in Morel, *Psychopathologie des Délires.* Hermann & Co., Paris, 1950, (186).

235. SHATTOCK, M. F. The Somatic Manifestations of Schizophrenia. A Clinical Study of Their Significance. J. of Ment. Sci., 96:32, 1950.

236. SHENKIN, H. A. and LEWEY, F. H. Taste Aura Preceding Convulsions in a Lesion of the Parietal Operculum. J. Ner. & Ment. Dis. 100:352, 1944.

237. SILVERBERG, W. V. The Factor of Omnipotence in Neurosis. Psychiatry, 12:387, 1949.

238. SILVERBERG, W. V. *Childhood Experience and Personal Destiny.* New York, Springer Publishing Co., 1952.

239. SMITH, R. B. The Aborigines of Victoria, 1878. Quoted by Werner, H. in *Comparative Psychology of Mental Development.* Harper, New York, 1940 (270).

240. SPIEGEL, R. Unpublished work. Quoted by Fromm-Reichmann, F. in Brody and Redlich, *Psychotherapy with Schizophrenics.* Internat. Univ. Press, New York, 1952.

241. STAERCKE, A. The Reversal of the Libido Sign in Delusions of Persecutions. Internat. J. Psychoana., 1: 1920.

242. STANTON, A. H. and SCHWARTZ, M. S. The Management of a Type of Institutional Participation in Mental Illness. Psychiatry 12:13, 1949.

243. STANTON, A. H. and SCHWARTZ, M. S. Observations on Dissociation as Social Participation. Psychiatry, 12:339, 1949.

244. STEINEN, K. Unter den Naturvölkern Zentral-Brasiliens, 1894. Quoted by Werner, H. in *Comparative Psychology of Mental Development.* Follet, Chicago, 1948 (270).

245. STERN, E. S. Acrocyanosis. J. Ment. Sci., 83:408, 1937.

246. STORCH, A. *The Primitive Archaic Forms of Inner Experiences and Thought in Schizophrenics.* Nerv. & Ment. Dis. Publi. Co., New York, 1924.

247. STRANSKY, . Zur Kentniss gewisser erworbener Blödsinnsformen. Jahrb. f. Psych. 24:1, 1903.

248. SULLIVAN, H. S. Schizophrenia: Its Conservative and Malignant Features. Am. J. Psychiat., 4:77, 1924.

249. SULLIVAN, H. S. Peculiarity of Thought in Schizophrenia. Am. J. Psychiat., 5:21, 1925.

250. SULLIVAN, H. S. Research in Schizophrenia. Am. J. Psychiat., 9:553, 1929.

251. SULLIVAN, H. S. The Relation of Onset to Outcome in Schizophrenia. In *Schizophrenia (Dementia Praecox)*, Williams & Wilkins, Baltimore, 10:111, 1930.

252. SULLIVAN, H. S. Socio-Psychiatric Research. Its Implications for the Schizophrenia Problem and for Mental Hygiene. Am. J. Psychiat., 977, 1931.

253. SULLIVAN, H. S. The Modified Psychoanalytic Treatment of Schizophrenia. Am. J. Psychiat., XI:519, 1931.

254. SULLIVAN, H. S. *Conceptions of Modern Psychiatry.* William Alanson White Psychiatric Foundation, Washington, 1946.

255. SULLIVAN, H. S. *The Interpersonal Theory of Psychiatry.* W. W. Norton, New York, 1953.

256. SUTTIE, I. E. *The Origins of Love and Hate.* The Julian Press, New York, 1952.

257. THOMPSON, C. Development of Awareness of Transference in a Markedly detached personality. Int. J. Psa., 19:299, 1938.

258. THOMPSON, C. *Psychoanalysis: Evolution and Development.* Hermitage House, New York, 1950.

259. THOMPSON, C. Sullivan and Psychoanalysis. In Mullahy, P. *The Contributions of Harry Stack Sullivan.* Hermitage House, New York, 1952.

260. THOMPSON, C. Counter-Transference. Samiska, 6:205, 1952.

261. TOWER, S. S. Management of Paranoid Trends in Treatment of a Post-Psychotic Obsessional Condition. Psychiatry 10: 157, 1947.

262. TYLOR, E. B. Primitive Culture. Quoted by Freud, Totem and Taboo, *The Basic Writings of Sigmund Freud.* Modern Library, New York, 1938.

263. VICO, G. *Principi di Una Scienza Nuova.* 1725 Naples.

264. VIGOTSKY, L. S. Thought in Schizophrenia. Arch. Neurol. & Psychiat., 31:1036, 1934.

265. VON DOMARUS, E. Uber die Beziehung des Normalen zum Schizophrenen Denken. Arch. Psychiat., 74:641, 1925.

266. VON DOMARUS, E. The Specific Laws of Logic in Schizophrenia. In Kasanin, J. S. ed. *Language and Thought in Schizophrenia: Collected Papers,* Univ. of Calif. Press, 1944

267. VON MONAKOW, C. V. *Die Lokalisation in Grosshirn und der Abbau der Funktionen durch Korticale.* J. F. Bergmann, Herde, Wiesbaden, 1919.

268. VON MONAKOW, C. V. and MOURGUE, R. *Introduction Biologique a l'étude de la Neurologie et de la Psychopathologie.* Felix Alcan, Paris, 1928.

269. WEIL, A., LIEBERT, E. and HEILBRUNN, G. Histopathologic Changes in the Brain in Experimental Hyperinsulinism. Arch. Neur. & Psychiat., 39:467, 1938.

270. WERNER, H. *Comparative Psychology of Mental Development.* Follet, Chicago, 1948.

271. WEXLER, M. The Structural Problem in Schizophrenia: The Role of the Internal Object. In Brody and Redlich, *Psychotherapy with Schizophrenics.* Internat. Univ. Press, New York, 1952.

272. WHITE, M. J. Discussion of Paper by Semrad, Menzer, Mann and Standish. Ref. 200. Psychiatry, 15:384, 1952.

273. WHITE, M. J. Sullivan and Treatment. In Mullahy, P. (ed.) Hermitage House, New York, 1952, (202).

274. WHITEHORN, J. C. The blood sugar in relation to emotional reactions. Am. J. Psychiat., 13:987, 1934.

275. WINKELMAN, N. W. and MOORE, M. T. Neurohistological Findings in Experimental Electric Shock Treatment. J. Neuropath. & Exper. Neurol., 3:199, 1944.

276. WITTE, F. Uber Anatomische Untersuchungen der Schilddruse bei der Dementia Praecox. Ztschr. f. d. ges. Neurol. u Psychiat., 80:1901, 1922.

277. YERKES, R. M. *Chimpanzees. A Laboratory Colony.* Yale Univ. Press, New Haven, 1943.

278. ZILBOORG, G. Malignant Psychosis Related to Childbirth. Am. J. Obst. & Gynec., 15:145, 1928.

279. ZILBOORG, G. The Dynamics of Schizophrenic Reactions Related to Pregnancy and Childbirth. Am. J. Psychiat., 8:733, 1929.

280. ZILBOORG, G. *A History of Medical Psychology.* W. W. Norton, New York, 1941.

INDEX

Abaissement du niveau mental, 27

Abraham, K., 355, 356, *bibl.* 489

Abramson, D. I., 391, *bibl.* 489

Abstract attitude, impairment of, 315-318

Acceptance of one's illness, 341

Accornero, F., 482, *bibl.* 489

Acetylcholine treatment, 480

ACTH hormone, 398-400

Acute course of sch., 79, 80, 324-327; prognosis 341

Addison's disease, 398

Adrenal glands, 398-400

Advanced, or second stage of sch., 346-349

Affectivity, Bleuler's study, 10, 18; Jung's study, 28; as prognostic sign, 335

Agnosia, visual, 369-371, 416

Alpert, H. S., 408, *bibl.*, 489

Altman, L. L., 427, *bibl.*, 489

Ambivalence, 16

Amenorrhea, 401

Analgesia, 373-378

Analogues, Jung's concept of, 30 *n*

Anesthesia, for pain, temperature and taste in regressed schizophrenics, 372-378

Animals, type of anxiety experienced by infrahuman, 44, 240; concept of time, 239-240; symbolization, 280-284; evaluation of experiments on, 292-293

Ann (patient), 145-155

Anthony (patient), 165-172

Anxiety, due to lack of satisfaction, 44; due to lack of security, 44; in childhood, 44-61; in schizoid personalities, 61-79; in stormy personalities, 76-79; in initial stage of sch., 324-334; as prognostic sign, 334; in second stage of sch., 347-348; in basic process of sch., 379-384; of the therapist, 442-443

Aphasia, 202 *n*, 420

Appetite, perversion of, 362-368

Appraisal, reflected from parents, 44-45

Archetypes, Jung's concept of, 30

Archipallium, 422, 429-432

Arieti, S., on psychodynamics of sch., 43-85; on stormy personality, 74-79; on paleologic, 186, 189-194; on Von Domarus' principle, 194-209; on connotation, denotation, verbalization, 209-219; on psychological causality and catatonia, 219-238; on conception of time, 238-243; on hallucinations, 243-253; on association disturbances, 253-264; on word-salad, 259-263; on magic, 263-266; on wit, 266; on desocialization and desymbolization, 279-305; on projection, 299-302; on interpretation of schizophrenic process, 314-318; on psychoses with pernicious anemia, 344; on the preterminal stage of sch., 350-360; on the terminal stage, 361-378; on schizophrenic regression, 379-389; on definition of sch., 384; on the psychosomatic involvement of central nervous system, 410-432; on the use of therapeutic assistant, 468-471; *bibl.*, 489-490, 494

© 219 238